Sainted Women of the Dark Ages

Edited and translated by

Jo Ann McNamara and John E. Halborg,

with E. Gordon Whatley

Duke University Press   Durham and London 1992

© 1992 Duke University Press
All rights reserved
Printed in the United States of America
on acid-free paper ∞
Library of Congress Cataloging-in-Publication Data
appear on the last printed page of this book.

With much gratitude to
The Friends of the Saints
A goodly company

Contents

Note on Language
and Abbreviations

Throughout our translations we have tried to indicate in the notes particularly difficult or debatable terms. In some cases, we have made consistent choices. Several terms are used to designate bishop, which we have reserved as a translation for *episcopus*. The term *antistes* has been translated throughout as primate and *praesul* as prelate. Pontiff has been left as is. *Pietas* is a complicated concept that should be understood, not in its modern sense but in its antique meaning, as a reciprocal relationship between unequals such as God and human, parent and child, ruler and subject, compounded of respect for the superior and care for the inferior. *Virtus* has many meanings. Where the text allows, we have translated it simply as virtue, but in other cases we have used power and even miracle.[1] Biblical quotes have been cited from the King James version to retain a traditional liturgical flavor, and there virtue appears as strength. The English language does not provide a workable alternative to *mother* to express the distinction our texts make between *genetrix*, the natural mother, and *mater*, the spiritual mother, or between *germana*, the physical sister, and *soror*, the fellow nun. *Sanctimonial* is the most common word for nun found in our texts. In the early lives of Monegund and Radegund, *monacha* is used, with a single appearance of *nonna* in Baudonivia's text. We have therefore used nun for sanctimonial and left the other usages intact. We have retained the slightly pretentious optimates for nobles where it appears, and Quadragesima for Lent. We have consistently translated Sabbath as Saturday.

1. Heffernan, *Sacred Biography*, 136–65, argues for translating *virtutes* as deeds and follows the thread of this definition to its classical and emerging Christian meanings. He sees classical virtue as correct social action and equates it to Jewish ideas of living correctly by the law prevalent in the Pharisaic movement. With the Christians, sensibility shifts toward a God-directed quality, divorced from social or public behavior. Thus it moved toward becoming a synonym for miracle.

Abbreviations in Footnotes and Bibliography

AS	*Acta Sanctorum*
ASOSB	*Acta Sanctorum Ordinis S. Benedicti*
c.	the numbered paragraphs in most standard Latin editions and in our translations.
CCSL	Corpus Christianorum: Series Latina
	Lexicon = *Lexicon Latinitatis Medii Aevi*
CIL	*Corpus Inscriptiones Latinorum*
CL	*Chronicorum Liber quartus cum continuationibus*
DACL	*Dictionnaire d'archéologie chrétienne et liturgie*
DHGE	*Dictionnaire d'histoire et géographie écclésiastique*
HE	History of the English Church and People, by Bede
HF	History of the Franks
LHF	*Liber Historiae Francorum*, ed. and trans. Bachrach
MGH	Monumenta Germaniae Historica
	AA = *Auctores Antiquiores*
	Diplomata = *Diplomata Regum Francorum e Stirpe Merowingica*
	Epistolae = *Epistolae Aevi Merovingici Collectae*
	SRM = *Scriptores rerum merowingicarum*
	SS = *Scriptores*
PL	*Patrologia Cursus Completus, series Latina*, ed. J. P. Migne
PG	*Patrologia Cursus Completus, series Graecae*, ed. J. P. Migne

Acknowledgments

No book can be written in a vacuum, and we have leaned hard on the sympathy of friends and colleagues for several years in creating this one. Some people, however, stand out "like lights upon a candlestick." We want to render special thanks to Bernard S. Bachrach and Patrick J. Geary for painstaking readings of the manuscript and suggestions that proved enormously helpful. William Daly shared his translation of the life of Genovefa and the drafts of translations of the lives of Radegund and Gertrude of Nivelles by the late John Cox. The members of the Hagiography Group of New York have been uniformly enlightening in our many meetings. William Tighe provided aid and comfort in the final stages. We acknowledge the friendly services of the staff at the Corrigan Library at St. Joseph's Seminary in Dunwoodie, New York, and the help of the late Magda Gottesman in charge of interlibrary loans at Hunter College. Richard C. Rowson and Reynolds Smith of Duke University Press have given us warm and unfailing support. The good cheer and encouragement of Edmund Clingan always command appreciation, never more so than in his assistance while we made the perilous passage from typewriter to computer. Finally, in many a stormy hour, we sought comfort from our respective cats, Pachelbel, Leibniz, Glatisant, Rollo, and Brumaire.

John Halborg and Jo Ann McNamara worked together on the initial translations. Gordon Whatley gave his critical attention to the lives of Genovefa, Clothild, Monegund, Radegund, Rusticula, and Balthild. The scriptural citations and liturgical notes are by John Halborg. The remaining notes, the Introduction, and the introductions to each saint's life are by Jo Ann McNamara.

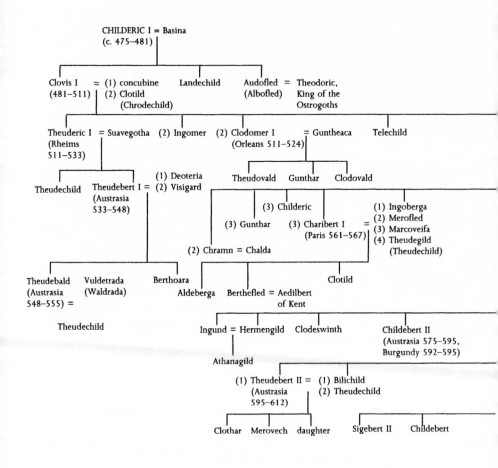

Wives, Concubines, and Children
of Merovingian Kings

Source: Suzanne F. Wemple, *Women in Frankish Society: Marriage and the Cloister, 500–900* (Philadelphia: University of Pennsylvania Press, 1981), viii–ix.

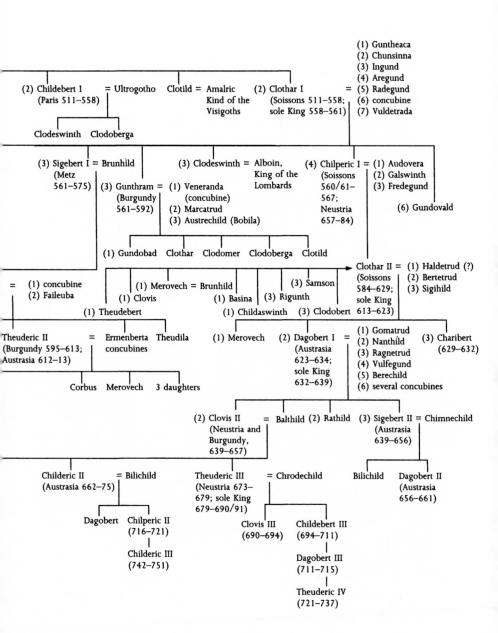

The Ancestors of Charlemagne

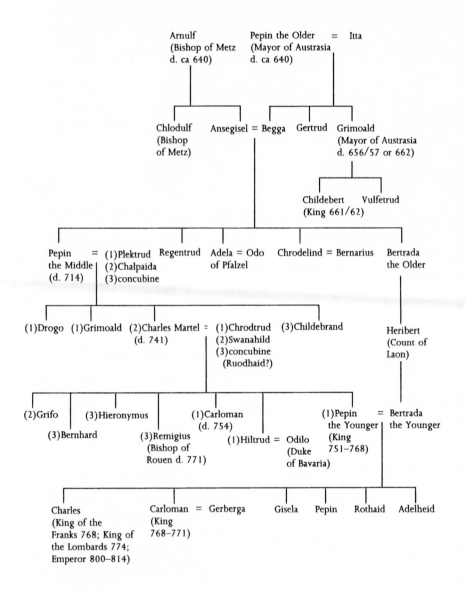

Source: Suzanne F. Wemple, *Women in Frankish Society:*
Marriage and the Cloister, 500–900 (Philadelphia: University
of Pennsylvania Press, 1981), x–xi.

Sainted Women
of the
Dark Ages

Introduction

Behold, here you have the deeds of a saint which you have read or heard piously that you may imitate them. Still in the maiden state, she despised the world and desired heaven. She tamed the lusts of the flesh to love virginity. She harnessed the concupiscence of the eye, which is curiosity, by meditating on divine readings. She trampled down life's ambition, which is pride, with her humility. She despised a mortal spouse to choose one who will never die. When she had riches, she put no hopes in treasures of money but wisely distributed all to the poor. . . . Therefore, imitate what you have read. Live as she lived. Walk as she walked and there is no doubt that you will go where she has gone with the help of the Creator who works His mercy in His saints and gives virtue and fortitude to His people, blessed be God forever. Amen.[1]

Here are the biographies of eighteen women who lived in the sixth and seventh centuries, sometimes called the Dark Ages. At the beginning of this book, the land they inhabited was called Roman Gaul. The population were the survivors of a vanished empire. Catholic Christianity defined their sense of identity, and their bishops struggled to maintain the remnants of civil authority against pagan Huns and Franks as well as other Germanic kings who had been converted by Arians, Christians branded as heretics by the Catholics because of their divergent ideas concerning the Trinity. This book introduces noble women who participated in Gaul's violent transformation into the Merovingian kingdoms of Neustria, Burgundy, and Austrasia. It ends just before Frankland, unified at last by the noble ancestors of Charlemagne, began its long career as "eldest daughter of the Roman church," Catholic Christianity's champion against the pagans of the north and the heretics of the south.

It is rare for any age to preserve so large a group of sources dedicated to women's achievements and rarer still for a period so impoverished in sources of any kind. Merovingian hagiography was a flourishing literary genre that offered a rough and inexperienced ruling class a new set of Christian

---

1. Hucbald of Saint-Amand, *Vita S. Aldegundis virginis*, 35, AS, January 30, 662.

heroic models. Holy women were set beside their violent mates. Their contemporaries worshipped them as saints worthy of the emulation and admiration of future generations. With scriptural quotations and analogies, their biographers stressed their adherence to Christian precepts and their likeness to early Christians martyred for their faith. Originality was no virtue. The cognoscenti were so attuned to the echoes of earlier lives that they could say that all saints shared but a single life.[2] The saints themselves sought out the similar threads that bound them in a single experience. Holy women, in particular, increasingly filed on to a single path embracing the common discipline of the monastic movement.

Grateful as scholars are for any light on "the dark ages," they have never reached a firm consensus on Merovingian hagiography.[3] Sometimes the saint herself has been dismissed as fictitious and her biography ascribed to Carolingian forgers pretending to work from older sources to give themselves a false credibility. Critics, particularly in the nineteenth century, were much in love with ancient paganism and developed fanciful ideas about race memory and the mechanics of cultural transmission. They were swift to discover doublets and *topoi*, reflections of local legends and ancient superstitions.[4] They came to believe that pagan deities had often been "baptized" as Christian saints by a rural population anxious to retain accustomed rites and cults.

The great modern hagiographer Hippolyte Delehaye broke through the overwrought techniques of literary criticism to secure the historical claims of many saints through coordinating their vitae with their feasts and cult centers.[5] The lives before us were intended for public reading on the anniversary of the saint's death, or of the translation of her relics, or of the dedication of her basilica, or some other important festivity.[6] Although debate still continues about the worth of various aspects of their biographies, none of the saints included in this book are now suspected of being ancient goddesses in disguise. Each of them lived a life in historical time. Each one left a legacy of property, a tomb, and her own body as a miracle-working relic, which in many cases is still preserved.[7] Their worshipers had a serious interest in remembering who they were and what their credentials were. Hagiographers recorded real estate transactions and promoted cults of monastic foundresses to attract new donors to their communities.

---

2. This is a concept recently elaborated from Gregory of Tours's introduction to his *Life of the Fathers*, by both Heffernan, *Sacred Biography*, and Wallace-Hadrill, *Frankish Church*.

3. For an overview of the problems of hagiography as literature, see Graus, *Volk, Herrscher*, chapter 1.

4. An excellent introduction to the problems of hagiography can be found in Aigrain, *L'hagiographie*.

5. Delehaye, *The Legends of the Saints*.

6. Collins, "Observations on the Form," *Columbanus and Merovingian Monasticism*, ed. Clarke and Brennan, 105–31.

7. McNamara has examined this question further in "A Legacy of Miracles," 316–52.

Most of these biographies were written by contemporaries. The lives of Clothild, Glodesind, Rictrude, and Waldetrude were written by Carolingians plausibly claiming to base their work on contemporary sources. In our notes, we have tried to summarize the current state of research regarding each one, and readers interested in literary forms may profit by a more detailed comparison of the idiosyncrasies of style than we have been able to provide. As Patrick Geary has pointed out, sainthood and miracles also have their histories. We have rudely cut short those lives that extend into the ninth century and beyond to avoid shifts in sensibilities when new demands were made of old saints.[8]

The vitae were intended for frequent recitation within monastic communities for the instruction of the sisters and for public liturgical reading. Carolingian editors often 'improved' the texts to purge them of their barbaric diction, but the wholesale charges of forgery based on literary analysis have now largely been discredited. Where we have both early texts and their Carolingian versions, it is apparent that the later authors concentrated most carefully on the literary ornamentation of texts they considered barbarous in the extreme. They also added scriptural citations with a heavy hand to improve their liturgical use and exegesis to improve their didactic value. They did not, however, add any significant narrative material. The ninth-century author Hucbald of Saint Amand, in his life of Rictrude, and the anonymous eighth-century author of the Life of Austreberta make passing reference to authorities with the power to judge the reliability of their work. Skeptics once assumed that the miracles were imagined by hysterical onlookers or cynically added by later scribes. Now, however, there is a growing awareness that chroniclers close to their subjects were as willing to credit the intervention of supernatural forces as more distant reporters. Modern scholarship has tended to beg the question by granting the miracles the reality of a constructed, literary, experience while frankly admitting that direct access to the event must remain out of reach.

Saints had a wide variety of functions in Merovingian Gaul. A hagiographer had first to prove that the subject was a saint. Emulation of martyrs, or at least a demonstrated willingness to be a martyr if necessary, was the first criterion. Some of our heroines faced threats of violence and others were tested by illness, but only Radegund suffered genuine physical torment—and she imposed it upon herself. With Athanasius' life of Antony, martyrdom was extended to the self-imposed suffering of asceticism. Merovingian Gaul inherited its hagiographic tradition from Sulpicius Severus, the fourth-century biographer of Martin of Tours, whose self-mortification was coupled with the

8. Geary, *Furta Sacra*.

threats and hardships of missionary life in a pagan countryside.[9] In all our other cases, God or destiny made happier uses of his consecrated servants. Consequently, the saint depended heavily on her *virtu*, God's miraculous power channeled through her, to prove that she was indeed his instrument.

At the beginning of our story, holy women were aligned with the poor and the conquered against unharnessed secular power. As a mediator between two cultures, a woman like Genovefa had to convince the conquering Franks that she and her God were allies worth having.[10] At the same time, her fragility as a woman without official status in the Gallo-Roman hierarchy rendered her innocuous in the context of secular power. Her most famous feat, the prayer marathon that warded the Huns away from Paris, inspired the besieging Franks with respect for Gallic saints. Her miracles proved that the king of Heaven was responsive to their requests. Power, as expressed through miracles, protected Childeric and his successors from the possibility that whatever mercy and indulgence they showed toward the saints and to the poor they championed might be construed as a sign of weakness unbecoming to a warrior.

Hagiographers shaped the historic destiny of the Franks as a divine mission in which women played a leading role. As Clothild's legend developed, the queen converted her husband and his Frankish followers to Catholic Christianity by promising that her God could deliver victory on the battlefield. Clothild matched Clovis's warlike prowess with her supportive prayers and gifts to the church. Within a generation, Frankish Christians adopted the Gallic saints as patrons. The generosity of Clovis and his successors with churches and other signs of honor assured their assistance in the consolidation of their power. They boasted, "The famous race of Franks, whose founder is God . . . is the race which, brave and valiant, threw off in battle the most hard Roman yoke from their necks, and it is the Franks who, after Baptism, have enclosed in gold and precious stones the bodies of the Holy Martyrs whom the Romans had burned by fire, mutilated by the sword, or thrown to the wild beasts."[11]

Even so, writers and readers, then as now, were ambivalent about miracles.[12] Ecclesiastical officials suspected anything that smacked of magic,

---

9. Translated by Hoare, *Western Fathers*, 3–46.

10. Van Dam, *Leadership and Community*, 261ff.

11. Salic Law, Longer Prologue (eighth century), trans. Hillgarth, *Conversion of Western Europe*, 89–90.

12. In a colloquium on hagiography published as *Hagiographie: cultures et sociétés IVe–XIIe siècles*, Vauchez remarks (259) that the expression of doubt is itself a topos of hagiographers. In "La controverse biblique," Van Uytfanghe notes (211) that by the early fourth century it was generally believed that miracles were no longer needed to convert pagans. As late as the 390s, Augustine thought their time had passed, but thirty years later he reversed himself and celebrated the miracles attributed to saintly relics. Van Uytfanghe cites further evidence for skepticism from Merovingian Gaul.

equally fearful of genuine diabolic powers and the fraudulence of the devil's more mundane human instruments. Martin of Tours and his successor Bishop Gregory prided themselves on exposing false miracles and failed pretenders to sainthood.[13] Genovefa enjoyed powers of discernment that often enabled her to uncover falsehood and hypocrisy. But despite the opposition of some writers, miracles won the day in Gaul.[14] The counterpower that gave saints, and by extension, their religion, an edge in dealing with the new warrior lords was simply indispensable.

Accordingly, the hagiographer's mission was to ensure that a saint employed "clean" power against "dirty" power, to use Peter Brown's felicitous concept.[15] The test of a miracle was its conformity to Christian teachings. Sulpicius presented Martin as Jesus's imitator, and insisted that his miracles did not stem from human magic but originated with God.[16] Miracles were certified by a literary process of "scriptural stylization," heavily underscoring their orthodox character with biblical citations.[17] Merovingian hagiographers were sensitive to "folkloric" miracles, and their influence weakened as the genre became more firmly articulated. Thus, Genovefa was credited with more purely magical feats, like her dragon-slaying adventure, than later hagiographers would allow. Even so, her biographer modeled her on Martin wherever he could. He carefully distinguished Genovefa from false wonderworkers by stressing the approval of Germanus of Auxerre, a leading Gallic bishop. He even inserted a greeting from Simon Stylites, a famous holy man of the east, to reinforce his heroine's position in the fellowship of the orthodox.

In the late fifth century, when the Gauls had to adjust to the loss of the Roman Empire, communal redefinition was linked to conversion of their conquerors. Martin of Tours became the focus for a new Gallic consciousness.[18] His ingenious successor, Bishop Gregory of Tours, wove an account of Martin's latest miracles into his concept of Frankish history as a divine plan.[19] He linked Martin's prestige with the labors of new saints like Monegund. Bishop Fortunatus also connected his heroine Radegund to Martin and to the saints of the east who sent their relics to help her in the Christianization of

---

13. Heinzelmann, "Une source de base," discusses the methods of Gregory of Tours and his contemporaries for verifying and recording miracles.

14. Van Uytfanghe, "La controverse biblique," 217, cites Bishop Hilarius of Poitiers on Saint Honoratus in particular.

15. Brown, Cult of the Saints, 168.

16. Van Dam, Leadership and Community, 131–32. Sulpicius said that to disbelieve Martin's miracles would be to disbelieve Christ (Dial. I. 26, 5; III. 10, 5 emphasizes the similarity).

17. For an expansion of this argument see Van Uytfanghe, "La controverse biblique."

18. Van Dam, Leadership and Community, 235.

19. Liber de miraculi S. Martini, libri quatuor, PL 71:913–1008.

Frankland. The homely medical skills of "wise women" like Monegund or Radegund based on cleaning, anointing, and herbal remedies were extended to divine cures beyond the power of earthly medicine. At its peak, healing power mobilized by the sign of the cross protected Rusticula and attested to her innocence of the charges brought by a murderous king and his jealous minions. The protests of demons as they were driven from the holy places they longed to infest, and from the bodies they had seized from unwary Christians, testified to a power that could effectively be deployed to protect holy things and property from the depredations of secular lords.[20]

Throughout the sixth century, saints stood between the conquered people and their rulers, mitigating the effects of their ongoing fratricidal wars. Radegund extended Genovefa's role as an advocate for prisoners and for humble people. Repeatedly, she begged God to help the sick and begged the king to help the needy, establishing a ritual whereby women could express the merciful side of royalty without softening the fierce warrior image of the king. This became a traditional role for Merovingian queens. Even Queen Fredegund, whose ruthlessness was far more widely celebrated than her tender heart, persuaded her husband to burn the old Roman tax records, claiming that God sent a plague that threatened her children in revenge for their oppression of the poor. The seventh-century queen Balthild took Radegund as her model and cultivated her spiritual power after she left her throne for a monastery. These holy women and the models they presented through their vitae thus played a vital role in the final amalgamation of Franks and Gauls into a working community.

Once the conversion of the Franks had been accomplished, cautious hagiographers began to circumscribe the powers attributed to their heroines. Even when there was no evidence of fraud, the church was wary of people who bypassed clerical intermediacy and tapped directly into divine power. With the seventh-century rapprochement between church authorities and secular monarchs, the power of female saints while they lived on earth diminished. Few of the seventh-century heroines performed miraculous cures until after they were safely dead and buried under the auspices of the local bishop.

In recent years, German historians have developed the thesis that the Germanic aristocracy sought to recover a charisma nullified by their conversion

---

20. In the lives of Burgundofara and Anstrude, particularly, the holy power of a saintly woman is dramatically opposed to the unholy power of the mayor of the palace, the highest secular official under the king himself. In this regard, we may place the frequent rescues of convicted felons whose only claim to mercy seems to be their faith in the saint's power.

by cultivating Christian sainthood.[21] To their unquestioned secular power, they added spiritual power by taking control of ecclesiastical offices.[22] The chapels and tombs of sainted relatives were transformed into focal points for family prestige. Women were particularly well suited to this role because they shared the noble blood of their families but could not actively enter into the violent competition of the secular world. They could, however, secure their dowries and inheritances from grasping monarchs by transferring them to God, as did the saints of the Dagobertian period. In the monastic life, they could use family wealth to create prestige on earth and favor in heaven. Like Rictrude, Sadalberga, and Gertrude of Nivelles, they could preserve that same wealth through a line of related abbesses.

Poverty, one of the three traditional monastic virtues, was no recommendation for a Merovingian saint. Our texts trace the patterns of womanly power in an age where caste often transcended gender in the division of social and political authority.[23] The outstanding virtue associated with sainted women in the sixth and seventh centuries was charity, viewed as an adjunct of noble lineage. The first barbarian kings were habituated to an economy of loot and gifts. They displayed their might and prestige by sharing the treasures garnered from their incessant warfare with their warrior companions and with their women. In turn, noble women acted as gift-givers to the poor, complementing the traditional role of men as gift-givers to their peers. Radegund obsessively moved the wealth her husband had won from his enemies (among whom were her own people) to the poor who gathered at her door during his nightly banquets. Monegund and Eustadiola lived more closely in the midst of the people they served, giving their husbands' wealth to the poor and to the church, which hagiographers consistently classed with the poor as joint recipients of the saints' largesse.[24]

As the Frankish ruling class was gradually Christianized, nobles took their places in the ecclesiastical hierarchy, creating the new religion's infrastructure with their money, influence, and administrative abilities.[25] Within the dynas-

---

21. Prinz, "Heiligenkult und Adelsherrschaft im Spiegel merowingischen Hagiographie," 532, builds on the ideas of Weber, *Kulturgeschichtliche Probleme der Merowingerzeit*, 348ff.

22. Wittern, "Frauen zwischen asketischem Ideal," 272–94, has summarized recent German scholarship that charts the shift from the heroic asceticism of the sixth century to the institutionalized aristocratic sanctity of the seventh.

23. Ibid., 272–94, interprets the "intention of the text" to propagate an image of proper Christian behavior of women in the lives of Radegund and Balthild, arguing for an increased institutionalization of queenly power from the sixth to the seventh centuries.

24. For further exploration of this notion, see McNamara, "The Need to Give."

25. Werner, "Le role d'aristocratie dans la christianisation du nord-est de la Gaule," in *Structures politiques du monde franc*.

tic patterns of the age, women played a central role in this development. Germanic laws protected the rights of women to share in the estates of both fathers and husbands as well as to accumulate gifts of unlimited size. They frequently chose to bring that inheritance to the church in the form of a monastery, which the landed aristocracy found convenient for storing family wealth beyond the reach of greedy suitors. The child Rusticula brought a huge family fortune to the convent in Arles where she was hidden after her rescue from the suitor who had kidnapped her. The crown often resented such sequestering of noble wealth and sometimes attacked it directly. The depredations of the mayor of the palace, Ega, who threatened Burgundofara's establishment, lie in the background of the hagiographer's tale of divine favors showered upon the monastery.

Like poverty, virginity was less highly regarded than in the ascetic models of the late classical world. Nearly half of our saints were married, and most of those had children. Only in the case of Genovefa, the closest to the Roman tradition, was virginity seen to have special potency. Their wealth made these women the objects of competition between their sovereigns and their parents, and even Christ appears as a contending suitor. In the story of Glodesind, a new theme emerges in which the heroine defies parental wishes in order to become a bride of Christ. Sadalberga's father feared to allow her to follow the same course and persuaded her to accept the king's matchmaking. In some cases, like that of Gertrude of Nivelles, the hagiographic convention may have masked paternal desire to keep a daughter and her wealth out of royal control. In that context, the sexual status of the saint—virgin, widow, or separated wife—made little difference, despite the rhetorical flourishes of some of the biographers. Wealth and noble status, rightly employed, were unabashedly offered as qualifications for sainthood. None of these women alienated themselves from their husbands or fathers so far as to lose them.

Family connections strengthened the natural administrative talents of great abbesses, while their active alliance with abbots and bishops (who were sometimes also their relatives) assured them the ecclesiastical support they needed without undermining the liberties of the communities. Their aristocratic rank and self-assurance enabled them to recruit members, publicize their communities, administer estates, and enhance their resources by deploying the spiritual attraction of miracles and relics. Their charitable services and spiritual offerings gave them a secure and necessary place in the developing structure of early medieval society.

Thus Merovingian Gaul produced a new model of sanctity: the great monastic lady, withdrawn from worldly power and worldly comfort but not from the world's misery and strife. Hagiographers praised her as a model of hospitality, a virtue antithetical to the original desert ideal. Abbesses entertained relatives and other noble travelers, neighborhood magnates, and prelates, who responded with generous gifts. They supported chaplains, working people, pilgrims, invalids, and beggars. They cared for the sick and the poor either temporarily or permanently, as seems to be the case with the five demoniacs housed in the upper stories of Anstrude's monastery. Some noble abbesses acted as peacemakers and as protectors of fugitives and prisoners. Unconsecrated women sought the convent simply for protection while their armed enemies prowled about the sanctuary. Family loyalty entangled the saints in political rivalries that brought violent men into the convent itself. Miracles assured the reader that a sainted woman was a powerful friend and a dangerous enemy, even against armed and violent men.

The clergy are usually classed among the poor beneficiaries of a saint's charity, and to some degree this reflected conditions during the conquest. In the sixth century, when bishops were more closely aligned to the conquered population than to their rulers, noble women enjoyed an independent footing in their relationships with the church hierarchy. The collaboration between Clothild and Bishop Remigius presented in our ninth-century text reflects the ultimate shape of a painfully developed tradition. In sixth-century versions of the story, the bishop appears only after Clothild had completed her risky venture. Bishop Médard was initially hesitant to support Radegund's decision to defy her royal husband. Bishops were subservient to the power of queens, as was Radegund's friend Fortunatus and Balthild's assistant Genesius. Indeed, when a contest of wills developed between her and her bishop, as in the case of her control of the powerful relic of the Holy Cross, Radegund was generally able to have her own way.

However, as the Frankish aristocracy integrated into the hierarchy, the bonds between sainted women and bishops tightened. Some clerical supporters were relatives or friends of the saint's family. Some were not. They provided a counterpower to those secular magnates who put obstacles in her path. Women often worked with bishops or abbots who validated their personal designs and served them as intermediaries with angry husbands, families, and even kings. Miracles during life gave way to visions supporting clerical preaching. Miracles after death depended upon clerical support for the saint's cult. The way to heaven was strait, and seventh-century visionaries were often reminded of the clergy, and of Saint Peter, who controlled its successful passage.

In a practical sense, bishops and abbots gave direction and support to women who wished to give themselves and their fortunes to the church. At the end of the sixth century, the Irish saint Columbanus organized a monastery at Luxeuil that became the center for resuming the painstaking process of converting the pagan peasantry. His monastic rule, which stressed internal discipline and encouraged external relations with the surrounding rural community, widely replaced the Rule of Caesarius of Arles that cloistered women within cities.[26] By 600, Pope Gregory I was promoting the Rule of Benedict of Nursia, written in the latter half of the sixth century, for women as well as men.[27] Although rarely adopted in its entirety, many of its elements were in use in Gallic communities. Two rules written expressly for communities of women by Bishop Donatus of Besançon and Abbot Waldebert of Luxeuil indicate that most communities combined individual elements of all these rules as best suited their own needs.[28] Bishops often took nuns out of one community and sent them to direct a new sisterhood, as the lives of Bertilla, Sadalberga, and Austreberta demonstrate. Such women with proven records in the communal life became solid links in the networks of women who flocked to the monasteries.

Many of our texts describe the saint as leaving father and mother or husband and children to follow after Christ, exchanging a mortal spouse for an immortal union. None so far despised the world that she did not secure the continued support of noble relatives in her project. They did not inhabit a world lacking in familial sentiment. The plaint of Rusticula's mother for her lost chick and Anstrude's terrible lament for her murdered brother exemplify the power of blood ties. Even the grim Rictrude was defended by her biographer as a proponent of the "spare the rod" school of child-rearing. But their scope was limited. Theis has criticized the popular thesis that seventh-century saints represented the aspirations of an extended kindred.[29] He notes that the texts reflect no blood ties beyond the immediate nuclear family.

Seventh-century noblewomen were in an unparalleled position to deploy their resources independently. Our texts insist that they seized upon the monastic life to liberate themselves from the violent secular world and that they sought their own spiritual self-realization. It would be foolish to become so fascinated by their structural position that we forget their own agenda. The monastic life itself was framed in terms of a better and closer family than the world could provide. Moreover, the aristocratic habit of keeping monasteries within the founding family made the community their adopted children. Thus Anstrude's nuns shared her sorrow for the lost Baldwin, and Gertrude's

---

26. *Regula S. Columbani*, PL 80:209–86.

27. Annotated translation in Meisel and del Mastro, *The Rule of Saint Benedict*.

28. Donatus episcopi Vesontionensis, *Regula ad virginis*, PL 87:273–98; McNamara and Halborg, "The Rule of Donatus of Besançon: A Working Translation"; Waldebert of Luxeuil, *Regula cuiusdam patris ad virgines*, PL 88:1053–70.

29. Theis, "Saints sans famille?"

daughters rejoiced in the care of her niece. While the physical mothers of saints are commonly called *genetrices*, the word *mater* was reserved for the role of the abbess within the spiritual family. Similarly *soror*, as opposed to the more physical *germana*, was reserved for sisters in the community. The greatest instances of grief, loss, and familial affection are reserved to the monastic daughters, who regularly bemoan their fate as orphans when their founding mother is taken away from them.

The saintly abbesses in our stories remained astonishingly free to invent their own way of life through the application and interpretation of rules written by men. Our texts helped them to profit from one another's examples. Radegund's correspondence with Abbess Caesaria illuminates a process of sharing experiences through a network of women and men devoted to the monastic experiment. Radegund adopted the rule composed by Caesarius of Arles for his sister's convent.[30] She employed his principle of claustration to protect herself from her husband but did not hesitate to correspond with her royal relatives or personally attend the visitors who converged upon her convent.

The care and nurturing of these communities clearly provided much joy to both the mothers and their daughters. But life in the convent was not all sunshine and light. Many women were hustled out of the world as soon as the monastery became an established institution in Gaul, and they had a tendency to pursue their own ambitions with little regard for communal peace. Other women lived temporarily or permanently in monasteries although they had no evident vocation for the religious life. Children were brought into the monastery in infancy. Some were raised to be nuns and successfully embraced their vocation, as did the nun Baudonivia who wrote one of the lives of Radegund. Others completed their education and married, like the niece of Abbess Leubevera, who catered her elaborate wedding party in the Poitiers cloister. Other women were formally imprisoned in convents.

Unlike later convents, the typical Merovingian institution housed women from every rung of the social ladder, and most of the saints used their fortunes to provide shelter for the helpless, like the six female slaves ransomed by Bishop Bercharius in 696 who formed the core of his community at Puellemoutiers. Although women of servile origins were unlikely to be the leaders of any attempt at insubordination, there is no guarantee that they were really prepared to live like nuns. They may have been more interested in improving their social status, a motive recognized and strictly forbidden in the Rules of Donatus and of Waldebert. On the other side, Caesarius had to

30. McCarthy, *Rule for Nuns of Saint Caesarius of Arles*.

restrain the noble sisters of Arles from attempting to turn their humbler sisters into personal servants, an impulse Austreberta punished with miraculous speed.

The lives of saintly abbesses were shaped to exemplify the need for stern discipline within the context of maternal responsibility. To maintain the community, nuns bonded in a fashion generally reserved to men. The imagery of virility, athletic competition, and military service runs throughout these lives. In patronizing the cults of sainted women and encouraging the composition of their vitae, the church not only rewarded women who contributed to the multifaceted monastic mission, but also forged a powerful didactic instrument for the training of new recruits, peculiarly suited to bridge the gaps between classes and races. Their rules firmly stated that the only acceptable distinctions within a community were those of virtue and office. Indeed, the offices themselves—the abbess and prioress elected by the community and their adjutants whom they appointed—were intended to be allotted also as rewards for virtue. The other sisters were ranked according to seniority in religion. The sisters who had been longest in the convent took the lead in choir, at table, and in all processional activity unless they were demoted for some lapse in discipline.

The abbess heard daily confessions from her nuns and gave them necessary penances.[31] In this manner, they were encouraged to police themselves and to forestall punishment by correcting their faults before they were translated into overt action. Within the community, elaborate lists of crimes and punishments were illustrated by the examples of saints and stories of divine intervention, which the nuns read constantly or heard during their meals and recreational periods.[32] In this sense, even our most high-flown miracle stories take on a historical life of their own, as instruments in the formation of the monastic community. The texts shaped the awareness of their hearers and provided them with models for their own lives.

This is particularly noticeable in the collection of stories reported from Faremoutiers in Jonas of Bobbio's biography of Burgundofara. Rewards and punishments for various nuns systematically point up the main characteristics of Columbanus' rule. Nuns were encouraged through their reading to believe that miracles would relieve their daily rounds of menial labor. These stories, preserved and ritually repeated in Merovingian convents, give shape

---

31. Donatus of Besançon, Rule, c. 23. Waldebert advised that a systematic review of faults be undertaken three times a day, rule, c. 6.

32. In "Columbanus, His Followers, and the Merovingian Church," Riché argues that private penance and constant reading joined with prayer were the hallmarks of Irish spirituality that left a lasting mark.

and meaning to a dreary and often unwelcome round of daily life for women who willingly or unwillingly struggled to live together in harmony. They illustrate the petty temptations against which the spirit of charity had to strive.

History favors success. To be remembered and serve as examples to the future, saints had to temper their own talents for innovation and leadership with qualities of humility and reverence that recommended them to the male hierarchy who controlled the historical tradition. We have no records of those women who may have attempted unorthodox experiments in living or whose communities failed through poverty or lack of discipline. We have only one example, the suspiciously late life of Waldetrude, of a woman who tried to withdraw totally from the world. Obedience and respect for priests ranks almost as high as charity among the desirable virtues listed in the texts. We might, therefore, best view these histories as a collaboration between the saint, her clerical biographer, and their audience. Initially, the subject framed her aspirations and began to work toward sanctity. Either she appealed to the church for support or the project was initiated by a missionary. The clergy set norms of behavior that would define her success. The saint then acted out the role provided by the clergy, who enshrined the results in a text that would provide guidance for the next aspirant.

At the same time, the texts are increasingly focussed on the rounds of prayer and liturgy that characterize the lives of consecrated women. The regular offices of psalm singing and praying in unison dominated the life of the sisterhoods. The rules they lived by outlined the round of chant adapted to the changing seasons and penalized any sister who put personal inconvenience or necessity above the chain of prayer that bound them together.[33] The monastery was the scene of an ongoing battle against the forces of evil. The nuns were military cohorts, living on the battle lines. The hagiographic texts themselves serve as training manuals and as inspiration. The presence of the devil as a tempter, as a possessor of the unwary, or even as an earthly enemy, is pervasive, replacing the old pagan persecutors as the agent of suffering and the reason for demonstrations of heroic faith.

Confronting demons, people possessed by demons, worshipers of pagan gods, and such representatives of earthly "evil" as the mayors of the palace Ega and Ebroin, the nuns relied on the solidarity bred of training and discipline. The results are first demonstrated in an almost miraculous strength and self-control in the face of both worldly and otherworldly force and finally demonstrations of the divine power at their command. In grief, they com-

33. For a discussion of hagiography as a tool for enforcing monastic rules, see McNamara, "Ordeal of Community."

forted one another, and in want they shared what they had. In times of danger, a cohort of psalm-singing sisters might even drive armed and violent men out of their cloistered precincts.

Throughout the seventh century, there was increased attention to the deathbed as the focal point where sainthood was proved. Abbess Bertilla was shocked when her candidate, Queen Balthild, seemed to die without warning. Fortunately, a discreet sister was able to reassure her that the saint had received all the required revelations of impending death and salvation but concealed them out of consideration for the abbess's own illness. A united sisterhood stood at a dying woman's deathbed to sing her into heaven while her parting revelations strengthened them for their unending struggles to perfect themselves. The troops were thus reassured that they followed a victorious general. The visionary content of seventh-century texts increased, and the saints were credited with powers of prophecy and illumination directed toward making the promises of bliss in another world concrete. As the saint's miracles in life decreased in number, the power of relics, tombs, and associated artifacts like oil, dust, funeral palls, and candles grew, weapons like the texts themselves in the ongoing battle.

The deeds and even the voices of women speak to us from these documents with a clarity rarely accomplished in historical texts. Although conforming to ecclesiastical prescriptions, at least two of the biographies that follow were written by women who knew their subjects. Others reflect the direct testimony of women within the cloister walls. They lived in a rough and brutal age, an age moderns have condemned as "the dark ages," but from the peril and suffering of their lives they shaped themselves as models of womanly power, womanly achievement, and womanly voices. They did not hide their lights under a bushel, but lit candles in the darkness and set them high upon a candlestick. Today, their light still shines.

Jo Ann McNamara

I
Genovefa
(423–502)

Germanus of Auxerre and Lupus of Troyes first encountered the child Genovefa in her hometown of Nanterre about 429. The Roman world was rapidly crumbling before the advances of Germanic tribes. To the south, Augustine of Hippo was soon to die while a Vandal army stormed the gates of his city. At the northern fringe, Patrick had barely begun his mission to Ireland before Anglo-Saxon invaders began to encroach on the Romanized Britons. The collapse of the Roman Empire left the Catholic church as the only outpost of Roman authority, but the church itself had to cope with various heresies that flourished among the barbarians who had heretofore received Christianity without its accompanying hierarchical structure. The two Gallic bishops were on their way to Britain to rally the Catholic people against the Pelagian heresy. In Roman Gaul, Arian Visigoths had infested the southern provinces and the pagan Franks had established a kingdom in the north around Tournai extending south in Genovefa's lifetime to Soissons, Laon, and finally Paris. The evangelization of the countryside had barely begun.

This translation is drawn from the edition in *AS*, January 3, 137–53, designated the oldest version by Kohler, *Etude critique*. Bruno Krusch supplied a later edition for MGH, SRM 3:204–38. He was convinced that many things about the vita, including the un-Latin name of the heroine, proved that it was a worthless historical document, a thesis he expounded in detail in "Die Fälschung der Vita Genovefa." In *Die Heiliger der Merovinger*, 190–96, Bernoulli went even further to argue that Genovefa's historical reality had synchretized with legends of antique Gallic goddesses of corn and rivers. Scholarly debate in the last decades of the nineteenth century and the first of our own reflected the nationalistic struggles which preceded World War I. French critics represented by Leclercq in the *DACL* and more recently by Riché, "Interêts historiques," have supported the defense of the Belgian hagiographer Kurth, "Etude critique," against Krusch. The entire argument has most recently been summed up by Heinzelmann and Poulin in *Les vies anciennes*. We have implicitly followed their arguments that the life is authentic, written as claimed by an anonymous monk about 520, in our decision to use the *AS* edition, which appears to lack many of the inaccuracies that so offended Krusch. We accept the opinion of Graus, "Die Gewalt," 192, that this is a Christian fable, not a pagan one. As we have done with all the saints represented in this volume, we have omitted material concerning miracles from a later period.

The little girl whom Germanus picked out of an admiring crowd as a candidate for future sainthood was destined to live a long life. She moved through a wild, half-pagan countryside and lived among excitable people easily moved to excesses of admiration and hostility. In 451, she rallied the people of Paris, her adopted city, against the Huns, led by their savage king Attila. A few years later, as their intermediary with the Frankish king Childeric, she gained the right to collect food for the besieged population and moved him to pardon his condemned prisoners. She was eighty years old or more when she died. Paris had become part of a Frankish kingdom, and its king had become a Catholic Christian. It is perhaps no small aspect of the Frankish success in winning Gallo-Roman loyalty that Clovis's consort Clothild may have commissioned Genovefa's biography and promoted her cult as patron of Paris.[1] The anti-Arian elements in the *Vita Genofevae* would then reflect the queen's own sentiments and her husband's policies.

Inspired by the saintly bishop of Auxerre, Genovefa dedicated her life and her virginity to the service of God. Her asceticism, however, was not defined and regulated by any established rule, nor was her life bounded by the walls of a conventual community. Asceticism had been introduced into Roman Gaul by the saintly Martin of Tours (d. 397) and achieved some popularity among spiritually ambitious aristocrats of the early fifth century. But in the north outside of Tours, it did not result in monasticism, which flourished in the more urban south of France. Queen Clothild retired to Tours after Clovis's death. In Genovefa's vita, anti-Arianism and the heavy use of Martin as a model strongly support the argument that the text originated there. Genovefa lived at home with her mother and then with her godmother. In her later years she may have set up housekeeping with a few companions, but her biographer indicates no formal arrangement and does not mention whether the women who came to her for guidance remained under her roof. The principal monastic foundations in Gaul in Genovefa's time, and the only ones we know of to accept groups of women lay along the Mediterranean, at Marseille, Lérins, and in the Burgundian realm, not very accessible to a Parisian girl.[2] The first written rule to make an impact in the north was that of the community of Arles founded about 510 by Bishop Caesarius.

---

1. Heinzelmann and Poulin, *Les vies anciennes*, 53, suggest that the author was a clerk or a monk from the *schola* of Tours patronized by Clothild during her widowhood. He could have been transferred to the Church of the Holy Apostles in Paris when she built it. He says himself, c. 51, that he decided to write the work eighteen years after Genovefa's death, ca. 520. Twice, c. 8 and c. 30, he declines to repeat things that Genovefa is said to have discerned about people's secret thoughts which suggests a reluctance to offend living persons. Heinzelmann speculates (80) that the author may have derived his material from the testimony of Bessus the priest, Clothild, and Genovefa herself.
2. Wood, "A Prelude to Columbanus," 3–32.

Thus, despite her consecration, Genovefa was not bound to a rule of stability or claustration. The enduring legend that she was a peasant has now been set aside, and she has been located among the Gallic upper classes.[3] She owned fields and went out to harvest them herself. She walked the city streets to church services and made use of the imperial transport services when her religious mission took her out of the city. In brief, whatever the actual date of composition, this life reflects an age when a saintly woman was free, indeed constrained, to create her own models and her own way of life.[4] Although her social status was higher than French popular tradition would suggest, Gallic instincts were correct. Uniquely among the female saints of Gaul and Frankland, she did not originate from the conquering aristocracy, but from among its victims. She lived in a turbulent age, and she played no small role in its events.

As with the subsequent lives in this volume, brief notices of scholarly criticism of this biography and of specific historical events noted in its pages appear in the footnotes.

The Life of Genovefa, a Virgin of Paris in Gaul
■

1. The blessed Genovefa was born in the parish of Nanterre which is nearly seven kilometers from the city of Paris.[5] Her father was called Severus and her mother Gerontia.[6] I believe that in her earliest years the faithful noticed first her religious devotion and then, in due course, the grace that God conferred upon her.

3. Heinzelmann and Poulin, *Les vies anciennes*, 28.

4. Some written models existed both in Latin and Greek. Jerome's lengthy eulogies of the noble Roman women who introduced the ascetic life into Italy, edited in J. P. Migne, *PL*, vol. 22, are partially available in English in the Loeb Classical Library edition. See also Gregory of Nyssa's life of his sister Saint Macrina, *Ascetical Works*, trans. Callahan, and Gerontius, *Life of Saint Melania*, trans. Clark. There is no indication in the biography that Genovefa had more than the most rudimentary knowledge of the ascetic tradition. Her biographer relies on the model of Saint Martin in framing her life as outlined extensively by Poulin in his half of Heinzelmann and Poulin, *Les vies anciennes*.

5. Millibus, units of roughly a thousand paces, has been translated as *kilometers* for convenience throughout the volume.

6. These names and Genovefa's own Germanic name convinced Heinzelmann and Poulin, *Les vies anciennes*, 28, that she was a noble from the Gallo-Roman aristocracy, which would explain Germanus's attention and later her ability to command the *annona*. In his section Heinzelmann supplies (28–31) a detailed set of references for the other proper names mentioned in the text. He also notes (81–82) that only the lives of Genovefa and of Severin of Noricum among saints of this period lack some indication of social status; since Severin was a consul, the lack of notice does not preclude a high rank for her.

2. The holy and venerable men, Bishops Germanus and Lupus, were setting out for Britain to conquer the Pelagian heresy which threatened those coasts.[7] Like tares sown over wheat, that heresy asserted that one whose parents were both baptized can be saved without baptism whereas all divine teaching has shown that no one can have eternal life who has not been born again with water and the Holy Spirit.[8] Triumphantly, they were to drive that heresy from the province with scriptural proofs and many powerful miracles. But as I have said, they were on the way to Britain, when they visited the aforesaid parish to stay a while and particularly to pray. Not far from the church, a multitude of common people came to meet them seeking their blessing and, through the Holy Spirit, Saint Germanus sensed from a distance the most holy Genovefa in the midst of the rushing crowd of both sexes, men, women and children. He asked immediately that she be brought to him. Kissing her on the head, he inquired among the crowd for her name and asked whose child she was. Straightaway, the bystanders told him Genovefa's name. Her father and mother were summoned and holy Germanus said to them: "Is this infant your daughter?" And they answered: "Ours, my lord." At that, Saint Germanus said to them: "Happy are the parents of such worshipful offspring! You should know that on the day of her birth the angels in heaven celebrated a mystery of great joy and exultation. For she will be great before the face of the Lord. Many people, marvelling at her life and holy conduct, will reject evil and turn from a dishonest and shameful life to God. So they will win forgiveness for their sins and the reward of life from Christ."

3. After a pause, he spoke to Genovefa: "My daughter, Genovefa." And she responded: "Your servant hears you, holy father. Tell me what you command." Saint Germanus said: "Let me ask, in case you are afraid to declare yourself openly, if you wish to preserve your body immaculate and intact, consecrated as a bride of Christ in sanctimony."[9] Genovefa responded: "Blessings on you, my Father, for your suggestion, which is perhaps your own wish, is indeed the very thing I long for. It is my wish, holy father," she said. "And I pray that the Lord will deign to answer my prayer." Saint Germanus

---

7. Germanus of Auxerre (d. 448) and Lupus of Troyes (d. 478). See a further account of their adventures in Constantius of Lyon, *Life of Saint Germanus*, in *Western Fathers*, ed. and trans. Hoare, 283–320, dating their first trip at 429. Their accomplishments in Britain were recalled by Bede, *History*, 1:10–18. In *Poetry and Letters*, Chadwick is but one critic of Constantius' claim that Germanus made two journeys to Britain in the same cause.

8. Evans, *Pelagius*, 78, cites Augustine, Sermon 294, 16–18, charging Pelagius with this doctrine, which seems a sufficient answer to the criticism raised by Krusch. Duchesne found the same "false" definition in the contemporary *Liber Pontificalis*, according to Leclercq, *DACL*.

9. The most common word for a consecrated woman in Merovingian texts is *sanctimonial* rather than nun. We have used nun throughout our book for simplicity of reading, but as it is used here the word is deliberately punned with matrimony, a practice that writers later expressed as *castimony*.

said to her: "Have faith, my daughter and act manfully. What you believe in your heart and declare with your mouth, you must strive to fulfill in your deeds. For the Lord will give you strength and fortitude for your adornment."

4. Then, entering the church for the celebration of the spiritual offices of *nones* and vespers, Saint Germanus kept his hand upon her head.[10] And when they had eaten and sung a hymn, he told Severus to lodge with his daughter in that same hospice for the night and bade him return to him at dawn before his departure. When sunlight was cleansing the world,[11] her father brought her back as directed. I don't know what celestial things Saint Germanus perceived in her, but he said: "Hail, daughter Genovefa! Do you remember what you promised me yesterday concerning your virginity?" To which Genovefa replied: "I remember, holy father, what I promised to God and to you. God helping me, I hope to keep my mind chaste and my body untainted to the end." Then Saint Germanus plucked a copper coin bearing the sign of the cross from the ground, where by God's favor it had fallen, and gave it to her as a great gift.[12] He said to her, "Have this coin pierced, and wear it always hanging about your neck as a reminder of me; never suffer your neck or fingers to be burdened with any other metal, neither gold nor silver, nor pearl studded ornament. For, if your mind is preoccupied with trivial worldly adornment, you will be shorn of eternal and celestial ornaments." And, in farewell, he besought that she would remember him often in Christ. Commending her to Severus, her father, the men continued on the road which they had been following with God's help.

II. Her sanctity during a paralysis is commended in several ways.

5. Some days later when her mother was going to church on a solemn feast day, she ordered Genovefa to remain at home. But by no means could she get rid of the weeping girl who was clamoring: "With Christ's support, I will keep the vow I made to Saint Germanus. I shall haunt the threshold of the church so that I may deserve to become the bride of Christ as was promised me by his blessed confessor." At that, her mother was so angry that she boxed her daughter's ears only to be struck blind herself on the spot. The divine majesty, to demonstrate Genovefa's grace, let her mother suffer that blindness for two years less three months. Finally, when she remembered what the highest bishop had said about her daughter, her mother summoned her and said: "Daughter, I earnestly beseech you to take the dipper and hasten to the well to bring me water." Speedily, she went to the well and there at the rim she began to cry because she had caused her mother's blindness. Then, stifling

---

10. The devotions of the hours of prayer in Gaul is discussed by Taft, *Liturgy of the Hours*, 100–115.

11. Virgil, *Aeneid*, 4, 6.

12. Dubois and Beaumont-Maillet, *Sainte Geneviève de Paris*, 21, discuss the several coins that meet this description issued in the fourth and fifth centuries.

her sobs, she filled the vessel with water and brought it to her mother. Sighing as she did so, she signed it with the power of the cross. Her mother stretched her hands toward heaven and, with faith and veneration took the water her daughter brought and dabbed some of it on her eyes. That soothed her eyes and she began to see a little. When she had done this two or three times, her sight was entirely restored.

6. Then, with two girls much senior to her, she was brought to Bishop Vilicius to be consecrated.[13] They were to be offered for consecration in order of their ages but the aforesaid Pontiff with divine perception saw that Genovefa's merits were far above those of the other virgins before him. So he said, "She who is coming last is to take first place for she has already achieved sanctification in heaven." And so, having been blessed, they all filed out of the Bishop's sight.[14]

7. When her parents were dead, the blessed Genovefa went to live in the city of Paris at her godmother's invitation. At that time, that the Lord might test her strength in infirmity and the grace conferred upon her by Christ might shine more brightly, her body was stricken with a paralysis that so weakened her limbs that her joints scarcely seemed to hold together. For three days, her severely afflicted body lay imprisoned by this infirmity, lifeless, save for a little blush in her cheeks. Later when she had regained health, she testified that her spirit had been led by an angel to the resting place of the just, where she saw the rewards which God prepares for those who love Him, in which infidels put no faith.

8. Then to many living in this world she clearly revealed their secret thoughts. But I prefer to be silent about this rather than make it known to the envious, on account of those presumptuous people who are excessively devoted to backbiting. For when they maliciously slander good people like her they plainly reveal their own blind prejudices.

9. After that, Saint Germanus came again to Paris, on his way to Britain for the second time and all the people went out from the city to greet him.[15] Before anything else he asked solicitously what Genovefa had been doing. But the common people who prefer to carp at goodness rather than imitate it,

13. The name of this bishop has caused much discussion. The editors of the *Acta* used Julicus and offered *Illico* as an alternative reading. Krusch reads it as *Vilicus* and, finding no bishop of that name in early records, added it to his evidence against the authenticity of the life. Leclercq, *DACL*, accepts Villicus but thinks it might mean *rural bishop*. Heinzelmann and Poulin, *Les vies anciennes*, 13, 28, persuasively identify him as Vilicius, Bishop of Bourges, considerably before 453.

14. Krusch criticizes this incident as incompatible with the activity of Genovefa's future life. Kurth, however, accepts it as proof of sixth-century authorship, predating the more formalized claustration of nuns in later centuries.

15. Heinzelmann and Poulin, *Les vies anciennes*, 73, n. 344, date this trip between 444 and 447.

asserted that she was not as great as he thought she was. Wholly despising that unjust voice, the blessed bishop entered the city and went to Genovefa's hospice and greeted her with such humility that everyone marvelled. Having prayed, he showed those who had scorned her how, in the privacy of her cell, she had turned the ground to mud with her tears. And sitting down, he told them of her early life just as it had appeared openly to all Nanterre. And likewise commending her to the people along the way, he went back to his road.

III. She repels the Huns from Paris by her prayers.

10. When it was noised abroad that Attila the King of the Huns, overcome with savage rage, was laying waste the province of Gaul,[16] the terror-stricken citizens of Paris sought to save their goods and money from his power by moving them to other, safer cities. But Genovefa summoned the matrons of the city and persuaded them to undertake a series of fasts, prayers, and vigils in order to ward off the threatening disaster, as Esther and Judith had done in the past. Agreeing with Genovefa, the women gave themselves up to God and labored for days in the baptistery—fasting, praying and keeping watch as she directed. Meanwhile she persuaded the men that they should not remove their goods from Paris because the cities they deemed safer would be devastated by the raging Huns while Paris, guarded by Christ, would remain untouched by her enemies.

11. But during that time, the people of Paris rose against her, saying that a false prophetess had appeared in their midst who prevented them from transferring their goods from the doomed city to safer towns. The citizens were conspiring to punish Genovefa either by stoning or drowning her in the boundless deep, when an archdeacon arrived from the city of Auxerre who had once heard Saint Germanus give magnificent testimony for Genovefa.[17] He went to the meeting place where the citizens had assembled to plan her slaughter. When he had discovered their plans he said to them: "Oh citizens, don't consent to such a crime! For we have heard our Primate Germanus say that this woman whose murder you are plotting, was chosen by God from her mother's womb. And behold, I present these eulogies direct from Saint Germanus."[18] When the citizens of Paris realized from Saint Germanus' testimony that Genovefa was truly a most faithful servant of God, and when they

16. This occurred in 451.

17. Germanus had recently died at the court of Galla Placidia in Ravenna, about 448. Lupus, his companion, was still alive when Constantius wrote Germanus's biography.

18. Again, Krusch attacks this tale, translating *eulogies* as *gifts*. Kurth responds that at most the word refers to *blessed bread*, in no way unsuitable to send to an ascetic; even likelier, it means simply *praise* or *greeting*.

saw the eulogies which the archdeacon had brought to present to her, the fear of God entered into them. Marvelling at what the archdeacon had said, they gave up their evil plan and made an end of their treachery.

12. On that day the Apostle's word was fulfilled: "All men have not faith. But the Lord is faithful who shall establish you and keep you from evil."[19] The Bishops Martin and Anianus have been greatly praised for their amazing virtues. One day, near the city of Worms, the former went into battle without weapons. Having thus allayed the fury of the opposing armies, he obtained a treaty.[20] And when the Huns besieged the city of Orléans, the latter by his prayers assisted the Patrician Aëtius and his Goths in keeping it from destruction.[21] Aren't the same honors due to Genovefa, who drove away the same army by her prayers so that it would not surround Paris?

IV. She built a basilica, now called the Priory of Saint Denis de Strata.

13. From her fifteenth to her fiftieth year, she never broke her fast from Sunday to Thursday and from Thursday to Sunday.[22] Thus, taking a little food only on the two sacred days of the week, Sunday and Thursday, she abstained during the rest of the week. In fact, her diet consisted of barley bread and beans, which she stirred with oil into a new batch every two or three weeks in an earthenware pot. In her whole life, she never drank wine or any intoxicating beverage. After her fiftieth year, at the urging of the bishops, whom it is sacrilege to contradict, she began to eat fish and milk with her barley bread, thus heeding the Lord's word: "Who heareth you, heareth me; who despiseth you, despiseth me."[23]

14. Every time she contemplated Heaven, she dissolved into tears. Since she was pure in heart, she is believed to have seen the heavens open and our Lord Jesus Christ standing at the right hand of God, as Luke the Evangelist says of Blessed Stephen.[24] For the Lord made no idle promise when He said: "Blessed are the pure in heart, for they shall see God."[25]

15. Each of the twelve spiritual virgins, described by Hermas in his book called *The Pastor*, kept her company. And they were called: Faith, Abstinence, Patience, Magnanimity, Simplicity, Innocence, Concordia, Charity, Discipline,

19. 2 Thessalonians 3:26–30. All biblical citations that match the Vulgate have been rendered from the King James translation to preserve their traditional quality. Where the hagiographers depart from direct quotation, so have we.

20. Sulpicius Severus, *Life of Martin*, 4, in *Western Fathers*, ed. and trans. Hoare, 16.

21. Wallace-Hadrill, *Frankish Church*, 150–62. Ewig, *Spätantikes und fränkisches Gallien*, 1:119, notes that Orléans was also Attila's objective.

22. In *Western Fathers*, 288, Hoare speculated that Genovefa may have been emulating the practice of Saint Germanus, *Life*, 3.

23. Luke 10:16.

24. Acts 7:55.

25. Matthew 5:8.

Chastity, Truth, and Prudence.[26] All these were inseparable and indivisible in Genovefa.

16. I cannot keep silence about her great love and veneration for Catalacus,[27] the village where Saint Denis and his companions, Rusticus and Eleutherius, died and were buried.[28] Blessed Genovefa's devotion was so fervent that she longed to build a basilica in honor of Saint Denis Bishop and Martyr but she lacked the means. One day when some of the city priests made their usual visit, she said to them: "Venerable holy fathers and my elders in Christ, I beseech you to take up a special collection to build a basilica in honor of Saint Denis." No one doubted the terrible and awesome quality of the site, but they said to her: "In our reduced condition, we haven't the means to build. We don't even have facilities for boiling lime."[29] Then the Holy Spirit filled Genovefa; her face shone but her mind shone still more brightly as she prophesied in plain words: "May it please your holinesses to go outside, and walk over the city bridge and report back to me what you will hear."

17. After they had gone out into the street, they lingered to see if they might hear anything pertinent to the holy virgin's wishes.[30] Soon two swineherds standing near them began talking and one said to the other: "While I was

26. Book 3, *Similitude* 9:15, in *The AnteNicene Fathers*, ed. Roberts and Donaldson, 2. The passage concerns the building of a mystical tower, and therefore might have seemed particularly apt to introduce the story that follows.

27. Krusch, ed., *MGH, SRM* 3:221, challenges this place name as proof of an eighth-century author, but Heinzelmann refutes his argument from the evidence of seventh-century coins, *Les vies anciennes*, 21. Wallace-Hadrill, *Frankish Church*, 182, identifies it as Roma Castellum and places it in the geography of Childeric's Paris by the single city bridge mentioned below. He defended the sixth-century date based on archaeological evidence from the site.

28. This reference to the apostolate of St. Denis provoked Krusch's criticism. The Bollandists omitted a paragraph of their base MS dealing with him and his apostolic commission on the grounds that it was lacking in other MSS. The A version as printed by Krusch (*MGH, SRM* 3:221) reads as follows: "Saint Denis was the first bishop of Paris, and submitted to martyrdom at the hands of his persecutors a mile outside that same city. As I have learned, from the elders' accounts of the story as related in his *passio*, he was ordained bishop in Rome by Saint Clement, the son of Saint Peter the Apostle in Baptism, and sent here to this province by him. The lection tells us that the first and second bishops of Rome were Linus and Cletus, both ordained by Saint Peter to perform, as it is written, the office of the episcopacy whereas Saint Peter fulfilled the role of apostle. The third bishop was Clement, whom Peter formally seated on his throne shortly before the day of his martyrdom. Clement it was, who set down in writing the story of Saint Peter's conflict in Caesaria with Simon Magus and the miracles and wonders everywhere performed by Saint Peter. So, now I have explained about Saint Clement, the successor of the aforesaid apostle, I will resume my original narrative."

29. For mixing in mortar; Bernard Bachrach, personal communication.

30. MGH has instead "They stood in stupefied amazement."

following some pigs wandering toward their pasture,[31] I found a huge lime kiln." The other herder replied: "And I found a tree in the forest uprooted by the wind. Under the roots, there was a similar furnace which looks as though no one has stripped anything from it." Hearing this, the priests lifted their faces aloft, fixing their eyes joyfully on heaven, and blessed God who deigned to confer such grace on Genovefa his servant. Following the swineherds' direction, they found the sites of the lime kilns and returned to report what the herders had said. At that, tears of joy spilled over her bosom. As the priests left her house, she sank to her knees and spent the whole night kneeling on the ground, weeping and praying, begging God for help and assistance to raise a basilica in honor of His high bishop and martyr, Saint Denis.

18. At dawn, her vigil ended, she hurried straight to Genesius the priest and pleaded with him that they might build the basilica in the said martyr's honor. She pointed out that God had already provided the lime for it. Indeed, when Genesius the priest heard about the lime he was overcome with awe. Prone on the ground, he honored Genovefa and promised that he would strive day and night to do what she had asked. Then all the citizens offered their help in answer to Genovefa's prayer and the basilica honoring the oft-mentioned martyr was soon built to its very roof-top.

19. The miracle the Lord performed through her demonstrates the value of the undertaking. Carpenters gathered in the forest and while some of them felled and sawed the wood for the building, others hauled it away in wagons. And they happened to run out of drink. Genovefa was unaware of this until Genesius the priest asked her to hearten the workers while he hurried to the city for drink. Hearing this, Genovefa asked them to bring her the vessel, called a butt, in which the drink had been kept. When it arrived, she ordered everyone to draw away from her. Kneeling on the ground, with flowing tears she prayed until she felt that she had won what she prayed for. Her prayers finished, she rose and made the sign of the cross over the vessel. Wonderful to say, the butt was instantly filled to the brim and the hired men, who drank copiously from it until their work on the basilica was done, gave God their hearty thanks.[32]

V. She cured a blind woman and a paralyzed woman by her prayers and she rekindled an extinct candle.[33]

20. It was her devout practice each Saturday night to keep vigil until the hour dawned, following the teaching of the Lord concerning the servant who

---

31. *Pastum vagantis*; the editors gave an alternative, *partum vacantis*: going to give birth.

32. Conceivably, this story provided a model for the Carolingian hagiographer of the *Vita Chrothildis*, c. 12.

33. As a result, the candle became Genovefa's traditional iconographical attribute.

awaited the master's return from a wedding.[34] Once, after a stormy night, when the crowing song of the cock indicated that the Lord's Day was near,[35] she went out of her cell to proceed to the basilica of Saint Denis. Suddenly the candle which was carried before her went out. All the virgins with her were frightened by the horrors of the night and the mud and the floods of water pouring from the clouds. Quickly, Genovefa asked for the extinguished candle and when she took it in her hand, it immediately lit up again. Holding it in her hand, she arrived at the basilica. There, shining before her, the burning candle was consumed by its own fire.[36]

21. Likewise, on the same occasion, she entered the church and lay down alone for a long time. Having completed her prayers, she rose from the pavement. A candle which no spark had touched kindled itself, by divine consent, at the touch of her hand.

22. They say that the candle in her cell lit up in her hand without being kindled by fire. And many invalids, instigated by faith, who procured a fragment of that candle were soon restored to pristine health.[37]

23. But another woman who secretly stole her shoes, lost her eyesight as soon as she got home. Then the little thief understood that Heaven had avenged Genovefa's injury on her. Led by another person, she returned the shoes and fell at Genovefa's feet, begging her to pardon her and restore her lost sight. Because she was kind, Genovefa, with a little smile, raised her from the dust with her own hands and, signing her eyes, restored her pristine sight.

24. The course of our narrative now requires us to recite a miracle the Lord did through her in the city of Lyon.[38] As she drew near to the town, a great part of the population came to meet her. Among them were the parents of a certain girl who had been paralyzed for nine years so that she could command no response from her limbs. The girl's parents, and the elders of the people persuaded Genovefa to go to the girl's house. Having prayed, she touched the limp members and ordered the girl to dress herself and put on her own shoes. Thus rising from her bed, whole and sound again she went

---

34. Luke 12:36; throughout, we have translated *Sabbath* as *Saturday.*

35. Pliny, *Historia Naturalis,* 10:21.

36. For a similar miracle, see the life of Aldegund, c. 18.

37. According to Constantius of Lyon, *Life of Saint Germanus,* 22, a woman named Nectariola performed similar miracles with straw the saint slept upon; so did the Empress Galla Placidia with bread and his wooden platter.

38. The text reads *Lugdunensis,* which provoked Krusch's skepticism. Kurth, "Etude critique," 82, made a strong case for Laon rather than Lyon, perhaps intending a "second Lyon" as Tours is called the "third Lyon," c. 44. Heinzelmann and Poulin, *Les vies anciennes,* 22, argue for Laon, attributing the confusion to an author not familiar with that area. They connect (101) her presence in Laon to her noble status and her relationship with Childeric shown in c. 25 because Laon is in his province of *Belgica secunda.*

directly to the church with the other people. And when the crowd saw the miracle, they blessed the Lord Jesus Christ who has deigned to confer such grace on them that love him. And Genovefa was led by the people from the town singing psalms and exulting.

VI. Gates, and hearts, open to her. Demons flee.

25. I cannot express the love and veneration that the illustrious Childeric bore her when he was King of the Franks. On one occasion, he went out of the city and ordered the gates closed so that Genovefa could not rescue some captives he meant to execute. But a faithful messenger conveyed news of the king's intentions to Genovefa and without delay she set off to save their lives. The people's amazement was wonderful to see when the city gate opened by itself when she touched it without a key. Then, gaining the king's presence, she persuaded him not to behead his captives.[39]

26. There was a certain saint in eastern lands, named Simeon of Cilicia in Syria, who was so full of contempt for the world that he sat on a column not far from Antioch for almost forty years.[40] And they say that he made eager inquiries about Genovefa from merchants going back and forth and asked them to greet her and convey his veneration for her; they also say that he earnestly desired her to remember him in her prayers.

27. A certain maiden of marriageable age named Cilinia, who had been betrothed, asked Genovefa to change her clothing that she might obtain the grace that Christ had conferred on Genovefa.[41] When the young man to whom she had been promised heard about this, he was filled with indignation. Without delay, he went to the town of Meaux, where Cilinia was staying with Genovefa. Hearing of the youth's arrival, Genovefa hurried to the church with Cilinia. As they fled to the church, a great miracle occurred, for the gate of the baptistery within the church opened of its own accord. Thus the girl was saved from the shipwreck and contagion of the world and she persevered in abstinence and chastity to the end.

28. At the same time, Cilinia brought Genovefa a maid from her retinue who had not been able to walk for two years because of illness. As Genovefa laid her hands upon her, she was immediately restored to health.

39. Critics again note that no parallel to this story appears in Gregory of Tours or other relevant material, but in "Etude critique" Kurth replies that in fact there are no sources of any kind for this period in Childeric's life. Heinzelmann and Poulin, *Les vies anciennes*, 73, suggest a date between 456 and 482.

40. Simon Stylites, d. 30 August 459.

41. "To change clothing" is a Merovingian commonplace for becoming a nun. Krusch believes this tale provides the key to the Carolingian forgery of this life. He identifies Cilinia with the mother of Saint Remigius and assumes that the document was intended to support a claim to her lands at Meaux by proving her son to be illegitimate. The story is refuted by Kurth, "Etude critique," 88.

29. Among the men and women who were presented to her, twelve in her own town of Paris were seriously troubled in spirit by demons. Invoking Christ to help her, Genovefa had immediate recourse to prayer. All of a sudden, the possessed people were suspended in the air: their hands did not touch the ceiling nor their feet the earth. Arising from her prayers, she ordered them to proceed to the basilica of Saint Denis the Martyr. The possessed cried out to her, that they were completely unable to walk out unless she set them loose. Genovefa made the sign of the cross over them and they were subdued. With their hands tied behind their backs, they proceeded in silence to the martyr's basilica. About two hours later, she followed them to the crowded basilica. Then, tearfully, she began to pray, lying on the pavement as was her custom, while the possessed clamored and shouted out loud that those whom she was entreating to come to her aid were already close at hand. Perhaps, as I believe, there were angels, martyrs and saints all gathered to help. At least, the Lord Himself was present Who is near to all who call Him honestly, Who grants the wishes of those who fear Him and Who hears the just pray that He save them.[42] Genovefa got up from her prayers and signed each of them in turn. And at once all those possessed by unclean spirits were cured. The nostrils of every bystander were filled with such a foul stench that they all believed those souls had been cleansed of the troubling demons. And the whole crowd magnified the Lord for such a sign.[43]

30. A girl came to Paris from Bourges whom the people believed to be immaculate though, in fact, she had polluted her body after her consecration.[44] Genovefa asked whether she was a consecrated virgin or a widow. She replied that she was consecrated as a virgin and worthy to offer herself to Christ's service with an intact body. But Genovefa revealed the place and the time and very man who had violated that body. And she who had professed herself falsely as a bride of Christ, overcome by her guilty conscience, fell at once at Genovefa's feet. Much could I tell of people like that! But because of the length of the narrative, I shall keep silent.

VII. She restored vision, strength, and life to various people. She procured supplies for the poor in time of famine.

31. Some time after that there was a woman with her whom she had

---

42. Psalms 144:18–19.

43. Constantius of Lyon, *Life of Saint Germanus*, 7, relates the story of a demoniac similarly prone to suspension in the air. Brown, *Relics and Social Status*, 13, discusses the role of the possessed in verifying the presence of the holy.

44. Heinzelmann and Poulin, *Les vies anciennes*, 73, put this in the context of the sack of Bourges during the Visigothic Euric's conquest of Aquitaine between 469 and 472. They suggest (97) that she was asked because consecrated virgins were exempt from certain taxes, whereas widows were not.

purged of a tormenting devil. She had a four year old son who tumbled into the well and lay submerged there for nearly three hours. Then, weeping and trembling, the mother got him out and, with pleading countenance, laid her dead child at Genovefa's feet. Genovefa took him and covered him with her cloak and, prostrate in prayer, she would not stop weeping until death abandoned the dead little boy. That was in the season of Quadragesima and the child who was still a catechumen was being initiated into the Catholic faith. Indeed he was baptized on Easter Eve. He was then called Cellomerus because he had recovered his lost life in Genovefa's cell.[45]

32. A man came to her in the city of Meaux whose hand and arm had withered to the elbow and prayed that he might be restored to health through her. Accordingly, she took hold of the withered hand and the finger joints and touched the arm, making the sign of the cross and in half an hour his hand was restored.

33. From the holy day of Epiphany even to the Cup's natal day, that is the Lord's Supper, it was blessed Genovefa's custom to remain closeted in her cell so that she could serve God more freely alone with prayers and vigils.[46] One day, a woman came there, moved more by curiosity than by faith, wishing to find out what Genovefa did privately in her cell. She had no sooner arrived at the door than she lost her eyesight. No doubt divine vengeance damned her crafty little scheme. At the end of Quadragesima, Genovefa came out of her cell and restored her sight with prayers and the sign of the cross.

34. When Paris had been under siege by the Franks for twice five years, as they say, the countryside was afflicted by such a famine that some people are known to have died of starvation.[47] Accordingly it was arranged for Genovefa to travel with a fleet of ships to collect the *annona* in the town of Arcis-sur-Aube.[48] They came to a place on the Seine where a tree in the rapids was

---

45. Critics compare this miracle to one attributed to Gertrude of Nivelles, c. 11. Krusch ridicules the name of Cellomerus but Heinzelmann and Poulin, *Les vies anciennes*, 25, supply a number of similar hybrids from the fourth through the sixth centuries and argue that the sixth-century practice of composing an individual name gave way by Carolingian times to the practice of repeating names in the same family.

46. That is, from the end of the Christmas season (January 6) to the beginning of the Easter celebrations, Paschal *triduum*, on Holy Thursday.

47. The skepticism of the author regarding a ten-year siege of Paris by the Franks has been echoed by modern scholars. It is generally conceded that it is a traditional reference to the siege of Troy, although Heinzelmann and Poulin, *Les vies anciennes*, 73, are more willing to credit it to the years 476–86, dating Genovefa's voyage to 480.

48. The *annona* was tax in kind, generally grain, introduced widely in the late Roman Empire. Geary, *Before France and Germany*, 22. We have translated *effectio* as fleet but Heinzelmann and Poulin, *Les vies anciennes*, 44, see it as *evectio*, the late Roman privilege of using public transport, reserved to people in the imperial service and certain nobles, as appears in the life of Melania the younger. Melania was

causing ships to sink and there Genovefa asked the sailors to get a little nearer to the bank. She said a prayer and ordered them to fell the tree. As her companions, the sailors, chopped away with their axes, she stood to one side praying until the tree was plucked up by its roots. At once, two varicolored monsters emerged from the place. For nearly two hours, they tormented the sailors with intolerable blasts of fetid stench. But since then, mariners say that no one has been shipwrecked in that place.

35. After that, as she entered the town of Arcis, a tribune named Passivus came and begged her to visit his wife who had long been immobilized by paralysis in order to cure her. Thus besought by the tribune and the elders of the place, she went into the house and approached the sick woman's bed. As was her custom, she straightaway gave herself up to prayer. When the prayer was ended and the woman invigorated with the sign of the cross, she ordered her to rise from her bed. Immediately the woman who, as they say, for nearly four years had been unable to move under her own power because of sickness and pain, rose up whole from her bed at Genovefa's command. And for that miracle all together magnified God who is wonderful in His saints.[49]

36. When she came to the city of Troyes, many people came to her bearing sick people whom she restored to health with signs and blessings. In that town, a man was brought to her who had been blinded by divine vengeance for working on the Lord's Day as well as a girl of nearly twelve years who had similarly been blinded.[50] She illuminated their eyes by making the sign of the cross, invoking each person of the Trinity.

37. A certain subdeacon, seeing how many miracles were done through her, brought her his son who had been afflicted for twice five months with fever and violent chills. Genovefa ordered water brought to her and, taking it, she blessed it with the sign of the cross,[51] invoking the name of God, and gave it to the sick boy to drink. Immediately, he was cured by the propitiated Lord, Jesus Christ.

38. At that time, many people who, full of faith, tore off the fringes of her garments were healed of diverse infirmities.[52] Similarly many were cleansed by her who had been possessed by demons.

---

known later to Sadalberga, although Heinzelmann and Poulin (6, n. 294) doubt that she was known in Gaul so early. However, Sulpicius Severus knew Melania the Elder and the author of Genovefa's life certainly knew his biography of Martin and perhaps some of his other work.

49. Psalms 67:36.

50. *Oblatus est* is used for "brought" here and in c. 37; it is doubtful that it had any technical meaning at this time.

51. The word is *vexilla* rather than *signum*, which is used elsewhere in the text. Perhaps she employed a physical cross.

52. Matthew 9:20; Sulpicius Severus, *Life of Martin*, 18.

39. Her return to her own city from Arcis was delayed for some days and the tribune's wife whom she had restored to health kept her company until she reembarked. During the return voyage, however, their ships were so buffeted by the wind and endangered among rocks and trees that the high holds fore and aft in which they had stored the grain tipped over on their sides and the ships filled with water. Quickly Genovefa, her hands stretched toward Heaven, begged Christ for assistance. Immediately, the ships were righted and thus through her our God and Lord saved eleven grain-laden ships. This was witnessed by Bessus the priest, whose bones had gone cold from fear.[53] In a clear voice, full of joy, he sang out: "The Lord is my strength and song, and he is become my salvation."[54] And likewise the rest made their cry to Heaven and, to the bosun's beat, they sang the canticles of the Exodus in unison magnifying God for He had saved them through the prayers of his servant Genovefa.

40. When she returned to Paris, her sole concern was to distribute the *annona* to all according to their needs. She made it her first priority to provide a whole loaf to those whose strength had been sapped by hunger. Thus when the girls who served her went to the ovens they would often find only part of the bread they had put in to bake, for she had privately given the greater part of it to the poor. But it was soon clear who had taken the bread from the ovens for they noticed the needy carrying warm loaves throughout the city and heard them magnifying and blessing the name of Genovefa. For she put her hopes not in what is seen but in what is not seen.[55] For she knew the Prophet spoke truly who said: "Whoever giveth to the poor lendeth unto God."[56] For through a revelation of the Holy Spirit she had once been shown that land where those who lend their treasure to the poor expect to find it again. And for this reason, she was accustomed to weep and pray incessantly: for she knew that as long as she was in the flesh she was exiled from the Lord.[57]

VIII. She healed various illnesses by the sign of the cross.

41. For four years, a certain *defensor* named Fruminius from the town of Meaux suffered from the closing of his ear passages. He sought out Genovefa at Paris, begging her to restore his hearing with a touch of her hand. And when she signed his ears with her touching hands, his hearing was immediately restored and he blessed the Lord, Jesus Christ.

53. Virgil, *Aeneid,* 3:308.
54. Exodus 15:2.
55. Romans 26:25.
56. Proverbs 19:17.
57. 2 Corinthians 5:6.

42. In their proper order, we shall tell in our text what miracles were done in the city of Orléans through her intercession. Hearing of Genovefa's arrival, a *materfamilias* named Fraterna, who was mourning her daughter Claudia who had been laid out for her passing, quickly sped to Genovefa to ask help. She found her praying in the basilica of Saint Anianus the primate. Falling at her feet wailing, she is said to have cried out: "Lady Genovefa, return my daughter to me." Seeing her faith, Genovefa is said to have answered: "Desist from injuring and molesting me. Your daughter is restored to you unharmed." At this response, Fraterna arose joyfully and returned with Genovefa to her tent. By a miracle, the power of God had healed Claudia and recalled her straight-away from the jaws of death. Unhurt, she met them at the entrance of Genovefa's dwelling.[58] And all the crowd magnified the Lord for Claudia's unexpected return to health by the merits of Genovefa.

43. And in the same city, she interceded with a certain man on behalf of his servant who had wronged him. But in his pride and stubbornness, he abso-lutely refused to forgive the servant. She is said to have addressed him thus: "If you despise my supplications, the Lord Jesus Christ will not do so, for he is all pious and clement to the forgiving." When the man returned to his house, he soon became feverish and all night he could not rest for freezing and burning. By dawn of the next day, his mouth gaping and drooling like that of an orochs, which is the everyday word for a bison, he rolled at Genovefa's feet and begged her to give him the pardon he had refused to his servant the day before.[59] And when she had signed him, all fever and illness left him. The master, then restored in mind and body, pardoned his servant in turn. There can be no doubt that the angel of the Lord afflicted him as he did Anicianus, the pertinacious judge of whom we read that Saint Martin stood before his gates on a stormy night begging for his captives. And the text relates that an angel boxed his ears so hard that he went outside the house and granted all that Martin asked.[60]

IX. She cast out a demon from human bodies.

44. She departed by ship from Orléans for Tours braving many perils on the

---

58. There is some confusion here. Fraterna is said to go with Genovefa to her *tabernaculum* (tent), but Claudia is in the entrance of the house (*domus*). Krusch's first and second MSS have *aditu* (dwelling).

59. The *Acta Sanctorum* text implies that the man had a disease called *quotidianus bos*. Krusch's edition reads "aperto ore secut [sicut] urus, qui cotidiana bos interpretatur lingua, sallivem distillans. . . ." Krusch quotes Macrobius to the effect that *urus* was the Gallic word for wild oxen (*feri boves*). Macrobius, *Saturn.* 6.4; Krusch, *MGH SRM* 3, 234. An anonymous reader for Duke University Press called our attention to the Greek term *boulimy* in Xenophon's *Anabasis*, which apparently described the same disease and possibly relates it to bulimia.

60. Sulpicius Severus, *Dialogues*, 3; *Gallus*, 4, in *Western Fathers*, ed. and trans. Hoare, 126–27.

River Loire. It is nearly six hundred *stadia* from the town of Orléans to the city of Tours, which is called the third Lyon.[61] When at last she came to the town gates of Tours, there came to meet her from the basilica of Saint Martin a crowd of people possessed by devils, most wicked spirits clamoring that the flames between Saint Martin and Genovefa were consuming them. And what is more they confessed that from jealousy they had caused the perils which beset her on the river Loire.[62] Meanwhile, Genovefa entered Saint Martin's basilica and cleansed many possessed ones with prayers and the sign of the cross.[63] And some whom the unclean spirits relinquished confessed that in their hour of agony the fingers of Genovefa's hand blazed up one by one with celestial fire. And this was why they had shouted and screamed so horribly that they were burning.[64]

45. Three men came to her whose wives were at home vexed secretly with demons, begging that she would cleanse them of the most evil spirits by a visit. And, being most kind, she followed them. She entered into each of the matron's houses with a prayer and blessed them and anointed them with oil, cleansing them of their troublesome demons.[65]

46. The next day, she attended the vigil of Saint Martin, and she stood praying in a corner of the basilica, blessing and praising the Lord, unnoticed in the midst of the crowd. One of the psalm-singers seized by a demon, began to mangle his own limbs, which in his captivated mind he believed to be someone else's. He hurried from the apse to Genovefa, who ordered the unclean spirit to abandon the man's body. The wicked spirit threatened to depart through the eyes but, at Genovefa's command, he was flushed through the bowels leaving a filthy discharge behind him. So with no delay, the demon had been speedily driven out and the person was cleansed. And everyone honored her in her comings and goings.

47. About the same time, Genovefa was standing in the entrance to her dwelling when she saw a girl pass carrying an overflowing vessel in her hand. She called out to her and asked what she was carrying. The girl answered, "It's a jar for liquids. Some merchants just sold it to me."[66] Genovefa spied an

61. One *stadium* equals about 625 feet, or the length of a runners' track.

62. Heinzelmann and Poulin, *Les vies anciennes*, see this connection with Martin as an argument for a Tourangeau author collaborating with Clothild in a plan to advance Genovefa as a protector of Catholic Gaul against the Arians.

63. Heinzelmann and Poulin say that would be the basilica built by Bishop Perpetuus between 458 and 489. Ibid., 74.

64. Similarly, a demon who was dislodged by Saint Martin testified to the fire in the saint's fingers, Sulpicius Severus, 17, in *Western Fathers*, ed. and trans. Hoare, 31.

65. Beck, *Pastoral Care*, maintains that the use of blessed oil, as well as holy water was common in the care of the sick. See also, "Possession diabolique," *Dictionnaire de théologie chrétienne*.

66. Krusch's base MS has *aputliquam*, not *ad liquamen* as in the *Acta*. He ingeniously emended it to

enemy of humankind sitting on the mouth of the vessel and she blew upon it with a threat. Immediately, that part of the mouth of the vessel broke off and fell; signing the vessel she bade the girl depart. Those who saw what had happened marvelled that no devil was able to hide itself from her.[67]

X. By her prayers, she dispels rain, wind and disease.

48. A little boy named Maroveus who was blind, deaf-mute and lame, was presented to Genovefa by his parents. She rubbed blessed oil on him and fortified him with the sign of the cross. At once his legs became strong enough for him to walk quite normally. He also regained full vision and was further able to hear and speak perfectly.

49. In the vicinity of the town of Meaux, the virgin, with a group of reapers, was harvesting her crops when suddenly a rainstorm with a whirlwind loomed over them. Genovefa went straight into a tent and, as was her custom, stretched herself on the ground and began to weep and pray. Christ showed her admirable virtues plainly to every witness. For when all the surrounding fields were drenched in rain, neither Genovefa's crops nor her reapers were touched by a single drop of the pouring water.[68]

50. Once when she was travelling by ship on the river Seine, as often happens, the serenity of the heavens unexpectedly changed and, in a rising tempest, her boat was tossed by the wind so that it could hardly keep afloat. Straightaway, Genovefa looked up to Heaven with arms outstretched and prayed God for help. Immediately, all was made tranquil. Without doubt, Christ was there who is believed to have command over wind and wave.

51. Often she restored the sick to health by rubbing them with holy oil. On one occasion, she wanted to anoint a person who was possessed of a demon but when she sent for the vessel in which she usually kept the blessed oil it was brought to her empty. Deeply troubled, God's servant Genovefa was not sure what she ought to do. For the bishop who should bless the oil for her had gone away.[69] She lay down on the ground begging help from heaven with her sacred prayers in delivering the afflicted one. As she arose from her prayers, the vessel in her hand filled itself with oil. In a single hour, by Christ's

---

Apuliquam, i.e., Apulian. Perhaps he felt it redundant to say what an ampulla is for in sixth-century Gaul.

67. This story is typical of the demonology of the age. Gregory the Great, *Dialogues* 1:4, tells a similar tale of a demon sitting on a lettuce leaf. In Krusch's edition of this vita, the word *homo* is once used for *girl*. Kurth, "Etude critique," 20, maintains that this was frequently done by Merovingian authors to designate a person of either gender.

68. A similar miracle is attributed to Saint Martin by Gregory of Tours, *Miraculi Martini*.

69. Marignan, *Etudes*, 2:xix, says that bishops customarily blessed large quantities of oil once a year and distributed it to parish priests as well as private persons. This was confirmed by a letter of Innocent I to the bishop of Gubbio, 416, cited by Dubois and Beaumont-Maillet, *Sainte Geneviève de Paris*, 61.

design, a pair of miracles were manifested through her: a vessel which had been devoid of oil was refilled between her hands; and the possessed one, anointed with that same oil was rescued from the demon's torments. And three times six years after her death, I myself saw that vessel with the oil which had materialized by her prayers and I decided then to write the story of her life.

XI. Miracles after her death; a basilica erected for her.

52. Adhering to the principle of brevity, I will keep silent about her departure from life and funeral honors which soon followed. She passed over in ripe old age, full of virtue. She dwelled for more than eighty years in the flesh as a pilgrim exiled from God in this world. And she was buried peacefully, 3 nones of January.[70]

53. To honor the place, I do not think it inappropriate to make known to the faithful how a man named Prudens achieved relief and healing at her tomb. He was so extraordinarily afflicted with the disease of stones that his parents despaired of his life. At Genovefa's tomb, with trembling and tears, they implored healing for his sickness. And that very day the stones generated by the sickness passed from him and he was never again troubled by that infirmity.

54. Both hands of a certain Goth who was working on the Lord's Day became contracted. All night he lay at Genovefa's tomb imploring that his health be restored. The next day, his hands were healed and he went forth cured from the oratory above the wooden sepulchre.[71]

55. Then Clovis, of glorious memory, fearful king by right of war, for love of the holy virgin, repeatedly pardoned criminals he had imprisoned in the *ergastulum*.[72] Often in response to Genovefa's supplications he let guilty men go free and unharmed instead of punishing them for their crimes. In honor of her merits, he began the construction of a basilica which was finished with a lofty roof by his most excellent Queen Clothild after his death.[73] A triple portico adjoins the church, with pictures of Patriarchs and Prophets, Martyrs

---

70. Her feast day is January 3, presumably the day of her death. The nones are the ninth day before the Ides (January 5).

71. Again, Kurth, "Etude critique," 69, dismisses Krusch's criticism that a Gallo-Roman Catholic was unlikely to have cured an Arian (presumably) Goth. Heinzelmann and Poulin, Les vies anciennes, 102, puts the incident in the context of the defeat of the Visigoths in 507, which would make the worker a prisoner. He believes that the wooden oratory was a temporary shelter for her tomb while the church was being built and the Goth was probably one of the construction workers.

72. A house of correction for slaves. This is a splendid example of the mediating role assigned to the "holy man" by Brown, Society and the Holy, 103–53.

73. Heinzelmann and Poulin, Les vies anciennes, 37, reads this passage to mean that the life was written between the death of Clovis (511) and that of Clothild (548).

and Confessors to the faith in ancient times drawn from pages of history books.[74]

And therefore, let all of us who adore the Father, Son and Holy Ghost as the substance of the deity and all who confess the unity of the Trinity, pray without cease, beseeching the most faithful servant of God, Genovefa, whom we have named so often, to beg forgiveness for the sins we have committed in the past and to stand surety for the sins we commit in the future and to procure for us mortals both angelic and corporal sustenance, so that, being reunited in the indivisible Trinity, we may rejoice in the splendors of the saints and magnify our Lord Jesus Christ to whom be glory and honor and the Kingdom and the power from everlasting to everlasting.[75] Amen.

74. This is the same task assigned by Gregory of Tours, History, 4:1, to the wife of Bishop Naumatius. Kurth, "Etude critique," 72, defends this passage against the criticism of Krusch, identifying it as the church of Peter and Paul, later renamed in honor of Genovefa. Wallace-Hadrill, Frankish Church, 183, note that construction was begun on the eve of Clovis's campaign against the Arian Visigoths in southern France. In The Catholic Encyclopedia, 6:414, McEnlean notes that Clovis began this church shortly before his death in 511. On her death in the following year, Genovefa was buried there, and her name was given to the church.

75. This final peroration is somewhat amplified from Krusch's text for better sense.

2

Clothild, Queen of the Franks

(d. 544)

The life of Genovefa was played out against a background of pagan invasion of Christian Gaul, first by Huns and then by Franks. That saint lived to see the conversion of Clovis, the conqueror of the Gallo-Romans. Her tomb was honored by his queen, Clothild, the daughter of a Gallo-Roman woman and a Burgundian king, Chilperic, who might have been converted to Catholicism by his wife.[1] She and her daughter, Clothild, set a pattern for a chain of Catholic female missionaries to the courts of the pagan and Arian kings they married. No one has really studied the attractions of Arianism for Germanic kings, but they must have perceived some advantage in it relating to their public life to have been so determined to retain a faith pronounced heretical by the Roman clergy who monopolized religious governance in their newly acquired lands. Clothild's life includes the sad story of her daughter and namesake, who vainly tried to win over her Visigothic husband. Her sister-in-law, Albofled, converted with Clovis, married the Arian King Theodoric the Ostrogoth, and probably procured the conversion of his daughter, Queen Amalsuntha. The work in Italy was continued by Clothild's granddaughter,

This life of Clothild is taken from MGH, SRM 2:341–48. The spelling of Merovingian names varies widely. In the text we have retained the Carolingian presentation, but in our own notes and introduction, we have preferred a spelling more recognizable to the modern reader. The vita translated here is a Carolingian version of the story written in the late ninth or tenth century, after Hincmar of Reims had composed his life of Saint Remigius, from which the author drew along with Gregory of Tours's *History of the Franks*. We have included it in this collection for several reasons. It fills a gap in our narrative of the saintly women of the age. It supplies the English-speaking reader with an otherwise inaccessible source. Finally, it provides an example of the more formal hagiography of the Carolingian period. As Graus, *Volk, Herrscher*, 406, points out, hers is a rather artificial ecclesiastical cult whose narrowness may be due to her failure to establish a lasting convent to serve as a center of her worship.

1. Wood, "Gregory of Tours and Clovis," 267, suggests that they may have conformed to an apparent Burgundian pattern of Catholic wives and Arian husbands.

Theodelinda, who married Alboin, king of the Lombards.[2] Another of her descendants, Bertha, brought Catholicism to Saxon Kent.[3]

This life of Clothild, being far removed from the complicated politics of early Merovingian times, makes only the briefest references to Clovis's relations with his wife's Burgundian relatives and gives no hint of the possibility that he may himself have been an Arian sympathizer before his marriage.[4] Clothild's uncle Gundobad, although an Arian, seems to have established a reasonably friendly relationship with the Gallo-Roman bishops in his kingdom.[5] Sometimes he was at war with Clovis, and sometimes he was allied with him, but his religion does not appear to have hampered control of his own kingdom. Like his contemporary, Alaric II of the Visigoths, he attempted to pacify his Roman subjects by the passage of a law code regulating their relationships with his own subjects.[6] His son Sigismund was finally converted to Catholicism, but his religion did not save him from the hostility of the Franks. He was attacked and his family murdered by the sons of Clothild, although this author did not blame her for that war.[7]

Clothild's story continued to fascinate succeeding generations as the centerpiece of a struggle between the old Catholic, Roman population against the Arianism of the Germanic tribes. Modern scholars can only dimly begin to calculate the depth of that hostility because our sources rarely go beyond the power struggles of the potentates of the age. Only occasionally can we see the ongoing violence that caught smaller fry than the bishops and nobles who plotted against Arian kings with Catholic support. The life of Saint Sacerdos, bishop of Limoges, for example, mentions almost casually that his mother, Saint Mundana, was murdered by Vandals when she refused to abandon her Catholicism at the demand of the Arian leaders.[8] Clovis's campaign against the Visigoths also entangled the saintly bishop of Arles in charges of treason. Caesarius, founder of the convent of Saint Jean, which we will encounter in later stories, was exiled to Bordeaux shortly before the siege of his city in 508.

2. See the letter to her from Nicetius of Trier in 564, MGH, Epistolae 3.

3. The subject of the conversion has further been treated in McNamara, "Living Sermons."

4. This possibility has been advanced by Wood, "Gregory of Tours and Clovis."

5. Wood notes that all the women of the Burgundian house seem to be Catholic in contrast to the men. On the other side, however, Clovis's sister Landechild was an Arian. Ibid., 267.

6. Gundobad was the promulgator of the Burgundian Code; see The Burgundian Code, trans. Drew. Wood is skeptical about this traditionally ascribed motivation. "Gregory of Tours and Clovis," 258. For general background on the Burgundian settlement, see the Introduction to the code by Edward Peters.

7. In contrast to the conflicting versions of her revenge in Gregory of Tours, HF, 3:6, and LHF, 20, a story Wood treats with great mistrust. "Gregory of Tours and Clovis," 253.

8. Vita S. Sacerdos Episcopus Lemovicensis, AS, May 5, 12–24.

After her husband's death, Clothild became closely associated with the diocese of Tours, where she spent most of her time near the tomb of Saint Martin, most popular of all the Gallo-Roman saints. Tours, along with the rest of Aquitaine, had been newly added to the Frankish kingdom by Clovis. The city had been long troubled with pagan elements, and the struggle between Catholic Romans and Arian Visigoths was particularly virulent. Mundana the martyr came from Bordeaux; Clovis himself appointed her son bishop of Limoges. Volusianus, bishop of Tours, and his successor Verus had each been exiled from their sees by Alaric, who suspected them of betraying the Visigoths to the Franks after the conversion of Clovis. The bishop of Béarn actually died in battle, leading his flock to Clovis's support. Gregory of Tours says Clovis even received supernatural support against the Arian armies: a ball of fire issued from the Church of Saint Hilary of Poitiers and lit up his camp outside the city at a crucial moment.[9] It is, therefore, possible that the residence of the dowager queen in that neighborhood, and in the city where Clovis first received his commission as patrician from the Roman emperor, was part of an ongoing Frankish policy of reaching a solid settlement with the old Gallo-Roman population.

Clovis died in 511, and Clothild survived him until 544. The vita outlines the tragic lives of some of her children but makes no mention of her daughter Telechild (Teutechild), who became a nun.[10]

The Life of Saint Chrothildis

■

1. The edifices of earthly stone and marble built in the city of Jericho were doomed to fall. But in the heavenly Jerusalem, the palaces constructed of the souls of the holy will never crumble but will stand forever. The gates of that city gleam with precious pearls which are the holy apostles, martyrs, confessors, virgins, widows, and spouses. Invisible and immortal, the King of that city takes servants unto Himself from all the people of the world, of both sexes. When they have been set free from the miseries of this life, he unites them with his bands of angels, within that city whose walls will never fall and gives them eternal bliss to enjoy. Behold! A chorus of virgins, dearest and most pleasing to God, garnished with fruit a hundred-fold, gleams in God's presence in His heavenly palace like stars in the sky. The flock of virgins is

9. Gregory of Tours, HF, 2:37.

10. Telechild, or Teutechild, enjoyed a limited cult as foundress of a monastery of Saint Peter at Sens, AS, June 28, 328–39, gives an outline of sources referring to her and reprints the foundation charter from Clovis.

followed by an assembly of holy widows and faithful wives who, though they cannot return fruit a hundred fold, harvest sixty and thirty fold and are numbered with all the saints justly rewarded with eternal felicity.[11] The blessed and venerable Queen Chrothilda is of that collegium. We will now pass on to generations yet to come an account of the nobility of her mortal lineage, who her parents were, how she scaled the heights of the kingdom of heaven, how she blossomed in holy works while she lived, and how she made an end and migrated from this world.

2. There was a certain king of the Burgundians, born of the family of King Athanaric, named Gundioc. From him, sprang four sons: Gundobad, God-egisel, Chilperic and Gundomar.[12] With his sword, Gundobad killed his brother Chilperic and ordered his wife bound with a rock tied to her neck to drown in the water.[13] Of his two daughters, Chrona the eldest was condemned to exile and changed her clothing. The younger, Chrothilda of whom we write, he kept in his house by God's disposition. For God who knows the future, foresaw that the seed of kings would spring from Chrothilda and that her progeny would hold imperium over Roman and Frank together.[14]

3. At that time, Flodoveus, son of Childeric, king of the Franks, frequently sent legations to King Gundobad in Burgundy.[15] Seeing the wise, beautiful, elegant and decorous maiden Chrothilda in the house of the aforesaid Gundobad, the legates asked who she was. And they were told that she was the daughter of King Chilperic whom Gundobad had killed. Therefore, returning to King Flodoveus, they advised him to have an eye to King Gundobad's niece who was famed for her manners and physical beauty for she was worthy of a royal marriage. Flodoveus was glad of these tidings. He told his trusty warriors: "My time of life demands that a noble wife should join me from whom royal progeny may spring to govern the kingdom after my death. King Gundobad has a niece whom I want to take as wife, if you so counsel me." Oh, highest wisdom and knowledge of God, whose will and prescience none can resist! All approved the royal will. Word came from the palace that the

11. This is an extension to the parable of the seed, Matthew 13:18–33; Mark 4:8. By Frankish times, its application to the three states of womanhood was a standard metaphor drawn from Jerome.

12. Gregory of Tours, HF, 2:28.

13. Duchesne, L'église au sixième siècle, 492, disputes this story identifying her mother as Caretena, whom Sidonius praised for her Catholic influence on the Arian Burgundians (Epistola 5:5–7), and whose epitaph commemorates her as a consecrated widow, died 506 (CIL, 13:2372). In DHGE Dumas cites a letter of Avitus of Vienne, who converted Gundobad's son Sigismund to Catholicism, describing Gundobad's grief at his brother's death.

14. The Carolingian author is alluding to the later Frankish Empire.

15. This name for Clovis does not appear in earlier sources.

most noble maiden Chrothilda be brought and made queen and was praised by all.[16] For it was fitting that from a royal stock, future kings of the Franks be born, destined to build for God, the immortal King, the many monasteries that now exist all over Gaul. It is fitting also that by building perishable churches they might gain the joys of the celestial Jerusalem, the church which endures forever! At that time there was a certain Aurelian at King Flodoveus' court who was skilled in worldly craft and privy to the king's secrets. The king sent him to King Gundobad in Burgundy to ask that his niece might be brought into Gaul and made queen. Now Chrothilda was a Christian and on a certain Sunday on her way to solemn Mass, as was her custom, she was distributing alms to the poor. In disguise, Aurelian sat among the paupers begging for alms. Blessed Chrothilda came to him and gave him gold and as she did so, he kissed her hand and drew back her cloak behind her. Later, Blessed Chrothilda sent her maid to bring Aurelian to her and said to him: "Tell me, young man, why are you disguised as a pauper and why did you pull my cloak away?" To which he said: "I beseech you that your servant may speak to you in private." She answered, "Speak!" He said, "My lord, King Flodoveus of the Franks, sends me to you. He wishes to have you for his wife. Behold his ring and other ornaments and the betrothal regalia!" Blessed Chrothilda accepted the ring and the rest of the gifts and deposited them in the treasury of her uncle, King Gundobad. Then she said to Aurelian: "My lord, I give salutation to King Flodoveus. But I do not know how I can do what you ask. For it is not lawful for a Christian to marry a pagan. Let no one know about this: let God's will be done. Go in peace and may you return safely to your own."[17]

4. Aurelian returned to meet Flodoveus and told him all that had happened. The next year, King Flodoveus sent Aurelian again to Gundobad ordering through him that he send Chrothilda to him as his wife. Hearing this, Gundobad trembled greatly in his heart and he said to his faithful followers: "King Flodoveus is looking for a chance to challenge me, he wants to invade my realm." And he said to Aurelian: "You have come to spy on our household for your king has never met my niece." And, responding to that, Aurelian said: "This is the command of my lord, King Flodoveus. Either send him your niece or prepare for war against him." Gundobad answered: "Let him come when he likes. He will perish and die and thus all those whose

16. After an earlier debate, Kurth, *Sainte Clothilde*, dates the proposal in 493, which Ewig accepts, *Spätantikes und fränkisches Gallien*, 1:114.

17. This rather confused tale has been given in more detail in the LHF, 11–12. There, Clothild pretended ingenuously that she placed the ring in Gundobad's treasury because her uncle customarily disposed of gifts in that way. But when he returned, Aurelian alleged that its presence in the treasury proved that his mission had been approved.

blood he has shed may be avenged." Hearing this, the Burgundians feared the anger of the Franks and counseled Gundobad, saying: "Give your niece to the King of the Franks and let there be firm friendship between you and him." Then he gave the Blessed Chrothilda, with the royal ornaments, to Aurelian. And she agreed that he lead her to King Flodoveus in the city of Soissons in Francia. There the king received her with joy and legally married her.

5. And when the king in his chamber had initiated her into the ways of the flesh, Blessed Chrothilda said to him: "Lord King, hear your handmaid and give me what I ask." And the king said: "Ask what you will and I will give it to you." The queen said: "I ask that you will believe in almighty God, Father, Son, and Holy Ghost, and that you will destroy the idols you worship and restore the churches you have burned."[18] The king answered: "I will not desert my gods and I will not pay honor to your God. If you will ask for something else, you will obtain it easily." And all this was done by the disposition of Him Who saves the unbelieving man through the faithful woman. For after that the queen conceived a son to whom she gave the name of Ingmar. The happy queen decorated the church with altar curtains and precious drapery. She ordered it prepared for a baptism and called the clergy to baptize the boy. But when he had been cleansed by holy baptism, he died in his white garb. At that the king was deeply grieved and exceedingly angry with the queen. He said that the boy would still be alive if he had been dedicated in the name of the gods. The queen answered: "I give thanks to God, for He has received this son who came from my body and yours in His kingdom." Thereafter another son was born and called Chlodomir in Baptism. And when he was sick, he was restored to health by his mother's prayers.

6. The queen did not cease to tell the king that he should worship God and desert the vain idols he honored. But in no way could she move his mind to belief until he went to war with the Alamans and Suevi. Then he was compelled to believe what he had denied before. For while Franks and Alamans fought, Flodoveus' men began to give way. Seeing this, Aurelian said to the king: "Lord King, believe in the God of Heaven Whom the queen honors and He will free you and yours from imminent peril and give you victory." Raising his eyes to heaven, with flowing tears, the king said: "I believe in You, Jesus Christ, who came to save the world. I adore you, true God, Whom I have refused to honor! Free me from present danger, for I am Your servant." When he said this prayer, the Alamans turned in flight, their king fell dead, and they submitted to Flodoveus. The king brought their land under tribute and,

18. Gregory of Tours, HF, 2:29, sets this conversation after the birth of Ingmar. LHF, 12, sets it before the marriage and couples the request for conversion with a plea for vengeance for her parents.

praising God for having gained the victory, he turned back into Francia and told the queen how he had merited victory by invoking the name of Jesus Christ. And this was done in the fifteenth year of his reign.

7. At this time, the great priest and bishop, Remigius strongly ruled over the cathedra of the church of Reims.[19] The queen summoned him from there, praying that he might show the king the way to salvation.[20] The bishop came before the king who received him with honors and said: "I hear you willingly, most blessed father, and I will follow your commands obediently." In answer, the Blessed Remigius said to the king: "God in Heaven is King of kings and Lord of lords, for He Himself has said: 'By me, kings reign.'[21] If you would believe in Him and be cleansed with holy baptism, you will reign with Him and will have remission of all your sins and you will conquer all your enemies and you will reign with Him forever in the life to come." Hearing these holy words from Bishop Remigius, King Flodoveus said with welling tears: "I believe in God. I want to be baptized. I desire to live through Him and to die in Him."[22] The holy Queen Chrothilda had prayed to God incessantly, supplicatingly beseeching that He might snatch the king and his people from the snares of the Devil so that, by the work of the Holy Spirit within him, he might be purged by holy baptism. Immediately, she decorated the church with drapes and cloaks and other ecclesiastical ornaments. Then the new Constantine came to baptism, Blessed Remigius in the lead and Blessed Chrothilda following. The Holy Spirit ordered these things to show their mystical meaning. For as was fitting in the pagan king's approach to baptism, Saint Remigius took the lead as they entered playing the role of Jesus Christ and the holy Queen Chrothilda followed as the embodiment of God's Church. The holy bishop consecrated the font. The king was stripped of his corporal vestments and baptized by the aforesaid bishop. And since there was not enough chrism, the Holy Spirit descended in the form of a dove,

---

19. "Great priest" may conceivably be an honorific title as in Bertilla, c. 4.

20. Gregory of Tours, HF, 2:31, and LHF, 15, characterize the summons as secret. In "Women as Proselytizers in Germanic Society," a paper presented at the Medieval Institute of Western Michigan, Schulenberg speculated that he had a hand in Aurelian's dealings regarding this marriage. In any case, he continued to exercise a pastoral responsibility toward Clovis, as reflected in his letters. PL 65:963–70, and Testament, PL 65:970–76. His first vita is no longer extant, but a later biography by Hincmar of Reims probably provided a model for the present work on Clothild, MGH, SRM 3:239–49.

21. Proverbs 8:15.

22. Gregory of Tours, HF, 2:15, also associates two of Clovis's sisters in his conversion. Albofled married Theodoric the Ostrogoth but died soon after. His sister Audofled apparently was an Arian, but his third sister, Landechild, was converted from Arianism to Catholicism (2:31), the subject of a lost homily of Avitus of Vienne, the converter of her cousin Sigismund. Duchesne, *L'église au sixième siècle*, 492.

carrying two ampoules full of oil and chrism which Saint Remigius devoutly received. With these he anointed the king according to the custom of the church and called him Ludovic, which means a laudable man.[23] Oh happy Gaul! Rejoice and exult, praise the Lord, delight in the true God! For through the prayers of Saint Chrothilda, the mystical embodiment of the church, your first king was chosen by the King of Heaven and torn from the cult of demons. He was converted to God by the preaching of Saint Remigius and baptized by him. His flesh was anointed with celestial chrism brought by the Holy Spirit and his heart was anointed spiritually with divine love. Then, with the counsel of Blessed Chrothilda, the king began to destroy the fanes and build churches in his land and endow them with copious gifts. He gave alms generously to the poor and helped widows and orphans and persevered sedulously and devoutly in every good work. Thereafter, Blessed Chrothilda bore a son named Lothar in holy baptism and that is what she called him.[24]

8. After that, King Ludovic, who had been Flodoveus, came into the city of Paris saying to his queen, Saint Chrothilda: "It is unseemly and indecent that Arian Goths should hold the greater part of Gaul. With God's help, let us go and drive them out of this land." This counsel pleased the queen and all the nobles of Gaul and Blessed Chrothilda said to the king: "If you wish, Lord King, to expand your kingdom on earth and to reign with Christ in his celestial kingdom, build in this place a church in honor of Saint Peter, Prince of the Apostles, that, with his help you will succeed in subjugating the Arian peoples to yourself,[25] and with him as your leader, return victorious." The queen's counsel pleased the king. Then the king went forth with a mighty army. The queen remained at Paris and built the church of the Holy Apostles. Having gained victory, the king returned and strenuously governed the Frankish kingdom. He built more monasteries for monks and, as he had promised Saint Remigius and Saint Chrothilda, he led a religious life even to the end. At last King Ludovic died, after five years of peace following his contest with Alaric, King of the Goths.[26] Altogether he ruled thirty years and was buried in the Basilica of Saint Peter the Apostle which he and his queen

23. This passage is heavily marked by the ritual and symbolism of Carolingian imperialism. The account of Gregory of Tours, HF, 2:31, makes no mention of the processional order or its typology. The story of the heavenly dove and the ampoule and the subsequent royal anointment appear to have been an invention of Hincmar, Vita Remigius, 38. Hincmar (39) also introduces the king's change of name of Ludovic (Clodovic or Clovis), which conforms to the growing popularity of the baptismal name from the ninth century. Dürig, Geburtstag und Namenstag.

24. Clothar I, husband of Saint Radegund.

25. This church housed the body of Saint Genovefa and was later renamed in her honor.

26. Alaric II, King of the Visigoths, killed in battle by Clovis (483), Isidore of Seville, History of the Goths, c. 36.

had built.[27] There were one hundred and twelve years between the passing of Saint Martin and the passing of King Ludovic.

9. After King Ludovic's death, Queen Chrothilda often went to the Basilica of Saint Peter in the city of Tours where she pursued good works in God's service.[28] She rarely went to the city of Paris. After the death of King Ludovic, his four sons, Theodoric, Chlodomir, Childebert, and Clothar, divided his kingdom equally among themselves.[29] Saint Chrothilda also had a daughter whom she called by her own name of Chrothilda and gave in marriage to Almaric, King of the Goths.[30] He hated her greatly because she was strong in the Catholic faith while he was polluted with the Arian faith and whenever she went to church, he threw dung at her. And he would beat her severely with whips but she would in no way let herself be torn from her Catholic faith.[31] Instead she sent a legation to her brothers and mother telling them how she was treated. Moved to wrath, they gathered a great army and went to war with Almaric until the Arian king and his followers turned in flight and sought to take refuge in a Catholic church. But before he could reach the entrance of the church, he was struck by a Frankish soldier's spear and perished cruelly—as he deserved. Then did King Childebert devastate Spain. He entered the city of Toledo and took great treasure and turned back for home with his sister. But some disease attacked her and she died of the illness on the road. Borne to Paris, she was buried beside her father in the Basilica of Saint Peter. And from the rest of the treasure Childebert carried off sets of ecclesiastical vessels, including sixty chalices from the most precious vases of

27. *Ecclesiae* were places of assembly dedicated to liturgical worship, and basilicas were temples where the bodies of saints rested. The latter were of three types: urban basilicas, which were a city's principal sanctuaries; monastic basilicas, an integral part of a monastery; and rural basilicas, some of which were parish churches. The oldest or most important urban basilica, the *basilica senior*, was normally the cathedral according to Salmon, *The Breviary*, 31–32.

28. This is apparently an error. Saint Peter's was in Paris; she went to Saint Martin's in Tours. Gregory of Tours, HF, 2:43. In 3:15, Gregory credits her influence with the appointment of two of his predecessors. Krusch, MGH, SRM 2:345, n. 1, suggests that the author wants us to believe that Clothild built a monastery for Saint Peter in Tours.

29. Theodoric was the son of one of Clovis' previous wives or a concubine. Geary, *Before France and Germany*, 94. He became the first king of Austrasia and founder of its line for two subsequent generations. Our ninth-century author draws a discreet veil over the tale (possibly untrue) that Clothild instigated her sons' attack upon Sigismund as found in Gregory, HF, 3:6, and later repeated in LHF, 20.

30. Amalric, son of Alaric II.

31. Two generations later, a similar experience was visited upon another Frankish princess. Clothar's son, Sigebert, married the Visigothic princess Brunhild, whose conversion to Catholicism was celebrated by Fortunatus, *Carmina*, lib. 6, 2. Her daughter Ingrid (named for her grandmother) returned to Toledo as wife of Hermangild, whom she successfully converted only to be faced with violent persecution by her husband's parents. Gregory of Tours, HF, 5:38.

Solomon, fifteen patens, twenty book covers for the Gospels with chased work in purest gold and jewels, beautifully ornamented. Not wishing to break them up, he kept them intact to share among the churches and they were all distributed to the churches.

10. At that time, Queen Chrothilda was living in Paris. Seeing that the queen was fostering the sons of his elder brother Chlodomir and that she greatly delighted in them, King Childebert thought that she planned to make them kings.[32] He said to his brother Clothar: "Our mother keeps our brother's sons with her and loves them dearly. She wants to elevate them to our brother's realm.[33] We must either shear them or kill them and divide the kingdom of our brother and their father, between ourselves."[34] Accordingly, they sent a nobleman, Archadius, to the queen at Paris saying treacherously: "Tell our mother the Queen to send us our brother's sons that we may make them kings." And she, believing this to be true, sent them gladly. Clothar killed them both while a third, named Chlotoald, escaped and left the world. Become clergy, ordained priest, enriched with good works, he migrated full of virtue from the villa of Nogent-sur-Coucy near the city of Paris on the 7th Ides of September.[35] Chrothilda the sainted queen bore the bodies of the two murdered boys to Paris with great psalm singing and immense lamentation and, worn out by her great grief, she buried them in the basilica she had built for the Apostles.

11. None would have thought that this holy woman, chosen by God before the beginning of time, who, sprang from stock royal in this world and rose to the highest place in the realm, suffered pain and torment in this life since she did not share the fire and sword of the martyr. But the sword pierced her soul in the killing of her father and her mother's drowning, the exile of her sister and her own marriage to a pagan king. Her sweetness softened the hearts of a pagan and ferocious people, namely the Franks, and she converted them through blessed Remigius with her holy exhortations and unremitting prayers. What great sorrow wore her down with the death of the king and of her daughter, Chrothilda, and the sons of her son Chlodomir? How she mortified

32. Ibid., 3:6. Clodomir, despite the warning of Avitus that he and his family would meet a similar fate, murdered Sigismund of Burgundy to avenge his mother's wrongs. He was killed in the same war, and the widow Guntheuc became one of the several wives of Clothar I.

33. By custom, Merovingian kings divided their kingdoms among their sons. However by a less reverent custom, they also tended to eliminate rival heirs and reunite the inheritance by violence.

34. This refers to the long hair that marked out a Merovingian king. Gregory of Tours, HF, 3:18, and LHF, 24, credit Clothild with the grisly but heroic choice of death rather than loss of royalty.

35. September 25. His feast is celebrated September 7. In his honor, the place was subsequently named Saint Cloud. Oddly enough, this vita omits the one miracle with which Gregory of Tours credits Clothild, a miraculous thunderstorm that prevented her remaining sons from fighting one another. HF, 3:28.

herself with abstinence, fasting, vigils, prayers and bodily penances! How she diminished the wealth of the royal treasury with the abundance of her largesse in distribution of alms! She, who was once clad by royal custom in most precious gilded garments, came to walk about dressed in wool and the cheapest garments. Rejecting delicious royal food, refusing to eat meat, she was refreshed by bread alone, and legumes and only water to drink. In several regions, she built many monasteries for the saints, especially the one in honor of Saint Peter the Apostle in the suburbs of Tours before the gates of Saint Martin's *castellum*. She built another monastery in the name of the Mother of God on the river Seine in a place called Les Andelys, not far from the walls of the city of Rouen. We should not try to conceal what occurred there while she stayed to begin the work but should manifest it to all the faithful.[36]

12. The kingdom was not fruitful in wine. Therefore, the builders of the monastery demanded wine from the queen, for it was a time of unparalleled shortage due to a bad harvest. Saint Chrothilda was very anxious about this problem but a spring of wondrous beauty rose from the ground near the site where the monastery was being built. Its appearance was delectable and its water healthful. In song, it is told that when the builders of the monastery sought her for a drink of wine, Blessed Chrothilda sent them a cup of water from that spring by one of her servants. But the following day, when the sun sizzled with the greatest heat, as is natural in summertime, the workers called out, shouting to Saint Chrothilda, demanding wine. As God instructed her, the holy handmaid of Christ quickly sent them a servant with a cup and, as they lifted it, the water was changed to wine and they said that they had never tasted better. Having drunk, they went to God's holy handmaid, bowed their necks to the very ground, and gave many thanks. They said they never had such good drink. When she heard this, God's chosen one credited God's goodness, not her own merits. She went on weaving in silence and spoke to the servants and told them not to tell anyone. Indeed, when anyone else drank from the fountain, they tasted water. But when the monastery builders took it, it was changed into wine every day until the monastery had been built. When it was completed, the fountain remained. And thereafter it gave the natural taste of water even to the present day.[37]

13. In the suburbs of the castle of Laon, she built a church in honor of Saint Peter where she established a clerical congregation. She expanded the church

36. Early chronicles make no mention of this foundation. The site is now occupied by the ruins of Chateau Gaillard.

37. There is still a spring dedicated to Saint Clothild in Les Andelys, although its water is now far from potable.

of Saint Peter within the walls of the city of Reims and enriched it with lands and ecclesiastical ornaments. Every day that she lived, she much loved and honored that church, for there her husband, King Ludovic, accepted the grace of baptism and there the Holy Spirit in the form of a dove brought him the oil and chrism.[38] From its foundations, she rebuilt that monastery of wondrous magnitude which was built in the time of Saint Denis in the suburbs of Rouen near the walls and dedicated to the twelve apostles by that same apostolic man, as was sculpted in stone at the altar's foundation, the first of September.[39] There she collected no modest congregation of clerks for the service of God.[40]

14. Thus Saint Chrothilda, her life filled with these and other holy works, who was once a queen and then the handmaid of the paupers and servants of God, despising the world and loving God with all her heart, grew gray in great old age to receive from Christ her everlasting reward. Thus, it happened that she proceeded to the city of Tours where it was her frequent custom to sojourn for the love of Saint Martin. Once, while staying there, she was told by angelic revelation that the day of her summons was near. Then she prayed, exulting in God, saying devoutly from the heart: "Unto thee, oh Lord, do I lift up my soul. Come and take me, Lord. In thee I take refuge."[41] Weighed down with corporal sickness, she lay upon her bed but never ceased from her prayers and almsgiving. But she, Christ's pauper, did not have anything to give, for she had diminished the royal treasury and passed it through the hands of the poor to heaven.[42] Then she sent a messenger to her sons, Childebert and Clothar, ordering them to come to her. As soon as they heard, they came quickly and the holy servant of God predicted many things to them as they were revealed to her by divine power. And they later came to pass. Thirty days after her calling, she was anointed as the apostle instructs, by priests with holy oil and given viaticum of the sacred body and blood of Christ. She shed her body confessing the Holy Trinity, and she abandoned the world. Angelic hands guided her soul to heaven and placed her amidst the multitudinous armies of saints. Now she went out of her body at the first hour of the night, on the third before the nones of June.[43] And at that passing,

38. Hincmar of Reims, *Vita Remigius*, 36.

39. September 4.

40. This monastery was subsequently dedicated to Saint Ouen.

41. Psalms 25:1.

42. The regularity with which female saints in Frankland and elsewhere diminish the gains of their warrior relatives by almsgiving suggests that they were playing a sort of structural role in the circulation of wealth, possibly as representatives of the more merciful or "womanly" side of monarchy. See McNamara, "Imitatio Helenae."

43. June 3.

the house was filled with immense light, as though it were the sixth hour of the day. Such an aroma filled the nostrils and mouths of all that they thought they were enveloped in the odors of thyme and every other aromatic perfume. The brightness and fragrance remained for a long time until daylight illuminated the earth and the sun shone at its brightest. Then she was brought from Tours by the two kings, Childebert and Clothar, her sons, and then carried to Paris. She is buried in the basilica of the Apostles Peter and Paul near King Ludovic. The body of Saint Genovefa the virgin also reposes in that basilica. How fitting it is that the church dedicated in the name of the Holy Apostle should be adorned by the body of that virgin and the limbs of so glorious a queen, so devout a widow, mother of Roman Emperors, and the genetrix of the King of the Franks.[44] Praise and glory to the Holy and Undivided Trinity, Father, Son and Holy Ghost, whose reign and power endure from everlasting to everlasting. Amen.

---

44. Again, by implication, the Carolingian author has added a nonexistent continuity between the Merovingians and the imperial successors.

3
Monegund, Widow
and Recluse of Tours
(d. 570)

The religious life of the Touraine was especially rich and dramatic in the sixth century. Circling as always around the tomb and reputation of the great Saint Martin, it was apparently fertile in small communities and establishments of ascetics. Grateful penitents and sufferers who had benefited from the blessings of the saint and his followers were generous in endowing old and new foundations around the cathedral core.[1] The basilica of Martin and its satellite shrines gained even greater luster from the publicity generated in the writings of their historian bishop, Gregory of Tours. He offset the violence and brutality of the secular life so vividly pictured in his *History of the Franks* with the miracles of the saints who shed grace on his diocese. He wrote the first account of Clothild's widowhood in Tours and of the trials of Radegund, her funeral, and the miracles he claimed to have witnessed on that occasion.

The lives of Clothild and Monegund, who migrated from outside the diocese, suggest that Martin's shrine was a powerful magnet for the spiritually ambitious of the age. Gregory filled two books with the histories of local saints and holy devotees of his patron. The story of the holy recluse Monegund is drawn from *De vita patruum*, written about 570. His active celebration of these holy persons may have represented an episcopal strategy designed to subject them to ecclesiastical authority.

Peter Brown has suggested that the presence of these little shrines and anchorages created centers of *praesentia* competing with the episcopal sees for the devotion of the faithful. Holy women and men, delivering inspired messages straight from God, threatened to rekindle the old quarrel between the clerical hierarchy and prophets and prophetesses that troubled the church in the second and third centuries. The struggles between unruly ascetics of the

This translation is taken from Gregory of Tours, *De Vita Patruum*, c. 19, AS, July 2, 275–81.

1. In *Leadership and Community* (231) van Dam describes the Martinopolis at Tours, which included the church, a baptistery built by Gregory, and at least two courtyards, one with a poorhouse.

wilderness and urban churches in the East were almost within the reach of living memory. Brown identifies these holy persons as representatives of the social misfits who "had been pushed tragically to one side by the rise of the Christian church and the extension of its structures into the countryside."[2] Gregory's method of reintegrating these persons back into the ecclesiastical mainstream is clearly demonstrated in his biography of Monegund. She appears to have become the leader of her community of worshippers through personal charismatic gifts that drew desperate invalids of the neighborhood to her for help. Gregory's version of her story emphasizes her devotion to his episcopal see and its great patron. Martin and the monastic foundation associated with him often fulfills this function in Gregory's plan to secure the adhesion of local saints to the main body of the church. Thus he associated the miraculous cure of a deaf mute, Theodemundus, with the charities of Queen Clothild, who placed him in a school to use his newfound skills in learning to chant the psalms and patronized his entrance into Martin's monastery.[3] The same monastery was associated with the aspirations of women through the story of Saint Papula, an obscure person who lived, according to Gregory, at the beginning of the sixth century.[4] He relayed a tradition that she desired to join a community of holy women, but her affectionate parents refused to part with her. When we recall the story of Saint Genovefa, we might add that there was probably no suitable community available in northern Gaul in 500. In any case, Gregory claimed that she disguised herself as a man and lived successfully among the monks of Saint Martin for thirty years, finally being elected their abbot. She disclosed her true sex on her deathbed to protect her corpse from being handled by men. Thus she is almost unique in representing a type of saint very popular in eastern hagiography, the transvestite saint. Gregory maintained that her tomb continued to produce miraculous cures in his day.

Elsewhere, Gregory described another tomb that attracted popular worship.[5] According to local tradition, it was the resting place of two consecrated virgins, Maura and Britta, who began to appear in visions, demanding a shrine to protect them from the rain. It required a second set of visions to coerce Gregory's aged predecessor Euphronius out into the inclement winter weather to bless the shrine, but once he had done so, the two virgins settled down as fruitful and cooperative spiritual agents of his diocese.

Gregory probably had similar hopes for the pious widow Ingitrude, who

---

2. Brown, *Cult of the Saints*, 123.

3. Gregory of Tours, *Miraculi S. Martini*, 7.

4. Gregory of Tours, *Glory of the Confessors*, trans. van Dam, 16.

5. Ibid., 17.

had settled in his diocese. He coupled her name with that of the sainted Radegund in one early section of his history.[6] Early in her career, Gregory associated her with a miracle of Martin himself. Ingitrude was in the habit of washing Martin's tomb, and during a drought God showed her His favor by changing jugs of wine into water for the purpose when she added a single drop of the holy water saved from prior ablutions.[7] In the end, Ingitrude disappointed Gregory. She founded a nunnery in the forecourt of Saint Martin's church and persuaded her married daughter to come there as future abbess. Gregory himself had to intervene and disabuse the daughter of her mother's notion that married people would be denied entrance to heaven. He sent her daughter back to her angry husband and continued to play an active role in the subsequent quarrels between husband and wife and then between mother and daughter, indignantly describing the final shambles of the family relationship. The mother disinherited the daughter, who later pillaged the monastery that the dead woman had finally bestowed upon a niece. The story of Ingitrude and her daughter finally emerged as an example of the conflict between episcopal interests and those of enterprising religious women.[8]

Monegund was more successful in making the transition. Her temperament was more modest than Ingitrude's, and possibly her social status was less exalted, although her husband had enough to support her in a life of service with a handful of followers. Gregory portrays her as an exemplary type of the married woman who, with her husband's support, turned the bitter disappointment of her children's death into a source of spiritual nourishment for others.

Monegund, a Widow and Recluse of Tours in Gaul

∎

1. Our senses cannot conceive nor words convey, nor writing recount the extraordinary gifts of divine blessings which heaven has granted to human kind. From the beginning of this rude age, the Savior of the world showed Himself for patriarchs to see, and prophets to foretell. At last he deigned to be received into the womb of the ever-virgin and intact Mary. The all-powerful and immortal Creator suffered himself to be garbed in the raiment of mortal flesh. He died to make reparation for mankind who had died through sin and

6. Gregory of Tours, HF, 7:36.

7. Ibid., 5:21.

8. Ibid., 9:33; 10:12. Graus, Volk, Herrscher, 118, emphasizes the need for married women to leave their husbands in order to be eligible for sainthood.

He rose again victorious. We were wounded by the arrows of criminal deeds and hurt by the blows of robbers who had ambushed us, but he cleansed us with a mixture of oil and wine and led us to the store of heavenly medicine, which is the dogma of Holy Church. He exhorts us with the gift of His incessant teaching to live by the saints' example. And as examples, He provides not only men but members of the inferior sex who are not sluggish in fighting the good fight but full of manly vigor. For He does not confer the starry kingdom only on men, who are expected to enter the contest; even women win the prize for their efforts. So blessed Monegund, like the prudent queen who came to hear the wisdom of Solomon, left her marriage bed and hurried to blessed Martin's basilica to marvel at his daily miracles, to drink from the priestly fountain so as to gain the power to open the gates to the groves of Paradise.[9]

2. The most blessed Monegund, a native of the city of Chartres, was joined in marriage according to her parents' promises. She had two daughters in whom she rejoiced with much delight, saying: "Behold, God has increased my family for unto me two daughters have been born." But the bitterness of this world cut short this earthly happiness. Struck by fever, the girls paid their final debt to nature. Mourning for them, bewailing her bereavement, the sorrowful mother never ceased to weep by day and by night. Neither her husband nor her friends nor any other intimate could console her. But at last she came to herself and said: "If I can find no consolation for my daughters' deaths, I fear I shall give offence to my lord, Jesus Christ. Now I will give up this lamentation and be consoled. Like the blessed Job, I shall repeat: 'The Lord giveth and the Lord taketh away: as it pleaseth the Lord so shall it be done; blessed be the name of the Lord.' "[10] So saying, she put off her mourning garb. She ordered a little cell prepared for herself, fitted out with a small window through which she might see a little light. Turning with contempt from the world and spurning the company of her husband, she devoted all her time to God alone, placing all her faith in Him, pouring out prayers for her own sins and those of the people. She had a single maid who ministered to her as a servant and brought her the water she needed. She would take barley meal, mix it with water strained carefully through ashes and knead the mixture into dough.[11] She would cook the loaves, shaped with her own hands, and eat them to revive her strength after long fasting. She distributed the rest of the food in her house to the poor.

9. Gregory uses *nemoris*, which may be a literary conceit or a conscious reference to Nemi, the grove sacred to Diana.

10. Job 1:21.

11. She seems to be making a primitive soda bread as prescribed in Bravé, *Uncle John's Original Bread Book*, 42: "Mix hardwood ashes with boiling water. Let ash settle and use liquid as baking soda."

3. One day it chanced that the girl who had been waiting on her was seduced, as I believe, by the cunning of the Enemy whom it is always customary to blame for harm done to good people. She decided to leave her service saying: "I cannot remain with this mistress who dwells in such abstinence. I'd rather enjoy myself in the world with plenty to eat and drink." After her departure, five days passed during which the religious woman had neither her usual flour nor water. She remained immobile, fixed on Christ, for whoever is founded or placed in Him will not be budged, neither by the tumultuous force of wind or pounding floods. For she thought that life depends not only on mortal food but, as it is written, also on the word of God, remembering the wise Solomon's proverb: "The Lord will not suffer the soul of the righteous to famish."[12] And also: "The just will live by his faith."[13] But since the human body cannot sustain itself without earthly food, she asked, prostrate in prayer, that He Who fed the people with manna from Heaven and produced water from a rock for their thirst, would deign to indulge her with similar food that her exhausted little body might be comforted for a little while. And immediately after her prayer, snow fell from heaven and covered the ground. Seeing this, she gave thanks and put out her hand through the window and collected the snow that was around the walls from which she extracted water and formed her customary loaves and provided herself with bodily sustenance for another five days.

4. She had a little pleasure garden near her cell where she used to retreat for recreation. One day, she went in and was walking about inspecting the herbs that grew there. A woman putting her wheat on the roof to dry, spied rudely on her from the higher place, her mind full of mundane things. Very soon, her eyes were closed and she lost their light. Recognizing her crime, she went and explained to her what she had done. And throwing herself into prayer, Monegund cried: "Woe is me! that the eyes of another are closed on account of my insignificant and sinful person!" Having finished her prayer, she placed her hands on the woman and, as soon as she had made the sign of the cross, the woman recovered her sight. And a man from the same country, who had lost his hearing sometime past, came devoutly to her cell because his parents prayed that the blessed woman might deign to place her hands upon him. She proclaimed herself unworthy that Christ might deign to work through her. Still she prostrated herself on the ground, as though humbly to lick the Lord's footprints, and asked for His divine clemency. And even as she lay there on the ground, the ears of the deaf one opened. Then, the cause of his sadness having disappeared, he returned to his own house with joy.

12. Proverbs 10:3.
13. Habakkuk 2:4.

5. Fearing that she might fall into vainglory because her own people praised her for these signs, she left her husband, her household and all her familiars and full of faith sought the basilica of the primate, Saint Martin. And when she was making her way there she came to a village called Esvres in the region around Tours where the relics of Saint Médard, confessor of Soissons, were kept.[14] That night the saint's vigil was being celebrated. While she was keeping her watch there in attentive prayer, the rest of the people came to solemn mass at the proper hour. While it was being celebrated by a priest of God, a certain girl, swollen with the poison of an evil tumor,[15] came and lay at her feet saying: "Help me! An evil death threatens to take my life." And, as was her wont, she prostrated herself and prayed to God, Creator of all. Rising, she imposed the sign of the cross on it and the wound burst open at the four points, the pus ran out, and importunate death released his grip on the girl. After that, the Blessed Monegund came to Saint Martin's basilica where, prostrate before the sepulchre, she gave thanks that she had deserved to contemplate the holy tomb with her own eyes. She settled in a little cell and spent her time in daily prayer, fasting and vigils. Her miraculous power did not lack fame in that place. For a certain widow's daughter came and showed her her paralyzed hands. Thus entreated, Monegund made the sign of salvation on her and with her own hand began to massage the girl's fingers. The fingers unfolded as the sinews straightened and she opened her unblemished palms. While this was going on, the blessed woman's husband heard of her fame. Gathering his friends and neighbors, he hurried after her, brought her back home and restored her to the cell where she had lived before. She did not desert the customs she had been keeping here but exerted herself in fasting and supplications that she might finally live in the place she longed for. So again, she took the desired road, imploring Blessed Martin's help, that he who had given her the desire, would give her its fulfillment and allow her to reach the basilica. Thus she returned to her original cell and remained there untroubled, for her husband asked nothing further from her. She gathered a few *monachas* there and lived with unbroken faith and prayer.[16] She ate only barley bread, took only a little wine on feast days and even that was greatly diluted. She had no soft bed of hay and straw but only the kind usually made

---

14. Médard, who consecrated Radegund in 550, died in 558. His relics were interred at Soissons, where Clothar built a church to honor them and for his own burial in 561, but may have been divided in some manner. Because the church at Esvres is still dedicated to Médard, this probably indicates the early spread of his cult outside of Soissons. See James, *Origins of France*, 156–57, n. 4.

15. Actually, *pustula mala*, but the illness seems far more impressive than a pimple or blister.

16. We have kept the relatively rare word *monachas* in order to reserve nun for the more common *sanctimonial*.

of rushes woven together in thin strips which are commonly called mats.[17] She would lay one of these over a bench or spread it out on the ground. It was her bench by day, and her mattress, featherbed and bedspread which was all the comfort she required of a bed. She taught those whom she admitted to her following to do the same. And there, as she pursued a life of praising God, she bestowed healing medicine on many sick people after praying for them.

7. A woman showed her daughter to her, covered with sores oozing pus. Assisted by the power of Him Who formed eyes for a man born blind with His sputum,[18] she prayed and took the saliva from her mouth and anointed the fierce sores, and made the girl whole again. Likewise, a neighborhood lad drank poison in a potion which, so they say, generated serpents within him. Their biting plagued him so much that nothing could calm him or give him a moment's rest. For he could take neither water nor food: when he got anything down, it came up at once. He was brought to the holy woman and asked to be cleansed by her power. She claimed that she was unworthy to do the deed. But his relatives' prayers prevailed and she gently touched the boy's belly, stroking it and feeling it with her palm where the iniquity of the venomous snakes was concealed. Then, taking a green leaf from a vine, she smeared it with saliva and fixed it on with the sign of the blessed cross. When she placed it on the youth's belly, it sedated his pain little by little and he, who hitherto had been kept sleepless by the insistent pain, now slept where he sat. After an hour, feeling the need to relieve his belly, he went out and brought forth the progeny of that pestiferous generation.[19] He gave thanks to the handmaid of God and departed singing.

8. Other people carried another paralyzed boy to her and begged the blessed woman for a cure. Prostrate in prayer, she poured out her plea to the Lord. When her prayer was ended, she got up, took the boy's hand and raised him up. Then she sent him away unhurt. A blind woman was led to her and prayed that she would lay her hands on her. And she answered: "What have I to do with you, people of God?[20] Doesn't Saint Martin live here, who daily shines in working famous miracles? Go to him, entreat him there that he may

---

17. An alternative is that *mattas* is a vernacular Germanic word in the singular and not the feminine Latin *matta* in the plural, which would agree with the (singular) bed Gregory mentions before and after this description of Monegund's bed. The *quas* in the phrase "*quas vulgo mattas vocant*" would therefore refer to the plural *virgulae* that are woven together in "what they call mats in the vernacular."

18. Mark 8:23.

19. Gregory appears to be implicitly comparing the boy's salutary bowel movement (or vomiting) to the birthing of monstrous babies.

20. John 2:4.

deign to visit you. For what can I, a sinner, do?" But the woman persisted in her petition, saying: "God does famous works daily, through all who fear His name. Thus have I come, a supplicant, to you in whom the divine grace of healing has been manifested." Then the servant of God was moved and laid her hand where the sight lay buried and immediately the cataracts fell away and she who had been blind looked forth upon the world opening wide before her. And she laid her hands on many possessed persons who came to her and, putting the wretched foe to flight, restored their health. Nor was there any delay in the cures of those whom the saint permitted to come to her.

9. But then, the time of her summoning was approaching. Exhausted, she was slipping out of her body. When the nuns who were with her saw that, they wept mightily saying: "And to whom will you leave us, holy mother? To whom will you entrust the daughters whom you have gathered in this place for the contemplation of God?" Weeping a little while, she said: "If you follow the way of peace and sanctification, God will protect you and in the holy Primate Martin, you will have a great pastor. Nor will I desert you. Invoke me and I will be with you in your charity."[21] And then they asked her: "Many of the sick will come to us begging for a blessing from you. What shall we do when they see that you are not here? Shall we send them away in our confusion when we can no longer contemplate your face? Since you will then be hidden from our sight, we ask that at least you will deign to bless oil and salt with which we may minister your blessings to supplicating invalids." Then she blessed oil and salt and gave it to them. They took it and saved it most carefully. Thus the blessed one died in peace. She was buried in that little cell where she has shown herself to posterity with many miracles. For after she passed over, many sick people received the blessings of health there as a result of the benediction we have described.

10. Boso the Deacon had a foot so swollen with pus that he could not take a step. He was carried to her shrine pouring out prayers. Taking the aforesaid oil that the saint had left, the maidens placed it on his foot. Straightaway, the poison flowed out from the open wound, and he was cured. A blind man led to her tomb prostrated himself in prayer. Weariness overcame him and he slept and the blessed woman appeared to him saying: "Indeed, I don't consider myself worthy to be counted with the saints, but you will now receive sight in one eye here. Then, if you will go as quickly as you can to the feet of Blessed Martin and prostrate yourself before him with compunction in your soul, he will restore sight to the other eye." When he awoke, the man had received sight in one eye. Then he went to the place where her instruc-

---

21. Possibly charity here is a special community meal; see chapter 12, c. 11.

tions had directed him to go and entreated the blessed Confessor to use his power. The night was dispelled from the blind eye and he left fully able to see. A mute came and lay prostrate at the tomb of this blessed woman. He had such compunction of faith that rivers of tears stained the pavement of the cell. When he rose, he went away with his tongue loosened by divine power. Then another mute came and lay down and implored the blessed woman's help with his whole heart, though his voice was tethered. And part of the oil and salt she had blessed was poured into his mouth. With an eruption of blood and pus, he deserved to recover the use of his voice. Then a feverish man came to the monument and touched the covering cloth. The contagion of fever was quenched and he was cured. A paralytic named Marcus was carried in the hands of others to the blessed woman's grave where he poured forth prayers for a long time. About the ninth hour, he stood up on his feet and returned home. A boy, Leodinus, overcome with grave illness was sick for four months. Because of the persistent fever he lost not only the power to walk but even to eat. Carried moribund to the sepulchre, he received a cure and rose, revived, from the tomb. How can I speak of all the other fever victims, most of whom were favored with remedies when they kissed the pall of her tomb in faith? What of the possessed ones? Whoever was brought to the blessed woman's cell and crossed the holy threshold was restored to wholeness of mind. For no evil spirit delays leaving a body when it feels the presence of the saint's power, working by agency of our Lord, Jesus Christ, who rewards those who fear His name with eternal blessings.[22]

22. Gregory made another brief note of her career in Glory of the Confessors, 24, where he appended to a reference to the present work: "Just this year, the maid servant of our archdeacon who was gravely ill of a quartan fever, was cured. She was left on the holy tomb by her parents and returned home healed."

4

Radegund, Queen of the Franks
and Abbess of Poitiers

(ca. 525–587)

None of the sources indicate whether or not Saint Clothild ever met the Thuringian princess who was one of the several wives of her son Clothar I (d. 561). Earlier, Clothar had married his brother Clodomir's widow. He murdered her sons, who were in their grandmother's custody, no later than 530 (the younger of the two victims was seven and Clodomir had died in 524). In 531, when Radegund first fell into the hands of her future husband, Clothild had already retired to Tours. Radegund herself spent about ten years growing up at Clothar's villa of Athies in Picardy.[1] Their marriage was probably consummated about 540, four years before Clothild died.

Whether or not they had the opportunity to compare notes, the older woman and her daughter-in-law had much in common. Radegund's early years were also passed in the household of an uncle who had murdered her father. Gregory of Tours says her aunt, a daughter of Theodoric the Ostrogothic king of Italy, provoked the quarrel because she could not bear being married to a man who had to share his kingdom with a brother.[2] Relations between the Franks and the Thuringians had been troubled for several generations. Clovis's mother was a Thuringian queen who, according to Gregory, deserted her husband because she considered the Frankish king Chilperic a better man.[3] Clovis and his sons came into conflict with the

---

The translations for Radegund are taken from Krusch, ed. MGH, AA 1:271–75, "The Thuringian War," and MGH, SRM 2:358–405. We want to thank William Daly for allowing us to see the translation of Fortunatus drafted by the late John Cox, whose work we have used with profit.

1. For a definition of the villa, see Murray, Germanic Kinship, 74.

2. Gregory of Tours, HF, 3:4. Note that Gregory was also the source for the accusation that Clothild was responsible for her sons' attack on Sigismund of Burgundy. Leaving aside the question of whether Gundobad murdered her parents, contradictions in the sources make the story hard to explain. Gregory may have suffered from the misogynistic tendency to blame the fury of women for certain particularly irrational exhibitions of male violence, although no one can dispute that women of the Merovingian age were quite capable of considerable violence themselves.

3. Gregory of Tours, HF, 2:11; for further details on her family, see Aigrain, Sainte Radegonde, 9–11.

Thuringians more than once and were provoked into a final deadly onslaught when Radegund's uncle broke his treaty with the Franks and ferociously murdered a number of women and children.

The revenge of the Franks was terrible and complete. The Thuringian ruling house was nearly obliterated in 531. Clothar gambled with his brothers and won the child princess, Radegund. He carried her off the battlefield to be raised at Athies as his future wife.[4] The trauma of that experience is vividly preserved in the poem "The Thuringian War," written more than thirty years later either by Radegund herself or by her friend Venantius Fortunatus (d. 609) with her verbal collaboration. By the time Clothar claimed her for his queen, he was somewhere in his forties, and several of his other marriages had already been consummated. The dates of these marriages and the fate of the five wives listed by Gregory of Tours for this period have never been satisfactorily disentangled, but it is clear enough that at least some of them were polygynous.[5] Contrary to the impression given by biographers, therefore, Radegund was probably not the only wife that Clothar had during the ten years of their marriage. His youngest son, Chramn, was born about 540, apparently just before his public espousal of Radegund.[6]

Radegund's achievements as queen and saint were widely celebrated. Like Clothild before her, she self-consciously played the role of a Christian queen in conjunction with the local ecclesiastical establishment.[7] She is perhaps the most richly documented individual of her time. Gregory of Tours described her life in *The History of the Franks* and details the events of her funeral, which he conducted, in his *Glory of the Confessors*.[8] Her lifelong friend and confessor, the poet and later bishop Venantius Fortunatus, wrote a full-length biography that was later supplemented with a second account by Baudonivia, a nun in Radegund's convent at Poitiers.[9] Both accounts follow. Radegund's biographers tactfully refrain from lengthy reflection on her reaction to the violent events that led to her marriage. The poem "The Thuringian War," also included in this chapter, is to her cousin Amalfred, who had escaped the tribal

4. The question of her age is unclear. Cautiously, Wemple, *Women in Frankish Society,* 39, says she was too old to be called *infans,* thus over six, but probably well below the legal majority of twelve because Clothar waited nearly ten years to claim his bride.

5. McNamara and Wemple, "Marriage and Divorce in the Frankish Kingdom," 103–18.

6. Aigrain, *Sainte Radegonde,* 21, lists the wives, their children, and probable dates. He suggests (29) an earlier date, but one somewhere between 536 when Ingund died and 540.

7. Graus, *Volk, Herrscher* 407–8 compares Fortunatus's portrait of the royal ascetic with Baudonivia's model nun. In "Frauen zwischen asketischem Ideal und weltlichem Leben," Wittern compares Radegund's asceticism to the systematic royal patronage of Balthild.

8. Gregory of Tours, HF, book 3, and *Glory of the Confessors,* 106.

9. Gordon Whatley is presently engaged on elaborating a gendered reading of these two texts.

disaster and taken service with the Emperor Justinian. It expresses a grief that was revived when her husband killed her surviving brother around 550.

Radegund, probably in her late twenties, then left Clothar, who was close to fifty, and retired to a villa at Saix, which was part of her dower. Despite the melodrama of her escape, recounted by Fortunatus, her own testimony emphasizes her husband's generosity in supporting her subsequent religious life until his death.[10] Clothar reigned for fifty years. The later years of his life were as violent as the first, culminating in the murder of his son Chramn, burned alive in a cottage with his wife and children after an unsuccessful rebellion. In 558, Clothar was in Tours, seeking absolution and repairing the Church of Saint Martin, which had suffered much the preceding year when Chramn burned the city. He apparently made some gesture that suggested that he wanted his wife back. Local tradition sets her flight from Saix to Poitiers in this context. Baudonivia claims that his designs on his former wife were frustrated by the intervention of Bishop Germanus of Paris. With his death in sight, Clothar may well have negotiated the endowment of the rich convent at Poitiers that Radegund then established, and it is probable that she finally settled there in 561 when she was a widow.

Both of Radegund's biographers imply by their silence that her life after Clothar's death was quiet and untroubled by the clamors of Frankish public life. In fact, however, Poitiers was in the thick of the bloody fratricidal strife that destroyed Clothar's sons. In 561, Fortunatus was in Metz, traveling from his Italian homeland toward Tours, where he had vowed to give thanks to Saint Martin for his deliverance from eye trouble. There he met the Visigothic princess Brunhild, who had just married King Sigebert. He addressed a poem to her in which Venus praises the new queen's charm.[11] Later, he wrote in praise of her sister Galswinth, who traveled through Poitiers on her way to marry Radegund's other stepson, Chilperic.[12] The marriage would end in Galswinth's brutal murder by her husband and his paramour Fredegund, followed by a long war of revenge and retaliation between Brunhild and Fredegund that ended only in 613. Radegund's community included a daughter of Chilperic's by an earlier marriage and an illegitimate daughter of Charibert (another son of Clothar), who was lord of Poitiers until he died in 567. Brunhild and Sigebert, who succeeded Charibert as lord of the city, enjoyed excellent relations with Radegund. Baudonivia testifies to the ongoing concern of the former queen with the public life of her successors.

10. Gregory of Tours, HF, 9:42, cites an undatable letter from Radegund to "the bishops," which could conceivably have been addressed to the prelates of the Council of Tours in 565.

11. Fortunatus, *Opera Poetica*, 6, 1, MGH, AA 41.

12. Ibid., 6, 5.

During the years of Sigebert's lordship, Fortunatus arrived in Poitiers and met Radegund and her spiritual daughter, the Abbess Agnes. He formed a bond with them that was to last more than twenty years until both women were dead. In 569, Radegund carried out her cherished plan of installing a relic of the cross in her monastery at Poitiers.[13] In honor of the occasion, Fortunatus composed his two poems, "Vexilla regis prodeunt" and "Pange lingua gloriosi," which are still actively incorporated into Catholic liturgy. His *Life of Radegund*, written at some time after her death in 587, dwelled heavily on her heroic qualities as an ascetic. Fortunatus was apparently determined to make good his claim for Radegund that she had earned a place among the martyrs. His occasional poetry reflects a far different picture of the life of the nuns at Poitiers, however. There he celebrates the pleasant feasts they shared and displays a long, affectionate intimacy based on mutual love of learning and poetry.

During those twenty years, however, Poitiers was far from peaceful and untroubled. The murder of Sigebert in 575 was followed by Brunhild's desperate gamble to secure the support of Chilperic's son, Merovech, by a precipitate marriage.[14] The outraged father and his murderous queen, Fredegund, pursued the young man through Poitiers and brought him to earth in nearby Tours. A few years later, the daughters of the warlike Count Guntram Boso were placed in sanctuary in a church in Poitiers while their father pursued the tangled political schemes that caused Chilperic to attack the town.[15] Chilperic's daughter Basina, the sister of the ill-fated Merovech, was sent to Radegund's convent in 580. After the saint's death, she would emerge as the leader of dissident forces that tore the convent apart. However, in 584, she gladly accepted the saint's help in avoiding the marriage to the Visigothic king Reccared that her father had planned for her. Fredegund's daughter Rigunth was substituted in the Spanish marriage. But by the time the princess passed through Poitiers, her father had died and her mother was desperately fighting to retain her son's right to a Frankish crown. Rigunth's escort gradually deserted her, taking her bridal wealth with them. Her remaining companions devastated the country around Poitiers before finally deserting the plundered princess in Toulouse.[16]

A year later, Poitiers was burned and looted in the strife between Childebert and Guntram. Neither Fortunatus nor Baudonivia saw fit to describe

13. Despite earlier uncertainties, Aubrun, *Radegonde*, 69, considers this an established date.

14. Gregory of Tours, HF, 5:2.

15. Ibid., 5:23.

16. Bernard S. Bachrach, personal communications, draws attention to the contrast between Rigunth's worldly wedding procession and Radegund's progress with her own wealth to her wedding with Christ.

Radegund's response to all this violence in her immediate neighborhood. Baudonivia claims that Radegund never tired of writing to all her royal friends, attempting to secure peace among them, but it must be clear that more than a raucous nightbird troubled the peace of the nuns. A final hint that Radegund kept up her connection to the political world comes with the mysterious appeal of Gundovald, a young man who claimed to be a natural son of Clothar, that Radegund and the holy woman of Tours, Ingitrude, could substantiate his claims.

Radegund was between sixty-five and seventy when she died in 587. She had outlived all her generation, and even the sons of her former husband had preceded her to the grave. She left a troubled convent that was to explode into violent strife within a few years, shortly after the deaths of the saint and the first Abbess Agnes. Basina, Chilperic's daughter with his first wife Audovera, had been forced into a convent when the ambitious slave Fredegund had replaced her mother in the royal bed.[17] Some years later, Chilperic attempted to reclaim his daughter, but she was apparently unwilling to accept his demand that she marry. On the basis of recent conciliar decrees, Radegund refused to release her back into the world.[18] Although Basina appears to have elected the nun's life, she later became discontented with the way it was conducted at Poitiers. She joined with Clothild, a natural daughter of King Charibert, in revolt against the incumbent Abbess Leubevera. Forty or more nuns joined the rebellion and left the convent. Some of them accompanied Clothild to King Guntram's court, while the majority took sanctuary in Saint Hilary's Church. There they tried to maintain some sort of communal life until Gregory of Tours dispersed them because they were unable to provide themselves with fuel for the winter.[19] Meanwhile, some of the nuns got pregnant and some married. Others recruited a gang of thugs and attempted to break into their old convent and kidnap the abbess.

When the bishops finally gathered to hear the rebel nuns, they were treated to a list of grievances that dramatically illustrates the dimensions of the communal problem. Leubevera was charged with providing poor food and allowing servants and workmen to use their bathroom. She was accused of playing backgammon, entertaining lay visitors, and dressing her niece in the altar cloths. The abbess replied that their food was at least plentiful; that the bathroom sharing was a temporary expedient during repairs; that the rule did not forbid backgammon; and that she followed the foundress's customs in

---

17. Gregory of Tours, HF, 5:39.
18. Ibid., 6:34.
19. Ibid., 9:31.

giving banquets to Christian travelers but did not eat with them. She admitted that she had outfitted her niece and held an engagement party for her that the bishop himself attended.[20] The abbess was acquitted of all charges. Basina returned to the monastery, where she can hardly have been a force for peace during the remainder of her life.[21] Both Fortunatus's and Baudonivia's biographies were written after the storm had been quelled. Possibly they wished to recall the community to an earlier and better time when they had lived as sisters under a woman who rejoiced to call them her chosen daughters.

The Thuringian War[22]

Oh, sad state of war, malevolent destiny
   That fells proud kingdoms in a sudden slide!
The rooves that stood so long in happiness are broken
   To lie fallen beneath the vast charred ruin.
The palace courts, where art once flourished
   Are vaulted now with sad, glowing ashes.
Towers artfully gilded, then shone golden-red,
   Now drifting ashes blur the glitter to pallor.
The captive maid given to a hostile lord, her power fell
   From the heights of glory to the lowest depths.
The entourage of servants, standing resplendent, her youthful peers
   Were dead in a day, besmirched with funeral ashes.
The bright attendant halo of powerful ministers

20. Ibid., 10:14.
21. Ibid., 10:20.
22. This poem is placed in Appendix 3 of Fortunatus's verses as a letter to Radegund's long-lost uncle who had taken service in Constantinople. Nisard, the editor of Fortunatus's *Opera poetica*, believed that she wrote the poem wholly or in part, and this opinion has also been embraced by Thiébaux, who includes it in *The Writings of Medieval Women*, 30–34. Allen and Calder have translated the poem among *The Sources and Analogues of Old English Poetry*, 137–40, attributing it without discussion to Fortunatus. Cherewatuk, "Female Personae," analyzed the piece as a direct expression of Radegund's voice; Wallace-Hadrill, *Frankish Church*, 84–85, defends Fortunatus's authorship by a comparison with his Lament for Galswinth. It seems at least likely that Fortunatus was following Radegund's account. Her competence to write such a work is attested by the letter Gregory of Tours transcribed in HF, 9:42, and by Fortunatus's own description of her learning and poetic talents. *Carmina*, 8:1. Aigrain, *Sainte Radegonde*, 25, is skeptical of the intensive patristic studies Fortunatus claims for her, but concurs that Radegund was well educated. Assuming the epistolary form of the work is not simply a poetic fancy, it is hard to understand why she waited twenty years or more to inform Amalfred of his nephew's death. It is likely that she composed the poem, or Fortunatus composed it for her, to be delivered by the ambassadors going to Constantinople to ask for a relic of the Cross.

Now lie still without tomb or funeral service.
The conquering flame belching, reddens the gold hair of her beloved[23]
   While the milk-white woman lies on the ground.
Alas, the corpses lie shamefully unburied on the field,
   An entire people, strewn in a common grave.
Not Troy alone must mourn her ruins:
   The Thuringian land suffered equal slaughter.
The matron was rapt away, with streaming hair, bound fast
   Without even a sad farewell to the household gods.
Nor could the captive press a kiss on the threshold
   Nor cast one backward glance toward what was lost.
A wife's naked feet trod in her husband's blood
   And the tender sister stepped over the fallen brother.
The boy torn from his mother's embrace, his funeral plaint[24]
   Hung on her lips, with all her tears unshed.
So to lose the life of a child is not the heaviest lot,
   Gasping, the mother lost even her pious tears.
I, the barbarian woman, seek not to count these tears,
   Nor to keep afloat in the melancholy lake of all those drops.
Each one had her own tears; I alone have them all,
   Anguish is private and public both to me.
Fate was kind to those whom the enemy struck down.
   I, the sole survivor, must weep for them all.
Not only must I mourn the near ones who died:
   I also grieve for those still blessed with life.
My face often moistened, my eyes are blurred,
   My murmurs are secret but my care unstilled.
Eagerly, I seek for some greeting borne on the winds,
   But of all those near ones, no shade comes near me,
He whose gentle looks once solaced me with love,
   Is now torn from my embrace by evil fortune.
Ah, doesn't my care gnaw at you in your absence?
   Has bitter destruction taken your sweet love away?
Oh Amalfred, remember how it was in those first years,
   How I was your own Radegund then.

23. *Amati*: Aigrain, *Sainte Radegonde*, 15, follows Nisard in changing the word to *amita*: "Her aunt lay on the ground. . . ." However, he adds that her only known aunt, Amalberga, the niece of Theodoric the Ostrogoth, survived and returned to the Ostrogothic court.
24. *Planctu*, a formal keening or breast-beating that the mother had no time to render. The same terminology appears later when Radegund bemoans her failure to provide her murdered brother with a funeral.

An infant, how you cherished me then,
   Son of my father's brother, kindly kinsman.
What my dead father could have done, or my dead mother,
   What only a sister or brother could be, were you to me.
With the press of a pious hand, sweet lingering kisses,
   Your tender speech soothed the little child.
Then there was scarcely an hour that you did not come to me:
   Now ages limp along without a single word.
How I writhed under the raging pain in my bosom,
   Trying to bring you back, kinsman, wherever you might be.
Once, if father or mother or the cares of ruling held you,
   However you hurried to me, you were always too slow.
Fate was warning that I might lose you, dearest;
   For I call you: impatient love cannot wait so long.
Then I was frantic when we did not share a house:
   If you went out of doors, I thought you had gone far away.
Now the sun rises where you are and sets upon us;
   The Ocean Sea binds me; the Red Sea holds you.[25]
All the globe comes between us dear ones,
   The world divides those whom no space parted once.
All that earth holds lies between our loving hearts,
   If the lands were broader, the road would stretch yet further.
But stay there, where the prayers of kindred may hold better things,
   More luck than Thuringian lands ever brought you.
But while I am here, I suffer more cruelly under my burdens
   For that you send no single sign to me.
The face I long for but do not see could be painted in a letter,
   A man's image borne from the place which holds him.
Your strength might recall our ancestors, your praise our kin,
   As your father's blush plays prettily on your face.
Kinsman, believe, you are not gone while a word remains:
   Send a speaking page to act as a brother to me.
Some have every gift while I lack even tears for solace.
   Oh cruel fate that the more I love, the less I have!
If the law of piety makes others seek out their servants,
   Why, I ask, should those of my own blood abandon me?
To save the home-bred slave, lords have often braved the Alps
   Where freezing snow has cemented the waters;
The lover enters the shadowy cave in the broken rock

25. This is Thiébaux's inspired reading for *unda rubri*.

Where no frost cools his burning ardor,
Barefoot, with none to guide him, he runs
    And snatches his plunder from the forbidding hosts.
The edge of the enemy's sword wounds him in passing
    But he takes his desire, for love spares not itself.
But I, listening every moment for you,
    Scarcely enjoy a moment with a carefree mind.
If a breeze whispers, I ask what place holds you now,
    If the low clouds drift by, I ask for the place.
Did warlike Persia or Byzantium choose you as leader
    Or the wealth of Alexander's royal city?
Do you live in Jerusalem near the citadel
    Where Christ our God was born of a virgin mother?
No letter on the page reveals where you are
    Whereby my sorrow takes on heavier power.
For should earth or sea send no sign to me,
    Then some swift-flying bird may bear a message!
If the monastery's sacred cloister did not keep me back,
    I'd come unheralded to the region where you bide.[26]
Swift would I pass by ship through tempest-tossed waves
    Racing gladly through the gales of wintry water.
For love of you, would I press more strongly through shifting tides;
    What sailors dread would never make me quake.
If the wave broke the keel in the perilous waters,
    I would still seek you rowing on the surface of the sea.
If by unlucky chance, the planks refused to bear me,
    I would come to you exhausted from swimming.
At sight of you, I would deny the journey's perils
    For that would sweetly take the sorrow from the wreck.
Yes, if fate had ripped from me at last my doleful life,
    I would have you bear me to a sandy tomb.
I would come to you a sightless corpse if your pious eyes
    Would turn at last to carry out my funeral rites.
Surely you, who spurn my living tears, would weep at my burial.
    Surely you, who deny me a word now, would make my plaint.[27]

---

26. This passage appears to confirm not only that Radegund had entered a monastery by this time, which she surely did before Fortunatus arrived in Poitiers, but also that she was already bound by the Caesarian rule of strict claustration. If this letter was sent in connection with her embassy to Constantinople (before 569), the reference appears to preclude a journey to Arles to obtain the rule in 570.

27. As in line 25, the formal *planctu*.

Oh, kinsman, why do I shun memories and delay my lament?
  Oh deepest grief, why are you silent about my murdered brother?[28]
How could the innocent have fallen into the wicked ambush,
  Or was he ripped from the world by men of a hostile faith?
Thinking of him in the grave, all my tears well up again,
  And I suffer again, and still speak tearfully.
While longing for you, he is eager to seek out your face
  But his love is ungratified while mine thwarts it.
He who never gave me a hard word, took all hurt to himself,
  That he feared to give hurt has become the cause of sorrow.
The youth was struck down while in his first downy beard,
  Nor did I, his absent sister, attend the dire funeral.
I lost him and could not even close his pious eyes
  Nor lie across the corpse in final farewell,
My hot tears could not warm his freezing bowels.
  I placed no kiss upon the dying flesh,
No embrace in my misery. I could not hang weeping on his neck
  Nor sighing, warm the unlucky corpse in my bosom.
Life was denied: how should I snatch the fleeting breath
  From the mouth of the brother to the sister?
I might have sent the fringes I made while he lived to his bier.
  Couldn't my love at least adorn the lifeless shell?
Brother, I salute you, and stand accused of this impiety:
  You only died because of me and I gave you no sepulchre.
Twice am I captive who only left my country once,
  Having endured again the enemy while my brother lay fallen.
Then, father and mother, uncle and kindred,
  This grief recalls them whom I should mourn in the tomb.
After my brother's burial, no day passed without tears;
  He bore my joy away with him to the land of the shades.
Oh, how can the sweet royal kindred end in such misery,
  The whole blood line from which he sprang?
I should have endured this evil, not bring it to my lips at present
  Nor be soliciting your comfort for my wounds.
Oh kindly kinsman, I beseech, send me a letter now,
  Sooth my raging fever with a friendly word.

28. Radegund had fled Clothar some ten to fifteen years earlier when he had her brother murdered. Assuming that he must have been born before the destruction of the Thuringians in 531, he would have been at least twenty in 550, somewhat old for the "downy-bearded" youth Radegund recalled. Aigrain, *Sainte Radegonde*, 40, connects the boy's death to the Thuringian revolt of 555; see Gregory of Tours, HF, 4:10.

This care for you is likewise from me to your sisters
    Whom I recall with cousinly love in my heart.
I cannot embrace the limbs of the kin whom I love
    Nor, like a sister, kiss each eye greedily.
If, as I hope, they remain alive, I ask you to salute them
    In greeting and send sweet kisses to me.
I pray that you may commend me to the kings of the Franks
    Who piously honor me as a mother.[29]
Health-giving breath and long life to you
    And may your offices renew my well-being.
Christ hear my prayer: may this page find out my loved ones
    And may a letter come back with sweet painted messages.
That my long delayed hopes after such suffering
    Will swiftly be fulfilled when your course is run.

The Life of the Holy Radegund by Venantius Fortunatus

∎

1. Our Redeemer is so richly and abundantly generous that He wins mighty victories through the female sex and, despite their frail physique, He confers glory and greatness on women through strength of mind. By faith, Christ makes them strong who were born weak so that, when those who appeared to be imbeciles are crowned with their merits by Him who made them, they garner praise for their Creator who hid heavenly treasure in earthen vessels. For Christ the king dwells with his riches in their bowels. Mortifying themselves in the world, despising earthly consort, purified of worldly contamination, trusting not in the transitory, dwelling not in error but seeking to live with God, they are united with the Redeemer's glory in Paradise. One of that company is she whose earthly life we are attempting to present to the public, though in homely style, so that the glorious memory that she, who lives with Christ, has left us will be celebrated in this world. So ends the Prologue.

Here begins the Life.

2. The most blessed Radegund was of the highest earthly rank, born from the seed of the kings of the barbarian nation of Thuringia. Her grandfather was King Bassin, her paternal uncle, Hermanfred and her father, King Bertechar.[30] But she surpassed her lofty origin by even loftier deeds. She had

29. Sigebert and Chilperic, who succeeded Clothar on his death in 561. Sigebert was murdered in 575.
30. Fortunatus tactfully suppresses the information that Hermanfred killed Bertechar and took his orphaned daughter into his own household. Gregory of Tours, HF, 3:4.

lived with her noble family only a little while when the victorious Franks devastated the region with barbaric turmoil and, like the Israelites, she departed and migrated from her homeland.[31] The royal girl became part of the plunder of these conquerors and they began to quarrel over their captive. If the contest had not ended with an agreement for her disposition, the kings would have taken up arms against one another. Falling to the lot of the illustrious King Clothar,[32] she was taken to Athies in Vermandois, a royal villa, and her upbringing was entrusted to guardians.[33] The maiden was taught letters and other things suitable to her sex and she would often converse with other children there about her desire to be a martyr if the chance came in her time.[34] Thus even as an adolescent, she displayed the merits of a mature person. She obtained part of what she sought, for, though the church was flourishing in peace, she endured persecution from her own household. While but a small child, she herself brought the scraps left at table to the gathered children, washing the head of each one, seating them on little chairs and offering water for their hands, and she mingled with the infants herself.[35] She would also carry out what she had planned beforehand with Samuel, a little cleric.[36] Following his lead, carrying a wooden cross they had made, singing psalms, the children would troop into the oratory as somber as adults. Radegund herself would polish the pavement with her dress and, collecting the drifting dust around the altar in a napkin, reverently placed it outside the door rather than sweep it away. When the aforementioned king, having provided the expenses, wished to bring her to Vitry, she escaped by night from Athies through Beralcha with a few companions.[37] When he

31. Again, Fortunatus omits Hermanfred's atrocities, which Gregory of Tours says provoked the Frankish attack. Ibid., 3:7.

32. Clothar was the third son of Clovis and Clothild, *Vita Chrothildis*, 9, 10, and shared his kingdom with Childebert until the latter's death in 558. One purpose of marriage was to prevent too much competition for these crowns. In 555, Clothar attempted to marry the widow of Theudebald, Clovis's grandson through another woman. Gregory of Tours, *HF*, 4:9. Episcopal opposition prevented him from doing so, and in 558 he contented himself with exiling Childebert's widow and her children.

33. This villa later formed part of her morning gift, and she established a hospital there. A parish was later formed in her honor. Higounet, "Saints mérovingiennes," 155–67.

34. See c. 26. This is a deliberate part of Fortunatus's hagiographical scheme.

35. Cox interprets this as mixing them a drink.

36. Although "with Samuel" seems clearly to indicate that she had the cooperation of a clergyman, it is also possible that Fortunatus intended to draw a parallel between his heroine and the prophet Samuel who was raised as a child in the Temple. I Samuel 2–4; Aigrain, *Sainte Radegonde*, 27. This is the meaning Cox prefers.

37. Krusch, ed., *MGH, SRM*, 366, n. 2, adds, "Nescio quid intelligitur." Variant readings supply "from Athies" as often as "to Athies." Aigrain, *Sainte Radegonde*, 29, n. 27, summarizes various attempts to associate Beralcha with Biaches on the Somme, not far from Soissons. Even more ingeniously, some

settled with her that she should be made his queen at Soissons, she avoided the trappings of royalty, so she would not grow great in the world but in Him to Whom she was devoted and she remained unchanged by earthly glory.[38]

3. Therefore, though married to a terrestrial prince, she was not separated from the celestial one and, the more secular power was bestowed upon her, the more humbly she bent her will—more than befitted her royal status. Always subject to God following priestly admonitions, she was more Christ's partner than her husband's companion. We will only attempt to publicize a few of the many things she did during this period of her life. Fearing she would lose status with God as she advanced in worldly rank at the side of a prince, she gave herself energetically to almsgiving. Whenever she received part of the tribute, she gave away a tithe of all that came to her before accepting any for herself. She dispensed what was left to monasteries, sending the gifts to those she could not reach on foot. There was no hermit who could hide from her munificence.[39] So she paid out what she received lest the burden weigh her down. The voice of the needy was not raised in vain for she never turned a deaf ear. Often she gave clothes, believing that the limbs of Christ concealed themselves under the garments of the poor and that whatever she did not give to paupers was truly lost.

4. Turning her mind to further works of mercy, she built a house at Athies where beds were elegantly made up for needy women gathered there.[40] She would wash them herself in warm baths, tending to the putrescence of their diseases. She washed the heads of men, acting like a servant. And before she washed them, she would mix a potion with her own hands to revive those who were weak from sweating.[41] Thus the devout lady, queen by birth and marriage, mistress of the palace, served the poor as a handmaid. Secretly, lest

---

have transcribed it as *per barcham* (by boat). Aubrun, *Radegonde*, 21, cites a local legend from Missy-sur-Aisne, ten kilometers from Soissons, where a rock has been preserved purporting to bear miraculous marks where the stone acted of itself to trap a soldier searching for the escaping bride.

38. Soissons was the capital of Clothar's kingdom. In "Queens as Jezebels," 34–35, Nelson discusses the problem of defining the office of Queen in this period. She is hesitant to accept the polygyny of Clothar, and therefore avoids the problem of whether his other wives also exercised the office. In any case, Fortunatus emphasizes more than once that Radegund was Clothar's official queen.

39. It is not clear what is happening in this passage—whether her "tribute" was a gift from her husband or an official income from the taxes. See Goffart, *Barbarians and Romans*, for a broad discussion. It is also unclear whether her dispensation of alms exceeded the expectations from a charitable queen, or whether it reflects the biblical tithe, or tenth. Nelson, "Queens as Jezebels," 36, discusses the role of Merovingian queens as receivers and distributors of wealth. Duby, *Early Growth*, 48ff., discusses the role of the church in facilitating the circulation of pillage into sacrificial gifts and charity.

40. A hospice dedicated to Radegund still exists at Athies.

41. Cox reads this to mean "workers worn out with toil."

anyone notice, at royal banquets, she fed most deliciously on beans or lentils from the dish of legumes placed before her, in the manner of the three boys.[42] And if the singing of the hours started while she was still eating, she would make her excuses to the king and withdraw from the company to do her duty to God. As she went out, she sang psalms to the Lord and carefully checked what food had been provided to refresh the paupers at the door.

5. At night, when she lay with her prince she would ask leave to rise and leave the chamber to relieve nature. Then she would prostrate herself in prayer under a hair cloak by the privy[43] so long that the cold pierced her through and through and only her spirit was warm. Her whole flesh prematurely dead, indifferent to her body's torment, she kept her mind intent on Paradise and counted her suffering trivial, if only she might avoid becoming cheap in Christ's eyes.[44] Re-entering the chamber thereafter, she could scarcely get warm either by the hearth or in her bed. Because of this, people said that the King had yoked himself to a *monacha* rather than a queen.[45] Her goodness provoked him to harsher irritation but she either soothed him to the best of her ability or bore her husband's brawling modestly.

6. Indeed, it will suffice to know how she bore herself during the days of Quadragesima, a singular penitent in her royal robes.[46] When the time for fasting drew near, she would notify a *monacha* named Pia, who, according to their holy arrangement, would send a hair cloth sealed carefully in linen to Radegund. Draping it over her body through the whole of Quadragesima, the holy woman wore that sweet burden under her royal garment. When the season was over, she returned the hair cloth similarly sealed. Who could believe how she would pour out her heart in prayers when the king was away? How she would cling to the feet of Christ as though He were present with her and satiate her long hunger with tears as though she was gorging on delicacies! She had contempt for the food of the belly, for Christ was her only nourishment and all her hunger was for Christ.

7. With what piety did she care solicitously for the candles made with her own hands that burned all night long in oratories and holy places? When the king asked after her at table during the late hours, he was told that she was

---

42. Daniel 1:12.

43. *Ante secretum.*

44. Krusch, ed., MGH, SRM 2:380, n. 1, notes the use of the term *mens intenta* by Baudonivia as a possible translation of Radegund's Germanic name.

45. *Monacha*, which also appears in Monegund's life, appears to have been common usage in the early sixth century, and we have retained it throughout. Thereafter, it virtually disappeared, to be replaced by *sanctimonial*, which we have translated as nun.

46. As we have done with other legal and institutional terms, we have followed our text in retaining *Quadragesima* instead of the more modern *Lent*.

delayed, busy about God's affairs. This caused strife with her husband and later on the prince compensated her with gifts for the wrong he did her with his tongue.

8. If she received a report that any of God's servants was on his way to see her, either of his own accord or by invitation, she felt full of celestial joy. Hastening out in the night time, with a few intimates, through snow, mud or dust, she herself would wash the feet of the venerable man with water she had heated beforehand and offer the servant of God something to drink in a bowl. There was no resisting her. On the following day, committing the care of the household to her trusted servants, she would occupy herself wholly with the just man's words and his teachings concerning salvation. The business of achieving celestial life fixed her attention throughout the day. And if a bishop should come, she rejoiced to see him, gave him gifts and was sad to have to let him go home.

9. And how prudently she sought to devote everything possible to her salvation. If the girls attending her when she dressed praised a new veil of coarse linen ornamented with gold and gems in the barbarian fashion as particularly beautiful, she would judge herself unworthy to be draped in such fabric. Divesting herself of the dress immediately, she would send it to some holy place in the neighborhood where it could be laid as a cloth on the Lord's altar.

10. And if the king, according to custom, condemned a guilty criminal to death, wasn't the most holy queen near dead with torment lest the culprit perish by the sword?[47] How she would rush about among his trusty men, ministers and nobles, whose blandishments might soothe the prince's temper until the king's anger ceased and the voice of salvation flowed where the sentence of death had issued before!

11. Even while she remained in her worldly palace, the blessed acts which busied her so pleased Divine Clemency that the Lord's generosity worked miracles through her. Once at her villa in Péronne, while that holiest of women was strolling in the garden after her meal, some sequestered criminals loudly cried to her from the prison for help.[48] She asked who it might be. The servants lied that a crowd of beggars were seeking alms. Believing that, she sent to relieve their needs. Meanwhile the fettered prisoners were silenced by a judge. But as night was falling and she was saying her prayers, the chains broke and the freed prisoners ran from the prison to the holy woman. When they witnessed this, those who had lied to the holy one realized that

---

47. See *Vita Genovefa*, 25. The intervention of women on behalf of prisoners may indicate an aspect of the division of labor whereby the harsh military face of kingship could be softened through the merciful quality of queenship without making the king appear weak or indecisive.

48. *Prandium*, a late breakfast or lunch taken about noon.

they were the real culprits, while the erstwhile convicts were freed from their bonds.

12. If Divinity fosters it, misfortune often leads to salvation. Thus her innocent brother was killed so that she might come to live in religion.[49] She left the king and went straight to holy Médard at Noyon. She earnestly begged that she might change her garments and be consecrated to God.[50] But mindful of the words of the Apostle: "Art thou bound unto a wife? Seek not to be loosed,"[51] he hesitated to garb the Queen in the robe of a monacha. For even then, nobles were harassing the holy man and attempting to drag him brutally through the basilica from the altar to keep him from veiling the king's spouse lest the priest imagine he could take away the king's official queen as though she were only a prostitute.[52] That holiest of women knew this and, sizing up the situation, entered the sacristy, put on a monastic garb and proceeded straight to the altar, saying to the blessed Médard: "If you shrink from consecrating me, and fear man more than God, Pastor, He will require His sheep's soul from your hand." He was thunderstruck by that argument and, laying his hand on her, he consecrated her as a deaconess.[53]

13. Soon she divested herself of the noble costume which she was wont to wear as queen when she walked in procession on the day of a festival with her train of attendants. She laid it on the altar and piled the table of Divine Glory with purple, gems, ornaments and like gifts to honor Him. She gave a heavy girdle of costly gold for the relief of the poor.[54] Similarly, one day she

49. See "The Thuringian War," and n. 22. This sequence of events likely occurred between 550 and 555, ending a childless marriage of ten to fifteen years.

50. Médard, d. 558, Bishop of Noyon and Tournai whose cult, patronized by subsequent Merovingian rulers, flourished locally from his own time. Wallace-Hadrill, Frankish Church, 194, sees him as one of the three great patron saints of the dynasty, along with Denis and Germanus. He remained a favorite with Clothar, who buried him at Soissons. Gregory of Tours, HF, 4:19.

51. I Corinthians 7:22.

52. Reginam non publicanam sed publicam: "a queen who was no whore but a lawfully wedded wife" (Cox).

53. The choice of deaconess rather than nun or sanctimonial seems to be deliberately indicated. Wemple, Women in Frankish Society, 142, gives a cautious overview of the questionable legal status of a deaconess in this period. There is no reason to suppose that a deaconess was bound to celibacy. Conceivably, Médard had found an ingenious solution to his particular dilemma in consecrating a woman who was still married to the king. On this point, Delaruelle, "Sainte Radegonde," 67, remarks that the promotion of women as saints and their role in the sanctification of public life was an innovation of Merovingian spirituality. He sees Radegund as exempt from the restrictions of claustration in Caesarius's rule because of her diaconal status, which explains her charity and social life. Our text however, suggests that once she entered her nunnery at Poitiers she did live as a cloistered nun, but that was after Clothar's death.

54. The belt is described as fractum auri; broken or unworked seem less appropriate than the less common translation, costly from CCSL, Lexicon, but Cox argues that the gold was broken up to be given away.

ornamented herself in queenly splendor, as the barbarians would say—all decked out for *stapione*.[55] Entering holy Jumerus' cell, she laid her frontlets, chemise, bracelets, coif and pins all decorated with gold, some with circlets of gems on the altar for future benefit.[56] Again, proceeding to the venerable Dato's cell one day, spectacularly adorned as she should have been in the world with whatever she could put on, having rewarded the abbot, she gave the whole from her woman's wealth to the community. Likewise going on to the retreat of holy Gundulf, later Bishop of Metz, she exerted herself just as energetically to enrich his monastery.[57]

14. From there her fortunate sails approached Tours. Can any eloquence express how zealous and munificent she showed herself there? How she conducted herself around the courts, shrines, and basilica of Saint Martin, weeping unchecked tears, prostrating herself at each threshold! After mass was said, she heaped the holy altar with the clothing and bright ornaments with which she used to adorn herself in the palace. And when the handmaid of the Lord went from there to the neighborhood of Candes whence the glorious Martin, Christ's senator and confidant, migrated from this world, she gave him no less again, ever profiting in the Lord's grace.[58]

15. From there, in decorous manner, she approached the villa of Saix near the aforesaid town in the territory of Poitiers, her journey ever prospering.[59] Who could recount the countless remarkable things she did there or grasp the special quality of each one? At table she secretly chewed rye or barley bread which she had hidden under a cake to escape notice. For from the time she was veiled, consecrated by Saint Médard, even in illness, she ate nothing but legumes and green vegetables: not fruit nor fish nor eggs. And she drank no drink but honeyed water or perry and would touch no undiluted wine nor any decoction of mead or fermented beer.

---

55. *Conposito . . . stapione.* Krusch, ed., MGH, SRM 2:369, n. 1 does not gloss the Germanic word *stapione*, but cites Graf, *Althochdeutsches Sprachschatz*, 6:655. This seems to refer to the old high German word that corresponds to the archaic modern German *Stapf, footstep*. A possible translation might be "with stately pace," but there is no apparent reason why Fortunatus should have used a vernacular word in place of the ordinary Latin *gradus*. Used in conjunction with *compositus*, as it is, it seems to have something to do with her outfit instead—possibly some slang version of "dressed for stepping out."

56. We have here translated *sanctus* simply as *holy* because the text seems to refer to a living hermit, and no Saint Jumerus appears in any of the standard reference works.

57. Krusch notes that Gundulf does not appear in any other sources as the bishop of Metz.

58. Gregory of Tours, HF, 1:48.

59. Discussing the spread of Radegund's cult, in "Saints mérovingiennes," Higounet shows that parishes were dedicated to her at Athies, where she grew up, near Tours, where she stopped on her way to Poitiers, at Saix, the site of John's hermitage, and at a variety of other locations in Neustria and Aquitaine. It is also worthwhile to note that Saix was given to Radegund by Clothar, as was the property where she built her nunnery in Poitiers. She was acting with his permission, however grudging it might have been, and she never went out of the lands that he ruled.

16. Then, emulating Saint Germanus' custom, she secretly had a millstone brought to her. Throughout the whole of Quadragesima, she ground fresh flour with her own hands.[60] She continuously distributed each offering to local religious communities, in the amount needed for the meal taken every four days.[61] With that holy woman, acts of mercy were no fewer than the crowds who pressed her; as there was no shortage of those who asked, so was there no shortage in what she gave so that, wonderfully, they could all be satisfied. Where did the exile get such wealth? Whence came the pilgrim's riches?

17. How much did she spend daily on relief? Only she who bore it to the beggars ever knew. For beyond the daily meal which she fed to her enrolled paupers, twice a week, on Thursday and Saturday, she prepared a bath.[62] Girding herself with a cloth, she washed the heads of the needy, scrubbing away whatever she found there. Not shrinking from scurf, scabs, lice or pus, she plucked off the worms and scrubbed away the putrid flesh. Then she herself combed the hair on every head she had washed. As in the gospel, she applied oil to their ulcerous sores that had opened when the skin softened or that scratching had irritated, reducing the spread of infection. When women descended into the tub, she washed their limbs with soap from head to foot. When they came out, if she noticed that anyone's clothes were shoddy with age, she would take them away and give them new ones. Thus she spruced up all who came to the feast in rags. When they were gathered around the table and the dinner service laid out, she brought water and napkins for each of them and cleaned the mouth and hands of the invalids herself. Then three trays laden with delicacies would be carried in. Standing like a good hostess before the diners, she cut up the bread and meat and served everyone while fasting herself. Moreover, she never ceased to offer food to the blind and weak with a spoon. In this, two women aided her but she alone served them, busy as a new Martha until the "brothers" were drunk and happily satisfied with their meal.[63] Then, leaving the place to wash her hands, she was com-

---

60. Krusch, ed., MGH, SRM 2:369, n. 10. St. Germanus was in fact content to mill and sift barley flour for his own bread. "Vita S. Germani Autisiodorensis episcopi," ed. Narbey, 47. In subsequent notes, Krusch indicates that many of Radegund's austerities appear to be inspired by Germanus's example.

61. Aubrun, *Radegonde*, 35, n. 15, suggests that this may refer to altar breads whose manufacture is still a major activity at Sainte Croix.

62. The recipients of her banquets are called *matriculam*, suggesting a regular role of dependent paupers. Salin, *Etudes mérovingiens*, 270, says that cemeteries in the Poitiers region yield evidence of widespread malnutrition, especially in women and children, and the remains even give rise to suspicions of cannibalism. More recent research supports this archeological hypothesis; see Bullough and Campbell, "Female Longevity."

63. Luke 10:40. Martha, as later texts will also show, is customarily presented as the type of the active religious life for women, whereas her sister Mary symbolizes the contemplative life. This public activity appears to mark Radegund's life at Saix before she built her nunnery.

pletely gratified with her well-served feast. And if anyone protested, she ordered that they sit still until they wished to get up.

18. Summer and winter, on Sundays, she followed a praiseworthy rule. She would provide an undiluted drink of sweet wine to the assembled paupers. First she doled it out herself and then, while she hurried off to Mass, she assigned a maid to serve everyone who remained. Her devotions completed, she would meet the priests invited to her table for it was her royal custom not to let them return home without a gift.

19. Doesn't this make one shudder, this thing she did so sweetly? When lepers arrived and, sounding a warning,[64] came forward, she directed her assistant to inquire with pious concern whence they came or how many there were. Having learned that, she had a table laid with dishes, spoons, little knives, cups and goblets, and wine and she went in herself secretly that none might see her. Seizing some of the leprous women in her embrace, her heart full of love, she kissed their faces. Then, while they were seated at table, she washed their faces and hands with warm water and treated their sores with fresh unguents and fed each one. When they were leaving she offered small gifts of gold and clothing. To this there was scarcely a single witness, but the attendant presumed to chide her softly: "Most holy lady, when you have embraced lepers, who will kiss you?" Pleasantly, she answered: "Really, if you won't kiss me, it's no concern of mine."

20. With God's help, she shone forth in diverse miracles. For example, if anyone was in desperate straits because of pus from a wound, an attendant would bring a vine leaf to the saint speaking with her about what was to be done with it. As soon as the saint made the sign of the cross over it, the attendant would take it to the desperate one, placing it on the wound which would soon be healed.[65] Similarly an invalid or someone with a fever might come and say that he had learned in a dream that to be healed he should

---

64. This formula, *signo tacto*, appears in different contexts in a number of contemporary monastic texts, including the Benedictine rule, c. 43, and that of Caesarius of Arles, c. 12. Herbert Thurston, *The Catholic Encyclopedia*, 2:418–24, interprets it as some sort of a bell, although he thinks that a gong or a clapper might have been used in some cases. He ultimately concludes that it would be more prudent to translate the term as *a signal*.

65. In this passage and in the preceding one concerning the lepers we have translated the word *ministra* as *attendant* to preserve the possibility that this person was more specialized in caring for the sick than an ordinary *ancilla* or *puella*. The practical nature of Radegund's nursing extended to cooperation with even more skilled medical practitioners, witnessed in Gregory of Tours, HF, book 9. Some years after Radegund died, rebellious nuns accused the Abbess Leubevera of harboring a lover disguised as a woman in the convent. The man at whom suspicion pointed came forward and claimed that he wore female garb to symbolize his loss of male potency. His testicles had been so diseased that, after consulting with Reoval, a surgeon, Radegund had advised his castration, and the operation had been performed (see n. 108).

hasten to the holy woman and present one of her attendants with a candle. After it had burned through the night his disease would be killed while the invalid was healed. How often when she heard of someone lying bedridden would she sally forth like a pilgrim bearing fruit, or something sweet and warm to restore their strength? How quickly would an invalid who had eaten nothing for ten days take food when she served it herself and thus receive both food and health together? And she ordered these things herself lest anyone tell tales.

21. Weren't there such great gatherings of people on the day that the saint determined to seclude herself that those who could not be contained in the streets climbed up to fill the roofs?[66] Anyone who spoke of all the most holy woman had fervently accomplished in fasting, services, humility, charity, suffering and torment, proclaimed her both confessor and martyr. Truly every day except for the most venerable day of the Lord, was a fast day for that most holy woman. Her meal of lentils or green vegetables was virtually a fast in itself for she took no fowl or fish or fruit or eggs to eat. Her bread was made from rye or barley which she concealed under the pudding lest anyone notice what she ate. And to drink she had water and honey or perry and only a little of that was poured out for her, however thirsty she was.

22. The first time she enclosed herself in her cell throughout Quadragesima, she ate no bread, except on Sundays but only roots of herbs or mallow greens without a drop of oil or salt for dressing. In fact, during the entire fast, she consumed only two *sestaria* of water.[67] Consequently, she

---

66. Fortunatus jumped abruptly over the end of Radegund's sojourn at Saix, the building of Holy Cross monastery, and her advent at Poitiers; see Baudonivia for an account of these events. Ever the courtier, the poet may have found the account too unfavorable to King Clothar, whereas Baudonivia, writing later, may no longer have been concerned with such repercussions. The publicity and the stress laid on the idea of enclosure within the small city built against the fortified walls of Poitiers facing the River Clain may reflect Radegund's fear of being forced to marry another king after Clothar's death. The powers and claims of widows in this age were not to be taken lightly, as the long war between Brunhild and Fredegund amply attests. Clothar himself, in 555, would have married his nephew Theudebert's widow, had not the bishops prohibited it, and he contented himself with exiling Childebert's widow Ultragotha in 558, Gregory of Tours, HF, 4:9, 4:20. Radegund was perhaps voluntarily emulating the forced imprisonment of Charibert's widow in the convent at Arles from which she had probably already received the rule from Caesaria II, who died in 558 or 559.

67. A *sestarius* is approximately a pint. In 1971, archeological exploration in Poitiers, guided by a map of 1787, uncovered Radegund's cell. Her isolation may mark her continuing peculiar status as a deaconess rather than a nun within the community. In any case, she could close herself away in this manner because, as she wrote "to the Bishops," she had appointed Agnes, "whom I have loved and brought up from childhood like a daughter," as abbess. Gregory of Tours, HF, 9:42. The date of this letter is unknown, but conceivably it was sent to the Council of Tours in 565. Germanus of Paris, who consecrated Agnes, was there. Chamard, *Histoire ecclésiastique du Poitou*, 2:401, also thought that

suffered so much from thirst that she could barely chant the psalms through her desiccated throat. She kept her vigils in a shift of hair cloth instead of linen incessantly chanting the offices. A bed of ashes served her for a couch which she covered with a hair cloth. In this manner, rest itself wearied her but even this was not enough to endure.

23. While all the *monachas* were deep in sleep, she would collect their shoes, restoring them cleaned and oiled to each. On other Quadragesimas, she was more relaxed, eating on Thursday and again on Sundays.[68] The rest of the time when health permitted, except for Easter and other high holy days, she led an austere life in sackcloth and ashes, rising early to be singing psalms when the others awoke. For no monasterial offices pleased her unless she observed them first. She punished herself if anyone else did a good deed before she did. When it was her turn to sweep the pavements around the monastery, she even scoured the nooks and crannies, bundling away whatever nasty things were there, never too disgusted to carry off what others shuddered to look upon. She did not shrink from cleaning the privies but cleaned and carried off the stinking dung. For she believed that she would be diminished if these vile services did not ennoble her. She carried firewood in her arms. She blew on the hearth and stirred the fire with tongs and did not flinch if she hurt herself. She would care for the infirm beyond her assigned week, cooking their food, washing their faces, and bringing them warm water, going the rounds of those she was caring for and returning fasting to her cell.

24. How can anyone describe her excited fervor as she ran into the kitchen, doing her week of chores?[69] None of the *monachas* but she would carry as much wood as was needed in a bundle from the back gate.[70] She drew water from the well and poured it into basins. She scrubbed vegetables and legumes and revived the hearth by blowing so that she might cook the food. While it was busy boiling, she took the vessels from the hearth, washing and laying out the dishes. When the meal was finished, she rinsed the small

---

the letter of the bishops to Radegund might have come from this council. See Gregory of Tours, *HF*, 9:39. Aigrain, *Sainte Radegonde*, 117, and more recently Labande-Mailfert in "Les débuts," disagree with this hypothesis, believing that Radegund personally went to Arles in 570 and did not adopt the Caesarian rule before that time.

68. See *Vita Genovefa*, 13, for a possible precedent.

69. The Rule of Caesarius of Arles, which Radegund adapted for her community, required that every nun except the abbess be required to spend a week in turn doing kitchen work. The passages just preceding in this text suggest that she introduced the same requirement for the infirmary.

70. Presumably left there by the monks attached to a small service community nearby, noted by Aigrain, *Sainte Radegonde*, 60–61, who thinks this may be the first of the great double monasteries of Gaul.

vessels and scrubbed the kitchen till it shone, free of every speck of dirt. Then she carried out all the sweepings and the nastiest rubbish. Further she never flagged in supporting the sick and even before she took up the Rule of Arles did her weekly tour of service preparing plenty of warm water for them all. Humbly washing and kissing their feet, the holy one prostrated herself and begged them all to forgive her for any negligence she might have committed.

25. But I shudder to speak of the pain she inflicted on herself over and above all these labors. Once, throughout Quadragesima, she bound her neck and arms with three broad iron circlets. Inserting three chains in them, she fettered her whole body so tightly that her delicate flesh, swelling up, enclosed the hard iron. After the fast was ended, when she wished to remove the chains locked under her skin, she could not for the flesh was cut by the circlet through her back and breast over the iron of the chains, so that the flow of blood nearly drained her little body to the last drop.[71]

26. On another occasion, she ordered a brass plate made, shaped in the sign of Christ. She heated it up in her cell and pressed it upon her body most deeply in two spots so that her flesh was roasted through. Thus, with her spirit flaming, she caused her very limbs to burn. One Quadragesima, she devised a still more terrible agony to torture herself in addition to the severe hunger and burning thirst of her fast. She forced her tender limbs, already suppurating and scraped raw by the hard bristles of a hair cloth, to carry a water basin full of burning coals. Then, isolated from the rest, though her limbs were quivering, her soul was steeled for the pain. She drew it to herself, so that she might be a martyr though it was not an age of persecution. To cool her fervent soul, she thought to burn her body. She imposed the glowing brass and her burning limbs hissed. Her skin was consumed and a deep furrow remained where the brand had touched her. Silently, she concealed the holes, but the putrefying blood betrayed the pain that her voice did not reveal. Thus did a woman willingly suffer such bitterness for the sweetness of Christ! And in time, miracles told the story that she herself would have kept hidden.

71. These and other extreme tortures appear to be unique to Radegund. No other saint in this collection imposed so much exotic self-inflicted pain. In fact, Gregory of Tours makes no reference to such mortifications in connection with Radegund. Fortunatus may have been overanxious to promote her claims to a place among the martyrs. Baudonivia refers only briefly to "greater tortures" than a hair shirt in connection with her frantic reaction to Clothar's attempt to remove her from the convent, c. 4. However, there may also be some penitential activity here if Radegund's final bargain with Clothar involved an exchange between his support for the community and her support for his absolution in heaven, particularly pressing in view of his brutal slaughter of his son Chramn and his family in 560. The spread of formal rules for monks and nuns in the seventh century would in any case put an official limit to similar exercises in endurance.

27. For example, a noble matron of Gislad named Bella, who had suffered from blindness for a long time, had herself led from Francia to Poitiers into the saint's presence.[72] Though won over with difficulty, she had her brought in during the silence of a foul night. Prostrate at the saint's knees, the woman could barely ask her to deign to sign her eyes. As soon as she impressed the sign of the cross on them in the name of Christ, the blindness fled; the light returned. Daylight shone on the orbs so long darkened beneath the shades of night. Thus she who had been led there, went home without a guide.

28. Similarly, a girl named Fraifled, whom the Enemy vexed, was violently contorted and most wretched. Without delay, she was found worthy of a cure at the saint's hands at Saix. Nor should we omit to mention the following miracle, revealed through the blessed woman at this time. The next day a woman named Leubela, who was gravely vexed in the back by the Adversary, was publicly restored to health when the saint prayed for her and Christ worked a new miracle of healing. For a rustling sound came from under the skin of her shoulder blades and a worm emerged. Treading it underfoot, she went home liberated.

29. What she did secretly was to become known to all people. A certain *monacha* shivered with cold by day and burned with fire by night through an entire year. And when she had lain lifeless for six months, unable to move a step, one of her sisters told the saint of this infirmity. Finding her almost lifeless, she bade them prepare warm water and had the sick woman brought to her cell and laid in the warm water. Then she ordered everyone to leave, remaining alone with the sick woman for two hours as a doctor. She nursed the sick limbs, tracing the form of her body from head to foot. Wherever her hands touched, the sickness fled from the patient and she who had been laid in the bath by two persons got out of it in full health. The woman who had been revolted by the smell of wine, now accepted it, drank and was refreshed. What more? The next day, when she was expected to migrate from this world, she went out in public, cured.

30. Let us increase her praise by recounting another miracle that has rightly not been forgotten. A certain woman labored so heavily under an invasion of the Enemy that the struggling foe could scarcely be brought to the saint. She commanded the Adversary to lie prostrate on the pavement and show her some respect. The moment the blessed woman spoke, he threw himself down for she frightened him who was feared. When the saint, full of faith, trod on the nape of her neck, he left her in a flux that poured from her belly. Also from small things great glory may accrue to the Creator. Once, a ball of thread which the saint had spun was hanging from the vault, when a shrew

72. Ewig, *Spätantikes und fränkisches Gallien*, 158, places much emphasis on this early appearance of the designation *Francia*.

mouse came to nibble it. But, before he could break the thread, he hung there dead in the very act of biting.[73]

31. Let our book include another event worthy to be called a miracle. One of the saint's men named Florius was at sea fishing when a whirlwind appeared and a mass of billows surged. The sailor had not even begun to bail when a wave came over the side, the ship filled and went under. In his extremity, he cried out, "Holy Radegund, while we obey you, keep us from shipwreck and prevail upon God to save us from the sea." When he said this, the clouds fled away, serenity returned, the waves fell and the prow arose.

32. Goda, a secular girl who later served God as a *monacha*, lay on her bed for a long time. The more she was plied with medicine, the more she languished. A candle was made to the measure of her own height, in the name of the holy woman, and the lord took pity on her. At the hour when she expected the chills, she kindled the light and held it and as a result, the cold fled before the candle was consumed.

33. The more we omit for brevity's sake, the greater grows our guilt. Therefore, as we dispose quickly of the remainder, our relief is slowed. A carpenter's wife had been tormented by diabolic possession for many days. Jokingly, the venerable abbess said of her to the holy woman: "Believe me, Mother, I will excommunicate you if the woman is not purged of the Enemy and restored in three days."[74] She said this publicly but she made the holy woman secretly sorry that she had been so slow to heal the afflicted. To be brief, at the saint's prayer on the next day, the Adversary went roaring out of her ear and abandoned the little vessel he had violently seized. Unhurt, the woman returned to the hospice with her husband. Nor should we neglect a similar deed. The most blessed one asked that a flourishing laurel tree be uprooted and transferred to her cell so she could enjoy it there. But when this was done all the leaves withered because the transplanted tree did not take root. The abbess jokingly remarked that she had better pray for the tree to take root in the ground, or she herself would be separated from her food. She did not speak in vain for, through the saint's intercession, the laurel with the withered root grew green again in leaf and branch.[75]

34. When one of the *monachas* closest to her suffered because her eye was flooded with a bloody humor, she laid hold of some wormwood which the

---

73. She had probably hung her distaff from a hook or niche in the wall beam.

74. Meaning to exclude her from the community meals, a common monastic punishment. Both stories here illustrate that the tartly jesting relationship with Agnes, whom Radegund had placed over her community, was not without its storms. Fortunatus, *Carmina*, app. 20, celebrated their reconciliation after one quarrel.

75. Aigrain notes that a laurel tree has customarily been cultivated near the site of Radegund's cell in Poitiers.

saint had about her breast for refreshment. When she placed it on her eye, the pain and blood soon fled and, from the freshness of the herb, the eye was suddenly clear and bright again. And that reminds me of something I almost passed by in silence. Children were born to the blessed one's agent, Andered, but he scarcely saw them before he lost them and the sorrowing mother had to think about burying her child even while birthing it. During the preparations, the tearful parents wrapped the lifeless babe in the saint's hair cloth. As soon as the infant's body touched that most medicinal garment and those noble rags, he came back from the dead to normal life. Blushing away his tomblike pallor, he rose from the mantle.

35. Who can count the wonders that Christ's merciful kindness performs? A *monacha* Animia suffered so with dropsical swelling that she seemed to have reached her end. The appointed sisters awaited the moment when she would exhale her spirit. While she was sleeping, however, it seemed to her that the most venerable blessed Radegund ordered her to descend nude into a bath with no water in it. Then, with her own hand, the blessed one seemed to pour oil on the sick woman's head and cover her with a new garment. After this strange ritual, when she awakened from her sleep, all trace of the disease had disappeared. She had not even sweated it away for the water was consumed from within. As a result of this new miracle, no vestige of disease was left in her belly. She who was thought to be ready for the tomb rose from her bed for the office. Her head still smelled of oil in witness of the miracle but the pernicious disease was no longer in her belly.[76]

36. Let us now tell a tale in which the whole region may rejoice.[77] One evening as twilight cast its shadows, the layfolk were singing noisy songs near the monastery as they danced around accompanied by musicians with cithars. The saint had spent some time exhorting two listeners. Then one *monacha* said, joking: "Lady, I recognize one of my songs being preached by the dancers." To which she responded: "That's fine if it thrills you to hear religion mingled with the odor of the world." Then the sister stated: "Truly, lady, I have heard two or three of my songs which I have bound together in this way." Then the saint said: "God witness that I have heard nothing of any worldly song." Thus it was obvious that though her flesh remained in the world, her spirit was already in Heaven.

37. In praise of Christ, let us proclaim a miracle from our own time

---

76. This story and the previous one are peculiar in that the saint herself seems to be entirely absent. They are the sorts of miracles generally associated with postmortem events. The context seems to indicate that Radegund was still alive, but Baudonivia, 15, says that her hairshirt, laid in a chapel where she was buried, cured the bishop. See also Baudonivia, 23.

77. Krusch, ed., MGH, SRM 2:375, n. b., c. 36, indicates that one manuscript offers *religio* as an alternative for *regio*, which might make more sense here.

patterned after an ancient model in the tradition of the blessed Martin.[78] When the most blessed female was secluded in her cell, she heard a *monacha* crying. At the signal, she entered and asked what was the matter. She answered that her infant sister was dead, and though still warm she was laid out and ready to be washed in cold water. Condoling with her, the saint bade her bring the corpse to her in her cell. There she took it into her own hands, closing the door behind her and ordering the other to withdraw to a distance lest she sense what she was doing. But what she did secretly could not be concealed for long. By time the services for the dead were prepared, she had handled the corpse of the dead little girl for seven hours. But seeing a faith He could not deny, Christ utterly restored her health. When the saint rose from prayer, the infant rose from the dead. The old woman got up when the infant revived. When the signal was repeated, she joyfully restored alive the one who was dead when she had tearfully received her.

38. And this noble deed should be commemorated. On the day the holy woman migrated from earth, a tribune of the fisc named Domnolenus who was wasting away with a suffocating disease dreamed that he seemed to see the saint approach his town in state. He ran out and saluted her and asked what the blessed one wished. Then she said that she had come to see him. And since it was the wish of the people to establish an oratory for blessed Martin, the most blessed one seized the tribune's hand, saying: "There are venerable relics of the Confessor here with which you could build a shrine which he would consider most fitting." Behold the mystery of God! The foundation and the pavement where a basilica had been built were revealed. Then, in addition, in his slumber she drew her hand over his jaws and stroked his throat for a long time, saying: "I came that God might confer better health on you." And he dreamed she asked: "On my life, because of me, release those whom you have in prison." Waking, the tribune recounted what he had seen to his wife, saying: "Indeed, I believe that at this hour the saint has gone from this earth." He sent to the city to confirm the truth of this. He directed the prison that the seven prisoners held there should be admonished and released. The messenger, returning, reported that she had migrated from the world in that very hour. And the saint's oracle was proved by a triple mystery: the relief of the prisoners, the restoration of the tribune's health, and the temple building.

39. But let this small sample of the blessed one's miracles suffice, lest their very abundance arouse contempt. And even this should in no way be reck-

---

78. Sulpicius Severus, *Life of Martin*, in *Western Fathers*, ed. and trans. Hoare, 7, described the first miracle of the saint as the restoration to life of a catechumen by stretching himself over the body in prayer for two hours, locked in his cell.

oned a small amount, since from these few tales we may recognize in the miracles the greatness with which she lived in such piety and self-denial, affection and affability, humility and honor, faith and fervor, with the result that after her death wonders also ensued upon her glorious passing.

Book II.

■

To the holy ladies adorned with the grace of virtuous living, Abbess Dedimia and all Holy Radegund's congregation, from Baudonivia, humblest of all.[79]

I can as easily touch heaven with my fingers as perform the task you have imposed upon me—namely to write something about the life of the holy Lady Radegund, whom you knew best. This task should be assigned to those who have fountains of eloquence within them. For whatever such people are commissioned to write is laid out generously in flowing song. On the contrary, people who are narrow of understanding and lack the full fluency of eloquence to relieve their own sterility and aridity—let alone refresh others—not only have no wish to speak out on their own but become terrified when they are commanded to do so.[80] For in myself, I know that I am weakminded and have but few intelligent things to say. For good as it is for the learned to speak, it is best for the unlearned to keep silence. For the former know how to produce something great from very little while the latter cannot even make a little from a great deal. Therefore what the learned seek eagerly terrifies the unlearned. I am the smallest of the small ones she nourished familiarly from the cradle as her own child at her feet! So that I may, in obedience to your most gracious wishes, compose, not the full story but a partial account in writing of her famous works, and so that I may offer a public celebration of her glorious life to the ears of her flock, in devout though unworthy language, I pray that you will aid me with your prayers for I am more devoted than learned. In this book, we will not repeat what the apostolic Bishop Fortunatus recorded of her blessed life but speak of what he omitted in his fear of prolixity, as he explained in his book when he said: "But let this small sample of the blessed one's miracles suffice, lest their very abundance arouse contempt. And even this should in no way be reckoned a small amount, since from these few tales we may recognize in the miracles the greatness with which she lived." Therefore, inspired by the Divine Power whom Radegund strove to please in this world and with Whom she reigns in

---

79. Krusch, ed., *MGH, SRM* 2:358–95.
80. We find that this phrase is unintelligible without the second negative Krusch found inserted in variant manuscripts.

the next, we will attempt to relate, in rustic rather than refined language, what she did here and to publish a few of her many miracles.

Here begin her virtues.[81]

1. With respect to the life of the blessed Radegund, her royal origins and dignities remain unknown to none since they are contained in the first book. Everyone knows how she conducted herself while living with her earthly prince and husband, the glorious King Clothar. She was a noble sprout sprung from royal stock; the nobility she inherited, she adorned the more by her faith. Though united with an earthly prince, the noble queen proved herself more celestial than earthly. For a brief while, in that union, she played the part of a wife only to serve Christ more devoutly acting as a model laywoman whom she herself might wish to imitate. For religion, anticipating the achievement of her soul's future condition, was adapted as an example of the monastic life while she was still in a secular habit. No worldly bonds fettered her but she was girdled about with obedience to God's servants, energetic in redeeming captives and profusely generous with alms to the needy. For she believed that anything that the poor received from her was their own in reality.

2. When she was still with the king wearing worldly garb, her mind was intent on Christ.[82] God be my witness, to whom the heart confesses though the lips be silent and from whom the conscience can hide nothing, even when the tongue is still: I swear that I am relating what I have heard and attesting to what I have seen. At the invitation of the matron Ansifrida, she was on her way to a noble banquet, attended by all her worldly retinue. About a mile from the blessed queen's route, there was a fane where the Franks worshipped. Hearing that, she ordered her servants to burn the fane revered by the Franks with fire for she judged that it was iniquitous to show contempt for God in Heaven and venerate the Devil's instruments. Hearing of it, a crowd of Franks tried to defend the place with swords and clubs shouting and all stirred up by the Devil. But the holy queen, who bore Christ in her heart, persevered unmoved, and did not allow her horse to go forward until the fane was consumed by fire and the opposing sides had made peace thanks to her entreaties. For when it was done, they blessed the Lord, admiring the virtue and constancy of the queen.

3. After that, moved by divine power, she parted from the earthly king, which her vows required and lived at Saix, in the villa which the king had

---

81. We have deleted the lengthy table of contents supplied by Baudonivia.

82. Krusch, ed., MGH, SRM 2:380, suggests that *mens intenta* is a pun translating the Germanic name "Radegund" into Latin.

given her. There, during the first year of her conversion, in a vision, she saw a man-shaped ship, with people sitting on every limb and she was sitting on the knee. He said to her: "Now, you are sitting on my knee, but in time you will find a place in my bosom." Thus was she shown the grace she would some-day enjoy. She related this vision privately to her followers, with earnest supplication that no one should know of it as long as she was alive. Such caution in conversation! Such devotion in every deed! She was always un-changed in prosperity and adversity, in joy and sorrow, neither broken in adversity nor rejoicing in prosperity.

4. While she was still in that villa, a rumor arose that the king wanted her back again, that he was grieving over the grave loss he had suffered in letting so great and good a queen leave his side and that within himself he had no wish to live unless he could get her back again. Hearing this, the blessed one shook with terror and surrendered herself to the harsher torment of the roughest of hair shirts which she fitted to her tender body. In addition, she imposed torments of fasting upon herself, and spent her nights in vigils pouring out prayers. For she scorned to rule her fatherland and she rejected the sweetness of marriage; excluding worldly love, she chose exile lest she wander from Christ. She still had with her from her queenly regalia, a "felte" cast in gold and studded with gems and pearls which was worth a thousand gold solidi. She had Fridovigia, a *nonnanem*[83] who was her closest companion, take it to a venerable man, Dom John, a recluse in the castrum of Chinon.[84] She asked him to pray lest she be turned back again to the world and to send her a hair cloth to scour her body. And he sent her a hair cloth wrap with which she made herself inner and outer garments.[85] She also asked this same man to inform her if he could discover anything through the Holy Spirit regarding the matter she feared so much. For she said that if the king truly did want to take her back, she was determined to end her life before she, who had been joined in the embrace of the heavenly King, would be united again to an earthly king. On the next day, after a night of vigil and prayer, inspired by divine power, the man of God informed her that this was indeed the king's wish but that, before he could take her again as his wife, he would be punished by God's judgment.[86]

5. Receiving this decision, Lady Radegund, mind intent on Christ and with

83. This unique use of the word nun appears in no other text we have translated.
84. Gregory of Tours, *Glory of the Confessors*, 23.
85. A similar practice is mentioned *Vita S. Germani*, 44.
86. Aigrain, *Sainte Radegonde*, 53, recounts the popular story of Radegund and the oat field that grew up to hide her as she fled from Saix before her searching husband. It was recorded in local folklore in the later middle ages, when a feast that had earlier been dedicated to the translation of her relics was renamed Saint Radegund of the Oat Field.

God's help and inspiration, and by arrangement with the excellent King Clothar, built a monastery for herself at Poitiers.[87] The construction was speedily completed with God's help by the apostolic Bishop Pientius and Duke Austrapius. Then, rejecting the false blandishments of the world, the queen joyfully entered into the monastery.[88] There, she would seek to gather ornaments of perfection, a great congregation of maidens for the deathless bridegroom, Christ. And in all things, she subordinated herself to the legally constituted abbess, reserving no authority of her own in order to follow the footsteps of Christ more swiftly and heap up more for herself in Heaven the more she freed herself from the world.[89] And soon her holy ways began to flower in humble demeanor, abundant charity, luminous chastity and heavy fasts. With all her love, she gave herself up to her celestial spouse embracing God with a pure heart. And she felt that Christ had come to dwell within her.

6. But, envious of the good, the Enemy of humankind whose will she hated to obey while she was in the world never ceased to persecute her. For now, through intermediaries, she learned what she feared most. The illustrious king, as though moved by devotion, had come to Tours with his son, the most excellent Sigebert whence he might more easily reach Poitiers and possess his queen.[90]

7. When she learned of this, the blessed Radegund, invoking God as her witness, wrote letters containing solemn imprecations to the apostolic lord Germanus, Bishop of the city of Paris, who was then with the king.[91] Most

87. The sequence of events is unclear, but 555 is the latest date for her leaving Clothar and the date of his frustrated effort to marry Theudebert's widow. Soon thereafter he may have made his approach to Radegund and frightened her into flight, but no further than Poitiers, which was still in his domain. Apparently they came to terms and the building of the monastery could then proceed between 555 and 560, when Radegund most probably wrote and procured the Caesarian Rule from Caesaria (d. 558).

88. Pientius and Austrapius appear in Gregory of Tours, HF, 4:18, as staunch supporters of Clothar against his son Chramn, who made war against his father in alliance with Childebert, Clothar's brother. Austrapius later became a bishop, Clothar's candidate to succeed Pientius. See c. 16 and Gregory's account of her death, ibid., 9:40.

89. Radegund placed Agnes over her community as a gesture of humility and possibly a recognition of the superiority of her virgin state. Fortunatus addressed his poem on virginity to her. See Gregory of Tours, HF, 9:42, for a transcription of Radegund's letter chartering her monastery.

90. The chronology of these events is obscure. It is, however, possible that this visit is the same as Clothar's pilgrimage to Martin's tomb at Tours. Gregory of Tours, HF, 4:21, relates that in 560, the year before his death, Clothar repented of all his evil deeds and prayed Martin to gain reconciliation for him with God.

91. Germanus (d. 576) is known to have consecrated Agnes as abbess, and this would perhaps be an appropriate point for that to have happened. The date of Pientius's death is unknown, but Gallia Christiana 2:1145, places it about the same time as Clothar's death. Germanus's intervention, therefore, might be because of an episcopal vacancy.

secretly, she sent these by her agent Proculus with gifts and eulogies. And when the God-filled man read what was confided to him in her letter, he prostrated himself weeping at the king's feet before the tomb of Saint Martin and solemnly entreated him in God's name not to go to the city of Poitiers.[92] Understanding that the petition came from his blessed queen, the king was full of sorrow. Led to repentance, he repudiated his evil counsellors. Judging himself unworthy to have such a queen any longer, he prostrated himself before Saint Martin's threshold at the feet of the apostolic Germanus praying him to ask blessed Radegund's forgiveness for obeying his evil counsellors and sinning against her. As a result, the same divine punishment soon struck those who acted against the blessed queen as struck Arius, who, for opposing the Catholic faith, lost all his bowels in a flux from his belly.[93] Then the king feared the judgment of God, whose will the queen had followed above that of the king while she lived with him, and he asked the holy man to go to her quickly. Accordingly, Lord Germanus, the apostolic man, went to Poitiers and entered the monastery. There in the oratory dedicated in the name of the blessed Mary, he prostrated himself at the holy queen's feet and asked pardon for the king. Indeed, she gave it generously, rejoicing that she had been snatched from the jaws of the temporal world. Then she prepared herself for God's service, hurrying to follow Christ wherever He might lead, speeding with devoted soul to Him she had always loved. Thus intent, she guarded her body through the night with an additional round of vigils as though she were its jailor. For while she was merciful to others, she judged herself. Pious to others but imposing hard abstinence on herself; generous to all but stingy with herself. Even the most exhausting fast would not suffice until she had triumphed over her body.

8. As the first book related, she occupied herself wholly in these efforts until she was totally and unreservedly at God's service.[94] And thus she ever more strongly armed herself, with ceaseless prayers and vigils, and devotion to reading. She administered food to pilgrims from her own table and

---

92. Germanus, bishop of Paris, 555–576. His life was recorded by Fortunatus, *Vita S. Germani*, in Krusch, ed., MGH, SRM 7:337–428. He sent a girl he miraculously resuscitated to be a nun at Radegund's foundation. Ibid., c. 34. In 567, he excommunicated King Charibert for following his father's example in marrying two sisters.

93. Athanasius, *De morte Arii*, 3:3 (PG 25:688). Gregory of Tours, HF, 2:23, also recalled the fate of Arius in a tale of a plot against St. Sidonius in which an evil priest died while defecating. Bernard S. Bachrach, personal communication, suggests that Clothar may have had some political motive for seeking to recover Radegund. If so, this reference may be a clue. The Franks remained the only Catholic barbarians in a world of Arians, and, as noted in the life of Clothild, Clothar's own sister had suffered much at their hands.

94. The section that follows seems to be a sort of gloss on parts of Caesarius's rule that were not emphasized by Fortunatus, showing particularly how Radegund respected chapters 7, 18, 22, 33.

washed and cleansed the feet of the sick with her own hands. She would not allow her maid to minister to her because she was anxiously bustling about being a servant herself. As far as her bodily weakness allowed, she kept herself to such a strict regime of abstinence that she had no craving for earthly food, her mind was so intent on God. And after she had donned the religious habit, she made up a small bed for herself which was painfully uncomfortable, never again lying in soft feathers. Nor did she cover herself with splendid linens but sackcloth and ashes were all her garments. The preceding book described many of the rigors of her abstinence and servitude. She made herself such a pauper for God that she became an example for others. She had no covering for her arms but two fingerless gloves which she made from her boots. But her behavior as a pauper was so discreet that even the abbess suspected nothing. Who can describe her patience, charity, fervor of spirit, prudence, beneficence, holy zeal, and incessant "meditating on the law of God by day and by night."[95] For when she seemed to cease meditating or preaching on the psalms, the lectrix, one of the monachas, did not desist from reading them to her. The praise of God was so ever-present to her heart and tongue that once when she saw Eodegund the portress crossing the yard and wished to call her, she shouted "Alleluia," instead of her name. She did that a thousand times but she never uttered any slander or lies, or curses against anyone. And not only did she speak no slander herself, she would not patiently listen to slander either. For she always prayed for her persecutors and taught others to do the same. She so loved her flock, which, in her deep desire for God, she had gathered in the Lord's name, that she no longer remembered that she had a family and a royal husband. So she would often say when she preached to us: "Daughters, I chose you. You are my light and my life. You are my rest and all my happiness, my new plantation. Work with me in this world that we may rejoice together in the world to come. With complete faith and hearts full of love, let us serve the Lord. Let us seek Him in awe and simplicity of heart so that we may say with confidence to Him: 'Give, Lord, what you have promised, for we have done what you commanded.'"

9. She never imposed a task on anyone that she had not done first herself. Whenever a servant of God visited, she would question him closely about his manner of serving the Lord. If she learned anything new from him which she was not used to doing, she would immediately impose it first upon herself and then she would teach her congregation with words what she had already shown them by her example. When the antiphonal singing of the psalter in her presence had come to its appointed end, her reading would continue and by day or by night it never stopped, not even while she gave her body its

95. Vita Caesarii 1, ASOSB 1:666.

meager refreshment. When the lesson had been read, she would say, with careful attention to our souls: "If you do not understand what is read, why don't you search for it diligently in the mirror of your souls?" There may have been a little irreverence in presuming to ask this question, but from pious concern and maternal love, she never ceased to preach on what the readings offered for the salvation of the soul. Just as the bee chooses various flowers from which to make its honey, so was she careful to pluck little spiritual flowers from the clerics she had to visit her.[96] So from them she could bring forth the fruit of good works in herself and those who followed her. Even at night or whenever she seemed to snatch an hour's sleep, she had the lesson read to her. Sometimes the reader began to feel drowsy and, thinking that Radegund was resting for a while, she might stop. But she whose mind was intent on Christ, as if to say, "I sleep but my heart waketh,"[97] would ask, "Why are you silent? Read on, don't stop." And even though she had completed the whole cycle of services earlier, and still had not had any sound sleep, when it was time to get up in the middle of the night she was ready at once. She would rise up rejoicing from her covers for the Lord's service, so that she might have said in all honesty: "At midnight I will rise up and give thanks unto thee, O Lord."[98] And often she seemed to be sleeping and yet chanting psalms in her slumber so that she might have said rightly and truly: "The meditation of my heart is always in thy sight."[99] Oh, who could ever imitate the ardent charity with which she loved all mankind? So many virtues shone forth in her: modesty with propriety, wisdom with simplicity, severity with mildness, teaching with humility! In sum, an immaculate life, a blameless life, a life wholly worthy of her.

10. So far did she alienate herself from everything that belonged to her that even if she wanted to give some undiluted wine to one of the sisters, she would not presume to touch anything from her own cellar. Knowing that, the venerable abbess gave her an eight-measure vessel which she committed into the charge of blessed Felicity, the cellaress, who from one vintage or another dispatched it every day wherever the saint ordered.[100] Yet it never diminished but always remained at the same level. Where did it come from, that new wine that filled her cellar? The barrel seemed to be filling itself! Great jars and barrels ran dry before this little cask, which met all the blessed woman's

96. Galatians 6:1.
97. Song of Songs 5:2.
98. Psalms 119:62.
99. Psalms 19:14.
100. Following the Rule of Caesarius, 28 for the role of the cellaress. The sentence is opaque. The mention of vintages seems almost to suggest an oenophile's miracle if the vessel was always filling itself as the subsequent passage implies.

demands. The Lord fed five thousand people with five loaves and two fishes. So whenever she saw people in want, His handmaid refreshed them all year round from this little supply.

She was always solicitous for peace and worked diligently for the welfare of the fatherland. Whenever the different kingdoms made war on one another, she prayed for the lives of all the kings, for she loved them all. And she taught us also to pray incessantly for their stability. Whenever she heard of bitterness arising among them, trembling, she sent such letters to one and then to the other pleading that they should not make war among themselves nor take up arms lest the land perish.[101] And, likewise, she sent to their noble followers to give the high kings salutary counsel so that their power might work to the welfare of the people and the land. She imposed assiduous vigils on her flock tearfully teaching them to pray incessantly for the kings. And who can tell what agonies she inflicted on herself? So, through her intercession, there was peace among the kings. Mitigation of war brought health to the land. Aware of her mediation, everyone rejoiced, blessing the name of the Lord![102] Despite having secured the triumph of the kings' peace from the King of Heaven, she devoted herself all the more eagerly to God and gave herself up to the service of all men, not caring what kind of slavish task that might involve. For she was eager to fill the needs of everyone. She washed the feet of all with her own hands, cleansing them with her veil and kissing them. If it had been permitted, like Mary, she would have wiped them clean with her own loosened hair. In return for this multitude of great good deeds which Divine Grace empowered her to perform, the Lord, Bountiful Giver of Virtue, rendered her famous for her miracles throughout all Francia. There, where once she had been seen to reign, He prepared a kingdom for her more celestial than terrestrial. To this day, in the oratory she built where she might invoke the Lord of Heaven whenever she could sneak away from the king, God manifests His miracles when people invoke her name, who prayed there so devoutly.

11. After Radegund had enclosed herself in the monastery, a matron named Mammezo got a cinder in her eye while she was travelling. She clamored night and day with one voice and one sorrow, for the Lord to reveal His faithful servant to her. And although she was not there in the flesh, that kindly one was present when her name was invoked. The Lord inspired the matron

101. For some account of Radegund's relations with Sigebert, Chilperic, and their wives, see the introduction to this chapter.

102. In fact, this was wishful thinking. The treaty was soon broken, and the struggle continued for decades after Radegund's death. But Aigrain, Sainte Radegonde, 73, notes that the French government recognized her efforts by making her feast a national holiday in 1921, fulfilling a vow taken in 1917.

to hasten to the oratory and to have faith that application to Radegund would save her. Leaning on the arms of her servant boys, and suffering the most intense pain, the sorrowing woman scarcely reached the oratory when she threw herself on the pavement and began to clamor: "Lady Radegund! I believe that you who follow God's will above man's are full of God's virtue! Good lady, full of piety, have mercy on me. Help an unhappy woman, pray that my eye will be restored for my spirit is grievously stricken by this tormenting pain." And she, who took everyone's sorrow upon herself alone, as long as she lived, responded kindly to the invocation of her name. Through her intercession, the Lord took pity, the pain fled and health returned. The eye was healed, which she thought she had lost while she could feel nothing but pain. Though she had not seen daylight and had eaten nothing for many days, she returned home on her own two feet with no one supporting her and even to this day she gives thanks to the Lord.

12. Let me add this miracle in praise of Christ, who makes his servants strike terror into others. Vinoberga was a housemaid who once, after the blessed queen had passed away, rashly dared to presume to seat herself in her high seat. For that deed, God's judgment struck her and she caught fire so that all could see smoke rising on high from her. Then she cried out in front of everyone confessing that she had sinned and was burning because she had occupied the blessed woman's chair. After enduring this burning for three days and three nights, she shouted out and cried: "Lady Radegund, I have sinned! I have done wrong! Forgive me, cool my limbs, for they are consumed by this cruel torture. You who are bountiful with your mercy and glorious in your good works, you who are merciful to all, have mercy on me." And seeing her in so much pain, everyone prayed for her as though Radegund were present (for wherever she is invoked in faith, there she is): "Good lady, spare her, lest her frightful agony should cause the wretched woman's death." And then, benignly, the most blessed woman answered her prayers. She quenched the blazing fire and the girl returned home unhurt. Such a punishment made everyone cautious and more devout.[103]

13. While she was still at the villa of Saix, her faithful and devoted mind intent on Christ, she determined, with great devotion, to collect relics of all the saints. At her request, a venerable priest named Magnus brought her relics of Lord Andrew and many others which she placed above the altar. When, at night, she lay prostrate in prayer keeping vigil according to the Formula,[104] a little sleep came over her while the Lord declared her wish granted, saying:

---

103. This story and the events surrounding the revolt of 589 in the nunnery provide depressing evidence that the monastic ideal of social equality was not observed at Poitiers.

104. Krusch, ed., MGH, SRM 1:946.

"Know thou, blessed woman, that not only the relics brought by Magnus the priest are here, but all those you gathered together in the villa of Athies are assembled here."[105] When she opened her eyes she saw that a most resplendent man had told her these things and she rejoiced and blessed the Lord.

14. After she had entered into the monastery, she assembled a great multitude of the saints through her most faithful prayers, as the East bears witness and North, South and West acknowledge. For from all sides, she managed to obtain those precious gems which Paradise has and Heaven hoards and as many came freely to her as gifts as came in response to her pleas. In their company, she gave herself up to chanting hymns and psalms continuously in ceaseless meditation. At last, news came to her that the holy limbs of Lord Mammas the Martyr rested at Jerusalem.[106] She drank the information in greedily and thirstily; as the dropsical only increase their thirst by drawing more water, so she, though refreshed by God's dew, was burning up.[107] She sent the venerable priest, Reoval, who was then a secular and still abides in the flesh with us, to the patriarch of Jerusalem to ask Blessed Mammas for a token.[108] The man of God received him benignly and, seeking the will of God, announced his request to the people. Three days later, after celebrating Mass, he approached the blessed martyr's sepulchre with all his people and, full of faith, proclaimed in a loud voice: "I ask you, Confessor and Martyr of Christ, that if the blessed Radegund is truly a handmaid of the Lord, you will make it known to all the nations by your power; permit that faithful soul to receive the relic she asks from you." At the end of the prayer, everyone responded, "Amen." Continually declaring his faith in the Blessed One, he went to the holy sepulchre and touched the limbs in such a way that the most blessed saint might indicate what he would give in response to the Lady Radegund's request. He touched each finger of the right hand and, when he came to the little finger, it came away from the hand it belonged to with a gentle pull.[109] Thus the blessed queen's desire was satisfied and her wish granted. With fitting honors, the apostolic man sent the finger to the blessed

105. LHF 1, 2, 4.
106. Delehaye, *Les origines du culte des martyrs*, 203–4 notes that Baudonivia may have made an error about the location of Saint Mammas's relics in Jerusalem. Both Theodosius and Nicetas (eleventh century) place his burial in Caesaria, where his feast on August 17 is a major event. For further development of the cult of relics and the idea that the saints themselves were instrumental in deciding their resting places, see Geary, *Furta Sacra*.
107. Horace, *Carmina* 2; 2.13.
108. Gregory of Tours, HF 10:15, names this man as the doctor who conferred with Radegund about the man mentioned earlier with diseased testicles who had to be castrated. One wonders whether the doctor's anatomical expertise had any relationship to the events that follow here.
109. We have preferred the variant *tractu* given in Krusch's notes to *tactu*.

Radegund and from Jerusalem even to Poitiers God's praises resounded in her honor. Can you imagine the ardent spirit, the faithful devotion with which she threw herself into abstinence while awaiting the prize, the mighty relic? And then on receiving the heavenly gift, her joy was ecstatic. She devoted herself and all her flock to psalmody, with vigils and fasts for an entire week, blessing the Lord that she had deserved to receive such a reward. For God does not deny the faithful what they ask of Him. Frequently she would say sweetly, in a sort of veiled figure of speech that none could understand: "Anyone who has the care of souls must be sore afraid of universal praise."[110] But no matter how much she wanted to avoid it, the Giver of Virtue labored more and more to display her faith to everyone. Thus, whenever the infirm invoked her, they would be healed of whatever illnesses imprisoned them.

15. The apostolic Bishops Leontius (of Bordeaux) and Eusebius (of Saintes) summoned the illustrious Leo to synodal council.[111] While he was on the road, his vision was seriously obscured, clouded by a bloody mist. Without his servants' support, he could hardly see to make his way. He reached the monastery of the blessed one, where, out of devotion to her, he had dedicated his daughters as the Lord's servants, and entered the oratory dedicated in the name of Lady Mary. After a prayer, he prostrated himself, full of faith, on the saint's haircloth, invoking her manfully. For a long time he lay on it, until the pain ceased, the mist dissolved, the blood coagulated, carried away with the help of the vein. He who had come supported by helping hands left with clear eyes, his health restored. From the blessed woman's hair shirt he gained light. Happy and uninjured, he walked to the synod where he had been heading. After that, the whole synod heard his account and he told it to us himself on the way back. Through devotion to her, he laid the foundations for a basilica for Saint Radegund and gave a hundred solidi for the construction of the fabric. Who can count how many of the sick were restored to health by invoking her? Who that ever saw her could believe her to be an earthly person? By God in Heaven, I say, truthfully and in good faith, that to every eye her face was always resplendent with the radiance of her soul, so that what appeared outwardly not undeservedly mirrored what occurred inwardly.

16. After having collected many relics of the saints, had it been possible, she would have petitioned the Lord Himself in the seat of His Majesty to dwell

---

110. Baudonivia takes every opportunity to emphasize Radegund's pastoral and semisacerdotal activities, possibly as a reproach to their neglectful bishop.

111. Perhaps the Council of Saintes called after Clothar's death, see Gregory of Tours, HF, 4:26. Perhaps there is a connection with her letter to the bishops, HF 9:42, or their letter to her, HF 9:39.

here in sight of all. But what she could not see with her carnal eyes, she could contemplate with her spiritual mind sedulously intent on prayer. Since the Lord withholds no good thing from them that walk uprightly,[112] and seek Him with all their hearts, minds and souls as did this blessed woman,[113] He showed His divine clemency in kindness to her in whose breast He lived both day and night. Thus, like Saint Helena, imbued with wisdom, full of the fear of God, glorious with good works, she eagerly sought to salute the wood where the ransom of the world was hung for our salvation that we might be snatched from the power of the devil.[114] When she had found it, she clapped both hands. When she recognized that it was truly the Lord's cross that had raised the dead to life with its touch, she knelt on the ground adoring the Lord and said: "In truth, you are Christ, the Son of God, Who came into the world and with your precious blood you have redeemed your own people, whom you created, from captivity."[115]

What Helena did in oriental lands, Radegund the blessed did in Gaul! Since she wished to do nothing without counsel while she lived in the world, she sent letters to the most excellent King Sigebert who held this land in his power asking that, for the welfare of the whole fatherland and the stability of his kingdom, he would permit her to ask the emperor for wood from the Lord's cross.[116] Most graciously, he consented to the blessed queen's petition. She who had made herself a pauper for God, full of devotion and inflamed with desire, sent no gifts to the emperor. Instead she sent her messengers bearing nothing but prayers and the support of the saints whom she invoked incessantly. She got what she had prayed for: that she might glory in having the blessed wood of the Lord's cross enshrined in gold and gems and many of the relics of the saints that had been kept in the east living in that one place. At the saint's petition, the emperor sent legates with gospels ornamented in gold and gems. And the wood where once hung the salvation of the world came with a congregation of saints to the city of Poitiers. The bishop of that place should have wished to welcome it devoutly with all the people but the Enemy of humankind, to subject the blessed Radegund to

---

112. Psalms 84:11.

113. Matthew 22:37.

114. Saint Helena, the mother of Constantine, to whom the discovery of the True Cross was attributed, was much admired as a model of medieval queenship. See McNamara, "Imitatio Helenae." Baudonivia's uses of earlier texts are analyzed in detail by Whatley, "The Earliest Literary Quotations."

115. Baudonivia has borrowed several phrases from the cross legend here, suppressing the role of Judas Cyriacus in favor of Helena.

116. In the partition of Clothar's lands among his sons, Tours and Poitiers had come to Sigebert (d. 575). The emperor was Justin II, and the date of the mission was 568–69.

trials and tribulations, worked through his satellites to make the people reject the world's ransom and refuse to receive it in the city.[117] So one and another played the role of the Jews which is not part of our story.[118] But they would see; the Lord knows His own. Her spirit blazing in a fighting mood, she sent again to the benevolent king to say that they did not wish to receive Salvation itself into the city. Until her messengers could return from the lord king, she entrusted the Lord's cross and the tokens of the saints for shelter in a male monastery which the king had founded at Tours for his own salvation, amidst the chanting of priests.

Thus envy inflicted no less injury on the holy cross than on the Lord Himself, who endured every malicious act patiently when He was summoned time and again by the minions of judges and governors so that the people He created might not perish. She cast herself into agonies of fasts and vigils lamenting and wailing with her whole flock every day until at last the Lord respected his handmaid's humility and moved the heart of the king to do judgment and justice in the midst of the people. Thus the devout king sent word by his trusted man, the famous Count Justin, to the apostolic Bishop, Lord Eufronius of the city of Tours, to deposit the Lord's most glorious cross and the relics of the saints with due honors in the Lady Radegund's monastery. So it was done. The blessed woman exulted in joy with all her cell when Heaven conferred this gift and perfect present on the congregation which she had gathered for God's service, for she had felt in her soul that they might have all too little after her passing. Thus, though she would always be able to help them when she was in glory with the King of Heaven, this best provider, this good shepherdess, would not leave her sheep in disarray. She bequeathed a heavenly gift, the ransom of the world from Christ's relics, which she had searched out from faraway places for the honor of the place and the salvation of the people in her monastery.[119] Thus, with the aid of

---

117. The bishop in question was probably Maroveus, but the date of his accession is unknown. Pientius, who had welcomed Radegund's convent, died sometime before 567. A rivalry between Austrapius and Pascentius for the bishopric of Poitiers developed in which Charibert supported Pascentius. The date and further mention of Pascentius are left obscure by Gregory of Tours, HF, 4:18, who says only that Maroveus, who later became bishop, was unremittingly hostile to Radegund throughout her life. Marignan, *Etudes*, 11, sees this conflict as evidence of the tensions between ascetics and bishops for the spiritual ascendancy in the Gallic church.

118. This is most likely another attempt to parallel Radegund with Helena, whose efforts to find and glorify the true cross were resisted by the Jews of Jerusalem.

119. Thereafter the monastery was named Holy Cross. Gregory of Tours, *Glory of the Martyrs*, 4, says he witnessed a constantly multiplying supply of healing oil from the lamp that lit the relic's sanctuary. The relic itself was rescued by the abbess when the convent was dispersed at the French Revolution and is still offered for veneration by the nuns of Holy Cross in their new location just outside the city.

God's might and heaven's power, the blind receive light for their eyes, the ears of the deaf open, the tongues of the mute resume their office, the lame walk and demons are put to flight in that place. What more? Anyone who comes in faith, whatever the infirmity that binds them, goes away healed by the virtue of the Holy Cross. Who could attempt to tell the greatness and richness of the gift the blessed woman conferred on this city? For this, all who live by faith do bless her name. And she solemnly called God to witness when she commended her monastery to the most excellent lord king and his most serene lady Queen Brunhild all of whom she loved with dear affection and to the sacrosanct churches and their bishops.[120]

17. After receiving this celestial gift, the blessed woman sent the aforementioned priest and other messengers to the emperor with a simple garment as a gift of thanks. On their return, the sea became rough and they suffered many dangers from storms and tempests beyond anything they said they had ever seen before. In the middle of the sea, for forty days and nights, the ship was exposed to these perils. Then despairing of life, with death before their eyes, they made peace among themselves as the sea prepared to swallow them alive. And seeing their great danger, they raised their voices to heaven, crying aloud: "Lady Radegund, help your servants lest we perish by drowning while in your service! Free us from peril of death for now the sea is ready to swallow us alive. You have ever been merciful to those who called on you in good faith. Pity us now. Help your own lest we perish." At these cries, a dove rose from the midst of the sea and circled three times about the ship. As it made its third pass, in the name of the Trinity which the blessed woman ever cherished in her heart, the holy Queen's servant Banissios, reached out, plucked three feathers from its tail and dipped them into the sea. The tempest subsided. When the Blessed Radegund's name was invoked, the dove appeared and returned her servants to life from the jaws of death. Great tranquility descended over the midst of the sea. So they cried out loudly: "You have come, good Lady, full of piety, to rescue your people from captivity lest they drown in the flood." By invoking her name, not only her own folk but all

120. The relic of the cross arrived in 569. Because of the difficulties caused by Maroveus, Gregory of Tours, HF, 9:40, says that Radegund and Agnes were forced to turn to Arles. He does not explain this statement. In *Sainte Radegonde* Aigrain argues that they actually traveled to Arles and there received the Rule of Caesarius, which severely restricted episcopal power. He denies the authenticity of Caesaria's letter, which would date the reception of the Rule back to before 559. Most recently, in "Les débuts," Labande-Mailfert defends the idea of the trip while accepting the authenticity of the letter. However, the trip is wholly inconsistent with Radegund's strong respect for her cloister and with her policy of staying within the protected boundaries of Clothar's kingdom (still ably administered by Sigebert at this time). Considering the rampant violence of the age and the attraction of capturing a rich widowed queen, it seems highly unlikely that the two women ever ventured abroad in this manner.

people are set free through the virtues of the Lady Radegund. And those whom she had rescued from death, brought the feathers here suitably framed and devoutly made a gift of them to this holy place.

She listens benignly whenever she is invoked. Anyone suffering from fever or smallpox or cast down by infirmity or prevented from reaching her by great distance, can dispel all illness by lighting a candle in her name. Who could venture to express how much she loved her flock? No, though the plectrum swept the strings of my tongue with a hundred tones, it would not suffice to perform the task. She ordained that a lesson would always be read while we were eating, so that we would not only receive food for the jaws but the word of God for the ears. In all that she taught others and all that she did herself, she always fulfilled the word of God. She did nothing and knew nothing carnally but when she prohibited something or avoided doing something herself it was in her zeal for God alone. Because she did not want any slovenliness to develop in the service of God, she insisted on prayers, reading, almsgiving and incessant daily preaching so that no one could use ignorance as an excuse to slack off.

18. She had so many gifts in herself through largesse of divine grace that, wherever she went, she followed the Lord in spirit imitating the teacher of humility who descended to earth from his heavenly throne. After her flock had retired for their rest, she would spend the night in prayer. With her holy right hand, she would protect her monastery with the sign of the cross. Once while the blessed woman was making this sign, one of the sisters saw a thousand thousand demons standing on top of the wall in the form of goats. When the saint raised her blessed right hand in the sign of the cross, this whole multitude of demons fled, never to be seen again.

19. Likewise, one night she stood before her cell, chanting the office as always in her heart and in her mouth—for the perpetual praise of God resounded in the secret places of her hidden heart. Meanwhile, a raucous night bird, hateful to mankind, was breaking the peace from a tree in the middle of the monastery. One of her companions said: "Blessed Lady, if you command, I will expel the bird in your name." To which she replied, "If it troubles you, go and make the sign of the cross over it in the Lord's name." Then she walked over and said to the bird: "In the name of Our Lord Jesus Christ, Lady Radegund orders you to leave this place unless you came at God's behest and presume to sing no more within it." Then, as if the creature had heard the words from God's own mouth, it took flight and was never seen again. She had earned the obedience of birds and beasts, for she had never failed to obey the Lord's commands.

And if she sometimes wished to rest because of illness, her spirit kept watch and she would say as if admonishing the person reciting the psalter:

"Go on! Recite!" There is no doubt that either she was with the saints in spirit singing psalms or sleep never overcame her in the first place. Her mind was so concentrated on Christ that even while asleep she would often preach of the future judgment and the eternal reward. And when she awoke she would say to us: "Gather, gather the harvest of the Lord. For truly I say to you that you will not have long to gather it. Mark what I say! Gather it! for one day, you will be seeking this time and the days you have wasted and you will earnestly desire to have them again." For although, in our slothfulness, we once accorded this a lukewarm reception, we see now that what she said has come to pass. For in us the prophecy is fulfilled: "I will send a famine in the land, not a famine of bread, nor thirst for water, but of hearing the words of the Lord."[121] We still repeat her teachings but her tireless voice has ceased, with its desirable admonitions and sweet affection. Oh God, oh Goodly Sculptor, who now can ever recapture her look, her form, her being? Indeed it is painful to remember what she was like. For we humbled ones long for her teaching, the form and face, person, knowledge, piety, goodness and sweetness that she had in herself from the Lord that made her special among other people.[122]

20. Her holy life was as sweet and pure as her face. Before the year of her transition, she saw the place prepared for her in a vision. A very rich youth came to her. He was most beautiful and had, as the young do, a tender touch and a charming way with words as he spoke to her. But she jealously protected herself and repelled his blandishments. So he said to her: "Why then have you sought me, with burning desire, with so many tears? Why do you plead, groaning, and call out with copious prayer, afflicting such agony upon yourself for my sake who am always by your side? Oh, my precious gem, you must know that you are the first jewel in the crown on my head." Who can doubt that this visitor was He who had her whole devotion while she lived in the flesh and that He was showing her what she was to enjoy in her glory.[123] She confided this vision most secretly to two of her faithful ones and made them swear to tell no one while she lived.

There are many more things to say about her, important things, but we pass over them, to avoid going on too long and arousing our audience's distaste for our prolixity instead of presenting them with something neat and pleas-

---

121. Amos 8:11.

122. This peroration is taken almost word for word from the life of Caesarius of Arles, 2:27, MGH, SRM 3:32.

123. Aigrain, *Sainte Radegonde*, 139, notes that at some later period a devotion grew up around a sacred stone in which the Lord was supposed to have left His footprint on this occasion, which is still on display at Saint Radegund's church in Poitiers, which also houses her tomb. The university of Poitiers instituted a pilgrimage to the old church of Pas-de-Dieu that housed it in 1642.

ing. And however much we recall of her love, nurturing, charity, teaching and all of her utterly holy way of life, however much we torture ourselves and grieve to seek again that great goodness, we cannot find again what we have lost. Oh cruel fate, which falls so unhappily upon us! Oh most pious lady, may the Lord in Heaven grant that you may herd before you the sheep you once gathered. Following the steps of the Good Shepherd, may you bring your own flock to the Lord!

21. Now we come to her most glorious passing, which we cannot speak of without a flood of tears. From our innermost selves, from our heart of hearts, the tears flow, wails and moans break forth and nothing can console us while we make our lament. For the less we say of her faithful devotion, the more we sin. Even to the day of her passing she never slackened in running the race and held fast in her heart to what she had begun as she who "endureth to the end will be saved."[124] Thus her holy little body came to the end of its life, that long drawn-out martyrdom for the love of God. The whole congregation of the blessed woman, weeping and wailing around her bed, struck their breasts with hard fists and stones and raised their voices to Heaven clamoring, and said: "Lord, spare us this heavy loss. You are taking our light. Why will you leave us in darkness?" And, since she had always chosen to do the things she cared most about on the birthday of the Lord, so she ended her most glorious journey on that day. Early on the Wednesday morning of the ides of August, she closed her eyes while darkness descended on ours.[125]

22. Woe unto us! Because we have sinned, our hearts are afflicted with sorrow. We weep and we mourn, because we did not deserve to have you among us any longer. On that same morning when this great evil befell us, one voice, one plaint, one clamor penetrated the very heavens. And masons working on the mountain heard an angel in the sky speaking to other angels: "What are you doing? Send her here." For the voices had come to the ears of the Lord. Angels bearing her [upward] responded: "Now it is done." What could we have done? Paradise received her and there she is in glory with God. We do not believe that we are cut off from her because she reigns with Him whom she wished to please. Therefore, it is a cause for awe but not for tears. In this present world we have lost our lady and mother, but we have sent her before us as our intercessor in the kingdom of Christ. But while she has become a source of wondrous joy in heaven, she has truly left us on earth in intolerable grief.

124. Matthew 10:22.
125. August 13, 587. The reference to the birthday of the Lord relates to the tradition that Jesus was born on a Wednesday, the day of the creation of the sun and moon, taken from *De pascha computus*, 243, by Talley, *Origins of the Church Year*, 90–91.

23. When her holy soul migrated to Christ, the local bishop was absent.[126] A messenger went to the apostolic Bishop, Lord Gregory of Tours, and he came. But in the Book of Miracles which he composed he included an account of all that he saw of her virtues with his own eyes before he buried her.[127] For, as he said tearfully afterwards, on his oath, as he came to the place where the holy body lay, he saw an angel's face in human form, a face refulgent with roses and lilies and he was stricken with fear and trembling, a devout man filled with God as though standing in the presence of the Lord's holy mother herself. They waited for the bishop of the place so that she might be interred with due honor. The whole flock stood around her bed singing the psalms. And whenever the psalms ceased for a space, they broke into intolerable plaints. Thus they delayed for three days for the bishop who was making his rounds. But when he did not come, trusting in love "for perfect love casteth out fear,"[128] the aforementioned apostolic man brought her to the basilica dedicated to Saint Mary where the bodies of the holy virgins of the monastery were kept. There he buried her with all honor.

24. Since it was ordained that no living person should issue out of the gates of the monastery, the whole flock stood on the walls while they bore the holy body with psalms beneath the walls.[129] They lamented so loudly that their grief drowned out the psalms, rendering tears for psalms, groans for canticles, sighs for alleluias. Suffering the loss of her most bitterly, they cried out from above that the bier on which the blessed woman was carried might pause under the tower. And as the holy body rested there, the Lord, to reveal his faithful servant in the midst of the people, gave sight to a blind person. One who had not seen the light of day for many years received the light. One who had been guided by another's hand, now followed behind the bier unassisted all the way to the holy grave as though he had never had trouble with his eyes. Even to this day he still sees clearly.

25. Nor should we omit another miracle. When the aforesaid bishop buried her, he could not close up the grave until the local bishop arrived. Female serfs, who had carried the candles before her, stood in a circle around the tomb, each bearing a candle with her own name written on it. According

126. Maroveus, bishop of Poitiers, 584–90. His hostility to Radegund had been evident for some years, although the reason is unknown. Gregory of Tours, *HF*, 9:40.

127. See Gregory of Tours, *Glory of the Confessors*, 104, where he includes the moving threnody of the nuns for their lost mother.

128. 1 John 4:18.

129. An indication that the monastery advocated the strict active enclosure introduced by Caesarius into his rule, and urged by his sister's successor at Arles in her letter to Radegund. See also, Schulenberg, "Strict Active Enclosure." Gregory notes that a group of possessed persons rushed forward to testify that they were being tormented by the presence of a saint's body.

to ritual, each then handed over her candle to one of the servants. But then there was an argument among the people. Some said that the candles should be placed in the holy tomb while others disagreed. While this was being debated, one candle escaped from the arms of the boy who held them all and flew on high above all the people and came to rest at the feet of the blessed woman in her holy grave, thus deciding what had been uncertain. When they looked to see whose candle it was, the name of Calva was discerned. Seeing this, the bishop and all the people blessed the Lord, admiring the virtues of the Blessed Radegund.[130] And who can count how many virtues were accomplished here, after her transition! How many were freed from demons, how many were restored to health from delirious fever?

26. An abbot named Abbo came from Burgundy with the apostolic Bishop Leifast.[131] While in the city of Poitiers, he developed a terrible toothache. Day and night, he was so overcome by pain that his one abiding wish was that death would come to him and rid him of the agony. But then, inspired by divine mercy, he asked to be taken to the saint's basilica. Having entered, he threw himself in an act of faith to the ground before her holy sepulchre. With death before his eyes, he took hold of the funerary pall over the holy tomb with his teeth. For seven days he had taken no refreshment of food or sleep. But with that bite, sleep came to him, the pain left and he returned to the hospice in good health. Many people learned of this afterwards and acknowledged that the virtues of the Lady Radegund had snatched him from the jaws of death.

27. It is the custom here for all the nearby monasteries to celebrate vigils together for the feast of Saint Hilary until the middle of the night. Then each abbot returns with his brethren to his own monastery to celebrate the office. While they were keeping vigil in the basilica of the blessed primate (i.e., Saint Hilary), those possessed by demons clamored all night among whom were two women gravely infested by the enemy. Indeed, one raved so violently that she shook the whole basilica with her roaring. After the venerable Arnegiselus, abbot of the blessed Queen's basilica, went with his monks to their own basilica, which Radegund had loved so well, to complete the office they heard the clamoring women coming after them. Vociferously, they entered the basilica and prayed that the Lady Radegund would spare them. One of them was gravely troubled—indeed her evil spirit had flagellated her

130. Aigrain, *Sainte Radegonde*, 145, thinks that the candles on the tomb (or in the burial chamber) would mark a saint's sanctuary and some were hesitant to proclaim a cult so soon after her death. Possibly the miracle is supplied to counter anticipated attacks by Maroveus, who regained control of the monastery and closed the tomb. Gregory of Tours, HF, 9:40.

131. Krusch, ed., MGH, SRM 2:394, notes that neither Leifast, who would have been succeeded by Siagrius as bishop of Autun, ca. 600, nor Abbo are named elsewhere, citing *Gallia Christiana* 4:346, 449.

for fifteen years. But while Matins was being sung, the raging enemy abandoned the vessel he had invaded. The other was freed at Terce before the gates of the same basilica. That most evil adversary never again had power to harm them afterwards. Oh, how bountiful and rich is the mercy of God that makes His own folk stand in awe of Him and seeks out the places where He may show His power to the faithful as the giver and dispenser of virtues. Some were liberated at the holy man's basilica while others were brought to Lady Radegund's basilica for, as they were equal in grace, so were they both shown equal in virtue.

28. If any invalid, even someone despairing of life was given a febrifuge, a cup of water into which the custodian of her holy tomb had dipped the bottom of the pall, immediately on drinking, the recipient fell into sleep before the holy sepulchre, and the illness left. By the largesse of Christ, many virtues are done here daily in the name of the Lord Jesus Christ where her remains are laid. So we venerate her with faithful devotion and due sedulity on earth. And we confide our souls to her rejoicing, and glorying that she shines forth in Heaven, where He Who lives and reigns with the Father and the Holy Ghost from everlasting to everlasting is above them all. Amen.

5
Eustadiola, Widow of Bourges
(594–684)

By the end of the sixth century, the popularity of the ascetic life as an alternative for women of means in Frankland was spreading widely. The customs of the time were fortunate for women who came from wealthy families or who married wealthy men. Barbarian law codes mandated a share of a man's inheritance for his widow and all of his children, including daughters. Marriage customs encouraged fathers to settle portions of the bride-price upon their daughters. She could usually add a morning gift and other gifts from her husband later in the marriage to this nest egg. Roman women and Frankish women whose families were influenced by Roman customs might do equally well from inheritances designated in individual wills. The church also encouraged men to be generous with women in every relationship.[1] Thus, many women, once widowed, were financially independent and well able to establish themselves in a semiretired religious life.[2] Eustadiola is but one of the women of Bourges in the sixth and seventh centuries who tailored individual lives with no apparent formal vows or submission to an outside rule.[3] In other cases, women supported the establishment of convents but ran them as deaconesses along lines that suited themselves, as did Saint Sigolena, who retained her virginity with her husband's consent. Once she was widowed, at the age of twenty-four, she refused to obey her parents and remarry.[4]

This life probably dates from the early eighth century, embedded in a life of Saint Sulpicius of Bourges, bishop from 624 to 647. This excerpt is from AS, June 8, 131–33.

1. There are many studies of women's control of property in this period. The classic is Herlihy, "Land, Family and Women in Continental Europe, 701–1200." Murray, *Germanic Kinship*, 81, has discussed the problem of female inheritance in the light of the *Edictum Chilperici*.

2. Even though a testament formerly attributed to Eustadiola has been judged a forgery by Aubert, DHGE, there is no reason to think that she lacked appropriate wealth.

3. De Laugardière, *L'église de Bourges avant Charlemagne*, 175–79, notes that several women in the city lived in a similar manner.

4. Verdon, "Recherches sur les monastères féminins," 122, considers her vita a pastiche from other lives. Wemple, *Women in Frankish Society*, 274, n. 81, agrees but believes her consecration as a

Eustadiola's life is typical of the urbanized asceticism of the sixth century characterized primarily by small communities with few permanent institutional qualities. It represents the sort of religious free-enterprise system that Pope Gregory I opposed in his patronage of the Benedictine Rule and that also concerned Gallic councils of the sixth century.[5] Such unsupervised and unregulated ways of life would gradually give way with the spread of the Irish system in the seventh century and its later amalgamation with the Benedictine Rule. The attention of hagiographers and institutional historians has focussed on the great foundations and their patronesses. Indeed, even the present record of the life of Eustadiola might not have survived had it not been embedded in the life of the sainted Bishop Sulpicius of Bourges. Nevertheless, it did survive and stands in this collection to remind us of the many forgotten individuals who pursued roads to sanctity not often commemorated by official historians.

Saint Eustadiola, Widow of Bourges

■

1. When the venerable Bishop Sulpicius most wisely governed the church of Bourges, a most noble woman name Eustadiola lived in that city. Even when she was still in secular dress, this woman lived the life of a religious. Sprung from most noble parents as the world counts rank, blossoms of the senatorial nobility, she was even more noble in Catholic learning, so strong that no heretic could seduce her. Noble in faith and nobler still in works, she was famous among her fellow citizens for worldly dignity and also in the precious grace of divine gifts.

2. While still in the bud of infancy, she was trained in sacred letters and became wise in religious ways. She submitted to her parents in all things so that she grew in the affections of all, even as she grew to maturity in the grace of prudence. Fearful lest a stranger might inherit their goods when they came to leave the world, her parents began to exhort and order her to marry in order to provide progeny for them. So they reminded her of the Apostle's word: "If a virgin marry, she hath not sinned."[6] For they were very wealthy in possessions and power throughout Gaul even to Aquitaine's far flung borders. They pressed their daughter until she allowed herself to be matched

---

deaconess may really have occurred despite the hagiographer's use of Fortunatus's diction. If our guess that Radegund's consecration as a deaconess was Médard's solution to the problem of her ongoing marriage is correct, the practice may have been adopted for other Frankish women following her example.

5. Wemple, *Women in Frankish Society,* 157, notes the concern of Gallic councils in the sixth century with the regulation of women practicing asceticism outside convent walls.

6. 1 Corinthians 7:28.

with a lawful husband. And once she had made an honorable marriage suitable to her rank and had been brought to an unstained bed, she bore a single son named Tetradius. Then her husband, coming to the end of this present life, migrated from the world.

3. When the noble maid had been widowed by her husband's death, burning worldly desires urged her to a new marriage bed with wealth and status. But she preferred to join with God in spiritual marriage, which begins with grief and leads to eternal joy, rather than subject herself to a carnal marriage which always begins with gaiety and leads to a tearful end. Freed from the governance of a husband, she followed the apostolic counsel, saying: "She is happier if she so abide, after my judgment."[7] Therefore, inspired by the Holy Spirit, she put off her secular garments so as to serve Christ wholly without worldly cares. She gave herself in all things over to the service of almighty God. She relinquished everything according to the Gospel, as the Lord said: "If thou wilt be perfect, go and sell that thou hast, and give it to the poor, and thou shalt have treasure in Heaven, and come and follow me."[8] So, according to the Savior's precept, she gave her goods to the poor, particularly to the poor who serve God. First of all, she dedicated the houses she possessed within the walls of Bourges as basilicas in honor of the Holy Mary Ever-virgin and the blessed martyr Eugenia.[9] From the abundance of her treasure, she adorned the churches with gold and silver vessels, choice pearls and various types of gems, having crosses, candelabra, chalices and other vessels fitting for the sacred mysteries made, as well as books and turrets.[10] Working with her maids, she made holy vestments, precious altar cloths and hangings for the walls, embellishing the elegant work with golden fringes and ornaments with her own hands. She built a monastery and a worthy convent for herself and her maids where she enclosed a large flock of the female sex prepared to live according to the norms of the Rule. Following the example of the blessed Eustadiola, they relinquished everything and devoted themselves to God with all their will, proposing to remain chaste and to strive to be adorned with other virtues.

4. Therefore when Saint Eustadiola had completed this monastery, she endowed it, assigning all her estates and powers to it by testament according to secular and canon law, retaining no hereditary rights for herself or any other.[11] So she would be one with those who had vowed themselves to

---

7. 1 Corinthians 7:40.

8. Matthew 19:21.

9. A martyr of unknown date buried at Rome. Her legend was of a common genre in which the heroine is falsely accused of sexual wrongdoing while serving in a monastery in male disguise. PL 73:605.

10. The latter are reliquaries or *ciboria* shaped like towers.

11. This does not appear to take any account of the rights of her son. If he were still alive, she was

Christ after her example.[12] Indeed several maidens followed her in aspiring to a heavenly fatherland and refused carnal spouses to win an immortal heavenly mate. Eustadiola, mother of the monastery, rejoiced in the holy zeal of her daughters. And who can tell how humbly she debased herself, how many abstentions she imposed on herself or how she lived in such charity and goodness? Through the space of seventy years, she never took the flesh of fowl or quadruped for her supper. If altercation or hatred sprang up among the powerful of the world, she would pacify them by a word if they were nearby or by a letter if they were far away. And none of them ever revived the original trouble. God performed many cures through her prayers. The blind received sight from the water in which she washed her hands and face and many were healed of various other weaknesses.

5. At one season, there was such drought that the heavens looked like copper and the earth was like iron. As was her wont, God's handmaid Eustadiola prayed daily in the basilica of blessed Paul the Apostle near the walls outside the gate where she delighted to spend days and nights meditating in prayers and reading. As she went there one day, the Holy Spirit inspired her to admonish the holy sisters in her service with smooth words, saying: "Beloved daughters, let us pray God for mercy and pardon for our sins. And tearfully let us supplicate, pouring out prayers, that he will deign to give us rain." Completing her prayers, she was on the way back to her convent with the procession from the basilica of Blessed Paul. Suddenly, thunder boomed and lightning flashed and Bourges was covered with darkest clouds. Soon they were so inundated with rain that the holy mother had to flee with her nuns, swiftly running to the monastery with utmost speed. Even so, their habits were soaked through as though they had sunk into a great flood.

6. Among other acts of piety, she washed the feet of wayfarers and cleaned their hair. Day and night she steadily poured out so many tearful prayers to God that she might rightly say with the Prophet: "My tears have been my meat day and night."[13] She was full of faith, ablaze with charity, affable of speech, amiable of aspect, endowed with prudence, famed for temperance, firm with internal fortitude, steady with just censures, great of spirit, robust with patience and gentle in humility. And with all these virtues, beauty adorned her with the jewel of wisdom. As the Apostle says, her speech was "seasoned with salt."[14] Consolation of many paupers, a humble staff of pilgrims, she fed

---

probably disposing of her own private rights of dos, dower, and morning gift; see McNamara and Wemple, "The Power of Women Through the Family."

12. This seems to suggest that not only her maids but also other women of the community were neither wealthy nor noble. For the question of the social status of women in Merovingian monasteries, see McNamara, "The Ordeal of Community."

13. Psalms 42:3.

14. Colossians 4:6.

the hungry, clothed the naked, supported widows and orphans. But no human tongue can tell all her bounties one by one.

7. The time came when she must relinquish the carnal habitation and, fully ninety years of age, migrate to the celestial kingdom. Hastening thence through good works, she knew, when she was old and full of days, having brightened her age with the consummate splendor of her merits, that the hour of her departure drew near. Exhilarated with a good conscience, she was prepared to appear at once before the Lord when He knocked. Giving thanks to God in her mind, like a stranger leaving an alien dwelling to go home, she breathed forth her blessed spirit with thanksgiving. And with an angelic company she sought the celestial realm where she gleams as an ornament among the fiery jewels of the heavenly King.

8. From all sides of the town, a crowd of innumerable people flowed together and all were overcome by infinite grief of spirit. Their bitter lamentations so often interrupted the spiritual hymns of the clerks that they could scarcely sing. Meanwhile she came to the basilica of Saint Paul which she had once built with great exertion. There she was buried in wondrous beauty to await the glorious triumph of resurrection. The religious bishop of Bourges, Rocco, who had been brought up at the king's court, and was at Eustadiola's funeral, attested that he had never seen such enormous grief at the death of a religious in church or even at the end of anyone in royal power. Whence it is clear that this handmaid of God was loved and mourned by all, as she was always so useful and beneficial to all. They mourned the absent one though they had not lost her but only sent her ahead. Soon in fact, she showed herself to be still present by restoring several people to health and through God's grace, so many mighty miracles were performed at her tomb that she shone like the sun. We wish to commemorate a few items from the wealth of similar deeds which may be inferred from them.

9. There was a priest named Leodebodus who had been struck blind. He had a strong belief, which never faltered, that if he could get a little dust from Eustadiola's tomb mixed with oil from the lamp before her sepulchre, and place it on his eyes, it would act as a heavenly medicine. For an angel had told him this by night. And when he had done that, light overcame the darkness in his eyes. Also, a man named Pretextus of the town of Poitiers received sight at once when he approached the sacred tomb with prayers to the Lord and was anointed with the holy liquor while invoking the names of Christ and blessed Eustadiola.

10. Another one named Theoderamnus was brought to the tomb in a vehicle by neighbors because the soles of his contracted feet had been drawn to his buttocks. Having invoked the names of the Savior and blessed Eustadiola, he regained the capacity to walk and returned to his dwelling hale

and hearty. And a woman named Leonichildis, lame of foot and contracted of arm, was brought before her tomb and soon returned home having received a wonderful cure. Another woman, named Bona, was brought to the tomb when struck by blindness. When she was anointed with the lamp oil by the priest to whom that office was assigned, she recovered sight and returned home rejoicing.

11. But these signs have multiplied beyond counting. Soon so many had received the gift of health that if each story were told separately they would fill a great volume. To this day, the sick are healed here daily to give evidence that Blessed Eustadiola lives with Christ and has influence with Him. For with her customary piety she has deigned to intercede for us that we may be snatched from the evils of the present world and deserve to share the joys of the just with her. Mercifully may our Lord, Jesus Christ grant this to us, Who lives with the Father and the Holy Spirit and reigns, God, from everlasting to everlasting. Amen.

6

Caesaria II, Abbess of
Saint Jean of Arles

(ca. 550)

The island of Lérins off the Mediterranean coast near Cannes was an early site
for the spread of monasticism into Gaul. Men and women, sometimes as
chaste clerical couples, took refuge there during the invasions of the fifth
century and experimented together with the ascetic life. From there, the
monastic movement spread up the Rhône Valley despite the continuing un-
rest of the late fifth and early sixth centuries. Indeed, female monasticism may
have been strengthened by the need to provide refuge for widows, orphans,
or other women endangered by continuous warfare. In Lyon, a nunnery
attached to the basilica of Saint Michael may have sheltered Clothild's mother
until her death in 506. Several convents, one attached to the cult of the local
heroine and martyr Saint Blandina, are known to have flourished at Vienne.[1]
Caesaria of Arles, sister of the bishop of that city, was trained at John Cassian's
foundation in Marseille before becoming abbess of Saint Jean.

Bishop Caesarius (d. 543) first planned to establish his sister Caesaria outside the city walls near the old Gallo-Roman cemetery called the Aliscamps.
This plan was violently frustrated in 508–9 when the Franks under Clovis and
the Burgundians under Clothild's kinsmen joined to besiege the Visigothic
incumbents of the city and destroyed the building. When the danger was past

MGH, *Epistolae* 2:450. Aigrain, *Sainte Radegonde*, 103, considers this letter fraudulent, believing that
Radegund obtained the Rule of Caesarius in person from Caesaria's successor Liliola after her
difficulties with the bishop of Poitiers in 569. Labande-Mailfert, "Les débuts," 42–44, while retaining
the idea of the trip in 570, supports the authenticity of this letter, which would have to be dated
before Caesaria's death in 561 and would thus conform to the probable time of Radegund's entry
into the monastery after Clothar died.

1. Wood, "Prelude to Columbanus," 9. Carolingian hagiographers claimed that before the devasta-
tions of the early eighth century, there were seventy-two monasteries of monks and nuns in the
diocese of Vienne, twelve in the city itself. The nunneries established by Leonianus in the city
housed more than sixty. *Vita Patrum iurensium*, ed. Martinez, 1:3, notes that Ansemandus founded St.
André le Bas outside the walls for his sister Eubona and his daughter Remila Eugenia. There were
two hundred nuns at Saint Jean d'Arles and Aurelian's nunnery of Saint Mary had more.

and Arles had passed under the powerful patronage of Clovis's brother-in-law, Theodoric the Ostrogoth, the convent was reestablished within the city walls and remained there until the French Revolution in 1789.[2]

Caesarius completed the convent in 512 and supplied it with an elaborate rule that was widely adapted in other female communities during the sixth century.[3] Radegund was in correspondence with the Caesaria II, who succeeded the foundress. Several scholars have interpreted a passage in Gregory of Tours to mean that she visited the abbey around 570 when it was under the rule of the third abbess, Liliola.[4] Under the fourth abbess, Rusticula, the abbey was rebuilt at the southeast angle of the city walls near the Tour des Morgues.[5]

Caesaria probably wrote this letter to Radegund about 550 when the queen first embraced the monastic life. It is interesting because it is an expression of the ordinary spirituality of a contemporary nun, trained according to the precepts of John Cassian. Caesaria's obedience to her mentor's command and her sister's tutelage is evident in her ready use of biblical texts, particularly psalmody, to illustrate her advice to Radegund.[6] In her brief letter, she summarizes the most important points of the Caesarian rule, urging attention to learning Scripture. She does not dwell on the bishop's command that the sisters support themselves by copying manuscripts. Perhaps she thought that so wealthy a foundation as Radegund's was more appropriately admonished to charity than to the problem of self-support.

Not surprisingly, Caesaria urged that constant prayer be supported by good works. She also urged the imposition of the cloistered life Caesarius considered a necessity for women.[7] It is not clear from the available lives how

2. Theodoric (d. 526) had married Clovis's sister Albofled, who did not, however, apparently attempt to convert him from his Arian faith. This is another example of the mixed marriages noted by Wood in the Burgundian family. "Gregory of Tours and Clovis," 267.

3. Caesarius's rule predates that of Benedict as the first systematic law for western monasticism. It is available in an excellent translation by McCarthy, *Rule for Nuns of Saint Caesarius of Arles.*

4. Gregory of Tours, HF, 9:40. The whole argument turns on the single word *expetunt*. Lewis Thorpe renders it plausibly into English as "they turned to Arles" when Radegund was in conflict with the bishop of Poitiers. However, this need not mean that she physically traveled there. Aigrain, "Le voyage de Ste. Radegonde à Arles," 119–27, and again in *Sainte Radegonde*, 103, buttresses his theory of a voyage with a passing mention of Agnes's presence in Metz by Gregory of Tours, *De virtutibus S. Martini*, 4, 26. Aigrain argues that this must have occurred before her acceptance of Caesarius's rule of claustration. Believing in the voyage, Gregory rejects this letter of Caesaria as a forgery. In "Les débuts," Labande-Mailfert accepts (43) Aigrain's arguments for the trip to Metz and subsequently to Poitiers and indeed, elaborates Gregory's remarks to support the idea.

5. Benoit, "Topographie monastique d'Arles au VIe siècle," 13–17.

6. The Rule (c. 18) enjoins that all nuns learn to read and write. The order of offices involves a constant daily round of psalm-chanting (c. 66).

7. Rule, c. 2. For further discussion, see Schulenberg, "Strict Active Enclosure," and Nolte, "Klosterleben von Frauen."

strictly sixth-century nuns observed that commandment. Certainly they did not interpret their claustration to mean that people should be kept out of the monastery. Radegund herself was in the habit of entertaining large numbers of the poor, the clergy, and possibly well-to-do people also at her convent. In chapter 7, we shall see that the Abbess Liliola had at least one conference with King Guntram, who might have visited her within the cloister. Rusticula herself is said to have had regular dealings with the workmen who built her new chapels. Both lives, therefore, seem to suggest that the advice to avoid the company of men was not understood too literally. The nuns of the period appear to have visited with clergymen fairly frequently, at least within the convent or the church, which was probably reached directly from the cloister. They also met workmen and others when it was necessary for the conduct of their business. On the other side, Baudonivia claimed that none of the nuns were allowed to go out of the cloister, and in "The Thuringian War" Radegund pled the constraints of cloister to explain her inability to go to Byzantium. Rusticula depended on her rule to prevent her arrest by the king's soldiers.

Perhaps the most interesting advice that Caesaria gave Radegund was the admonition not to be severe or excessive in her devotions. Roughly the same spirit was being expressed at about the same time in Italy by her great monastic contemporary, Saint Benedict of Nursia. However, as Fortunatus attests, Radegund was particularly in need of such a caution. It is possible that the saint's long life was at least in part due to Caesaria's timely intervention.

Caesaria the Insignificant, to the Holy Ladies Richild and Radegund[8]

∎

Having received your message and read it more than once, I am filled with inestimable spiritual joy at the heights of your holy piety. For you have chosen, and under God's direction I know you will hold to that which will prepare you for eternal life and thus you will acquire eternal wealth and exultation with the saints that has no ending. May the Lord our God who sets the prisoners free, the Lord who openeth the eyes of the blind, the Lord who raiseth them that are bowed down,[9] lead you in the right way, teach you to do His will, grant that you may walk in His precepts and keep His commandments and meditate on His law. As the psalmist says: "In His law doth He

8. The identity of Richild is unknown and her absence from the records of Saint-Croix provided Aigrain with an argument against the authenticity of the letter. Labande-Mailfert, "Les débuts," 42, following Voguë's work in progress which he shared with her, suggests that Richild may have been the original Germanic name of Agnes.

9. Psalms 146:7, 8.

meditate day and night."[10] And again: "The commandment of the Lord is pure, enlightening the eyes. The statutes of the Lord are right, rejoicing the heart."[11] As worldly men pay attention when royal precepts are read, so should you listen intently when divine Scriptures are read. Let the precepts of the Lord have your whole mind, your whole thought, your whole meditation. Take care to fear them, for "they are cursed which do err from thy commandments."[12] And the one who does not keep the least of the Lord's mandates is called least in the kingdom of Heaven.[13] May it be fulfilled: "let the meditation of my heart ever be acceptable in thy sight."[14] "Thy word have I hid in mine heart, that I might not sin against thee."[15] And because the Lord has deigned to choose you, my dearest ladies in Christ, for His inheritance, give thanks and bless Him all the time. Abstain from all vice and all sin because "whosoever committeth sin is the servant of sin."[16] Love and fear the Lord, for "the eye of the Lord is upon them that fear Him and His ears are open unto their cry."[17] Let your heart be pure and peaceful.

Remain mild and humble, patient and obedient. Hear the Lord, saying: "On whom shall I rest, but on the humble and quiet? He hath put down the mighty from their seats and exalted them of low degree."[18] Holy and good and laudable is the rule you have chosen to live by; but there is no teaching greater or better or more precious than the reading of the Gospel. See that you hold to what Christ, our Lord and Master, teaches by His word and fulfills by His example, Who works so many miracles in the world that they cannot be counted, Who patiently sustains so much evil from his persecutors that it is scarcely to be believed. For it is patience that God commends to us. Hear the Apostle: "all that will live godly in Christ shall suffer persecution."[19] As God rejoices in your incipient conversion, so the Devil bemoans it. He who has thousands and thousands of poisonous arts asks nourishment from God; likewise must you pray incessantly that God may resist him. "Be of good courage and He shall strengthen your heart."[20] Hear that scripture that says: "My son, if thou come to serve the Lord, stand in justice and fear and prepare thy soul for temptation."[21] For just as you would fight your enemies strongly

10. Psalms 1:2.
11. Psalms 19:8.
12. Psalms 119:21.
13. Matthew 5:19.
14. Psalms 19:14.
15. Psalms 119:11.
16. John 8:3.
17. Psalms 33:18; 34:15.
18. Luke 1:52.
19. 2 Timothy 3:12.
20. Psalms 31:24.
21. Ecclesiastes 2:1.

and manfully, if you were a man, lest your body be stricken, so must you fight constantly and manfully against the Devil lest evil counsels and thoughts should kill your soul. Cry out together to God: "Make haste, Oh God, to deliver me; make haste to help me, oh Lord."[22] "Oh God, be not far from me."[23] "Oh my God, make haste for my help. Leave me not, neither forsake me, oh God of my salvation."[24] Stand to attention when you say the psalm, for it is there that He speaks and instructs you: "Sing ye praises with understanding."[25] You must stand now as the Lord stood for you when He hung on the cross; crucify yourself with the work of God. Think of nothing else; presume to speak of nothing else; nor do anything else. Stand peacefully through everything for His place is a place of peace: "Blessed are the peacemakers, for they shall be called the children of God."[26] "Let not the sun go down upon your wrath."[27] "Great peace have they which love thy law: and nothing shall offend them."[28]

Virginity of the flesh has no value where wrath lives in the heart. And elsewhere Scripture says: "God ordains that there be peace and concord and harmony in His house." Though small and negligible, I ought to salute Him with more humility and charity than I can tell. I pray that God will so rule you that He will deign to protect and keep you and give you a good end, Who gave you this beginning. For it is not she who begins but she who perseveres even to the end who will be saved. As our humility exults and is glad for your beginning in the Lord, so may the Lord and His angels be gladdened by your perfection and behavior. I know you have abundant wealth. Give as much as you can to the poor: "lay up for yourselves treasures in Heaven."[29] Thus may it be fulfilled in you: "He hath dispersed; He hath given to the poor; His righteousness endureth forever."[30] As it is written: "As water extinguishes fire, so do alms to all sins."[31] Hope in God, for it is written: "Cursed be the man that trusteth in man."[32] Let none enter who do not know letters. All must be bound to memorize the Psalter for, as I have told you, you must all strive to fulfill all that you read in the Gospel. I have done what you requested: I am sending you a copy of the Rule which our blessed Father, Lord Caesarius of happy memory, made that you may see how you can keep it. In

22. Psalms 70:1.
23. Psalms 71:12.
24. Psalms 26:9.
25. Psalms 47:7.
26. Matthew 5:9.
27. Ephesians 4:26.
28. Psalms 119:165.
29. Matthew 6:20.
30. Psalms 112:9.
31. Tobit 4:11.
32. Jeremiah 17:5.

so ruling, be sure of my love for you, because if you live according to this you will gain a place among the wise virgins. The Lord will bring you into His kingdom and you will perceive "what eye hath not seen nor ear heard; neither have entered into the heart of man, the things which God hath prepared for them that love Him."[33] In the region of the living where the saints exult in glory, rejoicing and exulting in the Lord, you will say: "He that is mighty hath done great things to me; and holy is His name."[34] And also: "He brought His people with joy, and His chosen with gladness."[35] So the Lord will bring you immaculate to Him who reigns from everlasting to everlasting. Amen.

Come to me, for you have held back too much. Do everything reasonable if you would live for me and do as you are able. For if you fall ill through excess, which God does not will, afterwards you will need delicacies and you will lose time and you will not be able to govern the blessed ones. Hear what the Lord says in the Gospel: "Not that which goeth into the mouth defileth a man."[36] And the Apostle: "Your reasonable service."[37] Do all that you have in the rule that you have asked for, Lady, so that God may be blessed and praised in your behavior. And you will be an example to the faithful because "whosoever shall do and teach them, the same shall be called great in the kingdom of heaven."[38]

Therefore, rejoice and exult in the Lord, venerable sisters in Christ, and always give thanks to Him who deigned to call you from the darkness of worldly ways to the haven of quiet and religion. Always ponder whence you have been and where you will deserve to come. Faithfully turn from the shadows of the world and you will begin to see happily the light of Christ. Disdain the fires of lust and you will arrive at the coolness of chastity. Struggle will not be gone from you even to the end of life, for you will be secure from what is past only by remaining careful for the future. For I tell you that all our sins and crimes come back to us if we do not expunge them with daily works. Hear Peter the Apostle say: "Be sober, be vigilant, because your adversary, the Devil, as a roaring lion, walketh about, seeking whom he may devour."[39] As long as we live in the body, day and night, we must repulse the Devil with our Lord Jesus Christ as helper and leader. Those who think it is enough to change clothing are somewhat negligent and tepid. For we can put off worldly clothes and assume religious ones in a minute or an hour. But we

33. 1 Corinthians 2:9.
34. Luke 1:49.
35. Psalms 105:43.
36. Matthew 15:11.
37. Romans 12:1.
38. Matthew 5:19.
39. 1 Peter 5:8.

ought to labor with Christ our helper, always to maintain good customs as long as we live. One who desires to serve religion must struggle with the whole soul, with all the strength of faith to avoid gluttony, drunkenness, and lust so that the body will neither be weakened by excessive abstinence nor provoked to luxury by abundant delicacies. Therefore you should always be reading or hearing divine Scriptures for they are the ornaments of the soul: these are as precious pearls hung in your ear or rings or necklaces. As long as you perform good works, you will always be adorned with like ornaments. Indeed, anyone who desires to keep religion with pure heart and walk immaculate before the face of God, should never go out in public or only with difficulty. If you want to maintain chastity, avoid familiarity with men as much as you are able. Nor say to anyone: "My conscience satisfies me, whatever anyone cares to say about me." This is a poor enough excuse and hateful to God. For if your conscience is secure when you speak thus, you have not looked at that conscience! Most surely I think you know that the woman who does not avoid the company of men is lost one way or another. We must resist the vestiges of vice with all our might. But you never expunge vice unless you flee the consortium of men. If you are nobly born, you must rejoice more in religious humility than in secular dignity. Hear the Lord saying: "If you leave all and follow after me, you will receive back a hundred fold and you will possess eternal life."[40] One who is converted from poverty shall give thanks to God who saves the souls of the poor and frees them from the impediments of the world: The rich "lack and suffer hunger, but they that seek the Lord shall not want any good thing."[41] Love everyone if you want God to live in your own heart, for it is written: "He that hateth his brother or sister is in darkness and walketh in darkness, and knoweth not whither he goeth, because that darkness hath blinded his eyes."[42] Some may leave the goods of the parents and disinherit themselves because they hear the Lord saying: "Sell that ye have and give alms and behold the world is yours."[43] "He hath dispersed, he hath given to the poor; his righteousness endureth forever."[44] Run faithfully, that you may be able to arrive happily and stand rejoicing and exulting before the face of the Lord our God Who has deigned to choose you among the sheep of His pasture. As in terrestrial ministry, so He will grant to establish you in His kingdom before the celestial throne where He reigns from everlasting to everlasting.

40. Matthew 19:29.
41. Psalms 34:10.
42. 1 John 2:11.
43. Luke 12:33.
44. Psalms 112:9.

7
Rusticula, Abbess of Arles
(ca. 556–632)

After Caesaria's death in 559, Saint Jean was caught in a violent maelstrom of conspiracy, murder, and revenge. The old Roman city of Arles had fallen to the Visigoths and then the Burgundians early in the sixth century. The Roman population had never given these Arian barbarians their political loyalty. Bishop Caesarius himself was charged with treason as a Frankish collaborator against the Arian Visigoths.[1] Clothild's sons wrested the area from their Burgundian cousin Sigismund, and it finally fell, with all the Frankish domains, into the hands of Radegund's husband, Clothar I. At his death in 561, the realm was divided, and Arles fell to the share of Guntram, full brother of Sigebert and Charibert, half-brother of Chilperic.

Guntram's relationship with his royal relatives was typical of Merovingian family life. Shortly after Charibert's death, his widow engaged in negotiations to marry Guntram, whose own wife Austrechild had just died. Instead, Guntram robbed her of her treasure and persuaded Caesaria's successor, Liliola, third abbess of Saint Jean, to imprison her in a convent cell. Perhaps the abbess cooperated with Guntram in robbing and imprisoning Charibert's widow to secure a much-needed addition to their endowment. Caesarius's legacy, which had supported the convent, was probably running thin by the 560s. The heroine of this chapter, Rusticula, was about five when Clothar died

Krusch, ed., MGH, SRM 4:337–51. Krusch reverts to his favorite idea that the text was a forgery stemming from a Carolingian scriptorium based on certain aspects of the style and content of the text. Riché, "La Vita S. Rusticulae," has responded that the Roman heritage and ongoing literary tradition of the Rhône region refutes Krusch's claim that the style is too good for the period. In fact, Riché argues that interest in preserving the memory of a local saint and the talent to do so is more credible for the seventh century than for the ninth, when the area had fallen into devastation and neglect, prey to persistent invasion by Vikings and Saracens alike, as discussed by Weinberger, "Peasant Households in Provence."

1. See Life of Caesarius of Arles, in Hillgarth, Conversion of Western Europe, 31ff. Krusch views this incident as the model for the Life of Rusticula, which justified him for condemning it as a forgery.

and Guntram took control of Arles. She was heiress to an old Gallo-Roman fortune.[2] A greedy suitor abducted the child and would have brought her up to be his wife had Liliola not rescued her. In her turn, however, the abbess of Arles refused to release her and raised her instead to be the bride of Christ. The pleas of her grieving mother were lost on the king. Guntram owed Liliola a favor for guarding Charibert's widow, and Rusticula herself was apparently willing to remain in the convent. The case was not entirely unique. Gregory the Great (d. 604) some years later ordered his legates to restore a woman and her fortune to a convent in the same area after an ambitious suitor had abducted her.[3]

In 568, when Rusticula was just reaching puberty, Sigebert made a brief but unsuccessful effort to seize Arles from his brother. In 575, he was assassinated. Less than ten years later, Chilperic was also murdered. Both murders stemmed from the bitter vendetta of their queens, Brunhild and Fredegund, which began when Chilperic murdered his wife, Brunhild's sister Galswinth, at the instigation of the ambitious slave Fredegund.[4] Guntram steered a hazardous course between his brothers' widows and their children. Gregory of Tours says that Brunhild and Fredegund each threatened him with murder on various occasions.[5] Perhaps his lingering resentment of Sigebert led to his chivalrous dash to Paris to defend Fredegund and her infant son Clothar II in 584, but the alliance was short-lived. Within a few years, he had turned violently against Fredegund and even questioned her son's legitimacy. She was forced to secure the public testimony of a panel of bishops to certify that Clothar was indeed Chilperic's son. In 587, Guntram concluded a treaty with Brunhild and her son Childebert, making the latter his heir. When Guntram died in 593, the Burgundian kingdom reverted to Childebert and, after his death in 596, to his younger son, the nine-year-old Theuderic. The latter ruled Burgundy, including Arles, under the domination of his aged grandmother Brunhild until his own death in 613.

Rusticula's long tenure as abbess began at about the time of Sigebert's assassination in 575. In that capacity, she could hardly escape some involvement in the rivalry of Brunhild and Fredegund. Brunhild and her son intervened actively in the ecclesiastical life of the region. In 586, Brunhild intervened in the appointment of the bishop of Cahors by right of her inheritance of extensive financial rights in five southern towns from her murdered sister

2. Contrary to the clear implications in the vita, it is possible that the line did not end with her. In *Aristocracy in Provence*, Geary speculates (102) that Abbo, son of Rusticus, whose testament disposed of a major fortune in the early eighth century, may have been descended from the same family.

3. Gregory the Great, *Registrum epistularum*, 9:114.

4. Gregory of Tours, HF, 4:28.

5. Ibid., 7:34.

Galswinth. She endowed various monasteries in the region, which would surely commend her to the nuns at Arles. The queen obtained a pallium from Gregory the Great for Siagrius, bishop of Autun (d. 599). He was appointed papal legate with Vigilius, bishop of Arles, to carry out papal reforms of the Gallic church.[6] Brunhild remained close friends with him and may have been present when he entertained Augustine of Canterbury, who was going to begin his evangelical mission at the court of Charibert's daughter Bertha, who had married the king of Kent in England.

After Fredegund's death in 597, Clothar II never ceased to seek vengeance for his father against Brunhild and her descendants. Their violent conflict raged through the Rhôneland. In 603, the queen is believed to have cooperated with Bishop Aridius of Lyon in deposing Bishop Desiderius of Vienne, who was stoned to death in 607.[7] By 612, Brunhild's grandsons were at one another's throats. One of them, Theuderic, successfully wrested Austrasia from his brother, only to die within a year. Finally, in 613, the aged queen made a fresh attack on her dead rival's son, attempting to secure the Austrasian inheritance for her own great-grandsons. The result was a definitive victory for Fredegund's son, Clothar II, followed by the destruction of Sigebert's entire line except for the fugitive Childebert, who fled and was never heard from again. Brunhild herself, aged as she was, suffered a cruel death under the hooves of wild horses for her opposition to Clothar.

Her death brought a measure of peace at last to the Rhône Valley. Rusticula lived for nearly twenty years longer. The *Life of Rusticula* provides few clues as to the nature of the abbess's involvement in these intrigues, but the accusations of treason to Clothar II suggest a continuing loyalty to Brunhild and her supporters. Whether Rusticula's loyalty to the defeated kings of her country led her to shelter the fleeing son of Theuderic or whether she was suspected of some other plot, there seems to be no reason to dispute the probability of the account that follows.[8]

6. See Nelson, "Queens as Jezebels," 53–55, for a discussion of Brunhild's ecclesiastical policies.

7. Fredegar, CL 4:24, 21, sees this as an outbreak of her own irreligious temper. Nelson stresses (57) the politics of the attack and Sigebert's defense of Desiderius in his vita of the martyred bishop. She also ties it to the quarrel between Brunhild and Columbanus in 609 over the legitimacy of Theuderic's sons' claims. "Queens as Jezebels," 57. Bernard Bachrach, personal communication, suggests that Brunhild's supporters in Arles were those whose families were insiders in the foundation.

8. Geary, *Aristocracy in Provence*, 102, connects her to the plot to assassinate Clothar II around 613. Krusch feels that the story of her trial and vindication was simply a hagiographer's plot device modeled on a similar incident in the life of Caesarius of Arles, but we see no reason to credit this argument considering how well the story fits into the known events of the later period. On the other side, it is likely that Rusticula herself and her biographer consciously modeled her behavior on that of Caesarius in a similar situation.

The Life of Rusticula, or Marcia, Abbess of Arles[9]

∎

To the venerable lady in Christ, sister and mother of Christ's flock, head of the congregation, Abbess Celsa, from Florentius, a priest of the church of Tricastina, perpetual greetings in the Lord.[10]

Prologue

∎

1. Obedience deserves first place among the virtues when one, having carefully considered his own abilities, has performed a designated task. Thus, supported by divine Omnipotence and the aid of your prayers, I have written this little book, which I offer to be read aloud in your holy community, setting out in due order the origins and birth of Lady Rusticula, or Marcia, of holy memory, the quality of her life, the origins of her vocation and the saintly powers which she is said to have exercised through divine grace. Whence I entreat you to procure what you can for me through prayer lest, in fleeing blame for being contemptuous, I incur the guilt of being presumptuous. For I believe that by praying you will enable me to complete the work you ordered me to do. In any case, it is quite certain that if anything in this literary effort provokes criticism it will be because of my audacity. Indeed, I shall not escape blame if, in spite of your prayers, anyone sees that there is something superfluous or untrue therein, for she will know beyond doubt, that I have inserted it in this book. For you, venerable in Christ, have revealed to me by trustworthy account in simple and faithful writing what some believers have said in clear testimony that they have known and witnessed about the aforesaid woman's virtues. Therefore, I beseech you to pray, virgins of Christ, that while I submit to your authority, I may, by your intercession, deserve the help which I cannot obtain for myself.

9. This confusion about her name is unclear. Riché, "La Vita S. Rusticula," 371, notes that an inscription of Vaison, CIL 12, 1497, contains the name Rusticus, possibly the relative commemorated in her baptism. Bernard Bachrach, personal communication reflects that it sounds like a name from the maternal Namengut. Marcia, on the other hand, is the name by which a heavenly voice addressed her in a vision after her consecration so that it could be associated with her religious life. The possibility of a change of name in religion also underlies Voguë's theory concerning the identity of Richild as Agnes of Sainte-Croix, cited in chapter 6, n. 8.

10. Celsa was Rusticula's successor. Tricastina, now Saint-Paul-Trois Chateaux, is about thirty kilometers from Vaison, where a church still honors Rusticula's memory. Riché, "La Vita S. Rusticulae," 376, suggests that Florentius may have been raised in the convent and was perhaps present for her death or at least her funeral.

Here ends the Prologue.
Here begins the Life.

1. She was the daughter of Valerian and Clementia, a Roman couple of highest rank worshiping in the Christian faith with utmost reverence, who lived in highest honfor in the district of Hebocassiac situated in the territory of Vaison. A son was born to them and, after a little while, the Lord gave them the most holy child Rusticula.[11] By chance, on the very day of her birth, her father migrated from this light. Then, before many days had passed, the little boy also lay dead. After that, the mother cloaked her sorrow in widow's weeds. Grieving that her husband was gone and her son taken away, she took comfort in the daughter sprung from her womb's fertility. In holy baptismal water, her mother offered her solemnly to Christ in the font of regeneration and called her by her family name Rusticula. But she was called Marcia by the entire household.[12] She was beautiful of face and elegant of form. She was so loved by friends and acquaintances as well as the household that they all rejoiced as though she had been granted to them by heavenly grace.

2. One night, it seemed to her mother, as she lay sleeping in bed, that she was, in ecstasy, lovingly nursing two chicks of a dove. One shone white as snow and the other was covered by many colors. While she rejoiced over them with great affection, it seemed to her as though a servant had announced that Saint Caesarius, the Bishop of Arles, stood without.[13] Hearing joyfully of that most holy man's arrival, she hurried with delight to meet him. Saluting him most hospitably, she prayed most humbly that his advent might shower blessings on her home. And entering the house, he blessed her. With due honor, she prayed that she might be worthy to win his praise and that he might deign to take food and drink. He answered: "The Lord be with you, my daughter. I want you to give me the dove's chick which you seemed to be nursing so tenderly." Hesitating within herself at that, she thought: how did he know that she had them near her? And she said she had no such thing. Then he said to her: "Before God, I swear I will not leave here until you grant my request." Then she could not refuse but showed them to the holy man and immediately offered them to him. Then he was overjoyed and he took to

11. Valerian and Clementia are designated *clarissimus*, a Roman title of nobility. Rustica is an important name in the area of Vaison; its spread is discussed by Heinzelmann, "Les changements de la dénomination," 19–42, and *Bischofherrschaft in Gallien*.

12. This is probably a reference to her father's family, but the fact that the heavenly voice called her "Marcia" when she was in the convent (c. 9) suggests that *ab omni domus familia* might conceivably refer to her religious community.

13. Caesarius had died in 542.

his breast that chick which gleamed with such whiteness and withdrew bidding her farewell. Awaking then, she wondered within herself what this meant and asked herself why that man, who was dead, should have appeared to her. She did not realize that Christ had chosen that handmaiden for His spouse. For He has said: "A city that is set on a hill cannot be hid. Neither do men light a candle and put it under a bushel, but on a candlestick, and it giveth light to all that are in the house."[14]

3. When the virgin was five years old, she was abducted by a certain nobleman named Ceraonius.[15] Bringing her to his house, he entrusted her to his mother for nurturing so that he might couple with her in matrimony when she reached the legitimate age. But He Who never sleeps and has not slept through eternity, He Who keeps watch over Israel,[16] by His Holy Spirit revealed to the most blessed Liliola, Abbess of the monastery founded by Father Caesarius of most holy memory in the city of Arles, that she should ask the most venerable Bishop Siagrius how she might prevail upon the most glorious King Guntram to have her enter within the monastery enclosure.[17] When this was broached to the aforesaid Ceraonius, he entreated with many prayers and gifts that she be granted to him in marriage. But by concession of divine grace, the Lord imparted to the king's heart that he should send her to the holy Liliola through a certain abbot, a man of excellent behavior. For the Lord Christ had prepared her for Himself as a chosen vessel in sanctification of honor.[18]

4. Indeed, I will show that the Lord did wonders through her while she was still in her infancy.[19] As the order of the king was fulfilled, they took to the road and landed on the bank of the most noble river Rhône. Then her companions were surprised to find that they had provided themselves with far too little food. But the Lord does not withhold His goodness from them that walk in innocence. To snatch their souls from death and nourish them in their hunger, He bestowed a gift of His mercy on the needy ones through His handmaid. Thus, while the venerable maid walked with one of her attendants, she saw a huge fish near the river bank. Spreading the cloak she was

14. Matthew 5:14–15.

15. *Rapta* (raped) had the meaning of theft rather than assault on women in the early middle ages. Riché, "La Vita S. Rusticula," 371, notes the parallel to Radegund.

16. Psalms 121:4.

17. Liliola, third abbess of Saint Jean, 559–574, during whose regime Radegund acquired the fragment of the cross. Fortunatus mentions her; see *Carmen* 8, 3, 43. Siagrius, from a famous Gallo-Roman family, was bishop of Autun. See Krusch, ed., MGH, SRM 1:700, n. 2. Guntram (d. 593) was a son of Clothar and Ingund. Liliola's treatment of Charibert's wife is detailed in Gregory of Tours, HF, 4:26.

18. 1 Thessalonians 4:4.

19. Infancy generally means before attaining the age of reason, about six or seven years old.

wearing along the water's edge, she caught the fish and held it firmly. But then it began to struggle and to pull her toward itself. Truly, the grace of the Lord shed strength on His serving girl! She pulled her catch out with all speed and the fish was so large that it satiated all who were with her. Wondering at the deed, they said: "Truly, it appears from this that she will catch many souls with the word of God and consecrate them to Christ the Lord."

5. Then they came to the city of Arles where, at that time, the bishop was the apostolic man, Sapaudus.[20] They led her to the holy abbess Liliola, who rejoiced at her coming and took her with great celebration into the monastery enclosure where she brought her into the flock of Christ's virgins, teaching her all the holiness of the faith.[21] When her mother learned what had happened, weeping wildly with her sorrow, she sent to the bishop of the city entreating him with gifts and prayers to find an opportunity to return her own captive child to her. Thus she prayed him: "Have mercy, I beg, on my humility, most holy father, and relieve a woman afflicted by the loss of her only child. I look at the privileges of my house and its countless multitude of servants and I do not know to whom I can leave them. Give me back the fruit of my hopes! Who now will care for my old age when the only one I had is lost? I seek my little sprout and cannot find her! I know not where to run, where to turn! I pray your Beatitude for grace, and call God to witness that you should have mercy on me, stricken with such unbearable sorrow, and order my only child restored to me in my widowhood."[22] The man filled with God replied to this: "I long to give your nobility what you ask, but I dare not transgress the precepts of the Holy Name. The riches which you promise to give her will quickly come to an end. But the wealth that has been prepared by Christ Himself will be enjoyed in eternal bliss. Therefore I beseech you, sweetest daughter, console yourself. Do not weep for her whom you lost for we believe that she will reign with Christ." The mother took no consolation from this but suffered even greater sorrow. She sent some of her relatives with gifts of different sorts, riches and worldly ornaments to persuade Christ's virgin to renounce her holy vow. But the girl, whose faith was firmly founded on an unshakable rock, scorned them all as so much dung and persevered unmoved and unchanged.

---

20. Successor of Aurelian, he attended the council of Paris in 552 and was later appointed apostolic vicar for all Gaul. Krusch, ed., MGH, Epistolae 3:73. He died in 586. Gregory of Tours, HF, 8:30.
21. At best, she could only have conformed narrowly to the Rule, c. 7, which prohibits the entrance of infants before the age of six or seven, when they can learn their letters and submit to discipline.
22. Despite these complaints there is a strong possibility that some representatives of the family survived to produce Rusticus, the father of Abbo whose testament, about a century later, forms the centerpiece of Geary, Aristocracy in Province. It may even be that the widow subsequently thwarted them all by marrying again.

6. The Lord deigned to give her such grace and capacity of memory that, within a short space of time, she had learned all the psalms and memorized the entire scripture. It has been said that once, while the infant was learning the psalms, she fell asleep, as children do, leaning against the knee of one of the sisters who whispered the psalm in her ear. When she awoke, she recited it by heart as though she read it. Thus she fulfilled the scripture: "I sleep, but my heart waketh."[23] She showed such charity and humility in the holy congregation that all held her in greatest affection. For she was strong in all things, prudent in speech, well behaved, elegant of form, remarkable for her age, mild and gentle in every way and obedient to Christ's precepts. Thus she might testify by her acts to the fame of her propriety so that even at that time she deserved to hear her spouse's worthy voice saying: "Thou art fair as the moon."[24]

7. Therefore, when the blessed Liliola migrated from this light to the Lord, all that holy congregation felt that God's beloved Rusticula should be chosen as their mother. She refused, calling herself unworthy for this work. What more? With the Lord's favor, the devotion of God's handmaids was rewarded and the honor was imposed upon her. She kept watch at Christ's holy rudder over the souls that belonged to her. She was then about eighteen years old.[25] But she began to devote herself to abstinence and vigils taking food only every third day. She wore a hair shirt, fulfilling the words of the Apostle saying: "In many labors, in watchings, in fastings."[26] Indeed, in the nocturnal hours, while the other sisters slept, she remained all night long in the church praying with psalms, hymns and prayers for the flock entrusted to her and for all people with tears to the Lord.

8. So the holy virgin flourished and, prompted by the Holy Spirit, she conceived in her soul that she should establish a larger place of prayer for Christ's virgins. Meanwhile, she constructed temples with fortified walls for the saints. At the beginning, while the foundations of the church were being laid, exulting, the blessed mother brought stones to the workmen with her own hands. When that work was done, favored and inspired by the Lord, she built a church in honor of the Holy Cross. Then a building of wondrous magnitude constructed in Heaven was shown to her in a vision and she understood this to mean that the Lord was commanding her to build something similar on earth. Joyfully, she hastened to fulfill her Lord's orders faithfully and constructed a temple of sparkling beauty. Then it occurred to

---

23. Song of Solomon 5:2.
24. Song of Solomon 6:10.
25. Her rule extended from 575 to 632.
26. 2 Corinthians 6:5.

her that the Lord's cross should be moved to this building which was higher and that she should consecrate the one built earlier to the Archangel Michael.[27] She convoked Christ's holy priests and established seven altars there. The first was in honor of Christ's cross; the next for the holy Archangels, Gabriel and Raphael. After some years, she added those of Saint Thomas the Apostle, Maurice, Sebastian and Pontius. For as the Apostle says, the wise architect laid a foundation; what he built on earth he found afterwards in Heaven.[28] For those whom she venerably worshipped with such love on earth prepared starry mansions for her in Paradise by their appeals.

9. One day, around noon, as she rested in saint Peter's basilica, a voice spoke to her and called her name saying, "Marcia, imitate your Lord when He was hanging on the cross. Imitate your fellow servant Stephen when the Jews stoned him. Say, 'Father, forgive them, for they know not what they do.' "[29] After that, she woke up and wondered what the vision was for. But with his malign counsel, the Devil, who is always envious of the good, persuaded a certain bishop, Maximus by name but not by work, and a certain prince named Ricomer who was noble according to the world but not with God, to bear false witness against God's handmaid.[30] Going to King Clothar, they accused her of secretly supporting the king.[31] Hearing this, he was moved to violent anger and ordered the aforesaid prince to make careful inquiry into the matter and summon her. Coming into the town of Arles with many bishops and others like himself, he began rather to heap up threats than to inquire into the truth of things. When the holy flock saw their mother attacked with such lying words, in their usual way they seized weapons of celestial grace. Modulating their voices in psalms, they called upon the heavenly defender who sent Saint Daniel to save Saint Susanna from the condem-

27. This suggests that she had a relic of the cross, which might conceivably have resulted from the correspondence between Caesaria II of Arles and Radegund. Miracles recounted in c. 13 and c. 16 seem to refer to a relic of some sort that she carried with her.

28. Cf. 1 Corinthians 3:10.

29. Luke 23:34.

30. Krusch notes that Mabillon thought that Maximus was the bishop of Avignon but could find no confirmation. Riché, "La Vita S. Rusticula," 374, cites Duprat, Les origines de l'église d'Avignon, 72, that the relics of a bishop named Maximus were in the treasury in the ninth century. Ricomer was instituted a patrician by Theuderic II about 606 or 607. Fredegar, CL 4:29. "Prince" is thus an official title, probably indicating that he was governor of the province. Perhaps he was thus proving his loyalty to Theuderic's conqueror.

31. Krusch suggests that the king in question was Childebert, son of Theuderic II, who had just been killed with two of his sons and his grandmother Brunhild by the victorious Clothar II in 613. Fredegar, CL 4:42. Riché, "La Vita S. Rusticula," 374, points out that Guntram's treaty with Theuderic and his friendship with Liliola might have led to this suspicion, or might explain Rusticula's guilt. She would have been about fifty-six in 613.

nation of the impious.[32] One of the aforesaid man's friends, a certain abandoned person named Audoaldus who wanted to show his loyalty to the prince, sought to strike Christ's handmaid with his unsheathed sword. But the Lord, Who said through His prophet: "Their swords shall enter into their own hearts and their bows shall be broken,"[33] caused the raised sword to fall from his hands and saved the innocent from death. Indeed, the hands and feet of the man who had made the attempt were swiftly paralyzed. Then he raised his voice wailing: "Oh, pity me! I own that for my outrage of trying to slaughter God's handmaid, I deserve to be afflicted with these cursed and bitter torments." And so his life ended as he deserved.[34]

10. The said Ricomer then sent some of his retainers to the king to swear that Christ's most blessed virgin had been found guilty of this trumped up charge. Raging with greater fury, the king sent one of his optimates, named Faraulf, to bring her into his presence.[35] He arrived and gravely began to insist that the virgin of Christ be taken out of her holy sheepfold. She protested that she would rather obey the King of Heaven than of earth and would die rather than transgress the precepts of the holy father Caesarius.[36] Realizing that if he did not carry out his orders, he would himself be in jeopardy, Faraulf began to swear to Nymfidius, the governor of the city, with threatening words, that if he did not take her from the monastery that very day on the King's command, he risked losing his own head in the future. With tears and due humility, Nymfidius, who greatly venerated God's handmaid, begged her to come out voluntarily without violence, protesting on his oath that if any impious order were given, his own blood would be poured out with that of Christ's handmaid to his greater future joy.

11. Therefore was she taken from her sacred sheepfold, at the instigation of those who were there. No testimony to her innocence was heard nor the truth of the accusation questioned but she was condemned by false accusations and placed under guard in a cell of a monastery in the city. It is impossible to say how bitterly the flock she ruled with holy leadership was

---

32. Daniel 6:42–43.

33. Psalms 37:15.

34. This entire chapter throws much light on the reality of cloistering as it applied to the monastery. For a discussion of the contradictions in the principle, see Nolte, "Klosterleben von Frauen."

35. *Vita Lupi Senonensi*, 10, states that when Clothar took Burgundy from Theuderic II he appointed Duke Faraulf to clarify his regalian rights. Only his name links him to Charibert's chamberlain, who died shortly after being accused of attempting to assassinate Guntram in 573. Gregory of Tours, HF, 7:18. Ebling, *Prosopographie*, 149, is convinced that they are the same, as is Ewig, *Spätantikes und fränkisches Gallien*, 193.

36. According to the Rule of Caesarius, c. 2, "If any wish to renounce the world and enter the sacred flock, they should not go out of the monastery even to death, nor should they be seen at the gate of the basilica."

afflicted, seeing their pastor impiously ripped from them. They poured out their tears but there is none to give pious help or even the comfort of condolences. Christ's sheepfold, which had echoed with their modulating voices praising God in psalms, resounded with groans ululating for their absent mother. Day turned into night, sweetness into bitterness, canticles into dirges, light into darkness, life into death and all would rather die than live in the absence of their most pious mother. Meanwhile, as she kept her customary vigils of holy prayer in the monastic cell, as we said above, evil men armed by diabolical counsel came upon her, smothering the house with stones. But, protected as she was by the grace of Christ, nothing could harm her.

12. In this way, seven days went by before she was taken from the city on the journey she had begun. But the Lord, Who does not abandon those who hope in Him but exalts the humble, He Who sent an angel to free the sons of Israel from opprobrium, through the Holy Spirit revealed to a certain apostolic man, Domnolus by name and merits, bishop of the city of Vienne, that he should go on foot straight to the king and denounce him for giving grave offense to God by condemning Christ's handmaid through an unjust judgment.[37] For that unmerciful order, God would immediately deprive him of his son.[38] Hearing this, the king was gripped by fear and sent two counts, both God-fearing men, to lead her to him with honor and reverence and provide her with whatever she needed in every city.

13. I will now tell plainly how many miracles the Lord performed through her on the road. In the cities that God's servant approached, persons vexed with unclean spirits foretold her coming several days in advance, saying: "Behold, the handmaiden of God comes that she may torment us and evict us from our habitation." They went out to meet her about three or four stadia and humbly prostrated themselves confessing and saying: "Why do you come to torment us, servant of Christ, to expel us from our homes?" Then Christ's handmaid asked the men for what cause or negligence the evil spirit had entered into them. Each one confessed simply: one because he had

---

37. Domnolus had been appointed by a synod of bishops in Chalons in 603, when Theuderic II was king of Burgundy. Fredegar, CL 4:24, attributes his appointment to the machinations of Queen Brunhild and Bishop Aridius of Lyon, who wanted his predecessor Desiderius deposed and exiled. Domnolus attended Clothar's general synod at Paris in 614, and Riché thinks that he may have spoken for Rusticula on that occasion. Denounce is a rather strong word to use, but it reflects the legal character of denunciatio.

38. Krusch, ed., MGH, SRM 345 n. 2, believes this to be a reference to Maroveus, Clothar's son who had been captured in 604 fighting Theuderic. Fredegar, CL 4:26. When Clothar condemned Brunhild in 613, he named his son as one of the ten Frankish kings whose deaths he laid at her door. This implies that Maroveus's fate was still uncertain when Rusticula was taken into custody. Riché, "La Vita S. Rusticula," 375, thinks the language of the text points to another son living with Clothar.

drawn a cup of water without the sign of the cross, another because of gluttony, another for perjury, another for theft, another for homicide or for other evils. One of the demons told her that he had placed himself in a fountain so that when an unhappy man tried to drink its water without making the sign of the cross the evil spirit gained ingress into him. Then they called the cross and nails of the Lord to witness that she should not order them to leave their domiciles. But, praying lest she might shortly be overcome by their boasting, she laid the Lord's cross of redemption which she carried with her on their heads.[39] Immediately they were saved.

14. With much devotion she came to the basilica of the holy martyr Desiderius,[40] and discovered the gates locked where the holy corpse lay. Full of faith, she immediately called upon Christ's martyr: "Most blessed friend of God, come to me now in my tribulations and permit me to approach that I may prostrate my body at your holy feet and pray." As she spoke, the chains were broken and the door opened. Her whole body prostrate on the ground, she obtained by prayer what she had entreated in swift faith.

15. Since it would be tedious to tell in order all the miracles that were done through her in praise of the Lord's name in every city, let us go forward to the end. When she had been led before the king, she approached and greeted him with Christ as her guide. And once her own presence rather than common gossip testified for her, the king and queen and all their optimates began to venerate her with great honor and reverence. In fact, the king with his lords asked if the things said of her were really true. With God as her witness she made oath that they were not, nor could she even think of any such thing. While this was going on, anxiety filled the king's mind. His son whom he greatly loved was brought to the point of death. What had been foretold to him, that he would lose his son because of the unjust sentence he had laid on God's servant, was deservedly fulfilled. And when he was dead, the sorrowful and grieving king did not know what he should have them do with Christ's handmaid. Coming to him, the lords of his palace advised him to order that God's beloved Rusticula whom he had brought before him in great shame should be restored to her own in great honor. So it was done.

---

39. This strongly suggests that she not only may have had a relic of the cross at her convent but also carried it with her in some sort of standard.

40. Desiderius was deposed in 603, and Fredegar blamed Brunhild for his death in 607. The politics that drew him into the same cause with Domnolus is mystifying. Fredegar, an enemy of Brunhild, and the Visigothic author Sisebut of *Vita Desiderius* depict the bishop of Vienne as a victim of her hatred. But in 600, Gregory I refused Desiderius the pallium, tactfully alleging a lack of precedent. *Epistola* 9:112. However, the same excuse did not prevent Gregory from gratifying Brunhild's request for a pallium for Siagrius of Autun. Perhaps death had changed Desiderius's politics?

Provided with his authorization, the most blessed one returned to her own.[41] Who can describe how much joy there was in that province?

16. Then, as she came into the city of Sens, a man whom the Devil had seized threw himself out of an upper story above the litter in which the servant of God was being carried. Running swiftly, he tore aside the curtain which covered the litter's window, and putting his head inside tried to devour the blessed one's hand. She sat up quickly and, with her right hand, she laid the standard of the cross on his forehead. Prostrated on the ground, he vomited out blood as in the shape of a man and swiftly recovered his pristine health.

17. It would take far too long to tell all I could of her miracles but I will describe how her own people greeted her return with joy and exultation. When it was announced that the venerable handmaid of God was on her way back and was near the city, a great crowd of all ages and sexes ran out, religious, laity, nobles and commoners, rich and poor, natives and strangers. They all rejoiced; they all exulted. They all gave thanks to God for such an intercessor. They who had mourned the loss of such an intercessor rejoiced that she was restored by God's grace. And when her advent was heralded to the virgins of Christ, they were filled with unutterable joy and began singing hymns of exultation to the Lord who had restored the pastor to the afflicted sheep. Going once more into the holy sheepfold whence she had been torn, she was greeted by the modulated voices of her daughters chanting and saying: "Glory to God on high and on earth peace to men of good will."[42] Folded into the virgin chorus, the pious mistress again residing in her own seat raised her voice with theirs in thanks to the Lord, and, exhorting her disciples who had been excessively afflicted in her absence, the holy mother professed to believe that she had been restored by their prayers. Breaking into the psalmist's voice, she said: "Oh magnify the Lord with me," most beloved daughters, "and let us exalt His name together. I sought the Lord and He heard me and delivered me from all my fears."[43] "He hath made the barren woman to keep house, and to be a joyful mother of children."[44]

18. Not long afterwards, those hostile men who had accused Christ's handmaid came to her confused and repentant, humbly asking her pardon that she would forgive them punishment for their crimes. And, full of the

41. Bernard Bachrach, personal communication, suggests that this "auctoritas" was a document given her.

42. Luke 2:1. Following the rule of Lérins, Caesarius's Rule, c. 66, appoints this canticle to follow the Te Deum at matins, which Taft discusses in *Liturgy of the Hours*, 103.

43. Psalms 34:3.

44. Psalms 113:9.

sweetness of the Holy Spirit, she was swift to take them into her heart as though they had raised her up to great honors. Sweetly she said that she would pray the Lord for them, for she had read the Holy Gospel: "If ye forgive men their trespasses, your heavenly father will also forgive you."[45]

19. The storm having passed, she dwelt together with her daughters nurturing them sweetly for fourteen years, teaching them all the holiness of the faith. Then one of the sisters was totally exhausted by the dangerous infestation of a noonday demon.[46] She was utterly unable to raise her trembling body until the Lord, pouring out divine clemency, deigned to inspire another of the faithful sisters to burn some of the blessed mother's hair and give it to her to drink in pure water. Feeling her pristine health return immediately, she gave thanks with greatest devotion to God for her bodily recovery.

20. Another time, a terrible pestilence overwhelmed the people of the city and even some of God's handmaids met a sudden end and passed to Christ. The most blessed mother became most gravely afflicted for their sakes. Two of her sisters in turn were struck with blows from that sword. They were near to death, their eyes darkening so that they could not see the light of day. Scarcely able to speak, they begged the holy mother to pray for them. She went to the place where Saint Caesarius lay in the oratory. Prostrate on the ground, God's handmaid tearfully prayed God her Maker to restore life to those so near to death. When she arose from the office of prayer, she believed that she was to receive what she had asked from the Lord. She visited them and inquired how they were. Already convalescing, they thanked God and the mother, for her prayers had soon freed them from the threat of death.

21. Many things could be written at greater length about her miracles, but, lest the prolixity of my discourse should seem to generate boredom with reading, let us make an end to the work so that the words which are read may refresh the readers and the listeners, inspired by her example, and through intercession of good works, may partake of eternal life. For I believe, most beloved virgins of Christ, that your holy souls will be satisfied with what I have faithfully recorded, in my own insignificant words to the best of my ability concerning the virtues of the most holy mother, my lady Rusticula or Marcia, and her institutions and teaching, to the praise and honor of almighty God. Now since time presses, though I bring sorrow upon you, I will begin my account of how the Lord called her to those blessed rewards which are prepared for the just.

22. She had reached seventy-seven years of age. Strengthened with Christ's

---

45. Matthew 6:14.

46. A sudden and violent attack depriving the victim of her faculties is customarily attributed to the noonday demon. Graus, *Volk, Herrscher*, 82, sets this miracle in a broader context of contemporary beliefs in magic.

help, while she was on earth she could always triumph manfully against the Devil who attacked her incessantly.[47] At last, rejoicing, she was called to the reward prepared for her in Heaven, that she might receive what "eye hath not seen nor ear heard, neither have entered into the heart of man, the things which God hath prepared for them that love Him,"[48] because she had prudently and faithfully dispensed wheat from the Lord's storehouse to the household in her charge and because, aflame with the zeal of the Holy Spirit, she made firm God's tottering temples with the rigor of righteousness. This was her constant effort, her constant intent, that none of her flock should be afflicted with needless sadness or burdened with excessive labors or grow weary, but she, with a fervent spirit, would still herd them all to rest. It is a wonder how this blessed mother completed so many offices while her body was never free of daily sickness, yet it was so. The congregation she gathered from every part of the earth, breathing together in love, all called her lady and pious mother. They had all come to know her compassion for them, for she would count their sorrows as her own, suffering with their afflictions and reviving as they recovered. When the flock met to celebrate the holy offices together, she watered every heart from the rising font of celestial doctrine. I cannot express how she corrected them with such sweet words and pious charity that she did not punish them like a mistress but with a mother's loving kindness instructed them with beneficial advice. I declare I can barely think about it let alone describe it. Oh, truly blessed! Love for Christ filled her whole heart! Worthy as that steward who doubled his talents, she deserved to hear her master say that she was placed above many and might hear these words as a faithful and true description of her own guardianship of her flock: "Well done, good and faithful servant, enter into the joy of thy Lord."[49]

23. So it happened on Friday,[50] that she was singing the customary vespers with her daughters followed by the liturgy of the duodena.[51] She felt her body grow weak and drew on all her strength to recite the readings as was her

47. Krusch notes that if Rusticula were five in 561, the earliest date when Guntram could have intervened in her abduction, she would be seventy-seven in 632. This is not consistent with c. 19, which indicates that she died fourteen years after her trial by Clothar, which Krusch sets in the year of the king's accession, 613, putting Rusticula's death at 627. This chronological difficulty provides one of Krusch's arguments against the authenticity of the life, but Riché, "La Vita S. Rusticula," responds that none of these dates are securely established by the text.

48. 1 Corinthians 2:9.

49. Matthew 25:21.

50. The sixth day of the sabbath *sexta sabbati*.

51. Krusch interprets this as *duodecima*, or vespers sung at 6 P.M. as in Caesarius's Rule, c. 66, and discussed by McCarthy in the preface to her translation of the *Rule for the Nuns of Saint Caesarius of Arles*, 74–75. Taft, *Liturgy of the Hours*, 155, notes that in his sermon (136:1–4) Caesarius uses the word *duodena* to describe the monastic evening psalmody following vespers in southern Gaul.

custom. For now she knew that she was swiftly about to migrate to the Lord. Thus on the dawning of that Saturday, she began to feel moderate chills and all her limbs weakened. Lying in bed she was then overcome with raging fever but not so much that her mouth ever ceased praising God. With eyes intent on Heaven, she never relaxed her unconquered spirit from prayer. She commended her daughters whom she was leaving orphaned to the Lord and her strong spirit consoled those who wept. For then she was worthy to say with the Apostle: "I have fought the good fight, I have finished the course, I have kept the faith: henceforth there is laid up for me a crown of righteousness."[52] It was time for her to be called to rest, and to become one of the company of God's elect. By the next day, Sunday, she was yet more gravely ill. Though it was her custom that her bed was made only with the turning of the year, yet they asked the servant of God whether she would indulge herself a little with some softer straw to support her heavily fatigued body. But she could not bring herself to agree. Then on Monday[53] the feast of the birth of Saint Laurence Martyr, the strength of her body was yet further dispersed and phlegm sounded more strongly in her chest.[54] Seeing this, all the virgins of Christ were sorrowful. They wept and groaned and, when the third hour of the day was come, because of their excessive sorrow, the flock repeated their psalms in silence. Compassionately, the holy mother asked why she could hardly hear their chanting voices. They answered that the grief of their mourning disabled them. "Sing more clearly," she said, " that I may receive comfort, for truly the psalms are sweet enough to me." Yet another day her body remained with barely any vital motion, though her eyes kept their usual vigor, shining like stars. Looking here and there, lacking power to speak, she motioned silently with her hand to comfort the weeping. And, when one of the sisters touched her feet in order to see whether they were hot or cold, she said: "This is not the hour." But a little later, after the sixth hour of the day, her face lit up, her eyes shone as though smiling and her gloriously happy soul was borne aloft to heaven to join the countless choirs of saints.

24. Now for sure it is impossible to express the sorrow that struck the handmaids of Christ. None could stop groaning, weeping and wailing as they mourned the pious mother they had lost. They thought the roof of the oratory must fall at her departure. Universal love demanded universal mourning and the sorrow of all who loved her was a seedbed of tears. With failing voices their groaning and clamoring echoed and they cried: "Oh most pious Lord, why have you turned your face from us? Did we no longer deserve to

52. 2 Timothy 4:7–8.
53. "The second day of the Sabbath," *secunda sabbati*.
54. August 10.

be trained by so sweet a mother or nourished by that pious love? Of course, she is joyful, having migrated to heaven in reward for her righteous labors. But woe to us! For at the same time, she leaves us orphans on earth! Who now will show such sweetness to her children as our pious mother did to us! Who could ever express with her own lips how you bore the burden of our childishness, day and night praying to God incessantly for our sins?" But why prolong this? For the more you count up all you have lost, virgins of Christ, though we speak to commemorate such a handmaid of God with praising lips, the more your sorrow overcomes you.

25. So the holy body was laid out according to the custom of mourners and the diligent orphans multiplied their services with a great display of faith. And the next day the bishop of the city, Theodosius the Pontiff, together with all his clergy, came and took possession of the holy body laid out on gold and precious stones among crosses and tall burning candles of wax.[55] And not only the faithful but even Jews joined the throngs of people assembled to venerate her at these services and they all strove to outdo one another with their tears. Then, just outside the monastery, as her corpse was being borne before the weeping multitude of her virgins, honored by the psalm-singing chorus, one of the monastery's elderly servants loudly bewailed the loss of his eyesight. Asking to be set before the bier, he begged with the greatest display of faith that the Lord of all would restore his sight. And immediately the lost light and the power of sight were restored. Meanwhile, the venerable corpse was borne with due honors to the basilica of saint Mary and the mysteries of the holy altar were celebrated. The holy, radiant, shining corpse was laid in her tomb at the right side of the altar. And rightly so, she who dedicated the glory of her virginity to Christ in fullest faith, now is seated at the right side of the Lamb, honored with perpetual titles of praise, singing the new song, dressed in snowy white and decorated all over with precious gems amid the chorus of virgins in which the Blessed Virgin Mary holds first place.

26. But it would be a crime to pass in silence over what God has caused to be done through her prayers after her crossing that the merits of her virtues might be properly revealed. For example, one of the handmaids of Christ was tormented by a raging tertian fever. But with great faith, she took the cloth in which the body of the blessed mother had been wrapped and washed it in clean water which she then drank. And she was freed from the pain and fever and cured.

27. One of the servants of that monastery sorely lamented that he had lost the ability to walk because of an illness. In his sleep, he was ordered to ask the

55. Krusch, ed., MGH, SRM 4:350, n. 1, notes that Theodosius was deposed as bishop of Arles by the synod of Chalons in 650 for his indecent life.

handmaids of Christ to wash the four corners of the pallet where the holy mother had rested and give him the water to drink. When that was done, he immediately deserved to regain the best of health. And any sick persons, no matter how seriously afflicted, who placed the smallest scrap of linen or cloth from her garments on their bodies and appealed to her sanctity with fullest faith deserved to receive the body's recovery and the soul's salvation from the Lord.

28. Thus it is clearly to be seen that after her death, this most blessed mother exercised the same care and solicitude as when she was living in the body for the souls in her charge. Visiting each of them, she chastised and admonished them so that they should hasten to the holy work with fervent care.

29. Oh, most venerable handmaid of Christ! While, for your righteous labors, you exult with joy in Paradise, deign to offer prayers to God the Father for the flock under your care. Be an advocatrix for them to the Lord Jesus Christ that all may deserve to rejoice with you in that blessed state where is the bliss of angels, the joy of prophets, the praise of apostles, the victory of martyrs, the exultation of virgins, the glory of priests and the perpetual beatitude of all who praise God forever.

30. Therefore, I pray your bounty, holy virgins of Christ, that, through the ineffable omnipotence of God, as often as these deeds are recounted to you, you will always remember me in your prayers who wrote this work so carefully; that the Lord Jesus Christ, to whom the Father gave the judgment of all, will free my soul, chained by innumerable sins, from death and pluck it from the pit of Hell and bring me to the glory of the blessed souls in the bountiful gift of His forgiveness, Who lives, rules and reigns with the Father and the Holy Spirit, God from everlasting to everlasting. Amen.

8
Glodesind, Abbess in Metz
(ca. 600)

Glodesind is the first in a chain of saints associated with the Austrasian nobility. Her father, Wintrio, an Austrasian duke with extensive holdings in Champagne, was one of the most formidable nobles in the east Frankish kingdom. Her mother, Godila, was the daughter of another Austrasian duke. Wintrio's sister, Rotlinda, was abbess of Ören, a convent at Trier that may be the same house to which Oda retired when her husband, Arnulf, became bishop of Metz in 614. Arnulf (582–641) had probably already retired to Remiremont at the time of her first translation (i.e., removal of her body to another location), but his influence remained strong. His son had married Begga, the daughter of Pippin of Landen and sister of Gertrude of Nivelles, linking the family to the Carolingian dynasty. Although the problems inherent in eighth-century naming customs make it impossible to be sure, the Carolingian monk who recorded Glodesind's life and subsequent cult history seems to believe that she had some connection with the sainted bishop. If that is so, it would explain the late blossoming of her cult. Arnulf was one of the Carolingian family's most important saints, and Glodesind's biographer was clearly anxious to claim some kinship with him to enhance the reputation of his heroine. Her anonymous biographer emphasizes that the church where she was first entombed was later dedicated to the sainted bishop.

No miracles are claimed for the young woman in her lifetime. Although her memory was apparently revered locally, the miracles that established her claim to sainthood did not begin until a quarter of a century or more after her

Vita Antiquior, by an anonymous monk, AS, July 25, 198–224. The remarks of this biographer in c. 20 indicate that he wrote after 830 but that he probably consulted an earlier life used in the monastery. The final set of Glodesind's miracles were added soon after the episcopate of Walo (876–882) by the Bollandists' estimation. The ninth-century biographer claims Glodesind lived for about thirty years. Her exact dates are unknown, although the story is set in the waning days of the reign of Childebert II (d. 596). The editors of the AS argue that she must have been born around 578 and died about 608 in order to conform to her father's known date of death in 598.

death, when her body was translated from its initial resting place to the convent that later bore her name. The first record of her life, now lost, provided a source for the present rendition. In this context, her cult must be seen as part of a process of sacralizing the Carolingian family that culminated in the eighth century with their sacerdotal kingship.[1] Thus the life of a pious nun may have been transformed into full-blown hagiography with the rise of her family in the seventh century and its ultimate construction of a monarchy based on divine sanction.

Glodesind's brief life—she died when about thirty—was shadowed by the violence that swirled around the Austrasian court in her home city of Metz. There, about thirty years before this story begins, Radegund's friend, Fortunatus, first encountered the young Queen Brunhild on her arrival from Spain to marry Sigebert. Throughout her long life, as a ruling queen and then as a dominating dowager controlling the policies of her sons and grandsons, Brunhild was never absent from Austrasia for long, and its nobles were inevitably entangled in the bloody power struggles of the Merovingian royal families.[2]

In 590, Brunhild frustrated an assassination attempt against her son, Childebert II. This event may shed some light on the story of Glodesind and the unhappy fate of her young husband. She would probably have been about eleven or twelve in 590, old enough to marry but young enough to explain Obolenus's failure to consummate the marriage immediately. It is possible that he may have been involved in the conspiracy against Childebert, which would account for his year-long imprisonment and eventual execution by that king. The delay may have been an effort to hold him hostage against his father-in-law's good behavior. Obolenus was a great lord of Champagne, and Wintrio was there at this time.

In 591, Wintrio was ordered into Italy at the head of an Austrasian army intended to fight the Lombards. He gathered his troops in Champagne.[3] Then he and his companion, Audoald, decided to attack Metz first, where

1. Prinz, "Heiligenkult und Adelsherrschaft," analyzes this phenomenon at some length and believes that it represents an effort on the part of the Frankish nobility to regain a charisma lost to Christianity.

2. Brunhild's reputation swings from the extreme of wickedness to near-sanctification depending upon the political preferences of her contemporary chroniclers. Modern authors have not found a reliable way to assess her objectively. Her political capacities were certainly great to enable her to stay alive and in control of her husband's kingdoms, but her career was so intensely devoted to the effort to maintain that control that she had little time for more constructive efforts. At least one scholar, however, has attempted to see her as a benevolent influence on his native Lorraine. Huguenin, *Histoire du royaume*, 189, depicts her as a builder of roads and public fountains and the probable promulgator of the Ripuarian code of laws informed by the relative sophistication of Visigothic Spain.

3. Ibid., 252.

they callously ravaged their own home territories.[4] This ferocious attack, which dismayed Gregory of Tours, might be explained if, in the wake of her husband's execution, Glodesind had taken refuge in the cathedral, determined to avoid another marriage and preserve her virginity in the cloister. Glodesind's defiance of her father is a new theme in medieval hagiography. It may have been drawn from the antique story of Thecla, but if so, the hagiographer failed to draw the parallel. This suggests that perhaps it is an original story of a desperate girl, which provided a stock theme for later writers. The softer versions of the theme in some of the seventh-century lives that follow in this volume may be reworkings of the same story. The tale of the veil miraculously bestowed on Glodesind by an angel was adapted by Hucbald of Saint Amand in his redaction of the Life of Aldegund.[5] It thus appears to be a ninth-century topos, possibly intended to soften the exemplary strength of a virgin's defiance of her parents. The undisputed violence of Wintrio against Metz, however, lends support to the authenticity of the story at hand. A family squabble, an angry father, and a murdered son-in-law are more than sufficient to explain the violence of a Merovingian lord.

In any case, by 593, Wintrio had repaired his political position and was sufficiently friendly with Childebert and his mother to have joint command of the royal army that fell upon Fredegund's base in Neustria after Guntram's death in 593.[6] According to the highly partisan account of an eighth-century monk of Paris, their effort was frustrated by a humiliating trick of the Neustrians.[7] Thereafter, Fredegund pursued the fleeing Wintrio into Champagne and devastated the country. Incited by Brunhild, the people there blamed Wintrio for their troubles and rose against the duke. Later, however, they accepted his leadership once more.[8] Childebert died in 596, and Wintrio soon followed in 597 or 598. The chronicler Fredegar accuses Brunhild of his murder and implies that it may have been the reason why her grandson Theudebert exiled her from Austrasia. Thereafter, she moved to the court of her grandson Theuderic, who had inherited Burgundy and Arles, and launched a vain attempt to regain Austrasia for him.[9] The future saint Arnulf of Metz led the conspiracy of Austrasian nobles who betrayed Brunhild and her great-grandsons to Fredegund's son Clothar II in 613.[10]

4. Gregory of Tours, HF, 10:2.

5. See chapter 13, "Aldegund, Abbess of Maubeuge."

6. Their success gave Childebert the Burgundian throne, with the results already partially presented in chapter 7.

7. LHF, 36.

8. Gregory of Tours, HF, 8:18.

9. Fredegar, CL 4:18–19.

10. See chapters 7 and 12; Folz, "Remiremont," 15–28. Romaric, founder of Remiremont (see chapter 9) and Arnulf were close friends and united by their opposition to Brunhild. When

The following year, Arnulf became bishop of Metz and remained a close adviser to Clothar II and tutor to his son Dagobert for many years until he retired to the monastery of Remiremont in 629.[11] However, he had not yet become bishop in 608 or 609 when the young Glodesind was interred in the cathedral church in Metz. Her first translation and the miracles associated with her cult apparently began after he had retired into the monastic life.

Once Glodesind's family agreed to her consecration, they apparently supported her vocation generously. She trained with her aunt Rotlinda in the latter's monastery at Trier, which may be identified with Ören, where Arnulf of Metz's wife, Oda, and a succession of women from the Carolingian house later became nuns.[12] Her father endowed an establishment for her in Metz that supported a hundred nuns. A few years later, another duke of Austrasia, Eleutherius, who was distantly related both to the royal family and to the rising Carolingian family, built a second convent in Metz to house his kinswoman Waldrada.[13]

Glodesind's conventual practices are among the last we shall see in the tradition of the saintly women of the sixth century, the cloistered urban nuns who followed the customs of Arles.[14] At Trier, she learned "the rule," which may have been the Rule of Caesarius or simply the usage of the house in question. Despite the patronage of Pope Gregory the Great (d. 604), there is no reason to suppose that the Benedictine rule had yet gained currency in Frankland. However, his Benedictine missionaries to England did stop at Metz in 596 with letters for Brunhild. The lives of seventh-century saints no longer reflect the influence of Arles and Poitiers, but confirm the growth of the rural monasticism of Austrasia, where the rules of Benedict and Columbanus took root and flourished.

Columbanus (c. 540–615) was a fiery Irish missionary who combined a new monastic discipline based on confession and penitence with energetic missionary activity among heretics and pagans alike. His monastic foundations clustered around the wildernesses where Frankish Gaul was infiltrating the Germanic forests. Luxeuil in Austrasia, Bobbio in northern Italy, and Bregenz on Lake Constance were the major seats of his mission. Throughout the seventh century, his successors, Eustasius, Waldebert, and Amand, would spread his rule and his religion into modern Belgium, Frisia, and western

---

Theuderic occupied Metz, Arnulf fled. Romaric's biography says that his father was freed and his goods confiscated and only recovered when Theuderic died. The victory of Clothar II restored them all and provided a patron for the Columbanian movement.

11. See introduction to chapter 9.

12. See introduction to chapter 11.

13. See *ASOSB* 2:63, discussed by Huguenin, *Histoire du royaume*, 306–7.

14. Nelson, "Queens as Jezebels," 32–33.

Germany. The women of the Austrasian nobility, and particularly those of the Carolingian house, were among the pioneers who penetrated those northern lands.

Columbanus was in Austrasia by 590, and his angry confrontations with Queen Brunhild were surely known to Arnulf and his friends as well as to Wintrio and his allies. Glodesind was probably already dead by 609 when the rule of Columbanus's monastery at Luxeuil was conferred by Bishop Poppolus on a foundation near Metz. Nevertheless, Columbanus's reputation was high in her lifetime, and his form of monastic life was spreading quickly. His rule and his followers were soon associated with many of the leading aristocrats in Frankland, providing them with an ecclesiastical power base during the peak of Merovingian royal power represented by Clothar II and Dagobert I. Even if we do not unreservedly accept the thesis that the Germanic aristocracy was seeking to Christianize an old pagan charisma, the lives that follow in this volume will amply illustrate the importance of Irish monasticism in securing aristocratic control of the wealth that otherwise was vulnerable to royal ambition through the king's marriage strategies.[15]

Saint Glodesind, Virgin of Metz in Belgica Prima[16]

∎

1. Oh God, you Who created all things from nothing by the power of your virtue, have made woman's help indispensable[17] to man, for you have decreed that all virile flesh begin in feminine bodies. You have even consecrated conjugal copulation as an excellent mystery to presignify the sacrament of Christ's church in the nuptial union. Likewise, you conferred glory on the holy virgin Glodesind so that, scorning and despising the world, she might unite with your only begotten Son as a husband. I beseech you: Open our lips and our mouth that we may proclaim your praises and let us be worthy to praise you perfectly and fittingly. Give us strength to narrate the life and acts of the holy virgin Glodesind, in whose holy remains virgins may find an example of chastity. So will those who turn and run to you deserve to reach you by the prayers of this same holy virgin Glodesind.

2. In this little book, we shall inscribe a verse of ten lines in which number are contained the ten mystical virgins who took their lamps and went out to meet the bride and bridegroom. And, since five of them were foolish and five

15. Theis, "Saints sans famille?" challenges Prinz's theory of the *Adelskult* on the grounds that the defiance of the family is a more common theme in this hagiography than cooperation with its interests, which characterizes later saints' lives.

16. Later known as Lorraine.

17. We have translated *inseparabile* as *indispensable*, but it may carry an echo of 1 Corinthians 11:11.

were wise, five of our lines are hexameters and five pentameters: for none can doubt that a verse of six feet is a work of perfection.[18]

> Receive, Holy Father, our prayers through pleading Glodesind,
> The perpetual virgin, I ask piously:
> By Glodesind's prayers, omnipotent One, have mercy
> On us and everyone, I beg both day and night:
> And send us prosperity forever, Omnipotent One,
> By the glorified virgin Glodesind's prayers.
> May glory, praise and honor through every age rest
> With Almighty God on the virginal throne.
> Through holy Glodesind's merits, efface our crimes
> I pray God, and grant us peace.

3. It behooves us, brothers, to praise God the Father Almighty with all our strength, and His Son Jesus Christ, and the Holy Spirit, third in the perfect Trinity, the remission of sinners, hope of the miserable, refuge of the poor, comfort of the infirm. Amen. For the edification of holy mother church, redeemed by Christ's blood, who thereby shows herself His glorious spouse without stain or wrinkle, it behooves us to write the lives of the saints who shine like lamps in the world. Ignorant of darkness, free of error, they shed bright light on the hearts of the faithful. And we believe that the life and acts of the holy virgin Glodesind are no less deserving to be placed in their hearts. For it will be shown that she took the veil upon her head against her father's will and the plans of her other noble relatives, not from a human man but from an incorruptible angel. For had God not found her worthy and lovable, no angel would ever have draped divinity's veil over her with his own hands by the Lord's command, as we shall tell.

4. Therefore, holy virgin Glodesind, help us and give us strength, and pray the Lord that He will light the eyes of our hearts with the lamp of wisdom and intelligence and knowledge, so that we may be worthy to see clearly and tell the miracles of God and Our Lord Jesus Christ, that He has deigned to work in our time by your intercession. For, committing this to writing, we believe that the memorial we now record will gladden us in the present time and edify those who are to follow. For the same blessed virgin, whose merits when she was alive we are reporting, still acts in this age which is fully

---

18. The editors of *AS* suggest that by aligning the six-foot verse with the five wise virgins, the author is referring to the six days of creation. We have tried to keep each line separate but have made no attempt to reproduce their metrical "perfection." In a personal communication Stanislas Mosely indicates that Hucbald uses quantitative meter, as did the Greeks and Virgil for epic poetry. He believes that this is the perfection Hucbald tried to reproduce in contrast to the pentameter lines that reflect the five foolish virgins.

revealed by her miracles. For though hardly anyone in our times can do justice to the magnificence of her life, silence would be negligence.

I. The birth of Saint Glodesind; her marriage; her virginity protected by angelic help. The foundation of her Parthenon. Her holy death.

5. It is said that this holy virgin, Glodesind, lived at the time of king Childebert.[19] She was the daughter of a noble duke called Wintrio. Her mother was named Godila.[20] Suffice it to say that the girl was procreated from the stock of a noble race. When she was mature enough to be given a conjugal partner, her father began urging her to bear sons of like nobility and even settled upon a betrothal. When the time came for the wedding, her father and mother and her noble relatives gave Glodesind, the virgin and bride of the Lord Jesus Christ, to a certain noble man named Obolenus. He took her and brought her to rule over his house. Once having conducted that virgin and bride of Our Lord Jesus Christ, Glodesind, within the walls of his house, he wished to copulate with her. But, by an act of the Lord's providence, he never knew her, for all his efforts to that end were useless. The holy virgin had consecrated her body and soul to a celestial spouse.

6. In fact, by an act of Divine Providence, King Childebert summoned her husband on that very day so that he could not pollute the most sacred virgin. Thus her marriage involved no carnality and she renounced worldly pomp with all her heart. Meanwhile, Obolenus promptly and speedily headed for the palace with his followers. As soon as King Childebert heard of his arrival in the palace, he ordered him to be taken into custody for his nefarious crimes and his enormous iniquity. For a whole year, he was kept sequestered there behind strong walls and when the year had passed he was brought forth and his head was cut off by the king's command.[21]

7. Then the holy virgin's father wanted to unite her with another man in marriage. But she totally rejected this with all her strength. The day of the wedding came near when the blessed virgin was to be handed over to a corruptible spouse, to an enemy of her integrity who would soon putrefy into worms and dust. Spurning such a husband, she made herself a sacrifice to the Lord and desired only to be God's handmaid, leaving father and relatives and spouse for Christ. Then her father wanted to take the holy virgin

---

19. The editors of *AS* copied this as Childeric, which they point out is a mistake. Wintrio was the chamberlain of Childebert II, as noted by Gregory of Tours, HF, 8:18; Fredegar, CL 4:14; and LHF, 36. See also Ewig, *Spätantikes und fränkisches Gallien*, 141.

20. The editors of *AS* cite a shorter manuscript life at Metz that identified Godila as the daughter of a duke of Austrasia.

21. None of the dates are clear. The cause of Obolenus's execution is therefore unknown, but involvement in the assassination attempt on Childebert in 590 would fit the possible chronology and certainly qualify as nefarious and iniquitous.

to his sister Rotlinda who at that time lived according to the holy manner in Trier so that she might soften her soul with bland sweet words and he could give her to another man in marriage.[22]

8. Rejecting and detesting this, she did not wish to go there as her father planned. Instead she fled to the city of Metz to the church of the holy martyr Stephen where his relics and those of innumerable other saints are embalmed in the *confessio*.[23] She made this decision to run away, not because she had committed a crime but to avoid doing so.[24] She did not wait for the frightful ferocity of her kindred, because she was determined to die rather than surrender the flower of virginity and the ornament of chastity. Thus she set an example for future virgins by following Christ, the glory of all virgins, who was conceived by a virgin, born of a virgin and remained a virgin forever. Thus let not virgins reckon that true joy can be found in the chains of filthy marriage and in great possessions. These are often lost and after death nothing will sweeten the damage to their modesty.

9. But let me return to my proposed order. Her kindred were enraged, particularly those who had arranged the betrothal. Sadly deluding themselves, they decided to follow the handmaid of Christ and use whatever means they could to turn her from her intended path. But the blessed virgin Glodesind, rejoicing that she had reached the gate of peace, was neither shaken by their threats nor seduced by their blandishments. Then an alert guard was posted at the door of the basilica to watch for an opportunity to take the virgin by force and even punish her as an offender.[25]

10. But Christ's mercy transformed that inhuman fury and hatred for virtue into clemency. Parental insanity was commuted into benevolence for the daughter. They say that for six days she remained in the church of Stephen the Protomartyr in full sight of her kindred and many others. And she neither ate nor drank but was fully satisfied by bread from angelic dough.[26] And in that place she gave herself up with most intent and pure holy devotion to prayer. Then suddenly on the seventh day, which was the first day of the week, called the Lord's Day, a stranger with the face of an angel entered, followed by two boys. He laid the holy veil of religion over the holy virgin who had stationed

22. AS notes a mention of her in *Annalium Trevirensium*, 6:41. If this were the same foundation that Oda entered, the event would strengthen the notion of a connection between Glodesind and the Arnulf/Carolingian family who appear to have initiated the promotion of her cult. Ewig, *Spätantikes und fränkisches Gallien*, 196ff., provides greater detail.

23. This was a crypt beneath the altar in which relics were kept.

24. In other words, she was not asking for asylum as a criminal.

25. Again noting that the document gives no dates, this event could be linked to Wintrio's violent invasion of Metz in 591. Gregory of Tours, HF, 10:2.

26. Called *pasta*.

herself before the altar from fear of violence. And having done this, they left her veiled before everyone and passed out of sight.

11. No one asked what they had sought or what they were doing. All were frozen with fear and knew not what to do in the face of their terror. But when everyone had seen and understood the handiwork of the angels, they recognized that they should not persecute her as an impious girl but venerate her as a saint. Prostrating themselves, they all begged pardon that the holy virgin, God's beloved Glodesind, might forgive them. Thus they were reconciled and obtained pardon. Now let virgins, whose bodies are tickled by insignificant discomforts, hear how this holy virgin, who abhorred a husband's bed, prospered. For first the angel's hand awarded her the veil in this place of relics and secondly she won Christ as an inestimable spouse with a celestial and perpetual kingdom. And neither was she abandoned to insult in the present world.

12. For then the virgin quickly proceeded to Trier to come to her aunt Rotlinda. Living there with her monastically, she learned the holy Rule. Thus having been taught herself, she might give instruction to other nuns. Having done all this correctly, she went back to Metz and her parents gave her a certain place which she chose in that city. Then they endowed the holy virgin with even more possessions. Soon she built a monastery which was called Subterius [the Lower] Monastery, where she gathered a flock of about a hundred nuns.[27] And all the days of her life, she ruled and served them.

13. After the monastery was built and the community gathered and instructed in the Rule, they say that she lived regularly for six more years, faultlessly showing others how to follow her example. Thus her most holy virtues were displayed. After these six years, she migrated incorrupt to the Lord to whom she had vowed herself as an inviolate spouse and with whom she often longed to be joined. Some folk said that the whole course of her life was completed in thirty years. Then, as she had commanded, she was brought to the place then dedicated to the Holy Apostles where she had arranged to be buried.

II. The Saint's burial and first translation; her incorruption with several miracles.[28]

---

27. *Subterius* means lower in relation to the Abbey of Saint Peter, later Saint Arnulf of Metz, which was called *Superius*. Bateson, "Origin and Early History," 149, believes there was an earlier foundation, reestablished in 604. Wintrio died in 598, so Glodesind should have received her inheritance after that.

28. Thurston, *Catholic Encyclopedia*, 12:738, compares the solemn rituals of translation to canonization, a recognition of the heroic sanctity of the person whose remains are being transferred from one burial site to another. Van Dam, *Leadership and Community*, 59–60, sees the ceremony as a Christianization of the imperial progresses of antiquity.

14. At that time, the place did not yet possess the body of Blessed Arnulf the famous confessor.[29] Indeed, its name has since been changed so that it is called Saint Arnulf's or Holy Apostles. She had arranged to be buried there because her monastery, called Subterius, had no cemetery where the holy virgin's body could be buried. She rested peacefully in that place for twenty-five years. Then a divine annunciation was made to a certain religious nun in that same Subterius monastery that a church in honor of God's holy mother Mary was to be built outside the monastery walls. It seemed to that nun as though the holy virgin Glodesind spoke to her and stood on the city wall and threw a stone in a certain direction. And she ordered that on the spot where the stone fell, they were to establish an altar in honor of the blessed virgin Mary. And she showed her another place where a gate should be cut through the city wall through which the nuns of the said monastery would be able to enter the church of holy Mary.

15. But none who dwelled in the monastery dared act without the king's order and license. They sent messengers to the king and he conceded them what they asked. Also he ordered that they should establish a cemetery in the church of God's holy mother Mary, where the corpse of the holy virgin Glodesind might be entombed and where the bodies of other nuns might be buried. For the road to Holy Apostles, which is also called Saint Arnulf, was very long, and male laborers were needed to carry the bodies of the nuns to Holy Apostles, or Saint Arnulf's, or to the other churches around the town. So when the church had been built, they disinterred her from her previous resting place and carried her with psalms and hymns and spiritual canticles to Subterius monastery and buried her there in the aforesaid church of Saint Mary on the right side of the altar. And according to those who did that, she was as whole as she was on the day she died.

16. In fact, when they exhumed her from Saint Arnulf's cemetery, they put the holy virgin into a bath that her flesh might again be adorned with its original beauty. And there the wonderful power of Christ appeared. A certain religious nun, so ill that she scarcely remained alive, touched her finger to the holy virgin Glodesind's face from which, it is said, blood immediately spurted and appeared to many people.[30] And when the nun who had touched the face with her finger saw the blood pouring out of her, she understood that the term of her life had been extended by half a year. Thus she was buried in

---

29. Arnulf died in 641; thus the translation and associated miracles should be placed before that date.

30. *Ex qua* indicates that the face, not the finger, was the source of the blood, therefore suggesting that the saint's body was still functioning.

the church of the holy virgin Mary where she rested honorably until her body was translated into the monastery.

17. For then a certain nun who lived religiously, received a divine announcement that a mouse was fouling the body of the holy virgin Glodesind. And it seemed in her vision as though she was to open the sepulchre and throw out the mouse who had devoured the big toe of the virgin's right foot. At break of day, she related all this to her abbess and the other nuns. They understood that they should get Christ's religious priests to discover what they could achieve with a Litany and other holy prayers. And this they did. When the Litany and holy prayers were done, devoutly and piously with great trepidation, they opened the most holy virgin Glodesind's tomb and found that it was as the nun had reported. The holy virgin's right toe was stained with blood. They ejected the mouse and sealed up the hole where it had entered so that afterwards it could not enter again.

18. When the tumulus was again placed over the sepulchre and closed as before, she rested in peace in that place. Countless persons were cured there of various infirmities through her merits. And there she lay until the day before the Ides of March, when her body was translated into the church of the holy and inviolate virgin Mary near the monastery she had ruled. And she still rules though she rests in her grave. And faithfully, we shall note a few of her deeds which have come to us.

19. Now we come to another miracle. For about the year 830 from the Incarnation of Our Lord Jesus Christ, Pope Gregory holding the Apostolic See and Louis ruling with the imperial scepter and Drogo as Archbishop of Metz by divine pleasure, something so precious could no longer remain hidden.[31] The sepulchre in which the blessed virgin Glodesind lay entombed began to emerge from the earth in an extraordinary manner. For tombs that lay nearby in the same ground did not appear nor did those placed in the structure of the wall. When the said venerable bishop learned of this he could not suffer a matter of such dignity to be ignored in any way. The next day, he sent his auxiliary bishop with other religious priests to investigate for themselves whether these things were true.[32]

III. Another translation and the various miracles that followed.[33]

20. And when he arrived the most religious virgin's life on earth was related

---

31. Gregory IV (827–844); Louis the Pious (814–840); Drogo's rule is more uncertain but began between 823 and 830.

32. The later life, c. 32, AS, 216, suggests chief archdeacon.

33. This section opens up a ninth-century world of busy trade in miracles, the economy of a successful shrine.

to him. Then, by divine favor, they forearmed themselves with many prayers and soon bore her from that place to another. And when it was done and the holy corpse had been raised from the earth, she was provided with a sepulchre in the monastery's older church behind the altar which had been built and consecrated in praise of the holy mother of God, Mary, and Saint Peter, Prince of Apostles, and Saint Sulpicius, the famous confessor. And soon Christ's miracles began to radiate from there so that the blind could see and the lame walk and the infirm were restored to health most generously.

21. First, before her corpse was borne to the sepulchre, a man who had been blind a long time with no hope of seeing, received the light of his eyes through the holy Glodesind's merits. Then, afterwards, a woman named Andrea who had been blind for a long time was illuminated. Another woman called Rimberga who long had been blind hurried to the church where the corpse of the virgin Glodesind was buried as soon as she heard news of the signs spreading through the city. When she got there, the Lord showed a great sign of her merits. For she said a prayer and remained keeping vigil for a while and then received her sight.

22. Martina, Waldrada and Odegardis were all three struck with fever burning for a long time until they were almost dead. These women had in fact paid much of their wealth to doctors hoping to be healed, but no earthly physician cured them or even gave them comfort. But when they came to the threshold of the church and prayed by the merits of the holy virgin, no money was extorted from them and they received their pristine health without any human medicine concocted by carnal hands.

23. And another woman named Imma had languished for a long time, so weak she was scarcely able to breathe. She could get neither health nor soothing from any man and had no hope of recovery. But the Lord did not wish to leave her in despair for, as we believe, she had some spark of good works in her which He would not suffer to be extinguished. Therefore with God's approval, she took the road to the said monastery and, as soon as she entered the monastery walls, she began giving thanks to almighty God for there she deserved to feel a little strength though before it happened she would never have believed it possible.

24. As soon as she went through the gates of the monastery, she felt the sickness recede from her. The nearer she came to the church where the virgin's body lay buried, the more steadily did the infirmity recede, and she got better and better. As she passed through the church, she gave great thanks to God praying for her sins as she approached the altar and tomb of the holy virgin. Soon after, praying intently by the virgin's tomb in the same church, she was restored to her original health and so received a complete cure by the prayers of the blessed Glodesind.

25. Then on another day, while the nuns were most devoutly doing the offices in that church, a certain woman named Angelinda who had been born not far from the city of Metz, crossed the threshold of the church unawares and came to the steps before the altar. She had been blind for a long time and could not get around by herself without a guide. But it seemed as though the holy virgin Glodesind was leading her as she climbed the steps and came to the altar itself, though the blind woman did not recognize her as her eyes were just beginning to open. She only saw with her weak vision that she had a different guide than the one she was used to. Looking about and crying out, she began to call her guide by name but she could not find her. Still, with the Lord's help, she had a better and more beautiful guide.

26. So Saint Glodesind led her to the head of her tomb where she said a prayer. It seemed to her as though there were clouds about the virgin's tomb and she was amazed at clouds so near the ground, which was not the normal thing. Then little by little her eyes began to open so that she deserved to see the virgin's sepulchre. Not realizing where she was, she looked all about her, wondering how she had been separated from the unknown guide who had brought her there. For she could neither see nor recognize her. Then Divinity revealed to the grieving woman that Saint Glodesind herself had led her thither. Thus by the Lord's bounty, in the sight of many bystanders, she was granted clear vision. And after that she never needed a guide again but could go wherever she liked by herself.

27. And after that, another woman named Plectrude, who had not been able to see light for many days, came to the church. Soon she came to the virgin's tomb and sat near it. With innumerable other sick persons she lay there the whole night in vigils and prayer. Then, while the matutinal office was being performed it seemed to her as though the holy virgin opened her eyes with her own fingers and she was given to see the light by her merits.

IV. Further miracles.

28. There can be no keeping silent about the tenth miracle in the same place by which the Lord showed the holy virgin's merits. There was a man named Baldricus whose nostrils had been rotting for a long time so that scarcely anyone could bear to be near him because of the stench and putrefaction. He took medicine from many doctors for the said infirmity but nothing did him any good. So when he heard that the Lord was performing great deeds in the city of Metz through the virtues of God's beloved virgin Glodesind, he hurried to that city. As he came to the Subterius monastery where the holy virgin Glodesind's body lay entombed and entered the church, everyone began to flee because of the stench which he bore in his nostrils. But he, on the contrary, did not for that reason shrink back from God's mercy. With some bashfulness, he seated himself with the rest of the

sick, opposite one with an infirmity of the hand, and prayed that God would send him health from Heaven. Hearing the prayer, God cured him there and then through Glodesind's merits. Freed from the said illness, he was as well as he had been in his youth.

29. Nor in truth, will I be quiet about the eleventh sign. A woman named Benedicta who had been blind for ten years so that she could see no light nor anything else, came up to the monastery. For regarding her helplessness, our pious and merciful God had informed her by a certain secret sign that she should go to the monastery and when she got there, she hurried directly to the virgin's tomb. Sitting before the tomb, she heard the tumult of sick people ululating in loud voices and with all her might she began to accuse herself of her sins. Then God heard her and by the merits of the holy virgin she received light. And also Ansegardis and Lamberga, and Bercardis and Stangardis and finally Madelsinda, who all had lost the light of their eyes for a long time, were illuminated at the most holy virgin's tomb.

30. After these miracles, the seventeenth was a mighty sign. A woman named Bova who was paralyzed for three years in one hand and both feet was cured there. She had herself carried to Metz as soon as she heard the Almighty was doing many signs and wonders there, though she lacked strength to go by herself. As she was brought into the church where the holy virgin Glodesind's body lay in its honored tomb, she ordered herself placed on the pavement. Prostrate, she began to weep and pray to the Lord that she might have help to return to health, recognizing that her infirmity came to her because of her sins. Merciful God, the just and pious, heard her and restored the said woman to health before the eyes of all the witnesses.

31. And following that sign, many more were given. Several blind men or women received light: Madelberta, Abgenia, Baldrada, Adelbertus, Adalsinda, Ratbertus, Agidia, all were given to see the light of day in that monastery before the blessed virgin Glodesind's sepulchre, by her merits and prayers. Nor is it any wonder that there were so many signs in that place and the monastery to which we have referred so often. For her merits were declared even outside the monastic ground.

32. One day, a clerk of that monastery named Fulbert wanted to cross the river Seille.[34] Coming to the river bank and wishing to cross, he found no transport and sat down to wait for someone to bring a boat. The wait was most tedious. He was there for a long time and fell asleep in the place. On waking, he still saw no way to cross over the river. Turning within himself, he began to entreat the holy virgin Glodesind to ask God to send a boat in which her little servant might cross. And God, who is everywhere, heard him

---

34. It flows through Lorraine to join the Moselle at Metz.

clamoring. Through the virgin's prayers, He helped him to cross the river. For a boat, which no one was rowing, came to that clerk by itself. As soon as it appeared at the dock on the bank where he stood, he gave thanks to God who had given him the boat through the merits of his lady Glodesind and, entering it, he crossed that river.

33. Nor do I intend to be silent about a sign made by Glodesind's merits far from the city and monastery which became known to many people. A certain poor man wanted to go to the monastery where the holy virgin's body lay buried. However, he did not wish to go there empty-handed for he was heedful of the divine precept which we read in the law: "Thou shalt not appear empty before the Lord."[35] This poor man was skilled at fishing, so he went to the water with his tackle hoping to catch some fish there to offer the warden of the virgin's monastery so that he would get a better place among those praying there and be more kindly received among them.

34. When he began to draw his net through the water, he caught an enormous fish. But, when it felt the net, it freed itself and went back to the water. The fisherman began to cry out and entreat God and holy Glodesind that some small present of fish might come to him which he could offer at the place. And the merciful and pious God, who does not despise the clamor of the poor, heard his prayers and returned the same fish which he had earlier caught by his skill, but this time it was not captured by his cunning but by divine favor. For the fish returned, leaping spontaneously from the water, and fell right into the net just as though some helper had thrown it from the water into the net with his hand. And thus he received it and carried it to the said place and gave it to the warden of the holy virgin.

35. And in the same place, at a particular moment, wondrously a further virtue was shown by the Lord's favor at the holy virgin's prayer. There was a man named Odilulfus, an imperial craftsman from the villa called Judz.[36] He had been gravely troubled by a demon through the cycles of eleven years and had gone to many saints' places to receive health by expelling the demon. Thus he had been to Saint Sebastian and Saint Denis and Saint Quentin and the bodies of innumerable other saints. But he found the help he sought from none of them. And he had given out his substance to many carnal doctors to secure help but nothing did it profit him.

36. Then hearing that merciful and pious God who wants none to perish but all to be saved was doing acts of virtue through the merits of the blessed Glodesind in the town of Metz, he hurried to get help at the monastery where

---

35. Ecclesiastes 35:4.

36. On the Moselle about four leagues from Metz, mentioned by one of Charles the Bald's capitularies, *AS*, 196.

the virgin's body lay. And God, seeing his humility as he professed that he had deserved his scourge and vexation, gave heed to the holy virgin's prayer and restored his original health and ejected the demon from him with all his strength.

V. Further miracles.

37. Then a most wonderful mystery was revealed by the virgin's prayers in that same monastery. God impelled a man named Guntelinus, who was mute from birth so that he could not even mutter, to hasten hither. Here before the virgin's sepulchre he deserved to have his tongue loosened. And one Lord's Day, by the virgin's prayers, a woman who had been mute since birth gained speech in the same place before the tomb. And another woman named Teudrada came speedily when she heard that the Lord cast out many demons in that place by Glodesind's merits. On arrival, she was cured through prayer and the demon expelled. Nortpold, a native of Lorris, who had long been lame, was cured at that place before the virgin's sepulchre. Where his feet were weak before, he had received health and wholeness.

38. A woman named Aletrud from Argentiac villa heard of these signs and quickly made her way to the holy virgin's sepulchre.[37] For she had long been so blind that she could not see a single ray of sunlight. When she came to the place she began to pray, lying prostrate before the tomb for a while with the other infirm persons. And she received her pristine light through the merits of the holy virgin. Likewise blind Anstrada received light here by God's power. And Glumna was another blind woman who gained bright light before the virgin's tomb and all her shadows were dispersed. Innumerable other wonders through the blessed virgin Glodesind's merits were begotten by God the Provider,[38] from whom the majesty of divine power glowed revealing the shelter open to the human race.

39. Then when Bishop Walo ruled the church of the city, a sign was given which all the inhabitants of Metz considered a miracle.[39] For it was said that oil began to emanate from the feet of the Blessed Glodesind. A little while ago,[40] before the bishop's death, many people saw the oily liquor flowing from the holy virgin's feet and even spreading to her head. And they say that the virgin's tears implored God's mercy to save the city from impending ruin. And divine revelation disclosed to many men and women that her tears had gained such place with God that the town suffered no loss from ruin at that time. Accordingly, through Almighty God's clemency, it consecrated a court

---

37. The editors of *AS* venture Aurainville as the possible identification for Villa Auguntiaco.

38. *Patrata sunt* may simply mean "were accomplished," but the author seems to imply the further sense of sexual generation and legal fatherhood embedded in the word.

39. Walo ruled between 876 and 882, when the town was burned by the Norse.

40. *Nuperrime*, which suggests that this account was written before the close of the ninth century.

to the holy virgin where countless miracles still gleam forth. For as He took her to Himself in heaven, Jesus Christ made a memorial for her on earth, even He who is the Son of the Father most high and co-equal with the Holy Spirit who lives and is glorified God from everlasting to everlasting. Amen.

40. But when Bishop Walo had ruled the church for six years, he was slaughtered by the pagans. And a year after his death, Lord Rutpert was ordained bishop in the same holy see. During the time of his prelacy many wonders were done through God's power in the church consecrated to the virgin Glodesind. Oil was often seen to flow from the side of her sepulchre running down the side in a stream to the pavement. The custodians most reverently collected it from the altar with sponges and filled a certain glass vessel with it which they placed above the virgin's tomb.

41. About that time, a certain nun of the place, named Leudewidis, earnestly begged Doda, the custodian of that altar, to entrust her with the vessel which held the liquor, for she wished to bring it to the basilica of the Holy Cross within the monastery walls which she had in her charge and keep it there for religious purposes.[41] Doda put her hand in the place above the tomb, where she had put it earlier, but she could not find it. Trembling and stupefied, she gathered her other peers and, with lamps held aloft, they began to light the tomb diligently looking for it. When, after a long search, they finally brought the vessel to sight, they were scarcely able to reach it with their hands.

42. But when they took it up rejoicing, Doda separated part of the liquor and sent it to her brother Angelarius, a priest in the church of Metz dedicated to the Savior to serve as a relic in the cause of religion. At the same time, Leudewidis reverently accepted the better part of the liquor and carried it to the basilica of the Holy Cross. But when this was done, Doda was struck mad for her audacity so that she lost all control over her mind and body. Finally, sending to those churches, she acquired all the apportioned liquor and restored it, with the vessel in which it was first held, to its place above the sepulchre where Christ's handmaid, Glodesind, reposed. Two hours did not pass after this was done, before she was gratified by receiving renewed health of mind and vigor of body.

43. Then many persons with injuries to head or eyes or other members earned cures in that church from a touch of that liquid unction helped by the intercession of Christ's virgin. A woman named Hildegard who had been destitute of light for eight years, hearing of the virtue of the blessed virgin Glodesind, and having firm faith in the Lord that she could regain the light

41. *AS* notes that this church, consecrated by Brunhild and Sigebert in honor of Radegund's achievement, is called an oratory or shrine in other lives.

through her prayers, went reverently to the threshold of the church. One night before the sepulchre, she asked to be given divine aid. The shadows fled and that same night she received light.

44. An adolescent of Metz, long blind, who was not strong enough to take the road stayed within the monastery walls for quite a long time asking for God's mercy. By the prayers of the holy virgin Glodesind the blindness was expelled and he won the light. And a woman named Osa, who had limped for five years and was no longer strong enough to walk, asked to be borne into the court of the blessed virgin Glodesind. After waiting for half a year for divine clemency, she threw off her weakness and received health and she who was carried there by others' hands could leave stoutly on her own feet.

45. Then a certain cripple was borne into the court of the monastery on a couch about the vespertine hour. He asked praying that he might be allowed to pass the night lying before the altar of the blessed virgin which the custodian of the altar never allowed. He would not be parted from there but remained all night lying on his pallet before the entrance gates of the monastery. In the morning, he sprang from the cot healed, his strength renewed, and left that pallet before the monastery gates. On his own feet he came to the holy virgin's resting place and there he gave thanks to the Lord for all his gifts and, with open mouth, he testified with many prayers to the gift of health from the virgin Glodesind.

46. Another sick man who had lost all his physical strength, stayed in the holy place for a while asking for divine clemency. One day, deep in sleep, he had a dream and saw the blessed Glodesind by her altar. Imperiously, she commanded him to rise immediately from the spot and help the workers who were laying a pavement in the church. As soon as he awoke from this sleep he felt that there was nothing wrong with him. He swiftly rose from the place where he had lain so long and, as she had commanded him, joined the other workers who had been cured and helped them lay the needed pavement, knowing himself to have been healed truly by God through the virgin of Christ's prayers. We have omitted to record other similar stupendous miracles lest we bore our readers. But let us praise the wonders of Christ and the holy virgin, that they may have mercy and exhort them, with constant prayer.

9

Burgundofara,
Abbess of Faremoutiers

(603–645)

The monasticism of Gaul in the early seventh century was dominated by the influence of the monk Columbanus, whose rule was established at Luxeuil in present-day Burgundy and spread throughout Gaul, Italy, and into the Germanic lands to the east that had barely been penetrated before by Christian missionaries. His work and that of his followers was recorded by Jonas of Bobbio, one of the second generation of Irish monks in Gaul, who knew Burgundofara and the courtiers who made up the aristocratic circles of the age of Clothar II's son Dagobert and his successors. Columbanus (d. 615) was almost an exact contemporary of the long-lived Queen Brunhild. He came from Ireland as a missionary, intending to work in the pagan rural districts of Gaul, but his first efforts were aborted when, disillusioned by the vices and carelessness of the Breton clergy, he ran afoul of both the clergy and nobility of Neustria. Soon, however, he was brought to the notice of King Sigebert, who encouraged him to settle in Austrasia. Eventually, he established himself at Luxeuil, a spa where the Roman baths had fallen into ruin in a forest still haunted by old pagan idols.[1]

After Sigebert's murder, Columbanus apparently continued on good terms with the royal family for some years. Jonas states that Theuderic II was pleased to have him in Burgundy and often sought his counsel. Eventually, however, they quarreled. Jonas says that the monk angered the king's grandmother Brunhild by his refusal to bless the sons of Theuderic's concubines, whom she intended to place on the throne as his successors.[2] However, there may have been a more worldly political reason: Columbanus's followers were

---

Jonas of Bobbio, *Vita S. Columbani abbatis discipulorumque eius*, Liber II, in Krusch, ed., MGH, SRM 4:130–43. The text translated here is from Book 2, 11–22, which places the account of the convent of Faremoutiers between other chapters dealing with Columbanus's male disciples.

1. The story is recounted in detail by Jonas of Bobbio and translated into English by McDermott in *Monks, Bishops, and Pagans*, ed. Peters.

2. Jonas, *Vita S. Columbani*, 1:31–33.

among the leading families of Austrasia and Burgundy, opponents of Brunhild and friends of the family of Arnulf of Metz who came into favor with Clothar II's victory over the old queen in 614.[3] As a result, Columbanus was hounded out of the country in 609 or 610, twenty years after his arrival in Burgundy.

Leaving most of his Frankish followers behind him, he journeyed into the wilderness of the Austrian Alps to found a missionary center on Lake Constance at Bregenz.[4] In those years, his only companion was Burgundofara's brother Chagnoald, who was later entrusted with the supervision of his sister's convent at Evoriacum near Meaux. Columbanus met the young man in Austrasia when he stayed in the house of Chagneric, who was among the foremost nobles of the land. Jonas incorporated the story into his *Life of Columbanus*:

> Then Columbanus went to the city of Meaux. There he was received with joy by a nobleman, Chagneric, who was a friend of Theudebert, wise man and a counsellor grateful to the king, and was fortified by nobility and wisdom. The latter promised that he would take care of Columbanus until the latter reached the court of Theudebert, and said it is not necessary to have the other companions who were sent by the king. He declined the aid of others in order to keep the man of God with himself as long as he could, and in order that his house might be ennobled by the learning of the latter. Columbanus blessed his house and consecrated to the Lord his daughter Burgundofara, who was still a child, and of whom we shall speak later.[5]

Clothar II built his power on alliance with these great families whose rights and privileges he confirmed in his capitulary of 614. Frequently, their sons crowned a career in royal service with an episcopal appointment. Chagneric's son, Burgundofaro, became bishop of Meaux after a military career as count of the same district.[6] He also enjoys a cult as a saint along with his wife Bilhild, who entered a monastery herself to release her husband for episcopal duties. Indeed, her legend says that when Burgundofaro weakened in his resolve and tried to lure her back to their conjugal life, it was her determination that kept them both on their chosen road.

Jonas relates that Columbanus ended his life at Bobbio in Italy in 615. The

---

3. Folz, "Remiremont."
4. Jonas, *Vita S. Columbani*, 1:55, 57.
5. Ibid., 1:50, in *Monks, Bishops, and Pagans*, ed. Peters, 106.
6. Murray, *Germanic Kinship*, 93, notes that Fredegar, *CL* 4:41, appears to use "Burgundofarones" as synonymous with the Burgundian aristocracy or with the Burgundian leudes (followers) of the Frankish king.

monk of Bobbio then added a second part to his biography of the Irish saint, narrating the lives of his successors at Luxeuil and the other monasteries founded under his patronage. His account of Burgundofara's later life begins in the story of the life and works of Atala, second abbot of Bobbio. At that time, Clothar II sent Eustasius, to whom Columbanus had entrusted Luxeuil, to ask Columbanus to return because his enemy Brunhild and her descendants were all dead. But the aged saint declined to essay the Alps again. He kept Eustasius with him for some time and then sent him back to Clothar, who became an active patron of the Irish foundations in his unified kingdom.

The story of Burgundofara and her convent was continued by Jonas in the context of these travels:

As we said above, the venerable Eustasius returned from Columbanus in Italy to rule the company of monks in his charge with paternal affection and equity. Then, for the community's needs, he went to King Clothar who was living at that time at the ends of Gaul near the shores of the Ocean Sea.[7] His way took him through the woods and fields of Brie, where he came to Chagneric's villa where his master had previously stayed for some time. The villa was called Pipimisiac and lay about two miles from the town of Meaux. Chagneric lived there with his wife Leudegund, a Christian woman of sound mind. Their son Chagnoald, whom we mentioned above, was his servant.[8] Seeing Eustasius, Chagneric received him in great joy. At that time, their daughter, Burgundofara, whom Blessed Columbanus had consecrated to the Lord as we said above, was living with her father and mother. But when her father betrothed her and meant to give the girl in marriage against her will, she had been stricken with such an affliction of the eyes and burning fever that it was thought she could scarcely survive. As she lay at her last gasp, Eustasius rebuked her father saying it was his fault that she burned in such terrible agony because he had tried to violate the Man of God's interdict. Dissembling, he said: "Would that she might return to health and devote herself to divine service!" He also admitted that he should not stand in the way of such vows. Then, going to the girl's bedside,

7. Krusch associates this event with Fredegar's account of Bishop Leudemund of Sion's flight to Luxeuil in 613, c. 44. The bishop had borne a message to Queen Beretrude from a nobleman offering her shelter at Sion with her treasure if Clothar died within the year. In return she was to marry him and help him succeed to the throne. The queen divulged the plot, and the nobleman was executed; however, Eustasius secured a pardon for the bishop. Quotation is from Jonas, *Vita S. Columbani*, 2:7.

8. Ibid., 1:55, 57. Chagnoald was Columbanus's companion at Bregenz and later bishop of Laon, present at the council of Reims in 630. Her other brothers were Burgundofaro and Chagnulf, known only from Fara's testament.

Eustasius inquired if it were her own will to turn from her heavenly vows to earthly ways against Blessed Columbanus' interdict. The girl said that would be detestable. She would never allow herself to relax from such vows so as to change heaven for earth. But she said that she was and had ever been prepared to obey the blessed man's command. For she said she had seen a man-like shape during the previous night: "You are he, the one who will restore the light to my eyes." And at the same time she had heard a voice saying: "Whatsoever this man tells you to do, do it and you will be healed." So she said: "Speak into my ears what is intended for me and by your prayers drive away the pain the Lord has inflicted upon me." Then the venerable man, prostrate upon the ground, tearfully begged the Lord to bestow the promised favor. Rising, he pressed a cross on her eyes, stroking them with his hand, imploring the Lord to grant his protection. Health soon followed and the light was restored and the fever's fire went out. He commended the cured girl to the care of her mother saying that, when he returned from Clothar, he would robe her in the religious habit.

But when the father saw his daughter restored to health, he again decided to give her to a husband, consigning his earlier promises to the dark pit of oblivion. Discovering his intent, the girl took a friend's advice to flee away with her. Having agreed, they seized a happy opportunity for secret flight and reached the basilica of saint Peter, Prince of Apostles.[9] Discovering this, the raging father sent some boys after them and ordered them to kill his daughter cruelly when they caught her. Hurrying, the boys found the girl harbored in the bosom of the Church. Lingering on the spot, they threatened the girl with death to slake her father's wrath. And she said: "If you think death can frighten me, you may test it on the pavement of this church. For such a cause, I will gladly embrace death for Him who did not scorn to die for me." Without delay, Eustasius returned and, with many reproaches for her father, freed the girl from custody. Through Gundoald, bishop of the city, he invested the girl with the religious habit and consecrated her with salutary vows. Then she built a monastery of Christ's virgins on her patrimonial soil between the Grand Morin and Alba rivers.[10] He put some brothers in charge of the building and appointed the girl's brother, Chagnoald, with Waldebert, who became his successor, to train her in the rule.[11] In all of them many

---

9. Krusch, ed., MGH, SRM 4:121, n. 1, determines that the present church of Saint Stephen in Meaux was then dedicated to Saint Peter.

10. At first called Evoriacum by Jonas and then, after her death, Faremoutiers in her honor.

11. Waldebert succeeded Eustasius at Luxeuil, see chapter 10.

virtues were accomplished later which we will try to relate further on if life allows.

The tendency of many noble crown officers to end their career as bishops may reflect the use of the church as an alternative to the dangers of secular office or as a repository for wealth and influence to balance the powers of the crown. Likewise, the frequency with which noble women of this age entered monasteries with all their wealth suggests a family strategy that may have opposed the king's desire to dispose of heiresses among his own followers. The preceding story builds on a theme already noted in chapter 8. Jonas did not indicate who Burgundofara might have been destined to marry, but he provided her father with an iron-clad excuse if the king were pressing a candidate upon him.

An edict of Chilperic, Clothar's father, placed women in a favorable position in the inheritance system. Daughters were preferred to their father's brothers, and sisters were preferred to more distant male relatives. It is not certain whether the decree represented an innovation or an attempt to curb the tendency of fathers to treat their children equally regardless of gender.[12] In either case, it is clear that women of the seventh century were valuable repositories of wealth. Columbanus's rule and its adaptations were ideally suited to large foundations set in rural areas, and the great landed nobility of eastern Frankland promoted the new way of life enthusiastically.[13] It proved particularly effective for the establishment of female monasteries because it reflected the dynastic system of moving property and power through women to enable them to share in the responsibilities of the great families without risking the loss of patrimony to their husbands. An ancient document purported to be Burgundofara's will has been scrutinized by several scholars. Most recently, Guérout has argued forcefully that it is genuine.[14] The document introduces two members of the family unknown to Jonas: Chagnulf and Agnetrada, Burgundofara's brother and sister. Identifying Chagnulf with Arnulf, who was murdered in 641, Guérout dates the will between the death of Chagnoald, after his last official act as bishop of Laon in 632 and the death of Ega, the mayor of the palace (or prime minister), in 641. Guérout believes that the will was probably made following the illness that nearly killed Burgundofara sometime before Ega's attack on the monastery between 639 and 641.[15] She left all her property to the monastery, with the exception of a share

12. Murray, Germanic Kinship Structure, 81, takes the latter position.
13. Prinz, Frühes Mönchtum im Frankreich, advances this thesis throughout the latter part of his study.
14. Guérout, "Le testament de Sainte Fare."
15. Jonas, Vita S. Columbani, 2:2.

in a villa of Louvres that she gave up to her siblings in exchange for their agreement not to interfere with her bequest.

Columbanus left an extensive rule for Luxeuil and his other monastic foundations that was widely used in eastern Frankland during the seventh century, usually with some variations to suit particular houses. Eustasius became involved in a quarrel with a former notary of Theuderic's named Agrestius, who had been a monk of Luxeuil. Agrestius had criticized the harshness of the community's practices at the council of Macon in 626, but his complaints were rejected by the bishops. Then he successfully promoted his modifications of the rule at a monastery for women established by Saints Romaric and Amatus on the former's estates.[16] Jonas continues:[17]

> Agrestius then made his way to Burgundofara to try if he might defile her with his insinuations. But the virgin of Christ confounded him, not in a feminine manner, but with a virile response: "Why have you come here, you confuter of truth, inventor of new tales, pouring out your honey-sweetened poison to change healthy food into deadly bitterness? You slander those whose virtues I have experienced. From them I received the doctrine of salvation. Their erudition has opened the way to the kingdom of Heaven for many. Recall the words of Isaiah: 'Woe unto them that call evil good and good evil.'[18] Hurry and turn wholly away from this insanity." Thus confuted by the answer of Christ's handmaid, he fled back to Romaric and Amatus.[19]

After completing the life of Eustasius, Jonas turned to an account of certain events that occurred in Burgundofara's convent at Evoriacus. Jonas was in the neighborhood of Meaux in the 640s when he probably collected these stories. They are told in the first person, which suggests that they may have been sent to him by a nun of the community during the period he spent with Saint Amand in Elnone. The stories are in sharp contrast to the traditional hagiographical approach Jonas uses in talking of the abbots of Luxeuil, emphasizing the claims of many different nuns in the community to special

16. Ibid., 2:16, the foundation is Remiremont. Romaric was one of the principal nobles of Austrasia, a close friend of Arnulf of Metz who had been converted to religion about 618 by Amatus and served at Luxeuil for some years before making himself the director of the new foundation. *Vita S. Amati, AS,* September 4, 105.

17. Jonas, *Vita S. Columbani,* 2:10.

18. Isaiah 5:20.

19. Jonas goes on with the punishments that overcame Agrestius's followers. Romaric and Amatus repented and joined the ranks of noble seventh-century saints who flourished under the Rule. Folz, "Remiremont," 15–28, thinks that after the violent criticisms of Agrestius concerning the harshness of the Columbanian rule, Remiremont adopted the mixed rule of Waldebert.

graces rather than promoting Burgundofara herself. The chapter might even be considered the first in a tradition of "nunbooks" generally associated with the Rhineland in the thirteenth and fourteenth centuries.

Jonas gives no details of the convent's foundation or its way of life. He says that Evoriacus followed Columbanus's Rule, but Burgundofara probably introduced the mixed rule of Waldebert or a tailored rule like Donatus of Besançon's adaptation for his mother Flavia, who had been miraculously cured of barrenness by the prayers of Columbanus in her youth.[20] Donatus thus owed his life to the saint and showed his gratitude by promoting his rule. His adaptation combines elements of Columbanus, Benedict, and Caesarius, pointedly omitting Caesarius's requirement of claustration in deference to the practical necessities of a more rural way of life.[21]

Penitence was clearly at the center of their lives, which is typical of Waldebert's spirituality. After his rule was introduced at Remiremont, the dead founder Romaric appeared to a nun to remind her of a sin she had forgotten to confess to assure that she would do penance for it.[22] His friend Amatus introduced the *laus perennis*, another devotion popular among the followers of Irish monasticism. He divided the nuns at Remiremont into seven groups of twelve each to work in relays, which gives a population of at least eighty-four.[23] Jonas also mentions a convent under Abbess Aurea founded in Paris by Saint Eligius and one founded by the noble woman Berthoare in Bourges; two were also built for women by Theudulf at Carantomus and Nivers, which shows the extent of the movement.

The great foundations of this period are often called "double monasteries" because of the presence of both monks and nuns. The monks, however, did not occupy a prominent position. They seemed only to have menial positions. Possibly they were generally former serfs monasticized to perform manual labor for the nuns.[24] Even priests are not very much highlighted in these stories. Burgundofara herself heard the confessions of her nuns three times a day but apparently commanded no sacramental power of absolution. Communion appears to have been a relatively rare and special event, and the abbess apparently administered the Eucharist herself when a nun was on her deathbed, perhaps from a reserved supply.

11. On the death of Sisetrud and the singing of the angels.

Let me remind my reader that I promised above to disclose how many

20. Jonas, *Vita S. Columbani*, 1:22.
21. See Donatus, "Rule of Donatus," trans. McNamara and Halborg.
22. *Vita Romarici*, c. 15, in Mabillon, ed., *ASOSB*, 420.
23. Krusch, *Vita Amati*, c. 10, in *MGH, SRM* 4:218, n. 49, calls the groups *turmae*, a military term.
24. This is the opinion of Folz, "Remiremont."

different wonders the Begetter of All Things deigned to produce for the encouragement of his handmaidens in the community called Evoriacus, also following the rule of blessed Columbanus, which the memorable Burgundofara gathered with care and devotion. When, under Christ's captaincy, she was maintaining a cohort of many maidens assembled around her under regular discipline, Sisetrud, one of her subjects who was cellaress of the monastery at that time, was informed by revelation that her departure from this life had been decreed for forty days hence. She was ordered to prepare for the journey by correcting her ways and amending her life. For thirty seven days she carried out everything in religion: she wore out her body in labors of fasting, prayers and vigils with flowing tears, so that she might more easily open the way to the road where she was going. Then two youths with white stoles around their shoulders came to her and separated her soul from her body. Bearing her through the open air, they carried her to Heaven while subjecting her to close investigation. They introduced her into the white-clad multitude who associated with the angelic chorus and encouraged her to grasp her joyous triumph over the world. But just as she was rejoicing with ripe exultation that she was safe in eternal bliss inserted into the chorus of virgins, just as she was dancing in delight with glory in the highest, she came before the tribunal of the Merciful Judge and was ordered to be immediately returned to her body and to come again in three days. Thus commanded, they carried her back to her body so that she might have three more days of fuller preparations and the schedule of the forty days might be completed. Thus restored to her body, she called the mother and begged the whole troop of God's servants to give her the comfort of their prayers, swearing that her life was limited to the three conceded days. And when the third day came, she asked the mother to come and prayed that they would all attend her departure. All the witnesses present as she left this life confirmed that her body was secure and not out in the open, yet she saw two youths come to her from on high who asked if she was ready to go. And, rejoicing, she said: "I would go now, my lords. I would go and be detained no longer in this stressful life. Rather, I would return to that shining light from which I was snatched." When Mother Burgundofara asked to whom she addressed such words, she said: "No, don't you see the men standing here, garbed in their stoles, who conducted me to heaven three days since? Now they have returned when I am better prepared for the road." Then, with a last farewell to the marvelling mother and all the bystanders, she was taken from this present life. And all who attended this departure heard an angelic chorus singing in harmony, drawing sweet melodies through the air. Fear and joy percolated together through them all as they hurried out of doors from the cell where the cast-off hide remained, so as to hear as much as human ears could encompass of the singing angelic voices. And through this first lesson to the women of the community, the Lord wished to show the rest who remained behind that they should make every effort in their practice of religion.[25]

12. Of the behavior of Gibitrude and her exit from life.

Soon after this, another similar lesson followed. A certain virgin named Gibitrude, noble of family and religion, asked to be accepted into this convent as a convert from the world. The mother of the monastery, Burgundofara, who was closely related to her, rejoiced and received her as a welcome gift. She flickered with so bright a flame that the grace of the Holy Spirit blazing in her was evident in all that she did. Thus when she was still detained in her paternal home, she sought, under the Holy Spirit's guidance, to consecrate herself to the practice of religion. She asked her father and mother to build her an oratory where she could show her Creator her devotion. But her grudging parents, who were both from noble Frankish families, had not striven wholeheartedly to set themselves on the road that leads to the kingdom of Heaven, being more desirous of increasing their worldly importance. Because of this, they were more anxious to secure offspring from their daughter than to give her as a hostage for them in Heaven. But they could in no way turn the maiden's mind from her intention and finally gave in to her prayers and built the little oratory. The maiden haunted the place day and night until the enemy slyly began to cast his subtle darts at her. Through her nurse, he undertook to prepare obstacles which would keep her from frequenting the oratory.[26] But when the maid felt herself pressed, she began to ask the Creator's clemency. She prayed that the woman who sought to extinguish the light of her soul by preventing her prayers, should be deprived of her own external light. Nor did Divine Piety hesitate! Soon afflicted with an eye disease, she was deprived of her needed light. Her parents' fears were doubled when the Clement Arbiter seized her father with a violent fever. However puffed up he might have been with his nobility, he still aspired to fear and worship Divinity after his daughter's example. He asked his child to pray the Lord for her father and promised to do her will in everything if her intercession restored his health. His cure was not long delayed. Through her persistent entreaties, the fever's fire was put out and her father soon restored to pristine health. Then the maid asked to be allowed to enter the aforesaid convent.

After she had been practicing the religious life for the space of many years, Burgundofara was attacked by fever and everyone thought her bonds to the

---

25. *Ad cultum religionis*: religion is used here to mean the monastic life.
26. "Nurse" may be a poetic reference to her mother.

present life were about to dissolve. Gibitrude, seeing that the mother of the monastery was in *extremis*, went anxiously to the basilica where she implored the Lord with tearful voice to remember His former mercy and delay taking the mother in death until he had first received her and her companions in Heaven. Then he might order the mother to follow at the last. After these cries, she heard a voice from above saying: "Go, handmaid of Christ, you shall have what you asked. For she will still be joined [with you] on high but you shall be released first from the chains of the flesh." Nor was there any long delay. She was seized with fever and died, rendering up her soul at the final hour. Angels lifted her into the ether and brought her before the tribunal of the eternal judge. As she described it afterwards, she saw the white-garbed troops and all the militia of heaven standing before the glory of the Eternal Judge. She heard a voice from the throne saying: "Go back, for you have not fully relinquished the world. It is written: 'Give, and it shall be given unto you';[27] and elsewhere, in the prayer: 'Forgive us our debts as we forgive our debtors.'[28] But you have not settled with all your companions and you still nurse grievances for slights inflicted upon you. Bear this in mind: three sisters have borne witness against you for their wounded souls which have not been healed by the medicine of full forgiveness for the inflicted injury. Therefore, mend your ways: soothe these souls which you have soiled from indifference or neglect." Wonderful to say! She returned to her original life and, with sad lament, gave account of the judgment against her and confessed her guilt. She called her companions, against whose souls she had borne a grudge, and asked pardon lest by fraudulent silence she might lose her eternal life. And for six months after her return to health, she lived in the present age. After that she was seized by fever. She foretold the day and hour of her going, proclaiming her coming departure from the world. Thus she achieved such a happy exit that you would think that she was sweating balsam within the cell where her inanimate corpse lay. All of us who were there felt it to be a miracle. Thirty days later when, according to ecclesiastical custom, we went to make her commemoration by celebrating a solemn Mass, the church was full of such a fragrance that you would imagine that the aromas of all the oils and spices there are had been released. So, for their merits, the Creator of Things makes the souls of those who are consecrated to Him shine with His gifts so that for love of Him none would wish to cherish or love the world.

13. On the life and death of Ercantrude.

A certain girl named Ercantrude, whose parents were noble, entered the monastery as a convert while still an infant. After she had practiced the

27. Luke 6:38.
28. Matthew 6:12.

religious life for many years, the Just Arbiter determined to test her by punishing her temporal body. Accordingly, she suffered so many things in her tender years that, from the multitude of her sharp pains, you might believe that the example of Job was being repeated in her. But behold what patience she found in her youth! Wondrous was her virtue of humility! Wondrous her tranquility, her piety, her gentleness, her charity! The strength of her soul stood firm in the fire of pain. Her faith held unshaken; her goodness was unmoved; the floods of her tears were incomparable. As much agony as her body bore, so much hope of joy and exultation in eternal life gratified her soul. Our mother nurtured her so carefully within the convent walls that she could not distinguish between our sexual natures: for she counted male and female the same; female and male just alike. Her behavior was an example to all of the rich power of patience, of pious worship and loving gentleness. Yet, while she was always obliging, it happened that she once did something contrary to the tenor of the rule. The mother sentenced her to expiate the guilt of her admitted crime by submitting to the rule's penitential interdict depriving her of the Lord's body. When she heard that sentence, that she would be deprived of the Holy Body, she began to weep, wounded by the heavy blow. For on the next day the feast of the blessed primate Martin's death was to be solemnly celebrated. Therefore, she kept vigil through the night and prayed for absolution of her guilt lest for that reason she must suffer such loss, separation from the body of Christ for her own fault. After these tears and abundant groans and choking sighs, she earned forgiving consolation from God: "Go," He said, "and on this day be reconciled with the body of Christ because the fault has been forgiven as you asked. And you may so tell the mother by revealing what I have said." In the morning, she revealed it to the mother in humble confession, and was reconciled to the sacred body and afterwards achieved the religious life.

And when, after many cycles of time, the Creator of All wanted to bring her to Heaven, He infected her with burning fever. While she lay in *extremis*, she said: "Quickly, isolate the dead one in your midst and cast her out from the society of the others. For it is not fitting that those who are crucified with the pure Christ[29] should live with her and keep among themselves a woman who is dead and cut off from life." And when they all began to inquire among themselves and asked whom she meant, one of them, struck with fear and confusion fell on the ground, prostrate, and confessed her guilt, promising to amend everything. Though she had been parted from the world, she had never ceased longing for the secular life outside. Thus, she had lived entirely

29. *Mundo Christo*; an alternate reading might be "crucified to the world with Christ" echoing Galatians 6:14.

for the world and made no effort to offer any mortification. After that, as black night rushed in and the last glimmer of light winked out on earth, Ercantrude asked them to extinguish the flame lighting the cell where she lay. When the others asked why, she said: "Do you not see what splendor comes? Do you not hear the choirs singing?" When they asked what songs she heard, she said: " 'Oh give thanks unto the Lord; for he is good; for his mercy endureth forever; give thanks to the God of gods for his mercy endureth forever,' and all the rest that follows they harmonize with their mouths."[30] Thus, as they all marvelled, she took her last leave of the mother and her companions and sent forth her spirit. After the happy exit, she returned to heaven and deserved to possess eternal joy and won the reward of eternal life from present pain.

14. Of the death of Augnofledis and how the angels sang.

Yet another time, a virgin of Christ named Augnofledis who was drawing her last breath and, through losing the pain of the present life, collecting the reward of eternal life, deserved likewise to have her exit from this world accompanied by song. She joyfully sundered the bonds of the flesh. Even people from afar heard the sound of the song from her cell and their own voices broke forth: "Purge me with hyssop, and I shall be clean; wash me and I shall be whiter than snow. Make me to hear joy and gladness; that the bones which thou hast broken may rejoice."[31]

15. Of the adolescent Deurechild and her death.

The Author of Things never ceases through time's cycles to reward the innocent and accumulate just souls as ornaments for his majesty so that, being renewed by His encouragements, reinforcements might be added to religion. It happened that an adolescent named Deurechild with her mother was converted to the community.[32] After they had lived in the convent for many days, the tempter attacked the mother, seeking to distract her from taking the road to the celestial kingdom. But where the mother was driven back by imbecility and gave way to her fragile nature, in contrary wise, a reproof from her adolescent daughter dissipated the accumulating evil. So when the adolescent's spirit, though young, had yielded the abundant fruit of many seasons to her Maker, one day she saw the heavens open and with her own eyes she gazed upon Him who planted the eternal things. And attentive as she was, she simultaneously deserved to hear, from the clear light of Heaven: "Come to us and receive eternal light, freed from the bonds of the

---

30. Psalms 136:1.

31. Psalms 51:7–8.

32. Throughout this chapter, Deurechild's natural mother is called *genetrix* to distinguish her from the spiritual *mater*, Burgundofara.

flesh." Those who were there wondered what her gestures meant, or what her eyes beheld, so fixed on Heaven. They would never have known, from the flickering of her eyelids, what her eyes had seen, but she said she had been called above, and freed of the bonds of the present life. This was on Saturday. As the following day, the Lord's day, was dawning, the adolescent awaited her final departure in the grip of fever. Her anxious mother, seeing her only child about to go, with sobs and groans, begged her daughter to return from above if she could. Or she prayed that she might quickly be led after her from this life if her daughter's life had really come to its end. For she could not live after her child had gone. To this, she answered: "You have often provoked urgent desires in my flesh but I will grant your entreaties if I can. Christ willing, I shall draw you after me once you have taken the penitential medicine you need." Now in her last hour, she asked for the mother of the monastery without delay. And when the mother came speedily to do the last honors for a soul departing from the world, the girl rejoiced to see her. She commended her mother to her and bade farewell to all. She begged that they might keep silence among themselves. And while, in silence, they all awaited the departure of her soul, she said: "Give way, for my Creator comes to me; my Savior hastens to me." And she asked the mother to assist in saying the Lord's Prayer and the Creed, for with her trembling lips she could no longer express herself in words and lay motionless. And when this was done, her soul returned to her Creator with excessive pleasure. And the cell shone with light. And immediately her mother was stricken and her body was punished for a space of forty days. At the end of this forty-day cycle, she was first frightened by the sight of a terrible demon but then she was consoled by the power of the Giver. For her daughter's intercession had won her forgiveness and she returned to Heaven, her soul freed from the bonds of flesh. Indeed, she was given to understand that while she could not have escaped ruin in this world by her own merits, her daughter's intervention had won a little space for penitence so that she could be saved by the pains inflicted upon her.

16. Of Domna and the two adolescents who saw rays shining from her mouth.

If we insert something which helps to advance or augment the perfect or correct the delinquent, let no one by any means order us to delete it as unnecessary. For there can be no doubt that the losses of others give warning to many to be more vigilant in securing their profits.

Thus one Sunday Burgundofara with the college of her fellow handmaids attended solemn mass, partaking of communion with the sacred body.[33]

33. The use of the term *college* indicates that they were acting as an official chapter of canonesses.

When one of them named Domna had eaten of the Lord's body and drunk of the blood, she joined the holy chorus, singing with her companions: "Receive this sacred body of the Lord and the blood of the Savior for eternal life."[34] In her mouth, a globe of white fire shone, glittering and sparkling. While none of those who were near her spied the bright fire, two little girls whom innocence rendered immaculate, standing hand in hand, saw the glittering and sparkling rays escaping from her mouth between the modulations of the song. Not knowing enough to keep silent, they began to speak in amazement: "Look! Look at the sparkling globe shining from Domna's mouth!" When the mother heard, she rebuked them and ordered them to keep silence lest—as in fact it happened—the sin of vanity should darken her heart, from whose sweet mouth the flowing light of grace bestowed such sweetness. But the gift of the Holy Spirit had so puffed her up that her mind began to give way to fragility. Goaded by the spurs of pride, she incurred the guilt of contumacy, and exhibited the superciliousness of arrogance. Thus she spurned the mother, despised her companions and paid no heed to all their warnings. Seized by fever, she was without delay drawn to the extremity but she still made no attempt to mend her ways. And at the same time, Ansitrude, one of those who had seen her, got a headache but the other came down with fever and brought to the extremity they awaited their final going.[35] And when the cohorts of the sodality gathered and they prepared themselves for the parting to the singing of psalms from the office, one of them began to sing a song unheard by human ears. Sweet harmonies issued from her pious mouth praying the Creator with wonderful words, unheard prayers, ineffable mysteries.[36] And the cell was filled with an odor of wonderful sweetness. It was at the ninth hour of the day that the sweet odor filled her cell. The odor of balsam wafted from her breast so that through all the supervening night and the following day, even to the ninth hour following, the sweet odor and harmonious song persisted. Then they begged the mother to chant and announced their leave taking. And as the spirit went forth, the fragrant odor receded with their departure. We must believe this indubitable truth: that the glory of this good exit which they deserved to have would have been Domna's if she had not lost it through the vice of ballooning pride.

17. Of Wilsindane and her prophecy and the song of the angels.

Another lesson was supplied for the glory of this convent that through an

---

34. Mabillon notes the communion in both kinds according to Krusch. Warren, *The Antiphonary of Bangor*, 11, thinks the canticle was Gallican in origin.

35. There is a persistent problem with pronouns throughout the remainder of this tale. Ansitrude (see below, c. 17) apparently survived to be greeted by her sister Ansild in Willeswinda's vision. Although the last sentence here seems to state that two people died in addition to Domna, only one spirit departed in the odor of sanctity. Similarly, only one of the little girls sang the unknown song.

36. *Sacramentis.*

apparition of Divine Piety they should be more abundantly pleased with the rewards of eternal life. A certain woman, of Saxon origin, named Willeswinda was converted to that monastery.[37] She had practiced the religious life for many years, when, working one day in the garden within the monastery walls, she said to her companions: "Suddenly, I feel that one of us cultivating the vegetables in this patch is about to go and she should prepare herself lest she lose her eternal life through indifferent negligence." And when they asked who it was, she wished by no means to say. But before very long she herself was seized by bodily infirmity. And, while she suffered diverse torments, she began joyfully to turn her face to heaven and to expound pages of scripture previously unknown to her. She recited the books of Moses in order from the beginning and all the rest of the scriptures after, memorized in order. Then she recited the life-giving and apostolic mysteries of the Gospels after the ancient teaching. Lest those who survived her be overcome with sorrow, she said at that time that the Lord's promise to take vengeance on their enemies was to be given to them for consolation. For the monastery had an enemy named Ega, a man sublime in this world to whom the dying Dagobert had commended his son Clovis with his kingdom.[38] He set himself against the monastery and persecuted them whenever he found the occasion. He violated its boundaries, settling his own servants therein. But he did not remain master for long after these daring seizures. Soon he was smitten by the promised revenge and died.[39] Then she began to sing prayers and supplications with sweet modulations which were taken from the priestly offices. But then she filled the bystanders with violent amazement when she said to one of those who stood there: "Get out! Out the door! Throw that rubbish out!" And when the others asked what she was talking about, she said: "Don't you see how she has filled her slimy mind with filth? Nor has she even troubled to cleanse her breast through open confession of all the dirt staining it which she accumulated in the world before ever she was enclosed here." Struck with fear, seized with shame, and perceiving the light of the Holy Spirit in her who was speaking, the accused prostrated herself and laid bare her concealed vices in confession to the mother. And after this, she who

37. As noted in Bede, HE 3:8, Gallic monasteries drew Saxon women during this period when no convents existed in their own country.

38. Ega had been chief of Dagobert's councilors in Neustria and Burgundy for some years. His co-regency with Queen Nanthild after Dagobert's death in 638 earned him high praise from Fredegar, CL 4:79–80. A political coup at that time may have had repercussions on religious foundations. The famous saints of Dagobert's court who had actively patronized foundations in the Irish custom abandoned secular life one after the other: Ouen to become bishop of Rouen, and Eligius for Noyon-Tournai. Guérout, "Le testament de Sainte Fare," 25–26, says Burgundofara's brother Chagnulf, Count of Meaux, was assassinated by Ega's relative Ermenfred in 641.

39. Fredegar, CL 4:83.

was awaiting her exit from this life began to ask that they would make way to give room to those who were coming. And when they obeyed, she said with joyful face and bowed head: "Blessings, my ladies, blessings, my ladies." Asked who stood there, to whom she gave greeting, she replied: "Don't you see your sisters who have migrated to Heaven from your community?" And they asked if she knew any of them. In a loud voice, she said to one called Ansitrude: "Do you not know your sister Ansild who went to Heaven a little while ago? Now she has joined the white-garbed chorus." And as she spoke, her spirit slipped away from her body. As she went, an angelic chorus was soon heard in the air. Even people who were walking far from the cell where the lifeless body lay, heard the assemblage of angels echoing in song through the air. From that music, they understood that Willeswinda had been released from the bonds of flesh. Running, they discovered her corpse and the assemblage of sisters performing the offices of the dead and they realized that the psalms they had heard sounding in the air had been supplementing her exequies.

18. Of Leudebertana and the vision of Saint Peter, Prince of Apostles.

After that, His abounding goodness once more heaped up additional gifts and He did not hesitate to strengthen another virgin of the family named Leudeberta with salubrious warnings and heavenly proofs. After she had followed the holy life in this same community for some period of time, He warned her in sleep to prepare for her departure. When her limbs had relaxed into slumber, a voice told her that she should adhere to the mother's admonitions strictly for soon she would be taken away from on high. Nor did the blessed Giver of gifts hesitate to multiply the promised rewards. She was seized by illness and visibly approached her last departure. She lay in *extremis* with the mother and her companions waiting to honor her. Suddenly, her voice broke a long silence and she said: "Oh Peter, most glorious Prince of Apostles, what time do you want us to leave?" And when the others asked what was happening, she said: "Don't you see your patron, the glorious Prince of Apostles Peter, come among you to escort me from this life?" As soon as she had said it, she encompassed them all with a joyous face. She gave up her last breath and, leaving the upper air, was carried to eternal joy. Thus, after her long silence, the Maker of things had permitted her tongue to testify in that shaky voice so that others would be moved to follow the example of her life. And so He showed those who were leaving this light in awe and love, the abundance of His endless gifts from above.

19. On the punishment of delinquents and damnation of fugitives.[40]

---

40. Wemple, *Women in Frankish Society*, 157, notes that sixth-century councils were repeatedly forced to declare sanctions against virgins who abandoned their sacred vows.

The wickedness of diabolical fraud boiled up against these people of Christ. As it saw them grow in virtue, it attacked them with temptations to muddy them. Thus it tried to tear some of them, rendered unruly by unaccustomed discipline, from their bonds with the others by tempting them to breech the convent walls. It taught them to desire the deadly life of the world and to wish, like dogs, to eat their own vomit.[41] Thus several girls planned to carry out these insane counsels. In the dark shadows and thick silence of night, they attempted to flee over the secured monastery walls by means of a ladder. Just as they were leaving, a mass of flames burst forth from the dormitory lighting and illuminating the entire house. Then, in three separate balls, it progressed with a great thundering noise to the gateways so that there were as many fiery globes as the house had gates. The explosion wakened the sleepers and thwarted those who were going over the walls. Terrified by the noise just as their feet were thrown over the palisade, they sought to return inside the monastery walls. But they found themselves powerless to turn back. Instead, they hung there like leaden weights. For the Devil, as he could do by his craft, strove to weigh them down, whom divine punishment would not allow to perish. Thus confounded, they recognized their sins and revealed them to the mother through confession when they returned.

Then the ancient serpent attacked two others whom the new discipline rendered childish and totally silly. First he so tempted them that no true confession ever issued from their mouths. For it was the monastery's custom to observe the rule that each woman should purge her mind by confession three times a day, thus smoothing away any wrinkles and erasing the least hint of spiritual weakness by pious disclosure.[42] In this way, the devil's darts stained the minds of the girls with dishonor so that their lips never yielded any true confession of what they had done in the world or of what fragility drew them daily in thought, word and deed. Thus they could not regain health through the medicine of penance by true confession. When the lie-bearing serpent had gradually infused his venom into their hardening hearts, he was ready to reveal the evil his deceptions had instilled in their minds and then he struck. One night, they took flight outside the monastery walls, wishing to return to their own people. When they got out into the dense night, they could hardly have found a straight way through the fog except that the Devil assisted them in their rebellion with light in the form of an oil lamp which he was able to counterfeit through his arts. Then he showed them the

41. Proverbs 26:11.
42. Columbanus's Rule, c. 1, and "Rule of Donatus," trans. McNamara and Halborg, c. 19, prescribe this practice, which seems to have no sacramental dimension. At the end of this chapter, Burgundofara, as mother of the community, wanted to confess her dying nuns, and from the apparent absence of any priests she seems to have meant also to give them the Eucharist.

way back to the world and so aggravated their desertion. But when they had reached their destination, pursuing searchers found them without difficulty and they were returned with scowling faces to the community. And when their acts were scrutinized upon their return to discover the cause of their flight, they answered that by the devil's design they had been unable to control their own minds. For a long time thereafter the community tried to correct them but the criticism made no progress. Finally, divine vengeance struck them both with the punishments they had earned. And when the anxious mother of the monastery repeatedly asked why they were being punished, neither could tell her the truth though she warned them to reveal their crimes in confession even at their last hour. But as their obdurate hearts could find no remedy, they began to clamor in their sufferings: "Hold up a little! Hold up, don't press forward so eagerly!" When the others asked whom they were trying to delay, they said: "Don't you see that hoard of advancing Ethiopians who want to rape us and carry us away?" And while everyone there marvelled at these terrible words, they heard a noise above the cell roof. The doors were forced open with resounding blows and they saw black shadows standing there and heard numerous voices calling the pair by name. The witnesses, though armed with the sign of the cross and the chanting of their offices, were barely able to hold their ground. In this sorrowful and painful moment, the mother urged the two girls to reveal their vices in confession and be strengthened by communion with the Sacred Body. But at the very mention of the Sacred Body, their teeth began to chatter and they gnashed them, crying stridently: "Tomorrow! Tomorrow!" And all the while their voices kept repeating, "Wait! Wait! Hold up a little, hold up!" Among these cries, they finally breathed their last.

Since the mother of the monastery was determined that they could in no way be buried with the rest of the community, she ordered their tombs to be dug outside the boundaries in a segregated plot. During the next three years, a disc-shaped ball of fire frequently appeared over their graves which flared up most brightly during the forty days before the coming of Holy Easter or on Christmas Eve when a tumultuous crowd of many voices also resounded. Among those, two in particular broke through, ululating as though accustomed to scream in torment: "Woe is me! Woe is me! Woe is me!" Therefore, seeing the just sentence imposed by a just Judge on unjust souls, obviously a sentence of damnation, the mother of the monastery went to the tomb seeking to discover whether the cadavers were still there, however corrupt with putrescence. Six months after their bodies had been planted there, she discovered that the interior of the tomb had been burned out with fire. No vestige of earth or residue of the cadavers remained but glowing ashes. And the severity of the sentence lasted for three years so that terror of the damned should strike fear into their remaining companions. Thus the punishment imposed on the dead was a correction to the living and the health which threatened to fade from religion because of negligence or indifference or even hardness of heart was thus increased through the energetic efforts of the survivors.

20. Of the death of Landeberga and the angelic song.

After a while, further consolation was produced for our comfort. A certain virgin named Landeberga neared her last hour waiting to abandon the present life. She was looking forward to the comfort of leaving life with all its heavy cares, the blows of sorrow and the pricks of pain. When her summons came in the silence of the night, all those entrusted with watching the sick lay sunk into deepest slumber. Only one woman, Gernomeda, whose illness made her restless, kept watch among her companions. So when the awaited end came, she was dazzled to see the bed covered with a dense cloud and red lightning glittering. At the same time, she heard voices singing and exulting: "I will sing unto the Lord, for he hath triumphed gloriously."[43] As soon as she heard the singing, Gernomeda tried to rouse her care-worn companions but could by no means do so. With rapt attention, she awaited the end of things and saw the cloud gradually rise from the bed as the soul parted from the body. And when the cloud had risen on high and the singing voices could no longer reach her ears, the invalid was able to rouse her companions to render the chanting due to the dead. Then she warned them that she herself would be struck with grave fever within seven days and her life ended on the eighth day.

21. Of an effluence of oil and commutation of water.

Thereafter, the Institutor of Goodness and Favor never hesitated to bestow generous rewards from His piety. A certain maiden named Bithildis was converted to the convent during adolescence. After long discipline in the rule, she had at last been rendered unshakable and ardently desired her heavenly reward. As it happened, the Just Arbiter wanted to supply that just soul with an abundance of justice made full in Heaven. Thus, for several nights while she was in *extremis*, she asked them to place a burning light near her and put the message of sacred scriptures before her to be read. One of the watchers was supposed to refill the vessel with oil and water but was wholly overcome by sleep. Thus as night reached the end of its course, the sick woman spent the hours without the solace of her companions. But when the dawning day rushed in and they sang the matutinal praises of the Lord, it was apparent that oil had filled the lamp and the water had changed into milk. The attendant sought to discover whether one of her companions had changed it but they

43. Exodus 15:1.

asked: "Don't you know what happened? For this milk was not here." Then the sick woman said, "Don't wear out your wits over this work but make an investigation." And seeking more earnestly to understand, they called the mother and laid the case before her. She, to make more systematic inquiry, ordered the oil separated from the milk. And when they had skimmed off the oil and none remained on the semblance of milk, oil began again to increase and flow copiously from the vessel. Then the witnesses recognized the power of God and collected it with all care and stored it carefully in the sacrarium.[44] And these things were witnessed by Burgundofaro, Bishop of Meaux and Waldebert, Abbot of the community of Luxeuil.[45] Some invalids were restored to their original health when treated with this oil. But Bithildis awaited her happy end with all jocundity. And when she returned her soul to heaven, such sweet odors filled the cell that you would have thought she sweated balsam. For why did He turn His created water into the semblance of milk or order the flowing oil to multiply, except that Divine Mercy wished to show others how divine clemency visited the sick woman in the night? Though she had not wished to tell her companions what she had seen, the Omnipotent left this mark of His visitation and His power.

22. Of a beast seen because of food transgressions.

While we should not omit to transmit to posterity the many great things conferred as rewards for merit and the practice of religion, likewise we should reveal what we have found may be useful to terrify the hard or slothful mind. A certain girl of noble family came to the said community to bow her neck to the discipline of the rule. But the ancient serpent attacked her intention of a good life through the practice of religion. To tear her from Paradise by vicious transgression, he goaded her with greedy gluttony until she was driven to steal food to satisfy her hunger. For a while, she got away with this villainy undetected for none of her companions knew about it. Therefore, for a long time, avid gluttony soiled her mind until the Just Arbiter passed just sentence on the unjust soul. Her heavy fault was punished with heavier penance. Thus He excited her tired body with revulsion for lawful food so that her clouded mind rejected everything but bran and fronds and a mixture of wild herbs to eat. And when this punishment for her transgression had lain on her deluded mind for many days, and she asked to be given this food at the hour of refreshment, she saw the shape of a great boar eating with her, snorting grunts as he gobbled his food. Frightened, she asked what he

---

44. The sanctuary of the church or an ambry, a cabinet where sacred things are stored.

45. The bishop of Meaux was Burgundofara's brother. The similarity of the name Bithildis to that of his wife Bilhildis provokes some tempting speculation about the identity of the heroine of this story. Waldebert had become abbot of Luxeuil and had been appointed one of the directors of the convent. He also was the mentor of Sadalberga (chapter 10).

was. And the beast answered: "I am. Because up till now I have eaten with you the food which you gobbled up in your guilt. And from this, you may know that you will have to eat this food throughout the year's cycle." And thus as the year turned, her food remained limited. She could eat nothing but bran and tree leaves or wild herbs and the refuse cast out from the dregs of the brewing. And why should her fragile spirit have been thus scolded by a diabolic voice to make her conscious of the miserable transgression unless the savagery of present pain would spare her later from the agonies of the damned? Divine Piety wished by this to show the impropriety of consenting to him through whom sin spreads. Thus He made an example of how she had long complied with evil persuasion and through this punishment made it known that a creature ought to obey the Creator, not the Devil.

Similarly another girl named Beractrude lived in the community a long time but never made any effort to keep the precepts of the rule's discipline. The Devil instilled transgressions into her corrupt mind so that she would secretly eat whatever she could steal furtively. And when crime had long soiled her mind, the Just Arbiter gave her just sentence. She was struck with burning fever and began to cry out from the heat: "Woe is me!" After such cries, she slept so that all believed her dead. But after a space of many hours, she breathed and began to clamor: "Get the mother! Get the mother!" With rapid steps, the watchers went and called mother Burgundofara. When she saw her, she uncovered all her criminal intent through confession. And while all the bystanders expected the end of her life she returned as a convalescent. So afterwards, she lingered in this life, much troubled with attacks of fever until at last she ended her life.

[In one edition, the following spurious addition is appended to the foregoing part of the manuscript:]

After innumerable holy women had accomplished these diverse and disparate deeds under the rule of the Blessed Burgundofara, as we have told, they left this corruptible life for the quality of their merits. Even their venerable mother herself earned at last her celestial call. After she had most decently ruled the monastery of Evoriacus, she was seized by bodily illness, III nones April, the day of her end.[46] And she was gathered to her community of virgins to follow the Lamb wherever he went, that is the heavenly spouse, our Lord Jesus Christ who with the Father, and the Holy Spirit lives and reigns, God, from everlasting to everlasting. Amen.

Here ends the life of the holy abbess Burgundofara.

46. April 3.

10

Sadalberga, Abbess of Laon

(ca. 605–670)

Like Burgundofara, her contemporary, Sadalberga came from a family of aristocratic patrons involved in the evangelization of the Frankish countryside through the Irish monastic system. As was customary in that age of church decentralization, the generosity of these patrons was rewarded with the establishment of cults in their names. In the seventh century, saints tended to run in families. Thus Sadalberga was the daughter of sanctified parents and the mother of saintly children. She established at least two female monastic foundations from her inheritance, one of which she passed to her daughter Anstrude when she died. Her life spans the reigns of Clothar II and Dagobert (d. 639) and reaches into the troubled years of their successors. It was an age of increasing aristocratic self-confidence and importance. In 614, Clothar tried to stabilize their privileges in relation to the throne, but am-

This account is taken from *Vita Sadalberga abbatissae Laudunensis*, in Krusch, ed., *MGH, SRM* 5:40–66. Krusch believes the following extract from Jonas of Bobbio represents the only trustworthy information regarding Sadalberga. He condemns the life translated here as a ninth-century forgery and the biography of Anstrude as completely worthless, although he admits that a woman by that name did succeed Sadalberga at Laon. He believes that Sadalberga's marriage and five children were simply invented by the Carolingian author "to amplify his sterile material." Wemple, *Women in Frankish Society*, 153, accepts this condemnation without discussion. In fact, neither Sadalberga nor Anstrude have found defenders willing to examine the case in detail. We are not overly inclined to accept Krusch's judgment, considering his propensity to sneer at this material as we have noted in the introductions and notes for the lives of Genovefa and Rusticula. The anonymous author of this life knew Jonas's work, and his use of it demonstrates an ability and willingness to inflate his material without inventing any fresh narrative detail. From the dedication on, he conveys a vivid impression of being a near contemporary, which we cannot readily accept as witness to his strong literary powers. A telling argument against the authenticity of the document may be the lack of any church or cult at Laon to commemorate the two saints; however, it is hard to imagine who might have sponsored these biographies if no community stood to profit by the enhancement of the saints' cults. Sadalberga's establishment was probably Saint-Jean, which, in the twelfth century, was changed into a monastery of monks because the nuns there were charged with living too lax a life. The community has subsequently disappeared entirely.

bitious nobles continually threatened to escape royal control, or to take control of the palace administration and the persons of minor rulers. Meanwhile the royal family pursued its suicidal course of internal strife. Clothar yielded to Pippin of Landen's pressure to settle the old kingdom of Austrasia on his son Dagobert, although he attempted to keep his hold on Dagobert by marrying him to his own wife's sister. No sooner did Dagobert take over his new kingdom than he allowed himself to be persuaded to rebel against his father. In 629, he succeeded Clothar to the whole of Frankland, while Clothar's other son, Charibert, took over the government of Aquitaine. For ten years, Dagobert ruled a united kingdom, joined to a succession of three wives who seem to have represented various parts of the monarch's domains.[1]

Dagobert's personal life illustrates his keen understanding of the importance of well-chosen marriages. The role of women in family politics was firmly entrenched in the dynastic system of the seventh century. Sadalberga and the other women who appear in this chapter are not the unfortunate victims of a world wholly ruled by the sword as were their predecessors. By the middle of the century, the old legal restrictions on female inheritance of the family patrimony had been removed. Through marriage and motherhood, women bound the ruling class together, and they knew their own worth. Although they often ended tragically, they were not helpless pawns on a board controlled by men. Dagobert's attempt to force Sadalberga and other female saints of his circle into marriage should not be dismissed as literary romance. It was an obvious strategy to gain some control over his restless aristocracy and to prevent alliances that would be harmful to his own dynasty. The nobility's willingness to allow their women to choose a religious life should also be seen as a means of using their human capital to best advantage.[2]

Columbanus and his successors who promoted Irish monasticism had special affinity with this dynastic system, perhaps because Roman urbanization had never disturbed Irish rural and tribal structures. In any case, the Irish monk had discovered not only the family of Burgundofara on their rural estates but also the family of Autharius that produced the saintly brothers Ado and Dado (or Ouen). After Eustasius, his successor in Frankland, reclaimed Burgundofara, he discovered the youthful Sadalberga on the estates of her father Gundoin.[3]

---

1. Nanthild was later made regent with Ega for her son Clovis II in Neustria. The son of Wulfegund was destined for Austrasia. He repudiated Clothar's sister-in-law as soon as possible despite the violent reaction from her family and their supporters.

2. As Bateson was the first to point out in "Origin and Early History," her pioneering study of double monasteries, the power of the abbess reflected her social status.

3. Jonas of Bobbio, *Vita S. Columbani*, book 2, in Krusch, ed., *MGH, SRM* 4:121–23.

Returning to Luxeuil, the venerable man Eustasius prepared to fulfill the master's precepts to nourish the people of the vicinity with the food of faith. Therefore, going forth again, he preached to the Warascos who were given to the worship of idols and also to those stained with the errors of Fontinus and Bonosus.[4] Having converted them to the faith, he moved among the Boias, now called Bavarians, and, with much labor, correctly imbued them with the features of the faith and converted many to the faith. Having dwelt there for a while, he then sent out wise men who made mighty efforts to continue the work he had begun while he himself determined to return to Luxeuil. Hurrying on his way, he came to a certain Gundoin who was then staying in a villa called Meuse from the stream which flowed by the place. When he saw Eustasius, he received him joyfully in his home as a gift of grace. Having blessed the premises, Eustasius went into the place and asked to meet his children. Obediently, Gundoin presented him with two honest boys. "Is there," he said, "yet another child?" Gundoin confessed that he also had a daughter named Sadalberga who no longer possessed the light of her eyes. "Let her come here," Eustasius said. When he saw her, he asked whether her young soul aspired in awe to the divine service. She said that she had prepared herself as well as she could in her youthfulness to answer the holy call. Eustasius gave himself to his task. For two days, he prepared his body by fasting. He armed his spirit with faith. He poured the oil of benediction on her eyes. And she was worthy to have her blindness lighted through the holy man's intervention. Divine Piety by means of its servant restored her lost light that she, who received that light, might aspire after such divine benefits to worship God in awe. Furthermore, she not only gave herself to divine service for her own benefit but fittingly provided the chance to others.

The story of Sadalberga was then taken up by an anonymous author writing some time after her death at the request of her daughter and successor, Anstrude.

[Saint Sadalberga]
∎

Here begins the Prologue to the Life of Saint Sadalberga, Abbess, dedicated to the distinguished lord, decorated in honor with priestly insignia, in whom

---

4. Fontinus, Bishop of Sirmium, preached a sort of adoptionism condemned at the Synod of Rome

there has been an abundance of religion, to Omotarius neither pope nor priest, and to Abbess Anstrude, the most chaste virgin of Christ and Sadalberga.⁵

Oh, pride of venerable parents who were both kind and strong, I have not hesitated to obey your orders that with my pen I should hammer out the life of Sadalberga, most powerful nurturing mother and foremost woman of our time, and the order of her deeds as much as conditions allow and Divine Piety favors. But I feel myself unequal to this task, for I am barely imbued with the beginnings of letters and educated in Christian simplicity. Still, I remember our Lord and Savior's declaration: "Ask and it shall be given to you; seek and ye shall find; knock and it shall be opened unto you";⁶ and that psalmographic oracle: "Open thy mouth wide, and I shall fill it."⁷ Therefore, although I have attempted by a rash effort to weave her deeds together, I ask my reader, if such there be, to condescend to read caught up by love of the holy mother. Seek not here the eloquence of Tully, nor his great oratory, nor flowers of philosophy and the varied claims of the stoics, but only truth and the simplicity of the church.⁸ For the eagle does not always fly into the ether with wings spread wide but as frequently descends to earth with drooping feathers. And often, at the banquets of kings, the humble apple and the barnyard lettuce are most highly prized. Pray to God the Father that He will reveal the cloudy sense to the hardest and darkest heart. Pray our Savior, Jesus Christ, that He will deign to waft a breath of the Holy Spirit which, the darkness dispelled from our heart, will provide ease of speech. Thus we may be worthy to describe the acts of the venerable mother who always burned with love for monasteries and churches and pass them on to posterity briefly and succinctly. May He, Who makes the tongues of children eloquent, grant what I ask aided by your prayers.

End of Prologue.

---

(375) and the Council of Constantinople (381). Bonosus spread this teaching to the Danubian provinces; see Fontinus in *Encyclopedic Dictionary of Religion*.

5. Omotarius is unknown, although Krusch notes that Mabillon thought him bishop of Laon. For the description of him as "decorated with priestly honor," Krusch refers to a ninth-century formula. See Zeumer, ed., *MGH, Formulae*, 517, which uses the phrase *infula sacerdotalis honoris decorati*. The *infula* that designates his priestly honor is defined by the *CCSL Lexicon* as the headgear or pallium of an archbishop or priestly insignia. In his vast experience as an editor, Krusch thought the designation *papae necnon et sacerdoti* to be unique. Anstrude was Sadalberga's daughter and successor at Laon; see chapter 16. The dedication ends with "et Sadalbergae," who could be yet a third person. Krusch feels that it was meant to refer to Anstrude as Sadalberga's daughter.

6. Matthew 7:7.

7. Psalms 81:10.

8. Tully is the common medieval reference to Marcus Tullius Cicero.

Here begins the life of the Abbess Sadalberga

■

1. Sadalberga first entered into the human condition in the suburb of Leucus in the town of Langres, born of a noble family of the district called Uternus for the stream flowing by the place. But more illustrious or more noble than her birth was the solicitous care of her parents in nurturing her. At that time, the Bavarian *gens*, whom the most learned man and student of history, Orosius, named the Boias from an earlier usage, were settled at the ends of Germany.[9] Entangled in the reins of the ancient and clever enemy, they were infected with the error of Bonosus which the defenders of the holy church call the Bonosiacan heresy, and held [perverse notion!] that our Lord Jesus Christ was wholly human without the Father's Godhood.[10] To confute this nefarious and insane doctrine and cut it away, the venerable man, Eustasius was instigated by the Divine Spirit to journey forth from the monastery of Luxeuil in the wilderness of the Vosges which had been built through King Childebert's munificence with the greatest care and labor by a man of laudable fame and mighty sanctity, Columbanus, a pilgrim come out of Ireland.

2. But, though we have made mention of that great man Columbanus, it is unnecessary to weave his deeds into our work. For the most eloquent man Jonas, as he was burning the midnight oil, already showed how, amidst the tumults of the world in King Theuderic's reign, he suffered the sly treachery of nefarious enemies instigated by Queen Brunhild; how he was driven from his brethren by that reckless tyranny and went into Italy and built the monastery of Bobbio by permission and authority of Agilulf, king of the Lombards and gave a rule to the monks. Jonas published all that in the book of the life and miracles which proceeded from his pen.[11] Letters also survive from this same father Columbanus in which he mentioned his book On Pastoral Care to the most blessed and fluent man, Gregory, Pontiff of Rome, who at that time was held in great esteem and endowed with sanctity so that the secrets of Heaven stood revealed to him by the Holy Spirit's favor.[12] He discussed the nine orders of angels after the apostle Paul in a wonderful manner which was unique or very rare.[13] To this day, the entire west is enlightened by the beauty of his eloquent teaching and instruction in the medicines of penitence. But this same venerable man sent mellifluous writings to the aforesaid father.

---

9. Orosius 4:20, 11.

10. Citing Isidore of Seville, *Etymologies* 8:5, 32, in PL 82:302. Krusch shows this to be adoptianism (MGH, SRM 5:51, n. 3).

11. Jonas of Bobbio, *Vita S. Columbani.*

12. Krusch, MGH, SRM 5:52, n. 1, cites a letter from Columbanus to Gregory (MGH, *Epistolae* 3:159) referring to Gregory's book.

13. Gregory, Homily 34 in *Evangelio*, PL 76:1249.

3. To return to the subject, the Man of God Eustasius was going out to the aforesaid people in the heart of Germany so that the Creator's light should in no way be hid under a bushel but, placed on a candlestick, shine brightly on all, so that the talent should not be buried in the ground and lost but be presented with double interest. With the great sharpness of speech our Lord Jesus Christ conferred upon him, he cut the destructive doubt of that burgeoning error from the path of the gospel, preaching that our Lord Jesus had His divinity equally with God the Father and our human nature from His mother's body, which He Himself created and put on without sin and without diminishing His unity with God as He was always with His Father and nothing could weaken His dignity, whence Christ must be called true God and true man.[14]

4. Afterwards, following a hard trip to the Germans and Belgae, he was returning from the Bavarians when the famous man encountered a certain illustrious man of power and opulent wealth and secular fame, highest dignities and skill in courtly affairs named Gundoin. He was staying at the time in a certain villa called Meuse from the stream flowing by the place whose source, rising from the borders of Langres, after many bends and hidden circuits in the ground, after receiving flowing rivers into its sides, floods swiftly into the Rhine and at length pours itself into the barbarian Ocean. Gundoin having seen the venerable man received him as a most gracious gift. Furthermore, as he had usually to concern himself with human affairs,[15] among the salubrious words of pastoral encouragement in the conversation of men of faithful minds, the man of God began to inquire whether there were sprouts sprung from the root of that illustrious Frank. Indeed, I think that the man of God sensed that there was a child there predestined by God, as later events proved. Then the most illustrious Gundoin presented two good young sons with his wife Saretrude, a noble woman of elegant form, that they might receive the grace of benediction. Of these, the oldest was Leudinus, cognomen Bodo, and the younger was Fulculfus, who was also called Bodo.[16] But the man of God asked if there were not another child and they admitted to a maiden sister who was of a proper age but who had been blind for some time. The man of God said plainly, "Come, I entreat, let us take a look at her." For as I suspect, he knew in his heart that the Lord

---

14. Matthew 5:15 and Matthew 5:25 embellish this unwieldy sentence.

15. Krusch prefers the variant *fervere* over *favere*, citing Gregory the Great, *Regula Pastorum*, 2:7, PL 77:41.

16. One of these brothers later became bishop of Toul, installing his daughter as abbess in a new monastery near the city. It is not clear whether Odila, c. 18, was his wife or the wife of Sadalberga's second brother. Guérout, "Les origines," 25–26, also believes that Sadalberga was related to Agilbert, bishop of Paris, whose sister was second abbess of Jouarre. For more on the family network, see Ebling, *Prosopographie*, 166–67.

would confer health upon her. Then he fasted for three days before pouring the oil of benediction on the girl's eyes.[17] Wondrous to say! The girl was soon brought to pristine health through Christ's assisting grace. Nor was she undeserving, for Almighty God answers the prayers of servants who crucify their own wills for Him.

5. Then another splendid miracle followed. The same girl suffered for a long time from a flow of blood and, because of this grave illness, weakness had long restrained her body. Shrewdly, the great man ascertained this and prayed profusely, asking the wonted divine assistance. The eternal Maker of things, Who is at hand to those who fulfill His holy precepts with pious obedience, heard the prayers of His faithful servant. What more? The girl, having received health, was restored without injury.

6. When she reached maturity, her parents saw that the maiden grew, ornamented with good manners, graceful and fair of face. As is the case with many another enjoying good fortune after danger has passed, their minds grew cool. They thought about children to succeed them. Against her will, they gave the maiden to a certain mighty man of noble birth named Richramnus in marriage. But he had barely enjoyed his conjugal rights for two months when he was set free from human cares and deprived of life.

7. After all this was done, Eustasius returned to Luxeuil. Later, he proceeded to the Warascos who dwelt in part of the Sequani's province on either bank of the Doubs' flowing stream. Till then, they had been rotting away, stained by the same error of Bonosus and Fontinus themselves now grown old. The man of God came to them working with the plowshare of the Gospel and the cauterizing iron of holy Scripture, lest hardening clods should spread in the Lord's fields with tares and cockles suffocating the oats. Though with no lack of labor, he restored them to the bosom of Holy Church, and they still persevere in the way they learned from him, hoping for divine grace.[18]

8. Then after many hazardous adventures and immense labors against dire storms of heretics and the frauds of the schismatic Agrestius which are fully contained in his acts, Eustasius, his blessed life as a good athlete mighty with miracles ended, migrated to the Lord.[19] Third after his master's decease, he had guided and cared for his brothers with no less light. In his place (by a prior agreement), Waldebert of blessed memory was chosen to govern his brothers, a man of laudable fame and outstanding sanctity, with no small learning in

---

17. Compare this with the excerpt from Jonas of Bobbio, *Vita S. Columbani*, in which the fast lasted two days and her promise to consecrate herself to God precedes her cure, as in the life of Burgundofara. This discrepancy provoked Krusch to doubt the authenticity of the present text.

18. Jonas of Bobbio, *Vita S. Columbani*, 2:8.

19. Eustasius died April 2, 629. Ibid., 2:9–10.

church discipline, famous for goodness, piety, and charity, abounding in doctrine. In his time, bands of monks and holy maidens began to spring up through all the provinces of Gaul. They thronged not only through the fields, farms and villages and castles but even in the lonely wilderness. Monasteries began to blossom just from the rules of the blessed Benedict and Columbanus where only a few had appeared in the area before that time.

9. But let us return to the articulation of our tale. The most prudent woman, Sadalberga remained a widow for two years. Though she still wore secular dress, by earnest vigils and fasts and well-supplied almsgiving, as much as her strength would bear, she eagerly rendered to God what is God's.[20] Often indeed, she ruminated on the instruction she had received from the Blessed Eustasius which weighed on her mind like a burden on a beast. When she had undertaken all these things, she determined in her mind that she longed to flee to the refuge of that convent of holy virgins, the magnificent palace in the Vosges which blessed Romaric built after he had been converted by blessed Eustasius' exhortations.[21] She would have made binding vows if sex had not been an impediment and royal snares not entrapped her.[22]

10. For at that time, Dagobert held the scepter and governed the realm of the Franks, a man stamped with a sharp nature and princely glory. Not only his own subjects who had sworn him their faith, but nations near and far dreaded him because of his reputation. Gundoin, fearing to incite the king's wrath and ferocity because of his daughter, drew her cautiously back from the road where she had freely determined to go step by step.[23] For news of her intention had come to the king's ears. At that time, a certain strong man welcome in the royal council and greatly renowned among his own people, named Blandinus who affected the cognomen Baso, was staying at the prince's court. He, who came from the stock of a notable Sicambrian family, took Sadalberga in marriage, not by her own will, since she had not long

---

20. Matthew 22:21.

21. Romaric supported Agrestius, but was later converted to the support of Columbanus and his companions. His foundation of Remiremont long remained one of the leading female monasteries in Frankland; see Parisse, *Remiremont*; Constable, "The *Liber Memorialis* of Remiremont"; and Hlawitschka, "Studien zur Abtissinnenreihe von Remiremont." His establishment also provided hospitality for the retirement of Arnulf of Metz.

22. In the previous sentence, the author seems aware that there was a place for women in this retreat, but later he refers only to "monachorum" in both Romaric's houses. Possibly the impediment of sex is a bald reference to her lack of virginity.

23. For other examples of Dagobert's intervention in aristocratic marriages, see chapters 11 and 12. Another example, although only available in a twelfth-century version, is Godeberta, who was saved by the intervention of Saint Eligius. Krusch's skepticism about this marriage (MGH, SRM 5:42) should be balanced by the reasonable supposition that not every prospective bride who drew the king's attention was successful at defying or escaping him or was saved by a miracle.

before vowed to bury herself in divine precepts, but in obedience to her parents, by order of the King and for the procreation of children.

11. Thus she was joined with a worthy man. Although under marital law, they both performed Christian works and most devoutly kept themselves in baptismal purity. For they were hospitable and, following the greatest of preachers, blessed Paul, gave great alms to the household of faith,[24] and to pilgrims, obeying the servants of Christ with greatest veneration, mindful of the Savior's precept: "As you have done it unto one of the least of these, you have done it unto me."[25] And that of the Blessed Apostle Peter, "Use hospitality without grudging."[26] Strengthened by the Lord's help, they led a life of Christian vigor. Yet they had no children and the most Christian woman feared that she might be deprived of that privilege. Still she adhered to the faith of the holy women Anna and Elizabeth, who kept watch in the Lord's temple with vigils and prayers and, after a long period of sterility, deserved to procreate children.[27] She went to the basilica of Blessed Remigius, the Bishop who made the city of Reims in Champagne famous by his holy virtues and miracles. There she devoted herself to keeping watch in vigils and prayers and vowed that if Divinity would concede her a child she would consecrate her to the Lord. Then immediately on her return home, the Lord granted what she had asked so faithfully and anxiously. She conceived and bore a daughter whom she named Saretrude from her grandmother. Then she had another daughter whom she named Ebana. She bore yet a third daughter and called her Anstrude in the regenerative grace of baptism who in the course of time, by the will of the community, was to succeed her in the care and ruling of her sisters. She still survives and now rules under the auspices of Christ with divine privilege.[28] She had also a fourth child who was named Eustasius in the grace of baptism by the consecrated priests.[29] He died while still in infancy. Finally she bore a fifth child of good quality, a boy named Baldwin whom she consecrated to almighty God with the earlier children.[30] Christ's handmaid did this because she was absolutely determined that her whole

24. Galatians 6:10.
25. Matthew 25:40.
26. 1 Peter 4:9.
27. Luke 1 and 2.
28. If Krusch's argument that Sadalberga was a virgin and therefore childless is to be believed, this author would be engaging in an artistic but fairly outrageous and pointless lie.
29. Krusch notes that this Eustasius is noted for his relics reposing in a case in the monastery of Saint Jean of Laon, Sadalberga's foundation. Mabillon claims that the children of Sadalberga are commemorated in *The Calendar of Queen Emma,* for which Krusch refers back to his own criticisms (45).
30. Having borne a son who lived past infancy, Sadalberga may have felt, or may have persuaded her husband, that her dynastic obligations were fulfilled. The pattern of several girls and a final male child suggests that this was the condition of her release. For Baldwin's tragic fate, see chapter 16.

household, husband and children as well as herself, would form a church of Christ.

12. Meanwhile, the fame of Blessed Waldebert, whose reputation for sanctity we noted above, spread to the farthest boundaries of all the Frankish lands. By Christ the Lord without whom no good thing is done, the skill of his preaching enflamed them with the desire to worship God so that monasteries of men and virgins of Christ were established under his rule.[31] Blessed Sadalberga, who was soon to flower with exemplary virtue and blaze out on high, noted this and being assiduous to gather the flock torn from the jaws of the wolves, frequently summoned the servant of Christ and famous warrior to her home for his benediction and bestowal of grace. She received him rejoicing as a divine gift conceded by God and eagerly desired to drink words of salvation and fitting medicine for souls from his mellifluous mouth. Her soul insistently burned to ascend to the height of virtue, the apex of sanctity, despising worldly trappings and mundane pomp. In the Gospel, the Lord and Savior told of these heights, saying "Everyone that hath forsaken houses or brethren or sisters or father or mother or lands for my name's sake shall receive a hundred fold, and shall inherit eternal life."[32] "I am come to send fire on the earth; and I would that it were already kindled."[33] What more? Committing all her hopes to God the Creator and, after God, to the blessed man, she converted her husband and consecrated her children to God. She then took the religious habit and, with the counsel of Blessed Waldebert and the assistance of her living husband, undertook to erect a convent of maidens in the suburbs of the town of Langres on her paternal inheritance or succession. This she endowed with her own revenues from the lands of her hereditary paternal succession, nobly making Christ her heir.[34] To ease the work forward, venerable Waldebert offered and committed artisans and laborers to her. This place, though it was near the Austrasian border, was really in Burgundy, a little less than forty miles from Luxeuil.[35] There she

---

31. Waldebert was Eustasius's successor at Luxeuil and is credited with combining the Rule of Columbanus with that of Benedict whose influence was growing under papal patronage throughout the seventh century. Waldebert, *Regula*, PL 88:1053–70.

32. Matthew 19:29.

33. Luke 12:49.

34. About 650, Sigebert III of Austrasia added the formulas devised by a monk named Marculf (whose patron was Arnulf of Metz) to the Ripuarian Law. Book 2:12 states, "An ancient but unjust custom is observed among us: it directs that sisters have no part of the paternal estates with their brothers. But I, considering this an injustice and knowing well, my dear children, that the Lord gave you to me for that I should love with equal love, I institute you, my dearest daughter, my legitimate heir with your brothers that you should have a part no less than theirs in my land and goods." For further study of these legal formulas, see Murray, *Germanic Kinship*.

35. Butler, *Lives of the Saints*, September 22; identifies the place as Poulangey.

gathered more than a hundred women both from the free nobility and from her own service whom she gave to Christ the Lord.[36]

13. But when the greater part of the monastery's fabric had been erected, the handmaid of Christ, filled with God's spirit, began to have forebodings. Carefully in her mind, she began to weigh with her husband whether the place was safe for a convent of maidens since it had neither stability nor protection. For, though it was then far away from barbarians, secure within the king's frontiers, there were signs of those future perils which we have since experienced. There has been civil war between the Frankish kings, Theuderic and Dagobert, around these borders.[37] The neighborhood has been depopulated; fields and farms and buildings and, what is more serious, the bodies of saints have been incinerated. Whence it seems clear that she was imbued with the divine spirit when, long ago, she anticipated these hazards.

14. Therefore, she took counsel with the wise abbot Waldebert who was so endowed with ingenuity and vigorous wisdom and good nature in all these things. Thereafter, he became her travelling companion and the partner of her labors. And she chose the road where Christ led, following the example of the holy patriarch Abraham who went out of the land of Mesopotamia to Syria and lived as a settler among the Philistines where God promised that his posterity would come into the succession. Imitating him, the servant of God relinquished fatherland and patrimony, for she preferred to act with Christ rather than possess the profits of mammon. And she endured as many dangers when she set out for the city of Laon with the souls God had committed to her, carrying as many supplies as possible and provided with a stipend for life. That town could be walled from a siege by the enemy and it had a strong natural defense, sitting on a rocky height, so that it could not be broken into and was safe from barbarian threats. For in ancient times when Vandals, Alans, Huns and other German and Scythian peoples surrounded it in vain, no ballistics could make a dent in the rampart; neither siege engines nor thrown spears nor pounding battering ram availed. They all fell back frustrated, their labor wasted.[38] For besides the walled circuit extending

36. This seems to imply that both the servants and the ladies were admitted equally to the monastery, which would conform to the monastic ideal, although the rules of the period warn entrants against seeking to raise their social status by entering religion. See McNamara, "Ordeal of Community."

37. The war between Theuderic of Neustria and Dagobert II of Austrasia lasted from 675 to 679. See *LHF*, 46, and chapter 16 of this volume. Again, the author has achieved a vivid sense of being a contemporary that would be highly artistic if he were, in fact, writing in the ninth century.

38. Krusch notes that Jerome, *Epistola CXXIII ad Ageruchiam*, PL 22:1057, referred to this invasion.

outside on the heights of the peak, there was an equal circuit of earth within the walls so that no machine ever made could hope to reduce the town. On the other side, natural rock surrounds them. The town within was filled with wells; fountains flowed all year at the exits and gates, for the use of people, cattle and beasts of burden. Now as the venerable woman approached with her holy following to illuminate the town like the sun's rays, Attila, prelate of the city, came to meet her with the highest honors, as though a crowd of angels were coming as a divine gift. And he led the flock of Christ's holy handmaids into the city while a chanting chorus rejoiced with psalms and hymns of praise.[39]

15. But we must not be silent about the miracle, the magnificent thing that happened in the city that night. The bishop had ordered his boys and trusted servants to come and prepare a welcoming dinner for the handmaids of Christ the next day. As the servants hurried into the city by the night gate, they were astonished to see different sorts of beasts and wild things in their path. For one saw a wild ox, another a deer; one saw a bear, another a sow; some saw wolves, several foxes and still another a lascivious ass and a savage lion going away.[40] They were fleeing the city together with many other beastly monsters which I shall not name for it would make the work too prolix and thus subject the reader to boredom. Trembling at the miracle, all the servants marvelled. For such beasts never had appeared in this place before. What else could they suppose but that, unable to tolerate the holiness and vigor of God's handmaids, the ancient enemy was fleeing with his satellites? Nor was it unsuitable that he should deform himself into the shapes of wild and bestial monsters, producing various figments. For, having been created a good angel by a good Creator, he had swollen up with pride and said in his heart: "I will ascend into Heaven; I will exalt my throne above the stars of God: I will be like the Most High."[41] Now, ejected from supernal light and the delights of Paradise, he works the mystery of iniquity with his followers in the form of worms and mice and other deformed species.[42]

16. From ancient times—which many still remember, for there are those still living here who saw these crimes—worship of the ancient serpent cruelly flourished in this city and he used his cunning arts to sport with the rustic

---

39. Krusch notes that Attila had been appointed to the see by his brother Leudegisel, Bishop of Reims, sometime after the death of Chagnoald, Burgundofara's brother and the partner of Waldebert in the supervision of Evoriacus around 632. De Long, *Histoire ecclésiastique*, locates it at 640.

40. It is conceivable that this story was inspired by a Roman pavement still on view in the municipal museum at Laon, depicting Orpheus attracting some of these beasts with his music.

41. Isaiah 14:13–14.

42. 2 Thessalonians 2:7.

louts and stupid men. For it is written of him: "He injures by a thousand arts."[43] Under a form of idolatrous baptism, he claimed them for his own. In ancient times, they derived "idol" from *ludo*, sport.[44] Accordingly, the devil disported himself in their midst and many murders were perpetrated. And this most nefarious demon plied his crafty arts so that if a man were hurt in some way by his neighbor, he would cause his innocent relatives by consanguinity or affinity to shed torrents of blood. Thus over time, increments of evil accumulated through the abominable custom and the wicked robber claimed the miserable city for his own, entangled in his net.[45] But the omnipotent Lord, merciful in all things, Who will have all men to be saved, and to come unto knowledge of the truth,[46] looked kindly at the creatures in His keeping and uprooted the sacrilege and wicked crimes of the past from the city.

17. But now let us return to the narrative we had begun. Soon they had studied the layout of the place. Finding the most appropriate, gracious and least dangerous site, they began to lay the foundations of the church and houses within the fortifications. When it was properly completed, sprouts from both noble and servile stock began to gather to praise almighty God, our Lord Jesus Christ. For what powerful man or noble woman who lived in that place did not delight in love of blessed Sadalberga? She was always joyous and placid of face, full of chastity and humility, quick to give alms and devoted strongly to the worship of God. What more? Within a short space of time, about three hundred handmaids of Christ accumulated in this place or in an adjoining monastery and she dispensed the rule to these squadrons after the fashion of the monks of Agaune and Habenda.[47] Day and night she ordered the office to be sung, resounding to Almighty God and prayer without ceasing, according to the famous teaching of Paul.[48] And to this day, the convent still celebrates this custom auspiciously for Christ. Indeed the same fierce love still burns in the same desire to sing those songs.

18. As we said above, she gathered many thirsting nobles in Christ's service.

43. Sulpicius Severus, *Vita S. Martini*, 22:1.

44. Krusch tracks this reference to Isidore of Seville's *Etymologies* 8:11, 8, which refers to Prometheus making figures *de luto*, from clay.

45. Presumably the author was a churchman accustomed to Roman law and offended by the principle of collective responsibility that characterized all the barbarian codes.

46. 1 Timothy 2:4.

47. Agaune was Romaric's foundation in the Vosges; Habenda later became known as Remiremont. De Long, *Histoire ecclésiastique*, 66, says she built seven basilicas in her monastery, the fifth for the cross, which might suggest some connection with Poitiers. Echoes of an *imitatio Radegundis* appear throughout this work.

48. 1 Thessalonians 5:17. The *laus perennis* had been established at St. Denis and spread with the Irish rules.

And among other noble Sicambrian women, Odila who was mighty for good and of a nature both noble and clever, took venerable Waldebert's antidote and became marked for Christian health. She took counsel with her lawful husband the illustrious Bodo, whom we have named Leudinus above.[49] At that time, he was industrious, powerful and flourishing according to secular dignity. They laid aside the trappings of the world, converted to the Lord, and he conferred their goods on her monastery, taking the same road, hurrying to Laon after blessed Sadalberga. Abandoning the affairs of Caesar, Bodo observed the monastic offices as well as his affairs would permit, for he soon became Bishop of Toul.[50] Before long, he had paid his debt to nature. The venerable Odila put on the sign of Christ.[51] She joined the chorus of holy virgins living the blessed life under the rule of obedience until, as all must do, she too gave up her spirit.

Here ends the life.

Here begins the death of the Abbess Sadalberga

■

19. Thus the blessed Sadalberga spent her life piously with her sisters, grew old in sanctity and dignified of mien (as was said of Blessed Hilary). Once, a certain consecrated maiden, while singing the office in church, fell to the ground, with her mind all out of control, caught up in the furious disease of epilepsy. Quickly, holding her tenderly, the blessed and venerable mother prayed sedulously to God and with the help of divine grace purged her of the sickness and ordered her freely to proceed unharmed in the service of Christ.

20. There are many other well known things that our pen could insert in praise of the holy mother's memory which would be appropriate in this place. One time, when a visit from blessed Waldebert was expected and there was not enough wine, she ordered a drink called beer to be made from wheat or barley meal which, brewed by human skill, is much used in the nations of the west. When it was poured into one of those vessels which the vulgar call a tun, the strong liquor did not fill it to the brim. That handmaid of Christ who was in charge of the cellar that year according to the requirements of the rule,[52] came most humbly to the venerable mother and said: "Lady, mother,

---

49. Sadalberga's brother.

50. Krusch, MGH, SRM 5:60, n. 3, notes various charters identifying Leudinus as bishop of Toul in the reign of Sigibert II.

51. *Stigmate Christi*, for which Krusch refers to Ducange's definition, the veil of virginity.

52. Benedict, Rule, c. 31; "Rule of Donatus," c. 61 (based on Columbanus), both provide annual appointment of a cellaress.

what can we do? The brew didn't fill the vessel and it is fermenting in the air.[53] If the holy abbot's arrival is delayed, I fear the drink will sour to bitter vinegar." And she said to her, "Go and pour what was left when the liquor was prepared into the vessel." Never doubting that she could fulfill the holy mother's orders, she ran quickly back and found the vessel full so that the air space slowly disappeared. Such is the mercy of the omnipotent God! The mother was strong in her disciple. For divine power reached out to make the short draft grow larger. Returning speedily, God's handmaid humbly told the holy mother of the miracle and she gave thanks to the highest Creator of all things, Jesus Christ, Who is always with His servants in the way of truth.

21. Then another miracle was accomplished. One of the sisters, who was supposed to wash the clothes as is the custom, approached the workroom ceiling where it was normally done, holding the vessel she needed for the job and carrying a little wood. But the chain from which the vessel hung was too short and meager and the fire could not reach it. So the industrious servant of God bound another chain together with it. Then another sister, assigned to a similar task, came in with another copper vessel. Humbly, she asked her companion: "Sister, will you let me have one chain so we can both work more quickly?" And her companion said: "For the sake of charity, I will help you but the vessels are too high for the fire. Run and bring as much wood as you can so we can do our tasks." She went off then but could not find what she sought. Then both handmaids of Christ began to worry for they knew not what to do. Then, behold! suddenly, there was a great noise as though the workroom ceiling was about to collapse and it bent itself to the fire. The two handmaids of Christ ran out as all the sisters came to look, asking what made the crashing and clattering. Seeing the miracle, they were astonished at what had happened. Then the venerable mother ordered that the man of God, the priest Italus, prior of the community, come and contemplate this miracle. And when the man of God arrived, seeing that the ceiling was not destroyed by the crash but remained intact, he gave fulsome thanks to Almighty God, considering the merits of the mother who had such well-trained and devoted disciples that the elements served their ardent charity.

22. Then one day when she was walking outside the town walls, beneath the enclosure of the convent in the summertime, she saw Landefrid, the monk who was her gardener, examining the vegetables in the walled garden, for what reason I do not know. He was pulling up some innocuous plants. In a soft whisper which the other sisters could in no way hear, she said to him:

---

53. In brewing, it is necessary that fermentation be stopped by cooling the brew and protecting it from exposure to air. Here, the air threatened to contaminate the drink and heat it, starting the fermentation process again that would spoil it.

"Bring us some lettuce, brother Landefrid," communicating with him more by intimation than enunciation as the brother, who is still here, is wont to tell the tale. Wonderful to say! The voice which was but a breath of air heard by no other, came to the brother's ears as though she had spoken directly to him. Yet there was a distance of four stadia or more between them.[54]

23. Then another sort of miracle occurred. Once she was serving her sisters for her week in the office of cook as was the rule.[55] There was but small store of the little fishes and other things suitable for monastic uses. Basinus the archdeacon was resting in his house in the same town when, behold!, a voice sounded in his ear saying: "Didn't you know that the abbess is cooking for the sisters? It's a sight worth seeing. You should run over there." But, taking it lightly, he ignored it. He had to be told three times and even threatened with a whipping. [Then he wondered] what he should do and what modest gift he could bring to so great a mother [for] at least he had some task of that sort. Just as he went out of the house, he found a man at her guest entrance carrying a wonderfully huge fish. Believing it had been sent by divine favor, he paid the proper price for the fish and brought it to the blessed mother. She served it as a meal to the sisters and it filled everyone very comfortably. And let none believe that this happened by any human labor but it was prepared for their refreshment by Divine Favor.

24. Indeed, we cannot hide in silence that almighty God loved her in this life with so great a love that He purged her like purest gold. Once her blood boiled with such a fever that it carried grave illness throughout her body and she lost the power of speech. But when she recovered with the help of Christ, the sisters asked, indeed entreated her, to know what had set her right. She answered with fervent spirit: "Oh, sweetest sisters, why do you seek for the cause of things? I was being strangled by exceedingly harsh and raging spirits. But then I began convalescing when two wings emerged from my back and circled about. The sight of them was more beautiful than the purest gold and I sensed that their edges were clearly sharper than a two-edged sword. When they protected me, the most abominable spirits fled." What might we understand by this, except that God Almighty purges His creatures in the present life and gathers them with the saints in the protection of his strong right hand? For by the wings, we are to understand the higher powers of Holy Scripture. With her body regaining strength and with a stronger mind, she lived nearly a year and nine months free from attack.

25. Who can worthily put into words the astute nature of her holiness and sagacity whose charity and humility governed all her subjects in wonderful

---

54. About 740 meters.
55. As in chapter 4, a practice taken from the Rule of Caesarius of Arles.

sweetness and loving bounty? For she had a smiling face and lovely looks. She was swift to speak but her words were moderate, and her advice prudent. Particularly in ordering the affairs of the monastery, she was wise by nature. She loved to give alms and was never sluggish in hospitality. She was distinguished in the practice of her rule, imitating the holy women Melania and Paula[56] As Jerome said, Melania was the noblest of Roman women, daughter of the former consul Marcellinus. She journeyed to Jerusalem where she lived in such humility and with such remarkable charity that she might take the name of Thecla.[57] And in like manner he said of Paula that she left her urban patrimony of the noblest Gracchan line, and went to rural Bethlehem to live a life of goodness and humility, pouring out her holy spirit to the Lord.[58] And, as I said above, Blessed Sadalberga imitated the Augusta Helena, mother of the Augustus Constantine, who, as the Ecclesiastical History says, put off the pomp of the world to mortify her fleshly limbs, daily serving God as a handmaid.[59] She personally did everything that might be useful to the convent and assigned herself the task of cleaning. She did the cooking and other business customary to the monastic life in her weekly turn.[60]

26. With these and other good habits she grew so strong under Christ's rule that in the house where she was accustomed to dwell, she saw a tabernacle descend from on high of wondrous and splendid brightness, spacious beneath and steeply peaked above, which sheltered a wonderful white bird, shining in splendor. The bird carried her, caught up in a state of ecstasy, across the river and put her down in an exceedingly pleasant meadow where various flowers generated fragrant scents. And among the bright lilies and blushing roses she saw a crowd of children of both sexes playing in snowy robes and crowned with laurels. And the little boy, Magobert, stepped out from among them.[61] Seeing her, he said, "Do you know me, mother?" She said, "I don't." The boy answered, "I am Magobert, Amiliana's son, whom

---

56. Melania, Paula, and Helena are no doubt being offered as models because they were married women who had borne children before consecrating themselves to religion.

57. Jerome, *Chronicle*, anno 376. Thecla was a popular early Christian saint believed to be the first woman to consecrate herself to the life of virginity as preached by Paul.

58. Jerome, *Epistola* 108, PL 22:878ff. For further discussion, see McNamara, "Cornelia's Daughters."

59. Helena was a popular pattern for noble women. Krusch identifies the "ecclesiastical history" cited here as Rufinus, *Historia*, 10:7–8.

60. As in c. 23, and also on the model of Radegund, the author is anxious to emphasize that his heroine did not take advantage of the abbess's exemption from the menial labors of the community provided by the Rule.

61. If Sadalberga's daughter Anstrude was the intended recipient of this work, presumably she knew who Magobert and Amiliana were. The boy might have been a godchild of Sadalberga's or a child who was raised in the convent and then died.

you have sent before you. And I live in this light, as you see." And soon she saw a blessed man, the venerable bishop Anseric coming to meet her. He said to her, "Do you know me?" And, when she confessed her ignorance, he said: "I am Anseric, Bishop of Soissons, whom you have seen often visiting in your house. Come, I will show you the gates of Paradise."[62] And he showed her the city of the most high God, and the seats of the twelve Apostles shimmering with gold and gems. And he said to her, "Behold! Your own place is prepared. But because the Blessed Mary cannot endure the prayers of the sisters who need you still, her eyes are bejewelled.[63] She has beseeched her Son that you might return a while to them before you collect your reward from God." Then the bird snatched her in its mouth and returned her, breathing once again, to earth.

27. And while she rested in the night, the angel of the Lord appeared to her for the third time, as might be expected, in the shape of the venerable man Waldebert. And she saw him draw off the girdle from his loins to wear it no more. This meant, I think, that his honor would increase in succeeding generations.[64] As she often said, he shone with stunning whiteness. In a loving voice, he said to the woman: "Oh, sweetest daughter, prepare to claim your prize. Get ready to come away for I also long to receive an award for your victory. Your summons will come a hundred days from now. Then the fruit of your labors, which you have sought with much exertion, will be given you with multiple interest from the Lord's storehouse." Hearing this, she summoned one of her familiar sisters and revealed the dream and its meaning. The sister spread the word among the others that the angel of the Lord had admonished her to complete the psalter through each day and night of the hundred remaining to her. So she began that day to worship the Lord more fully in vigils, fasting, psalms and prayers, with a firmer devotion and swifter service.

28. The twentieth day before her calling, her feet gave out and she took to her bed, as was said of the perfect man: "The almond tree shall flourish, and the grasshopper shall be a burden and desire shall fail because man goeth to his long home."[65] Finally she had completed her duties. The flock of sisters was summoned and she told them in her own voice: "Persevere in the service

---

62. Anseric died between 627 when he attended the Council of Clichy and 659 when his successor issued a privilege. Krusch, MGH, SRM 5:65, n. 1.

63. *Ingemmati*. The author seems to be trying to make the poetic suggestion that the virgin's tears turned into jewels.

64. Waldebert died about 670. Krusch notes that the belt of a newly married man is loosened to symbolize his readiness to beget children.

65. Ecclesiastes 12:5.

of the almighty God, oh handmaids of Christ, for as the divine oracle says, it is not the one who begins but she who perseveres even to the end who will be saved."[66]

29. Meanwhile, as affairs involving wealth usually generate discord among our nearest kin, her brother Bodo had, by illicit usurpation, retained the farms which she had bestowed on the convent through a series of charters.[67] But hearing of his sister's illness and that she had anxiously appealed to the Lord in the matter, he hastened to her side. Soon, with God's mediation, they mutually confirmed those charters and they remain legal to this day.[68] When she felt herself leaving her body, she said farewell to her sisters and called Italus the priest so that, as is customary, he might perform the funeral offices for her. And with these entreaties, she sent her holy spirit to be gathered into the assembly of the saints. By His gift, she received double measure of eternal glory from Him to Whom be honor and glory and power and ruling from everlasting to everlasting. Amen.

30. The said handmaid of God died on the tenth calends of October on which day we celebrate the passion of St. Maurice of Agaune Captain of the Theban legion.[69] And her relics were conducted to that place at which tomb the fame of her virtues was revealed after her death.

Here ends the death of the Holy Abbess Sadalberga.

---

66. Baudonivia, *Radegund*, 21. It is impossible to tell whether it was the author or Sadalberga herself who was inspired by the earlier saint's example.

67. Presumably this is her second brother, Fulculf-Bodo, and not Odila's husband, Leudin-Bodo, bishop of Toul. Possibly the difficulty involves the newly decreed hereditary rights of women.

68. McNamara has examined the uses of hagiography in strengthening the economy of conventual communities in "A Legacy of Miracles."

69. September 22.

I I

Rictrude, Abbess of Marchiennes

(ca. 614–688)

Rictrude was born about 614 in Gascony, a land that had never been thoroughly brought under Frankish control. It had a strong Gallo-Roman population mixed with Gascons and a troubled history of Visigothic authority in the sixth century. In addition, it was constantly plagued with Basque raiding parties, a fact that would still be vividly known to the early tenth-century author of the present life. Rictrude's meeting and marriage with the Frankish noble Adalbald, therefore, occurred in the context of this Frankish settlement and internal turbulence.[1]

When she was a child, the country was relatively peaceful. Clothar II had delegated its government to his son Charibert, who continued to hold it from his half-brother Dagobert I, who succeeded to their father's kingdom in 628. Dagobert soon repudiated his first wife Gomatrude (the sister of Charibert's mother) in favor of a new queen, Nanthild.[2] However, he left Charibert in control of Aquitaine despite his uncle's rebellion in the north, which resulted in his execution.[3] The saintly missionary bishop, Amand, was also caught up

This account is taken from Hucbald, monk of Saint-Amand, *Vita sanctae Rictrudis*, AS, May 12, 78–98. Hucbald was a popular Carolingian hagiographer and wrote this work about 907 from earlier sources, some of which have since vanished as he explains in his prologue. Van der Essen, *Etude critique*, 260–65, establishes that Hucbald used the *Vita Arnulfi* (MGH, SRM 2:426–46), *Vita S. Amandi* (MGH, SRM 5:395–449), Pseudo-Fredegar, and Isidore of Seville, *Etymologies*. Geary, *Aristocracy in Provence*, 132, n. 23, adds Alcuin's *Vita Richarii* (MGH, SRM 4:381–401) from which the story of saving the child of a holy woman named Rictrude derives.

1. The family's continuing ties to the south are traced by Geary, *Aristocracy in Provence*, 145, in references to an eighth-century revolt, some years later, against the growing power of the Carolingians led by a man named Maurontus, who is likely to have been the descendant of Rictrude's son of the same name.

2. For an outline of this queen's career, see Wemple, *Women in Frankish Society*, 67.

3. Charibert was the son of Clothar's second wife, Sichild, whose sister, Gomatrude, had been repudiated by Dagobert.

in this storm.[4] The king exiled the holy man, and he went on an evangelizing mission to Aquitaine.

In 631, the half-brothers were reconciled, and the saint returned north for the baptism of Dagobert's son by Regentrude, his Austrasian wife. The meeting and marriage of Rictrude and Adalbald occurred somewhere in that period of conflict. After Charibert's death, Basque raiding again intensified, and in 636 Dagobert sent a substantial army into the country to pacify the people there. Adalbald's return to the south and subsequent death may have been connected to that strife. He was one of Neustria's leading nobles, brother of Erchinoald, who served Dagobert's son (Clovis II) as mayor of the palace.[5] Rictrude's resistance to Dagobert's demand for her remarriage must be placed in this highly political context. Her son Maurontus grew up to be a court official, and his own retreat into the monastic life may have been connected to the political crises following Erchinoald's death and the rise of Ebroin, although the dates and even the names of the kings casually embedded in Hucbald's rendition of her biography are not recoverable.

Rictrude may have encountered Amand during his earlier trip to Gascony. If not, she certainly established a friendship with him after her marriage brought her north to Dagobert's court. There she formed ties to aristocratic families who patronized the Columbanian movement and used the religious life to enhance their worldly prestige. This involved transferring property commanded by women to monasteries. Noble women, sometimes in family teams, embraced the religious life and endowed lasting establishments in the north and east of the kingdom. Rictrude's mother-in-law, Gertrude of Hamay, had retired to a convent in the half-pagan north country and was destined for sainthood. Her husband enjoyed a cult after his untimely death at the hands of her relatives, as would her son Maurontus and three daughters. Rictrude herself is still actively honored at Marchiennes in modern Belgium, where she built a monastery on Adalbard's allodial property between Douai and Saint-Amand.[6]

This policy was complemented by aristocratic appointments to bishoprics that enabled aristocrats like Arnulf of Metz who wanted to resist royal centralization to concentrate land and power out of the reach of secular politics. Dagobert and his successors countered this by securing episcopal appoint-

---

4. Amand (584–679) will appear in chapter 13 in association with some of the saints of the north where much of his career was spent.

5. See introduction to chapter 14.

6. In part, this may represent a systematic family strategy of diverting wealth and women away from the predatory king and his ambitious courtiers. It also reflects a practice of deploying women in religious service involving both administrative and, above all, charitable activities. See McNamara, "The Need to Give."

ments for their own court officials. In addition to Amand, Philibert, Eligius, and Ouen started life at court as secular officials, moving later to a clerical vocation, bishoprics in the northern missionary centers, and finally sainthood.

The alliance between these ambitious aristocratic families and the Columbanian monastic leaders fits into a larger pattern of evangelization spreading in the north in the latter part of the seventh century. In 663/4, a synod at Whitby, an English convent with ties to the Frankish convent at Chelles, guaranteed the inclusion of the Anglo-Saxons and ultimately the Irish into a unified ecclesiastical administration. The event strengthened the connection of the Franks and the islanders in the work of converting the north. In 678, Wilfred of York came through Frisia on his way to Rome. Irmina, abbess of Ören near Trier, supported Willibrod, the great evangelist of the north.[7] Other representatives of insular culture appear in the life of Gertrude of Nivelles and in the life of Balthild, the English queen of Neustria.

In the monasticizing of the north, Rictrude and her daughter Eusebia were members of a large company of women that included Oda, wife of Arnulf of Metz; Ida, the wife of Pippin of Herstal; and her daughters Begga and Gertrude of Nivelles.[8] Together, they pursued a *Klosterpolitik* that tied the Carolingian family closely to the church and contributed to their ultimate replacement of the Merovingian dynasty in the mid-eighth century. Rictrude's own influence was long-enduring. Her vita was extended by various authors far into the twelfth century with accounts of her ongoing wonder-working. Here, it ends after her convent was destroyed by Vikings in 879. The subsequent account of its gradual decay into poverty and the usurpation of its land and titles by a company of monks, who accused the sisters of dissolute and irreligious lives, is omitted.

The Life of Rictrude, Abbess of Marchiennes

■

To the Lord Prelate Stephen, garlanded as his name suggests,[9] who grows more honorable as he is more highly placed in the framework of Christ's body, now crowned by men with the insignia of apostolic reverence, but at last to be crowned with insignia by God because of his merits with those whom he follows in his turn, Hucbald, most insignificant of priests and

7. Probably the same monastery that earlier housed Glodesind's aunt, Rotlinda.
8. The life of Eusebia may be found in *AS*, March 14, 445–56. We have omitted it from this collection because it contains little material not to be found in Rictrude's life.
9. The name Stephen means "garlanded" in Greek.

monks, wishes the joy of a crown of the same incorruptible and verdant flowers of virtue.[10]

1. I have been asked by the clerks and nuns of the congregation of God's beloved servant, Blessed Rictrude, to take up my pen anew to write of her acts and her children.[11] Long and hard have I resisted, knowing my paltry knowledge to be inadequate to the subject. Moreover, much time has passed and I had neither seen nor heard that there was any trustworthy narrative in writing. Thus I feared to assert doubtful things as sure and falsehood as truth. But, then they showed certain samples of her history to my reluctant self confirming what certain, not inconsiderable persons swore to me had once been set down in old writings which had vanished in the wake of the Norman depopulation. Invoking the name of Divine Majesty, trembling I acquiesced. So let me begin, if not as well as I should, then as best I can, not aspiring to verbal ornamentation but to comfort and edify my reader or listener.

2. In truth, when this little work was handed over spread out for Your Excellency's recitation or, rather, examination, it seemed to Your Prudence and those from whom it is customary to require an authorized corroboration of each book by Scholastics, to lack something: an attribution with time and place. Now it seemed enough and more than enough, that the many names of famous persons, deeds and places mentioned in the text should blot out the writer's name and provenance lest, like a black cloud, it seem to obscure stars of such splendor. Still, because it pleases Your Holiness, the shining lamp of your own famous name and even our own, though vile, shall cast light upon the shadows. So, where the preface of this book praises the famous Prelate Stephen of Liège, it mentions our own insignificant person. But as to my place: as you know, it is no longer in this famous city as once it was. Rather I might be preening myself on being the lowest of the monastic congregation of the most Blessed Amand, Confessor of Christ and your one-time predecessor, except that, for my pressing sins, I had been forced to flee more than once for fear of invading barbarians.[12] How can I speak of that time? For we might say that worse things have been seen and thus proclaim like the Psalmist to God: "Make us glad for the days wherein thou hast

10. The addressee is Stephen, Bishop of Lièges, 901–20.

11. Marchiennes, like other religious foundations in northern Frankland, was burned and devastated by the Vikings in the late ninth century. It was reconstituted as a convent with some auxiliary contingent of priests, but never recovered its former prosperity. It is likely that their appeal to Hucbald arose out of the need to revive the cult of their saints in order to improve their revenues. In the early eleventh century, the nuns were accused of incompetence in dissipating the property and displaced in favor of monks.

12. The Viking attack occurred about 879, less than thirty years before Hucbald was writing.

afflicted us and the years wherein we have seen evil. Let thy work appear unto thy servants."[13] Then we must hear the warning of the Apostle: "Redeem the time, because the days are evil."[14] But lest I seem to ignore the authority of your orders, I note, omitting the names of native kings, that 907 years have run their course from the time of the birth of our highest King, Christ, to the tenth indiction of the year of this writing. For the help of the Catholic Church, I pray that you will prosper happily in the prayers of our community.

3. May your wise prudence, which sheds a sweet smell of fame everywhere, smile on our enterprise, that a worshiper of truth may strip away the clouds of falsehood. May you deign to look upon this our work with complacent countenance and mend its faults, if evil error has inserted any therein, by balancing the scales with just weights. For if no unbalanced part tilts the turning scale, then no fraud mars it. Renowned Father, you know that the just are glad when a pious work has been accomplished. For we know that in this life we are moved to give due thanks to God, while we hope rather for the joy of true life which Lord Jesus gives us likewise to assume by the prayers of the saints whose acts we record.[15]

I. Saint Rictrude, born of the Gascon nobility, married to Saint Adalbald, has four sainted children and mourns for her husband's death.

4. When the Frankish nation had, in its primordial past, migrated from lesser Phrygia and propagated its nobility from the royal stock of Troy, Divine Grace wished it to come to knowledge of the truth, after it had, for a long time, been deluded by the fanatic madness of idolatry. For before the beginning even to the end of time, It had predestined that when the diligent King Clovis held sway over this nation, he would condescend to gratify the devout importunity of the blessed Prelate Remigius. This most holy bishop, by the holy probity of his behavior and the powerful virtue of miraculous signs, taught the Catholic faith to that king and even the greater part of his army and, gaining chrism from on high,[16] as they say, he imbued about three thousand with the charism of Christ's baptism in a single day. And from that day, more and more, holy religion has increased among the Franks even as their domination has grown over kingdoms beyond their borders in certain distant places. This success was not obtained by their savage customs (though there are those who think that they are called Franks because they have a naturally ferocious temperament and very disorderly habits).[17] Rather, it rested on

---

13. Psalms 90:15–16.

14. Ephesians 5:16.

15. The whole of c. 3 was written in a poetic form that we have not attempted to reproduce here.

16. By ninth-century legend, from a dove descending from heaven.

17. As we shall see below in c. 5 and again in c. 8, Hucbald was given to rather fanciful etymologies. We have no idea how he derived this one.

mighty twin columns which are seen to support the whole state of the entire church: clearly, the authority of holy bishops, who each in turn served outstandingly in that honor, and the strength of prepotent kings administering public affairs with wisdom in all things. Thus by divine grace, prevenient and subsequent, they were led to ever greater heights.

5. And since, wherever sin abounds there also does God's grace superabound, so, as Heaven is decorated with the varied beauties of the stars from the Father of Light from whom all good and perfect gifts descend, does the land of the Franks shine with the brightness of its multiplicity of perfect saints both native and immigrant from other regions, of both sexes and all degrees. From which sacrosanct college, like a star of splendid beauty, shines Rictrude, devout bondwoman of Christ, most acceptable to God, lovable to all good people, laudable for justice and deserving of sanctity. She began with fame enough from her family origins, the noble Ernold being her father and Lichia her mother, from the agile and warlike Gascon people. Of old, these people were first called the Vaccaei from a certain walled town of the same name near the Pyrenees. But afterwards they were named Wascones, as the C in Vaccones changed to an S and that the same region before called Vacceia was now called Wasconia. And, though its natives were at that time given over to the worship of demons, Rictrude was predestined by God to spring from that same impious and godless people as a rose habitually flowers among the thorns.[18] From that cradle, she came to maturity confirmed and lofty in honest customs.

6. This was at the time of King Clothar the Great, fourth of the Frankish kings after Clovis who, as we said, was first to convert to Christ,[19] and of his famous son, Dagobert, nurtured by the blessed Arnulf, Bishop of Metz, to share the realm and then succeed his father, of whom it is written, he was worthy and diligent with his power.[20] When Clothar died and Dagobert took up ruling with the royal scepter, he was pleased to concede the lands and cities south of the Loire as far as the Gascon frontiers even to the Pyrenees to the government of Charibert, his brother by a different mother. This practice sprang from wise counsel, for thereby a firm pact was made that his brother would never struggle against him for more of the patrimony. Holding his seat in Toulouse, Charibert ruled part of the province of Aquitaine and in time subjected the whole of Gascony to his power. But, while he maintained the highest royal rights in many things, King Dagobert was excessively given over

18. The Basques were still largely pagan in Hucbald's time.

19. Clothar II, son of Fredegund and Chilperic (585–628). Hucbald has subtracted the line of Sigebert and Brunhild from this genealogy.

20. Arnulf may have had a connection to the family of Glodesind. He was one of the family of Pippin of Herstal, father of Gertrude of Nivelles and ancestor of Charlemagne, and assisted in the overthrow of Brunhild and her grandsons in favor of Clothar II in Austrasia in 614.

to the love of women. Having found that the woman who had fallen to his lot in marriage appeared to be sterile, he repudiated her and took another whom he wished to make his queen.[21] For this crime, he was denounced by the bishops, particularly the most holy man and wonder-working prelate Amand. Moved with indignation and pride, the King expelled that same venerable pontiff from his whole realm, not without injustice. Amand bore that persecution imposed on him patiently for the sake of truth, which is Christ. Indeed, he most freely chose to pour out his own blood to sow the seed of the divine word in various places. Thus, among other regions, he came at last to Gascony, Rictrude's original fatherland, for he yearned that by the light infused in him by Heaven, he might irradiate this beautiful star and many more; and there he hoped to obtain the palm of martyrdom from this savage people.

7. Meanwhile, the said Prince and King Dagobert, when he had no son in whom he could rejoice as a successor, was overcome with sorrow and admitted yet a third wife to his bed.[22] The prayers of many men turned pleading to the Lord, and, by God's generosity, he had a son from her that same year, acquired by many prayers and largesse of alms. And most solicitously he moved toward his powerful cleansing in the holy font and his introduction to divine law. As he himself had had the Blessed Arnulf for his pedagogue, so he wanted his son educated in the practice of the Christian religion by one of God's greatest servants. Remembering and repenting all that he had done before when he had imposed so much shame on a man of sanctity, he sent servants out in every direction to find the Pontiff Amand and recall him most respectfully. What more? That true preacher and doer of the Gospel, the venerable Bishop Amand, was returned from exile like a new John the Evangelist coming back from Patmos. The King and his nobles alike made great rejoicing together and all the people danced in solemn celebration of his return.[23]

21. Dagobert was the son of Beretrude and Charibert, the son of Clothar's second wife Sichild who had secured the marriage of the young Dagobert to her sister Gomatrude. Around 630, some conspiracy caused Dagobert to execute his wife's uncle, Brodolf, and repudiate her in favor of Nanthild. Hucbald's claim that it was because of Gomatrude's infertility is unconfirmed by any earlier source. It probably grows out of a greater sensitivity to the church's demand for monogamy which characterized Carolingian Christianity. See McNamara and Wemple, "Marriage and Divorce in the Frankish Kingdom."

22. This is presumably Regentrude, who in 631 gave birth to Sigebert III, king of Austrasia (634–56). However, Hucbald is white-washing Dagobert. Nanthild continued to be his queen until his death. She also had a son, the future Clovis II, in 631, who was to marry Saint Balthild. When Dagobert died in 639 he left her regent for Clovis II under the protection of Ega.

23. Tripudium, a religious dance, is the term used and may accurately describe the event, as Amand's successors in the north celebrate the dance of Saint Willibrod on his feast day. See Duckett, The Wandering Saints, 192.

8. Therefore, the king asked pardon, prostrate at Amand's feet, and obtained it most readily. But when he poured out prayers for his son, his petition was refused. For our own Paul answered three times in the voice of the Blessed Paul that it was not suitable for a soldier of God to mix in the affairs of the world. Saying this, he turned from the king's face but the royal will lost none of its fervor. He finally succeeded in accomplishing what he had been unable to do for himself by the persuasions of good men. For the king sent Ouen and Eligius, proven executors of his will, after him. These men, foremost in sanctity and prudence, were very dear and familiar to Amand, who loved their virtues.[24] The holy man consented to the petition of these saints, for he could refuse them nothing, and obeyed the king's pleasure. Therefore the royal infant, who had been alive only about forty days from his birth, was brought to receive holy grace by the priest's blessing. But now the etymology of Amand's name must naturally be given. For, when he was being made a catechumen, no one in all the multitude answered 'Amen' at the end of the prayer. But it is said that the Lord, who opened the mouth of the mute and made the tongues of infants eloquent, opened his mouth. Everyone heard him, not like an infant but a boy, respond in a clear voice, 'Amen.' It was stupendous enough for the people there to be silent against all habit but it was even more marvelous that, contrary to nature, this one had spoken. Let us delay no more. The holy pontiff regenerated the child with life-giving baptism and announced his name to be Sigebert. King Charibert, the king's brother, took him from the sacred cleansing. And the Lord who did wonders in His saint, magnified him in the sight of kings. And all the troops following both kings were filled with great joy and wonder by this sign. The next year, King Charibert died. Nor did his infant son linger but died soon after him and King Dagobert recovered the whole land, with Gascony, into his power. I have inserted all this preceding material for the sake of what follows so that my readers or hearers will know how Blessed Rictrude came to be in Francia.

9. So at this time, when Gascony was being repeatedly infiltrated with Franks, the good-natured girl Rictrude had become nubile. A certain Frank—born Adalbald, child of a just and noble stock, saw her, loved her and chose her for his own. His mother, Gerberta, was the daughter of Saint Gertrude who rests in the monastery which she built which is now called Hamay. She

---

24. Ouen, or Dado, was one of the sons of Autharius, consecrated by Columbanus as a child. He was Dagobert's keeper of the seals until his retirement as bishop of Rouen and ultimate withdrawal to monasticism. From his retreat in Normandy, he continued to influence Neustrian affairs through the period dominated by the mayor of the palace, Ebroin. Eligius, or Eloi, was master of the mint before becoming bishop of Noyon and Tournai. They head the Neustrian branch of Dagobertian saints, as Arnulf of Metz heads the Austrasian group.

had imposed the highest standard of discipline on the boy who grew strong, rich with copious lands, and was greatly loved and honored at the king's court. He was a full worthy man who would take the worthy Rictrude in marriage. Thus, despite the opposition of some of her relatives, she was espoused to him according to custom, dowered and brought into matronhood. He took a wife, not for incontinence, but for love of progeny. In both of them, those things which people customarily expect in choosing husband or wife were combined. The man had strength, good birth, good looks and wisdom which made him most worthy of love and affection. And the wife had good looks, good birth, wealth and decorum which should be sought above all else. So let us remember the words of the Apostle on honorable marriage and an unsullied bed, for the apostolic word did not fall on deaf ears: "Know ye not that your body is the temple of the Holy Ghost which is in you, which ye have of God, and ye are not your own? For ye are bought with a price: therefore glorify and carry God in your body."[25] "Let the man pay his debt to the wife and likewise the wife to the husband."[26] And again, "Defraud ye not one the other, except it be with consent for a time, that ye may give yourselves to prayer."[27] And further: "This is the will of God, even your sanctification, that ye should abstain from fornication that every one of you should know how to possess his vessel in sanctification and honor; not in the lust of concupiscence."[28] Therefore, let married people keep their faith with the Apostle before their eyes: "Let everyone of you love his wife as himself; and the wife see that she reverence her husband."[29] And again, "Wives, submit yourselves to your own husbands as it is fit in the Lord. Husbands, love your wives, and be not bitter against them."[30] Therefore may they join together in faith and charity that they may be two in one flesh and no more two because the flesh is one. Together in one voice, acting in concord, they honored God, the Father of our Lord Jesus Christ, and served the Lord all their days in sanctity and justice in His presence who have lived together in one house.

10. And children were given to them, according to the first blessing that God gave to man, "Be fruitful and multiply."[31] Their first-born was named Maurontus and, afterwards, he became a holy priest and abbot. And their three daughters were holy virgins: Clotsendis, who ruled this monastery after

25. 1 Corinthians 6:19–20.
26. 1 Corinthians 7:3.
27. 1 Corinthians 7:5.
28. 1 Thessalonians 4:3–4.
29. Ephesians 5:33.
30. Colossians 3:18–20.
31. Genesis 1:28.

the death of her mother; Eusebia, a great worshipper of God according to her name's meaning;[32] and finally Adalsendis. As their parents were righteous, they were educated to serve God by them and their familiars, growing trained from infancy in fear of the Lord and in celestial blessings. The worthy and venerable priest Richarius was Maurontus' spiritual father and regenerated him in God through holy baptism. The famous Bishop Amand rendered Clotsendis worthy before God in every way and with his own holy and worthy hands took her from the font to be saved. Dagobert's wife, Queen Nanthild, took Eusebia from the sacred cleansing.[33] Oh progeny truly blessed and pleasing to God! Of such it is rightly said: "Oh how beautiful is the chaste generation with brightness!"[34] Verily, the just are even as amply enriched with spiritual gifts as with temporal goods, as the Psalmographer says: "Blessed is everyone that feareth the Lord; that walketh in his ways. For thou shalt eat the labor of thine hands: happy shalt thou be, and it shall be well with thee. The wife shall be as a fruitful vine by the sides of thy house: thy children like olive plants about thy table. Behold, that thus shall the man be blessed that feareth the Lord."[35] Though these words should be understood spiritually, yet sometimes prosperity is gained fairly and temporally.

11. After this, the devout handmaid of Christ Rictrude's husband, Adalbald of good and praiseworthy memory, sadly took the road from Artois, where he was rich with many possessions, to Gascony. The noble matron Rictrude went part of the way with him but then, as he ordered her, she soon returned home in sorrow. For even while she was still in ignorance, her mind had a presage of the dolorous future which hung over her. Thus she was already mourning what she had not yet suffered. What more? The just man was set upon from ambush by certain wicked people, obviously [her relatives] who had been displeased by their holy matrimony, and he was wounded, and perished.[36] As was fitting, he was given a most honorific burial service. Dead to the world, he lives in God. He lives, I say, for his happy soul lives close to Him who is the true life and signs from his dead bones have frequently declared his merits. There was small delay before God's servant Rictrude

---

32. *Eusebia* is piety in Greek.

33. This seems to provide a base date between 632 (the earliest date at which people married after 628 could have had three children) and 639 (the death of Dagobert, after which Nanthild would probably be designated as queen or Clovis II's mother rather than Dagobert's wife).

34. Wisdom 4:1.

35. Psalms 128:1–4.

36. The Basque uprisings of 636 that caused Dagobert to send an army south seem to provide a handy setting for this story. Geary, *Aristocracy in Provence*, 131, says that Adalbald was the brother of Clovis II's major-domo, Erchinoald. If so, his death may have had some relation to the power struggles of the Arnulfings.

heard what had happened. She was so stricken by the news that her mind was afflicted with deepest sorrow, a sorrow that slowly grew by the sorrow of her sorrowing children. And her tears were multiplied with tearful tears among the domestics.

12. Still as the worst time of weeping passed, she began to take healing counsel from familiars who shared her love for Christ, especially Amand, God's most holy bishop.[37] At last, he offered the words of Paul the Apostle, a true consoler of the spirit: "The wife is bound by the law as long as her husband liveth; but if her husband be dead, she is at liberty to be married to whom she will, only in the Lord. But she is happier if she so abide, after my judgment."[38] And she gave her ear to those words and also she gave her mind. For from him she heard and gave heed to that sweet and swelling evangelical voice of Christ's servant: "If any man will come after me, let him deny himself and take up his cross, and follow me."[39] And, "whosoever that forsaketh not all that he hath, he cannot be my disciple."[40] And again, "If thou wilt be perfect, go and sell that thou hast, and give it to the poor, and thou shalt have treasure in Heaven, and come and follow me."[41] And again, "Everyone that hath forsaken houses or brethren or sisters, or fathers or mothers, or children, or lands for my name's sake, shall receive a hundred fold and shall inherit everlasting life."[42]

II. Of Saint Rictrude, holy widow, in the monastic life with her daughters and the priestly Maurontus.

13. Rictrude, widowed by Adalbald but loving God and beloved by God, fixed these holy and life-giving words as an anchor in her mind. Putting aside all wavering deliberation and turning from all that would delay her, she promised herself to find refuge in these salubrious admonitions. But lo! the envy of the devil strove by stealth to thwart the healthful advice of the Prelate and the pious vows of the holy matron. Nor did he move the weak or middling by his evil disturbances but the highest princes of the world: for he tried to sway the king's mind with the idea of joining her with a certain optimate in a second marriage. And when she spurned that utterly, he vainly poured out many blandishments and flatteries. And when this wholly failed to move her from her fixed stand in God, he tried the terror of royal threats, but to no avail. For she was equally contemptuous of his raging and his

---

37. Wallace-Hadrill, Frankish Church, 72–73, sees Amand as an initiator of the alliance between missionary work and political assimilation developed by the Carolingians.

38. 1 Corinthians 7:39.

39. Matthew 16:24.

40. Luke 14:33.

41. Matthew 19:21.

42. Matthew 19:29.

blandishment. From the three parts of philosophy, she had learned the greatest, which is to act in conformity with a just cause, which Greeks call Ethics and Latins Morals, mistress of the good life. And this is divided into four principal virtues: prudence and justice, fortitude with temperance. And each of these guided her. Through justice she was disposed to obey God before man; fortitude kept her from bending to enticement or breaking in adversity; through prudence she acted cautiously to save herself from royal anger and temperance enabled her to keep the rule of humility as a way of life in all her words and deeds. Following the counsel of the initiate in the mysteries, the Godbearer, Amand, she dissimulated for a time, while she remained constant in her proposed vows to serve God. Meanwhile, he pledged to use his influence to obtain the king's agreement to what he judged was most useful for her.[43]

14. Why linger longer? She encouraged the king to imagine that she was ready to yield to his will and arranged a convivial gathering of splendid magnificence worthy of a king at her estate in the villa called Baireius.[44] She invited the king and his optimates and, with the salty seasoning of the banquet, they all enjoyed the sweetness of her talk. "Afterward, when hunger was repelled and love increased by eating, and they were convivial with Bacchus' bright exhilaration," she rose.[45] Not haltingly but steadily, not coolly but warmly, not sluggishly but sharply, not womanlike but manlike, she perfectly carried out the plan she had made. First, she entreated the king to allow her to do what she liked in her own house and to use that power freely in his presence. And he agreed promptly, her raised cup suggesting that she would command him to drink, as is the custom with many. He supposed that she sought to please him and his company. Following the salubrious advice of her renowned counsellor, the Prelate Amand, she invoked help from the terrible name of God and, to the stupefaction of the king and all the others, she covered her head with a veil blessed by that holy bishop which she drew from her bosom. The king was stirred to wrath and left the banquet, abandoning the unwelcome food. And she, pinning her thoughts truly on the Lord, committed herself and hers totally to His will that they might be nourished by Him and always comforted in the solace of His mercy.[46]

43. Geary, *Aristocracy in Provence*, 147, fits Rictrude's family into a pattern of southern men brought up at the royal court in the seventh century and then restored to the south as bishops and other officials. The court cooperated with Luxeuil in bringing the two aristocracies together according to Prinz, *Frühes Mönchtum*, 121–51.

44. The Bollandists place this as Bray in Artois, halfway between Douai and Arras.

45. We have used quotation marks at this point to indicate that Hucbald here broke into verse.

46. The king is not named, but the best candidate is Dagobert (d. 639) when Rictrude was in her early twenties. Otherwise, a long wait for Clovis II to grow up would have to ensue, which would be utterly incompatible with the chronology of Eusebia's life.

15. First, she prudently ordained the distribution of the powers and posses-sions left to her and wholly extirpated the thorny cares of the world from the soil of her heart. What she had borne three-fold in the conjugal life was then doubled, for in widowhood her seed yielded fruit six-fold. At first, satisfied to serve Christ in His members, she was Martha. But then, sitting at His feet listening and storing up His words, she became Mary. And thus, by Christ's own testimony, she chose the higher part which would not be taken from her, and for that same better part she deserved to receive in recompense the reward of the elect and beloved. Indeed, to appear outwardly as she was inwardly, she changed the habit of her mind as she put a new habit on her body. She threw off the elaborate clothes which adorned her in marriage when she thought of worldly things, how she might please her husband. But one who has stripped away all the burdens of the world, though she appears as a widow divided from a husband, is not divided in mind but is always solicitous for the things of the Lord only, how she might please God.[47] She put on garments of widowhood which expressed her contempt of this world through her appearance. For just as white garments are fitting for exultation and solemn joy, so do black belong to humiliation and lugubrious sorrow. Whence the head, the principal part of the body, is veiled in vile draperies that the principal member of the spirit, the mind, should be shown as veiled with sorrow and penitent mourning. Thus, to be brief, her consolation would soon be wrought, I would say instantaneously, as it says in the Lord's Gospel: "Blessed are they that mourn: for they shall be comforted."[48] And again: "Amen, Amen, I say unto you, that ye shall weep and lament, but the world shall rejoice and ye shall be sorrowful, but your sorrow shall be turned into joy."[49]

16. In order to subdue her body which had been accustomed in the past to pleasures and was now troubled by demonic suggestions, she imposed repeated fasts upon herself with strenuous vigils and continual prayers. She clothed herself in a haircloth shirt whose insistent prickling smothered the pricks of desire for, as the Poet says, "Venus freezes without Ceres and Liber."[50] Truly she might sing with the Psalmist: "When they were sick, my clothing was sackcloth. I humbled my soul with fasting and my prayer re-turned unto mine own bosom."[51] Then she chose a fitting place, a monastery called Marchiennes which the same pontiff had built on the river Scheldt, where she might carry out her spiritual exercises, with the prelate's advice

47. 1 Corinthians 7.
48. Matthew 5:4.
49. John 16:20.
50. Terence, *Eunuchus* 732.
51. Psalms 54:13.

and help in private counsel. The prelate had assigned his venerable disciple Jonatus, whose holy body is still resting in that monastery, as abbot for its completion and ordering. For Blessed Amand had intended to install an order of monks there: but the abbot gathered nuns instead as had been shown to him.[52] So God's servant Rictrude hurried to this opportunely remote place. With the consent of blessed Amand who mediated a reconciliation between her and the king, she received privileges from royal authority. There, though she occupied a fragile body, she strongly subdued its physical desires and not only them. Struggling towards Heaven against the powers of the air, against the worldly rulers of this darkness,[53] against spiritual wickedness, while conquering the world as well, she awaited her triumphant victory when she would receive fitting rewards from the supernal Spectator.

17. For the happy accomplishment of her aims, that she might be a public example to all, she began her conversion with the perfection advised by the Gospel: "Let your light so shine before men, that they may see your good works and glorify your father which is in Heaven."[54] Casting from her the burdens of estates and the baggage of wealth, making profession of widowed continence to God and assuming the holy habit of a nun, she showed herself holy as a living sacrifice. Nor was she content to please God in herself alone. For she offered the first fruits of earth, that is her womb, holy and excellent, to the undivided Trinity: that is, her three daughters, white as doves, as most gracious offerings that with immaculate body and soul, preserving perpetual virginity they might follow the Lamb, Son of a virgin mother, where he led with sincerity of heart and flesh, blooming with unfading flowers of virginity in body and glittering with inviolate purity of truth in heart; that they might be always without stain before the throne of God singing to Him a new song, that is, rejoicing perpetually with Him about the uncorrupted flesh. For though they can hear the song, none of the saints can sing it but the white-robed throngs of the uncontaminated.

18. Oh, hear these most truthful things, I pray! Let your ears receive them all—you who have ears to hear, to whom it has been given to rise to chastity, the privilege of angels, and thus to acquire the society of the most famous companions to sound out the sweet melody of the new song. Hurry! Hasten!

---

52. At the time Hucbald was writing, the nuns who had hung on after the Vikings burned the monastery were already in the straits that would eventually lead to their eviction in favor of monks in the eleventh century. Hucbald was a monk of Saint Amand, whose institution would later benefit from the claim that the nuns had wasted the property and that Saint Amand had originally wanted to put monks in the place and only changed his mind to accommodate the pressing need of Rictrude for a retreat. *Miracula S. Rictrudis*, 1, 3, AS, May 12, 92.

53. Ephesians 6:12.

54. Mark 5:16.

Run! Remember Lot's wife and never seek to look back.[55] Flee lust with disgust and trample down carnal concupiscence. "All flesh is grass and all the goodness thereof is as the flower of the field."[56] May these exhortations sink into your inmost heart, for they do not come from me but from the words of the famous Father Augustine. They are drawn from the Doctor's words exhorting virgins: "Hasten," he says, "holy boys and girls of God, men and women, celibate and unmarried; continue persevering unto the end. The more sweetly you praise the Lord the more constantly you will think of him. Hope more happily in Him and you will serve Him more swiftly. Love Him more ardently and you will be more attentive to please Him. With girded loins and burning lamps, await the Lord when he is coming to the wedding. You will present a new song at the wedding of the Lamb, and play it on your cithars as no one can but you." And a little after, this follows: "You will follow the Lamb for the flesh of the Lamb is also virgin. You will follow Him with your virgin heart and virgin flesh wherever He goes. For what is it to follow except to imitate? Because Christ suffered for us, leaving you an example that you might follow in His footsteps."[57]

19. Therefore, the faithful woman of God who had devoted herself to Him in holy continence, Rictrude espoused her three daughters at one time, while they were still young, to Christ as husband.[58] So they might always follow in the footsteps of the Lamb and that song which she could never make her own could be made to sound for her on her daughters' cithars. With all things thus wisely disposed and stripped of every worldly care as in the customary nudity of the palaestra, she entered the monastic gymnasium where she would run, competing in the arena of this present life, struggling in contention against the Devil.[59] She was anointed with the oil of celestial grace lest the wicked adversary get a hold to restrain her. And besides contending in the contest, as the Apostle said, she abstained from all things and taught her

55. Lot's wife was turned to a pillar of salt when she looked back with regret to Sodom. Genesis 19:26.

56. Isaiah 40:6.

57. Augustine, De sancta virginitatis, 16.

58. Geary, Aristocracy in Provence, 132–35, suggests that the entrance of the whole family into the cloister may have been connected to the rise of Ebroin as mayor of the palace, a bitter rival to their own family and thinks he might have been involved in the death of Adalbald. However, Ebroin's rise was not until 658. The Eusebia incident has to be between 647 and 653 if the girl taken from the font by Nanthild (d. 642) was not yet twelve. That would be in the era of Erchinoald's (Adalbald's brother) power and subsequently Balthild's ascendancy. Assuming Maurontus was born by 632 (to allow for his three sisters to be born by 636), he was twenty-six when Ebroin rose and could well have been married and even possibly had a child despite Hucbald's disclaimer. Thus it would be quite possible that Ebroin drove him (but not the rest of the family) into the cloister.

59. 1 Corinthians 9:24.

daughters to live by her example. Meanwhile her first born, Maurontus, still did service to the king in lay habit and fought his wars with his body rather than his spirit. We will spare a few words for him at a subsequent opportunity.

20. In those days, Adalsendis, the youngest of her daughters died. She who entered most lately through the gate of this present life was first to enter the gate of death. And wherefore do we say she was dead? She went with the annual cycle of the turning year, at the sacrosanct solemnity of the Lord's birth when He came as a remedy for the sins of this world putting Death and his prince to flight. So, will she not rather be exalted in perpetual light and life than in death? And what did good Rictrude, strong and long-suffering in adversity, do then? With her mind running in two contrary directions, did she rejoice or did she mourn? While the whole world listened to the angel intoning: "Behold, I bring you good tidings of great joy which shall be to all people,"[60] she had her dead daughter before her eyes. But did she give in to the natural sorrow of her condition? The strength of the manly mind within her overcame her womanly feelings. Sorrow for her daughter's death was not suffered to dominate her nor sadness allowed to enter where the birth of Life was celebrated. Let me absolve myself briefly of the worthy memory: the due office of burial was completed according to the custom of the faithful, but the custom of mourning her loved one was set aside. Then in sequence the solemnities of the first, second and third days were celebrated.[61]

21. Then, on the fourth succeeding day, when Holy Church recalls the massacre of the Innocents slaughtered by Herod for Christ and the misery of their bereft mothers, prudent Rictrude knew how she should spend the time. For there is a time for all things under heaven: a time for joy and yet a time for tears. She did not mourn during the explication of the mystery where honor is shown to the holy martyrs in praise of God; for then ceremonial devotions are tendered, not tears. But when she was going with the other nuns for bodily refreshment, she gathered them all and said: "Now, oh beloved sisters, let your company's charity proceed,[62] and rejoice, giving thanks together for God's gifts. For myself, I will follow the example of those ladies, the mothers of the most holy innocent children—so like my own little innocent—for whom much mourning and wailing is heard today. For now, it is permissible to mourn this one snatched too soon to death." And she asked a friend for a private place to mourn so that her grief might be satisfied as is compatible with nature. Oh, praiseworthy woman, example of prudence, long-suffering

---

60. Luke 2:10.

61. That is, the three days of Christmas, the feast of Saint Stephen and the feast of Saint John the Evangelist.

62. A *caritas* is a festive meal in the monastery.

and patience, "let her works praise her in the gates."[63] Oh, strong woman with loins girded up in chastity who persevered in good, and strengthened the good works of her arms! Her light will not be extinguished in the darkness.

22. We mentioned the blessed man, Maurontus, earlier and it does not seem out of place to say a little about him here. As we said, in Baptism he was a spiritual son of the famous priest of Christ, Richarius. One day, that same venerable priest came on horseback to visit the blessed Rictrude, both for the sake of holiness and friendship. And after their holy colloquy, partaking of the food of heavenly life which was equally sweet to both of them, the man of God mounted his horse, intending to return home. From love, God's bond-woman slowly went with him a little ways from her house, bearing one of her natural generation in the crook of her arm—the little son who was also his by spiritual generation. She followed his steps, asking that the boy be fortified with his paternal blessing. The man of God, sitting on his horse, took up the child in his hands either to bless him or kiss him. An envious devil, one of the enemies of good, infected his horse with unaccustomed ferocity. He burst out insanely at the delay and, with gnashing teeth and thrashing hooves, impetuously hurled himself forward with excessive strength, striking both the priest and the mother with the same fear. The priest feared for himself and for the boy: the mother for the priest and her son. And what did the anxious one do? Almost lifeless, as the imminence of death hung before her eyes, she turned away her tear-blinded face so she should not see the pair's miserable fall. And the grief-stricken household, weeping and wailing, gathered in great lament at the spectacle. But God's servant poured out prayers to God lest he fall holding the child in his hand. As he finished, the child fell to the ground unhurt, as lightly as a bird's feather. Then the horse reverted to his usual manner, gentle as a sheep. And recovering her spirits, the mother took up her unharmed son and carried him laughing in her arms. Thus enormous sadness was turned to great joy for all who were there. No one ought to dispute the great merits of both. For such is Almighty God's mercy that, where a malign enemy makes more and more progress and opens his jaws to seize the just, he is so used by blessed men that the attack contributes to the perfection of virtue. For believing within himself that, while the lord God was proceeding to the redemption of human kind, He made an example of humility instead of a display of pride by not riding on an ornamented horse but being borne on an ass led by the Apostles, he was ever afterward borne in the same way whenever necessity required him to travel.

63. Proverbs 31:31.

23. Later, when he came to manhood, the same venerable Maurontus adhered unswerving to the king's side as his nobility required and it is said that, in the service he had contracted, he was joined in the bonds of matrimony. But he had no sooner placed his feet in the voluptuous bondage of carnal love, than he dissolved the bond.[64] The prelate Amand, profitmaker of souls, suggested the sweetness of spiritual love to him and the suavity of eternal jocundity. But when he confided to his holy mother that he wished never to make use of his wife's companionship, she feared that by turning too abruptly from lasciviousness, he might, as young people do, be deciding to follow the broad road to hell. Accordingly, her mind stricken with these cares, she asked Amand, doctor of sick minds, to help her. And coming to Marchiennes, he soothed her with gentle words, bringing her relief. Thus with her original alacrity, she turned back to God. Then it happened that while the Pontiff was celebrating solemn mass with Maurontus standing in his presence, he saw a bee circle three times around the man's head. And the man of God fully understood what this prophetic sign portended. By that witness, he warned him speedily to complete the work he had begun in his heart, for he had understood what had been revealed by God's auspices. And he delayed in no way to do that.

24. Then the most holy Pontiff Amand, blessing him according to the ecclesiastical custom, cut the hair off his head in clerical tonsure and made the sign of the cross on his brow, showing that what was done on the outside was to serve as a sign of what was inscribed within. Clearly the denuded top of his head signified that all the secrets of his heart were bare and open to God and every secret act and thought revealed to all eyes. Verily, frequent shearing of hair signifies the frequent shearing of superfluous evil thoughts. And that adornment of the crown symbolizes both the tiara of high priesthood, and the diadem of royal dignity. Thus he knew that he belonged to the regal priesthood. And so, after completing the endurance of diverse temptations and proving his patience in this manner, he would be worthy of the crown of eternal life which God has promised to those who love Him. For the same holy man, Maurontus, committed many readings and admonitions to memory, not only from the salubrious legacy of the prelate but even from the reading of holy Scripture and devoutly strove always to fulfill his tasks assiduously. For being made a Levite, he took care that his life and deeds would be suitable to that title and office. And, as he sprang from the bright nobility, he

---

64. Hucbald seems uncertain about this marriage. If, as Geary suggests in *Aristocracy in Provence*, 128, Maurontus, a dux in Provence in 735, was a descendant of this line, the marriage must have borne fruit. Perhaps Hucbald did not want to associate his pro-Carolingian hero with an opponent of Charles Martel's rise to power.

shone even more brightly in the king's court, honored with royal bulls as one might expect, a prudent notary writing out edicts containing royal commands. To which, seizing and storing up emoluments of holy behavior, God added the holy association of the holy man, Bishop Amatus. That holy man, who was chosen and raised to the bishopric of the town of Sens,[65] was falsely accused of treason at the time when King Theuderic exercised his wicked tyranny and ordered him to submit to exile in the monastery of Péronne in Vermandois where the holy Abbot Ultanus presided.[66] After Blessed Abbot Ultanus' death, he was turned over to the aforesaid servant of God, Abbot Maurontus, for custody in that monastery called Breuil which he had built in the territory called the Lys.[67] Having accepted him, as he was experienced in religious usages, he [Maurontus] made every effort to act as his servant all the days of his life as though storing up treasures in heaven, for in him [Amatus], he had a most beautiful mirror of life and sanctity for himself and his brothers.[68]

III. The Acts of her daughter, Saint Eusebia; Her death; the deaths of Amand and Maurontus and Saint Rictrude herself.

25. Meanwhile, God's servant, Gertrude, grandmother of Adalbald, Ric-

65. The Bollandists follow several sources in calling him archbishop of Sens, although modern scholars have assigned him to the see of Sion (Sitten) in Switzerland. Hucbald may have been the first source, but by the tenth century his name was inserted into the episcopal lists of the see.

66. Ultanus was brother of Saint Fursey, the founder. In 670 Theuderic III, third son of Saint Balthild and Clovis II, succeeded to his brother Clothar III with the help of the contentious Neustrian mayor of the palace, Ebroin. Hucbald's characterization of Theuderic as a tyrant indicates his Carolingian loyalties because his opponents were the Arnulfing family led by Pippin II, Austrasian mayor of the palace. Amatus, Bishop Chramnelenus of Embrun, and Philibert of Jumièges supported the effort to restore Dagobert II in 676, for which Amatus was accused of infidelity and imprisoned at Péronne, formerly under the control of Erchinoald until 680. This tangled tale of interwoven family loyalties is outlined in Geary, *Aristocracy in Provence*.

67. Ibid., 135. Nearness of property suggests relationships between the brothers Adalbald and Erchinoald and Ansfledis, Waratto's wife. Waratto, the majordomo after Ebroin, also had land in Normandy. Waratto and Maurontus cooperated in the affair of Amatus. In 680, Ultanus died, Ebroin was murdered, and Waratto succeeded. These related persons formed an alliance of aristocratic groups between Rouen and Douai like the alliance of the Arnulfings and Pippinids in Austrasia. Bishop Austrebertus in Vienne (726–730) was a native of Normandy with estates near those of Waratto and Ansfledis and was also an opponent of Charles Martel. Moreover, Prinz (275–78) argues a relationship between the Rhône and Neustria by the introduction of the Benedictine-Columbanian rule in three Provençal monasteries at the end of the seventh century: Lérins, Grosseau, and Douzère. The reformers can be shown to relate to Neustrian houses. Both areas supported nobles supporting the claims of Childeric II against the Arnulfing domination, and the appearance of the Dux Maurontus seems to provide a final tie.

68. *Vita Amati, AS,* September 4, says that Maurontus knelt at his feet to beg pardon for acting as his custodian.

trude's venerable husband, went the way of all flesh. In a long life, she had accumulated good works at the monastery she had built at Hamay. There she had brought up the holy virgin Eusebia, her great granddaughter. A girl of good quality, Eusebia succeeded her in the ruling of the place, but she was as yet hardly old enough, being but twelve years old. A true servant of Christ, her mother Rictrude, was guided by deeper counsel and prudence, well knowing that the malign enemy, by his cunning, seduces even more mature folk with much training in virtue. She feared for her daughter, lest having too much liberty while still immature, she be too strongly tempted by the serpentine fraudulence. Therefore, she wished her to come and live with her. Eusebia refused, wishing to remain at Hamay. Her mother was compelled to put a word in the king's ear by whose authority she could recover her daughter. He agreed and sent letters ordering her return. Sorrowing, the holy Eusebia went back to her mother's monastery at Marchiennes with the body of her great-grandmother, Saint Gertrude, and other relics of saints kept there. Her entire flock came with her. And having gained control of her daughter, the mother gave her many admonitions to train her to serve with her in God's militia. And most freely obeying these precepts, she settled to the yoke of divine service. But she could not turn her mind from her love of that other genial place.

26. Whence, almost every night when Vespers were over, in the dead of night, when she was supposed to be resting her body with the others, she would deceitfully leave her sandals by her bed and silently proceed to Hamay, with her prayer book and a harp which she considered the comrades of her secret. There, she celebrated the vigils and offices of the hours. Having finished this truthful deception, she would return to the monastery of Marchiennes in good spirits never being caught absent at the evening or matutinal hours. But it did not fail to reach her mother's ears. Calling her again, she was compelled to punish her; both soothing her with sweet blandishment and terrifying her with harsh words, she sought to recall her to her will, knowing surely that she could contain her body but not her mind. And when she saw that neither she nor her friends or familiars could succeed, she took counsel with her son Maurontus, urging that she should be punished with a whipping for her disobedience and a certain pertinacity of mind. Her brother agreed to carry it out when it suited her mother.[69] He ordered the servants to hold her tightly by the arms and she was subjected to the decreed correction.

69. This must have taken place before 650, because Eusebia was taken from the baptismal font by Nanthild in Dagobert's lifetime (d. 639). Presumably Maurontus was still a layman in royal service, probably at the court of Clovis II, husband of Balthild and perhaps working in association with his father's brother, Erchinoald.

One of the boys who held her was girdled with a sword and while the virgin twisted this way and that under the pain of the whips the hilt struck her tender ribs. This so wounded her that, through the rest of her life, pus and blood sometimes mixed with the saliva which she spat from her mouth.

27. Still she would not desist from carrying out her intention. They called bishops, abbots and other important men of the neighborhood who all met with the holy virgin to try to persuade her in diverse ways to give up her desire. However, with great constancy, she opposed their advice and exhortations. When they saw how inflexible her mind was, they counselled the mother to let her go back to her chosen place. Though unwillingly, she agreed, stiffening her religious habits with persuasive admonitions and commending her to God in her holy prayers. Thus she achieved what she had desired for so long. With all her little following, she took up the body of her grandmother and the venerable saints' relics and walked back to the monastery of Hamay full of joy. Living there the life of an angel on earth, she was carried off to the chamber of her heavenly spouse in the middle of her adolescence. For, as Scripture says: "Lest that wickedness should alter his understanding or deceit beguile his soul,"[70] she achieved much in a short time and ended her life quickly. For her soul was pleasing to God and he hurried to take her from the midst of the wicked.[71]

28. Now, despite a certain clumsy garrulity, we are pleased to sharpen our pen a little in order to confound those who would slander the righteous with forked tongues and misplaced pride. Such folk would lay their tongues to heaven itself and still not fear to malign people who are free of earthly burdens and, as we believe, reigning with God in heaven. So in their cunning they have observed: 'Look who they are calling saints: a mother who attacked her innocent daughter for wanting to serve God; a daughter who detested her own mother and fled her as an enemy; a son who, with his mother's consent, branded his sister like a fugitive taken away in secret, or like a condemned thief whipped her so viciously that she nearly died. And even though she did not perish on the spot, she wasted away in slow agony. Is this how they make saints pleasing to God? What sanctity is here? What peace? What charity?' Now, how can we answer the madness in men's heads? Oh, foolish arrogance

---

70. Wisdom 4.

71. A life of Eusebia was included in the AS, March 16, 445–56. Like this life of Rictrude, it was produced in the tenth century, and the style suggests that it was also by Hucbald or someone enamored with his overwrought style. It adds no substantial information to this account but does contribute a fanciful tale that the whips used on Eusebia later burst into blossom. According to that life, c. 12, she lived in virtue thirty minus seven years. Van der Essen, Etude critique, 261, like the Bollandists, reads this to mean twenty-three years after her return to Hamay and puts her death at forty-six, clearly at odds with this text.

of minds gone mad! Oh, rabid fools, yapping like dogs rather than men! What will be given—what assigned—to the accursed tongue? Only the sharp point of the arrow, that is, the lance of God Almighty's word from the quiver of the Holy Scripture! For [these weapons] can not only transfix the loquacious mouth but also the clouded heart.

29. And first they are struck with the thunder of the Gospel: "Judge not, that ye be not judged,"[72] He says, "Condemn not, and ye shall not be condemned."[73] Then sounds the trumpet of the Apostle Paul: "Why dost thou judge thy brother?"[74] "Who art thou that judgest another man's servant."[75] To this is added: "Judge nothing before the time until the Lord come, who both will bring to light the hidden things of darkness, and will make manifest the counsels of the hearts: and then shall every man have praise of God."[76] And now hear James: "Speak not evil one of another, brethren. He that speaketh evil of his brother, and judgeth his brother, speaketh evil of the law and judgeth the law."[77] But God himself speaks through the Psalmist: "Thou givest thy mouth to evil, and the tongue frameth deceit. Thou sittest and speakest against thy brother."[78] And a little while after: "I will reprove thee, and set them in order before thine eyes."[79] And again: "The Lord shall cut off all flattering lips and the tongue that speaketh proud things."[80] And again the Scripture says: "Who calumniates the brethren shall be eradicated. Why do you not fear exceedingly this misery?"[81] "How long will ye love vanity, and seek after falsehood? Thou shalt destroy all that speak falsehood."[82] And, "Thou lovest lying rather than to speak righteousness. Thou lovest all devouring words."[83] That means the blasphemies of the deceitful tongue and so, "God shall likewise destroy you forever."[84]

30. Listen if you can, and pay attention: the holy mother Rictrude did not persecute her innocent daughter. Rather, she considered her immature age, knowing that everything has its time and there is a time for every business. As

72. Matthew 7:1.
73. Luke 6:37.
74. Romans 14:10.
75. Romans 14:4.
76. 1 Corinthians 4:5.
77. James 4:11.
78. Psalms 50:19.
79. Psalms 50:21.
80. Psalms 12:3.
81. Psalms 4:2.
82. Psalms 5:6.
83. Psalms 52:3.
84. Psalms 52:15.

Solomon, the most wise, said: "A child left to himself bringeth his mother to shame."[85] And she heard the Scripture say: "Hast thou daughters? Have a care of their bodies,"[86] and thought she would be better to remain with her, in order to achieve greater perfection by more powerful exhortations and examples. And her daughter Eusebia, though betrothed to the heavenly King, did not spurn or despise her blessed mother for she knew that her Spouse commanded: "Honor thy father and thy mother that thy days may be long upon the land."[87] Still she confided in His grace Who affianced her with a ring. She wished only to delight in Him and show no other love, not even affection for her mother, lest it should detract from her love's immoderate fervor. Nor did her brother, the minister of Christ Maurontus, whip his sister from hate or cruelty but rather from fraternal charity for her insolence and disobedience (as he was given to understand) to her parent. As her age required, he punished her infancy, knowing the Scripture: "He that spareth the rod, hateth his son."[88] Correction and the rod bestow wisdom. What wonder that a mother and her son might be mistaken in their human judgment? They corrected the holy virgin, not yet knowing of the divine grace that was in her. With the holy prophets, they made a human judgment as though from the Spirit of God. Cease therefore, cease your vain and foolish chatter! For no work that springs from the root of charity can be called a work of iniquity. Truly is it said: "Therefore if thine eye be single, thy whole body shall be full of light."[89] And as to the blessed virgin's endurance of such infirmity as long as she lived, who would not see it as the crowning pinnacle of the accumulated grace built up in her? For while her body weakened, her spirit grew stronger, as the Apostle says: "When I am weak, then am I strong."[90] Therefore let us stop up our mouths against wicked gossip. As the divine voice intones in the prophet Isaiah: "I will direct their work in truth, and I will make an everlasting covenant with them. And their seed shall be known among the Gentiles, and their offspring among the people. All that see them shall acknowledge them, that they are the seed which the Lord hath blessed."[91]

31. In effect, God's good worshiper, Eusebia, died full of virtue on March 16, which is the seventeenth calends of April. After that, the Lord assumed the holy bishop and beloved monk, Amand from these troubled wanderings and

85. Proverbs 29:15.
86. Ecclesiastes 7:24.
87. Exodus 20:12.
88. Proverbs 13:24.
89. Matthew 6:22.
90. 2 Corinthians 12:10.
91. Isaiah 61:8–9.

hard labors to the heavenly fatherland on the ides of September.[92] Having his holy body in possession, the priest Maurontus buried it honorably: he had given the whole of his inherited estates over to him through the instrument of charters. And this same venerable Abbot and worthy Levite of God, Maurontus, survived his mother in life afterwards completing his pious duty of administration. On the third nones of May, his debt discharged, he was borne to a heavenly palace to receive the reward worthy of his labors in eternal life rejoicing with Christ, joined with Him in glory.[93]

32. But let us return to the explication we had begun. Rictrude, God's most devoted handmaid, gave her whole mind and her whole bodily strength to good works, pacing from strength to strength as she hastened with swelling heart indefatigably in the way of God's mandates over the field of faith and justice drinking into her open ears: "Walk while you have the light that you may be worthy to receive a heavenly prize."[94] She showed herself in all things most perfect by imitating Him who said: "I came not to do mine own will."[95] Subjecting herself to the rule of others she appeared most obedient to their orders serving others as a servant that it might be said: "I did not come to be ministered unto but to minister."[96] She kept this always before her eyes: never going anywhere outside her monastery walls, an example in herself of good works, she offered it to all in humility, obedience, patience, chastity, fasting, vigils and constant prayer, long-suffering, gentleness, modesty, and benignity. And what more? As a daughter of God she walked forever in daylight and all her fruit is goodness and justice and truth. Thus persevering in holy virtues, she completed seventy-four years. On the fourth ides of May her long desired joy was gained and, leaving her little body on earth, she returned her soul to heaven.[97] She was honorifically buried in the same holy place by priests of God and others doing service in the order of ecclesiastical dignities. Men of the Christian religion flowed from every direction to the services of such a mother, sorrowing for her temporal absence but rejoicing that her eternal glory blossomed in Christ. And now, with ineffable joy and hope, she awaits the great day of her greater glorification when what was sown in corruption shall rise incorruptible; and what was sown in ignominy shall arise in glory; and what was sown in infirmity shall arise in strength;[98]

---

92. Van der Essen, *Etude critique*, 341, places the date of Amand's death in 679. His life appears in the *AS*, September 13.
93. May 5, 701.
94. John 12:35.
95. John 6:38.
96. Matthew 20:28.
97. May 12, 688.
98. 1 Corinthians 15:42–43.

and then, with that happy resurrection, she will be glorified with double glorification arising once more in blessed glory with all the saints on the right side happily crowned with the merits of their acts.

33. And, lest anyone doubt of the lasting efficacious life-giving merits of God's servant, our experiences yield many true signs of virtue demonstrated by the lifeless limbs of her corpse. For here the blind see, the deaf hear, the mute gain the use of words, the lame walk and those laboring with fever and various illnesses often received relief and still receive relief when praying with faith. And witnesses of these many things still live who have seen those who sought health healed. Seeing the wonders God does through His saints, they have rejoiced praising them and His benefits. Therefore, thou holy servant Rictrude, beloved of God, we pray with all the love in our hearts that by your merits and intervention with holy prayers, we shall be loosed from the bonds of various infirmities and, most of all, from the chains of our sins. By the grace of benign Jesus, rescue us on that terrible day of His judgment, when heaven and earth shall burn so we may be snatched from the flames of Gehenna and taken with you to enjoy eternal felicity with Him whose pity and mercy have no end, eternal with God the Father and the Holy Spirit, whose kingdom and power, honor and glory are forever from everlasting to everlasting. Amen.

12

Gertrude, Abbess of Nivelles

(628–658)

Gertrude was the daughter of the leader of the east Frankish nobility, Pippin of Landen (Pippin the Elder), founder of the dynasty that would later be known as Carolingian. In 622, he was instrumental in persuading Clothar II to crown his son, Dagobert I, as king of Austrasia. The new king appointed Pippin as mayor of the palace, and with Arnulf, bishop of Metz, he remained a principal counsellor. Arnulf retired into religion on the death of Clothar in 628, but he retained his close connection with Pippin's family through the marriage of his son, Adelgisus, with Gertrude's sister Begga. Like Arnulf's wife Oda, Begga retired into monasticism in her widowhood, and two years before her death founded an abbey at Andennes.[1]

When Dagobert succeeded his father, the court moved west to Neustria, and although he retained his Austrasian office, Pippin went with the king. He remained at court until Dagobert's death in 639, an honor that may have been thrust upon him against his will. The chronicler Fredegar emphasized Pippin's great popularity in Austrasia, which may have roused the king's suspicions.[2] Gertrude's life begins with her refusal of a suitor who had the king's patronage and who is designated as son of the duke of Austrasia, possibly a usurper or a competitor for Pippin's position. Like Sadalberga and Rictrude, Gertrude was the object of one of Dagobert's marital schemes. Her indignant refusal to marry the king's candidate for her hand and her determination to

Vita Sanctae Geretrudis, in Krusch, ed., MGH, SRM 2:447–74. Krusch provides transcriptions from two manuscripts, with a preference for the B version. We have also followed B with an occasional interpolation from Life A for the sake of clarity. From internal evidence, Krusch attributes the manuscript to a monk attached to Nivelles, writing after Begga's death in 693. He accepts the author's claim to have been an eyewitness of several of the incidents in the biography, notably Gertrude's death and the last recorded miracle. Van der Essen, *Etude critique*, 13, confirms Krusch's belief that one of the monks of Fosse wrote this piece. John R. Cox, whose draft translation has been made available by his executor, William Daly, adds a note from Bieler, *Ireland: Harbinger of the Middle Ages*, 101, calling this biography "one of the earliest monuments of Irish hagiography."

1. Ewig, *Spätantikes und fränkisches Gallien*, 221ff.

2. Fredegar, CL 4:85, 4:68, adds that Dagobert hated Austrasia when he was king of Neustria.

enter the religious life, which certainly had her mother's support, may also have been dictated by her father. The girl herself might have been infected by the tension generated by her father's delicate position and sought escape in celibacy.

During her childhood among the nobility at Dagobert's court, Gertrude must have received some impression of the political role of sainthood in Dagobert's kingship. Her father's close ally, Arnulf, was only one of several leading courtiers who capped a distinguished secular career with an ecclesiastical post and eventual sanctification. Moreover, she and her mother Ida were, at the very least, aware of the accomplishments of the saintly women who left royal circles to found convents. Ida, like Rictrude, came from Gascony, which makes some acquaintance with Adalbald's wife, as well as with Saint Amand, a likely possibility.[3]

In 640, after Dagobert's death, Pippin returned to the east, bringing his daughter with him. Austrasia had been entrusted to Dagobert's son Sigebert III, son of his Austrasian wife Regentrude.[4] Pippin soon died, and Gertrude and Ida took the veil and founded the monastery at Nivelles.[5] By doing so, they kept their portion of the family fortune out of royal hands. The monastery, passed to Gertrude's niece Wulftrude, was still under their control when the Carolingians secured the throne.

After Pippin's death, his son Grimoald became mayor of the palace, dominating the young Sigebert, who was only twenty-six when he died in 656.[6] Thereafter Grimoald attempted a coup, anticipating by more than a hundred years the successful action of his descendant Pippin the Short, Charlemagne's father. Queen Himnechild bore Sigebert two children. Grimoald enticed her son, the young Dagobert II, to go on a pilgrimage that ended in his involuntary sojourn in an Irish monastery. Grimoald then installed his own son on the empty throne and attempted to cover the illegality by calling him a "king's son," possibly alluding to some baptismal relationship or some relationship through a Merovingian woman who may have married one of his ancestors.[7] For many years, Dagobert's mother apparently believed that he had been

---

3. For the relationships of these families, see Geary, *Aristocracy in Provence*, particularly 145ff. We have used the modern Ida for Gertrude's mother, though she appears variously as Itta and Itana in the texts.

4. Meanwhile, Neustria passed to Nanthild's son Clovis II, with Ega and then (in 641) Erchinoald, Rictrude's brother-in-law, serving as mayor of the palace.

5. For further information on the early years of the institution, see Hoebanx, *L'abbaye de Nivelles*.

6. For Grimoald's history, see Ewig, *Spätantikes und fränkisches Gallien*, 1:573–77.

7. The story exists only in LHF, 43, where it is brief and not very clear. Geary, *Before France and Germany*, 191, outlines modern evidence that suggests that Dagobert II actually ruled until 661 before the attempted coup. He also suggests the matrimonial connection with the Merovingians, whereas Bouquet, *Rerum Gallicarum et Francicarum Scriptores* 3:545, prefers the baptismal relationship by analogy with Saint Beuve, abbess of St. Peter of Reims.

shipwrecked and drowned. She took her daughter Blichild with her and retreated into Neustria, where Bilichild married Queen Balthild's son Childeric II, later king of Austrasia. The two eventually helped Himnechild drive Grimoald's son off the Austrasian throne, and eventually both father and son died in an ambush at the hands of a discontented Neustrian nobleman. Gertrude had no apparent active role in her brother's ambitious attempt, but her ultimate contribution to the family's success was better rooted.

This life was written after her sister Begga's death in 693, when Pippin II had a firm hold on the office of mayor of the palace. Within half a century, the family would replace the Merovingians on the Frankish throne. Gertrude was destined to become one of the most enduringly popular saints of northern Europe. The importance of this sacral connection to the rise of the Carolingian family cannot be overstated.[8] Eventually it was to provide the theoretical base that enabled them to supplant the Merovingians permanently. Moreover, it gave the dynasty the ecclesiastical legitimation that did so much to stabilize the entire institution of kingship in the later Middle Ages.

Gertrude, Abbess of Nivelles[9]

∎

By the unstinting bounty of holy charity, we believe and we hold with steadfast and inviolate faith, that it will help those who seek the road to the heavenly fatherland and utterly to relinquish earthly profit in order to win the eternal prize, if I strive to record in writing or preaching some small part of the lives and conduct of holy men and women, virgins of Christ, for the advancement and edification of my neighbors. Thus the examples of holy virgins, men and women, who came before us may illuminate the darkness in our hearts with the flames of charity and the heat of holy compunction.[10] Therefore, with the help of the Holy Spirit, Maker of All Things, I have undertaken to present to your charity, in writing, the example and deeds of the blessed virgin Gertrude, mother of the family of Christ, who lived regularly according to God and the discipline of the Rule under the arch of

8. The broad implications of these aristocratic *eigenklosters* are discussed by Prinz, *Frühes Mönchtum*, particularly 493, and Ewig, *Spätantikes und fränkisches Gallien*, 199ff. Graus, *Volk, Herrscher*, 414, suggests that her later appearance in popular religion dates from the thirteenth century. Wallace-Hadrill, *Frankish Church*, 31, notes that Nivelles means *Niuwale*, "the new place of sacrifice," suggesting that it replaced an ancient pagan shrine whose burning sparked a riot in the sixth century. See Gregory of Tours, *Life of the Fathers*, 6:2.

9. We are grateful to William Daly for sharing the draft translation made by the late John Cox in the final phase of our work.

10. *Ardore* has been inserted from Life A.

heaven from the testimony of what we saw ourself or heard from witnesses with the help of Christ, the abbess Dominica, a holy maiden, and the holy women of the congregation of Nivelles where the holy virgin ruled.[11] It would be a lengthy business to insert the genealogy from which she will have drawn her earthly origins into these remarks. But who among the inhabitants of Europe is ignorant of the name and location of her most high-placed family?[12]

1. When she was in her parents' home, at the feet of her mother, Ida of blessed memory, God's holy maid Gertrude grew by day and night in word and wisdom. She was dear to God and more lovable to men than all her generation. I have learned about the origin of her election to Christ's service from a just and truthful man who was present. Pippin, her father, had invited King Dagobert to a noble gathering at his house. The son of the Duke of Austrasia was also present.[13] In the way of the world, to satisfy earthly ambition as well as for mutual liking, he asked the king without consulting her parents to grant him the virgin Gertrude in marriage.[14] The request was pleasing to the king and to the maid's father and he suggested that the girl should be summoned with her mother into his presence without letting them know why the king wanted the child. Then, between the courses, her father asked if she would like to have that boy, dressed in silk trimmed with gold, for a husband. She lost her temper and flatly rejected him with an oath, saying that she would have neither him nor any earthly spouse but Christ the Lord. The king and his nobles marvelled greatly at those things which the little girl said under God's direction. The boy left in confusion, filled with anger. But the holy maid returned to her mother and from that day her parents knew by what manner of King she was loved.

11. Because the author is generally conceded to have been an Irish monk, the Rule was most probably the Rule of Columbanus, although as seems to have been customary, Gertrude may have made her own adaptation.

12. Cox notes that this use of "Europe" predated any cited by Hay in *Europe: The Emergence of an Idea.*

13. Glodesind's father had the same title and was associated with Arnulf of Metz and therefore Pippin's family. There is no indication here whether this young man could have been his son or whether the duke of Austrasia in question may have been a newcomer, possibly being positioned by Dagobert to counter the power of Pippin and his allies. Another intriguing possibility is that the young man could have been Ansegisel, who later became duke of Austrasia and married Gertrude's sister Begga around 628 or 630 after Pepin and Arnulf had campaigned together against the Saxons. See Melin, *Une Cité Carolingienne,* 16–19.

14. The earlier draft, Life A, described the young man as "pestiferous" but says less contentiously that "he asked the king and her parents." Life B seems to wish to imply that Pippin had not consented to the request, but does not offer any open opposition either. Although the author carefully says that Gertrude was taken unawares, it is not inconceivable that a prior contingency plan had been reached, as Saints Rictrude and Sadalberga had already done or attempted to do.

2. Fourteen years later, when her father Pippin had migrated from this life, she lived with her mother in her widowhood and served her steadily in obedience according to God's commandments.[15] While the *materfamilias* Ida thought daily of how she should arrange things for her orphaned daughter, the man of God, Bishop Amand, came to her house preaching the word of God.[16] At the Lord's bidding, he asked whether she would build a monastery for herself and Christ's handmaid, Gertrude. Readily perceiving that the idea would be healthful for her soul, she took the holy veil and turned herself and all she had over to God. But, at the instigation of the enemy of human kind, who has been envious of good works from the beginning and hardens the hearts of the wicked to oppose them, she suffered no small opposition from those who ought to have helped her in doing God's will. It would take long indeed to relate the injuries and indignities, even penury, that this handmaid of God and her daughter endured for Christ's name if it were told in detail. But great as they were, she was equal to them in her determination and desire. To prevent violent abductors from tearing her daughter away by force into the alluring charms of the world, she snatched up the barber's blade and quickly cut her hair around her maidenly crown.[17] Blessed Gertrude gave thanks to God and rejoiced that, for Christ's sake, she deserved to take this crown on her head in this brief life which would in heaven be a perpetual crown of integrity in body and soul. Then merciful God, helper in tribulation, quickly recalled her adversaries to the concord of peace. They ceased their strife and the Devil's party was overcome. The *materfamilias* Ida offered her daughter to the Lord's priests and, once she took the consecrated veil with her companions, she appointed her as the leader of a holy flock as Christ had ordained. In her habitual continence, sobriety of mind and moderation of speech, she behaved as though she were wholly mature. She was endowed with charity: fair of face but more beautiful of mind, generous with alms, integral in chastity, excelling in fasts and prayers, provident in care of the poor and pilgrims, pious to the sick and aged. She was rigorous in support of the church, treating its vessels with pastoral care. Through messengers, men of good repute, she obtained the patronage of the saints[18] and holy books from

15. Pippin died about 640 having returned to Austrasia following Dagobert's death. *Mandatum* (commandments) has the additional meaning in monastic parlance of ritually washing the feet of the poor.

16. Presumably this was before, or at the beginning of Amand's evangelical mission to the north.

17. Wallace-Hadrill, *Frankish Church*, notes that this is the only mention of the round or crown-shaped tonsure for a woman. As in the *Life of Rusticula* and, with less violence, the lives of Rictrude and Sadalberga, it is clear that these noble women were highly vulnerable to forced marriage for the sake of their wealth. Rictrude, Sadalberga, and Ida all saw the monastery as a way of maintaining their inheritance and passing it to their daughters.

18. Literally, as exercised through their relics.

the city of Rome[19] and places overseas for teaching divine song to ignorant folk.[20]

3. So everything was disposed by Divine Ordinance. At sixty years of age, twelve years after the death of her Lord Pippin, full of days and perfect age, leaving an example of good works to posterity, Ida migrated to the Lord commending her spirit to God and His angels, at the monastery of Nivelles and was honorably buried under the protection of Saint Peter the Apostle. When her mother had died and all the work of ruling fell solely on God's blessed virgin, Gertrude thought within herself how she would rather contemplate celestial things far from the clatter of the world. Thus she commended the stewardship of external affairs to good and faithful brothers and committed the care of the household within the monastery to sisters.[21] In this way, she could struggle night and day against spiritual iniquities in holy combat with vigils, prayers, readings and fasts.[22] And the result was that she committed a whole library of divine law to memory and could publicly clarify for her auditors the shadowy mysteries of allegories which the Holy Spirit revealed to her. She erected churches to the saints and other distinguished buildings from the foundations and she ministered to orphans, widows, captives and pilgrims with daily sustenance and all largesse.[23]

4. Nor do I think we should overlook what the handmaid of God herself told us trembling in fear. Once when she stood at the altar of the holy martyr,[24] she saw a sphere of bright flame descending above her so that the whole basilica was illuminated by its light for about half an hour. In a little while, it receded whence it came and afterwards in the same manner it appeared to other sisters. What could this manifestation of light have meant,

19. Vogel, *Medieval Liturgy*, 147, notes this rare piece of evidence for the penetration of the Roman liturgy into Gaul before Pippin III.

20. Saint Amand was a friend of Pope Martin and traditionally credited with at least one trip to Rome. He spread the cult of Saint Peter. This may reflect the competition with the Irish over the extent of papal authority, which boiled up at the Synod of Whitby in England in 664. The people "from places overseas" are probably Irish or English monks connected to the Irish, an oblique reference to the connection between Nivelles and the Irish monks who manned its partner monastery, Fosse.

21. The manuscripts differ: Life A gives *septa monasterii* (within the monastery walls); Life B says *septem sorores* (seven sisters).

22. This is the most concrete example in these lives of a double monastery. The nuns of Nivelles were partnered with Saint Follian and the monks of Fosse. *Additamentum Nivalense de Fuliano*, MGH, SRM 4:428–29, gives an account, missing here, of the murder of some of the monks of Fosse by brigands and of the monks' attendant miracles.

23. This practice probably accounts for the widespread custom of dedicating hostels to Saint Gertrude that prevailed in northern Europe and still marks the frequent naming of streets in the area.

24. Life A identifies the martyr as "St. Sixtus."

unless it were a visitation of the true light that never ceases to illuminate the saints praying for themselves and all others?

5. One day, when we were in peril of the sea, our appeal to blessed Gertrude opportunely helped save our lives. For the monastery's utility, we were sailing over the sea when, from afar, something appeared alongside of us which looked like a ship of wondrous magnitude. As it drew near, the sea swelled with mighty waves. And, lo, the earth shook and a terrible monster appeared as though cast from the depths. We could not see it as a whole but only partly from the back side. The trembling sailors abandoned hope of life and invoked their idols while we invoked the name of the Lord and waited for our last hour. But one of us, who is still living, cried out three times saying: "Holy Gertrude, help us as you promised!" And for sure, I swear to you, I saw and heard, at the third repetition of the word, the whale sought the abyss! That night, we made port happy and untroubled. For Christ had saved us from death through our prayers to His handmaid.

6. After several years, her little body became fatigued from too much abstinence and ceaseless cares and great illness. She knew by divine revelation that her departure from this light drew near. With advice of the priests and handmaids, she completely abandoned herself to the love of Christ relinquishing all her temporal offices and the care she had been taking for her flock except in spirituals. She appointed her niece, Wulftrude, who had been imbued and nourished at her feet under the holy rule from the cradle to govern her flock and care for the poor in her place. This consecrated girl, Wulftrude, was then about twenty years old, springing from a noble old family of the Franks. She was of serene countenance, loved by all the household, gentle to the humble, dreadful to the proud, generous to the poor, pious to her parents, smooth of speech, pure in love of God and neighbor. But it so happened that from hatred of her father, the spiteful queens wished, first through persuasion and then through force, to take her from her place and wickedly possess the goods the blessed maid administered.[25] But God's mercy and the prayers of the saints protected her from all adversaries and in a wonderful way, Christ, for whom she had such devotion, restored everything to her. The Lord conferred such grace on her that those who had so lately

---

25. Wulftrude was the daughter of Gertrude's brother Grimoald whose ill-fated attempt to overthrow Merovingian rule in Austrasia probably accounts for his daughter's difficulties. For the chronology of the period from 656 to 662, see Fischer, *Der Hausmeier Ebroin*, 17–74. Life A adds "kings and even priests" to the list of her enemies. The kings are Clothar III and Childeric II. The queens are Balthild, widow of Clovis II, and Himnechild, regent for her son Dagobert II after the death of Sigebert III in 656, when Grimoald had him kidnapped and informed his mother that he had died. Wulftrude was abbess from 658 until 669, when Himnechild was backing Neustrian claims against Grimoald.

been raptors afterward appeared as defenders and then benefactors giving endowments with all largesse. And when everything had been most carefully disposed and the church restored, eleven years after the flock had been entrusted to her, a heavy languor forced her to lie for fifty days and more upon her bed. By her custom of care for the poor and sharing great alms with the needy, she had paid her debts to all, according to the gospel, and from all she received peace and blessing. Comforted among the spiritual handmaids of God, with faith and hope in Christ, in the thirtieth year of her life, she commended her joyful soul to God, 9 calends December.[26] With every care, she was brought to burial in the basilica of the blessed apostle Peter in a marble tomb and awaits the day when all the saints will be rewarded.

7. But now let us return to the road from which we digressed. When the blessed Gertrude had released her conscience from the chains of office, she prayed incessantly for three months, exhorting and preaching the word of the Lord to herself and others. Joyous in hope, patient in tribulation, with devout mind and serene countenance, she waited her last day when she would leave. She was hurrying from prison to the kingdom, from darkness to light, from death to life, for she was here in body only. Daily with continuous prayer she sent her soul to eternity with singular affliction and abstinence. Secretly she put a harsh hair shirt on her little body, so that she would have no sweet refreshment in this life but only where the just will gleam like the sun in their Father's kingdom. And when she came to her last days, she decreed that neither linen nor woolen clothing be laid over her where she was buried but only a single cheap veil which a certain pilgrim nun had brought a few days earlier to cover her head, with that same hair shirt underneath. She could rest in peace with no other covering but these two: the hair shirt which she wore with the old rag to cover it. For she said that such superfluous things could give no help to the dead, which all wise people affirm. And when the day of her assumption drew near, she called one of the brothers and gave him instructions, saying: "Go in haste to that pilgrim who is far away in Fosse monastery and say to him, 'The virgin of Christ, Gertrude sent me to ask you to name the day when she will migrate from this light. For she tells herself to be afraid but she rejoices at the same time.' And that one will tell you what you ought to announce. Go and have no doubts." And her orders were soon carried out and the servant of God without delay responded to her message. "Today, is the 16th calends of April. Tomorrow, during the solemnities of the Mass, God's virgin Gertrude will migrate from her body. And say to her that she should neither fear nor tremble because of her death but proceed with joy for the blessed Bishop Patrick with God's elect and His angels is prepared

26. Wulftrude died November 23, 669.

to receive her in immense glory.[27] Go speedily." The brother who had been sent, asked him whether he had seen this through divine revelation that he might reveal all to her in order. And he said, "Go brother and hurry. You know this: Tomorrow is the day. Why ask me more?" And, returning, he announced to Christ's handmaid what had been said to him. And she, as though waking from slumber, gave thanks with joyous exhilaration to God that he deigned to console his handmaid through her fellow servant.[28] And she continued to be happy because of these promises. Through the whole night she led the sisters in prayer at their vigils. The next day, Sunday, about the sixth hour, following the words of the man of God, she received viaticum of the most sacred body and blood of Christ. And when the priest had ended the Secret, she breathed forth her desiring soul on the 15 calends of April in the thirty-third year of her life, giving thanks to her Maker who saw fit to call her without corruption to His kingdom.[29] Then I was summoned, with another brother named Rinchinus. And calling me by name, the servant of God Rinchinus asked, "Do you notice anything?" And I answered, "No, except that I see the sisters in great grief." But just as he spoke, there came the sweetest odor, as a fragrance of ointments and the whole cell where the holy body lay was redolent and as we walked we sensed this wonderfully sweet odor in our nostrils. When everything was done about the blessed corpse and the offices finished, the body of the most blessed virgin of Christ, Gertrude, was laid in her sepulchre in an underground grave that she had prepared for herself in the past with praises by the priests and handmaids of God.[30] There daily benefits of prayer are shown through our Lord Jesus Christ who reigns with the Father and Holy Spirit from everlasting to everlasting. Amen.

27. Gertrude shares the feast of Patrick, March 17. There may be some deeper significance intended because Fosse was a monastery of Irish monks, following the model of Columbanus in attaching themselves to communities of women and working in a complementary relationship with them.

28. Krusch cites a variant manuscript of Life A that gives the monk's name as Ultanus. It is possible that he is the same Ultanus who was abbot of Péronne eighteen years later when Amatus was imprisoned there.

29. The Secret is the silent prayer that the priest says preceding the preface of the Mass. This reference predates the traditional date of its introduction by almost a century. See Jungmann, *The Mass of the Roman Rite*, 2:90. The text also suggests that Gertrude was given viaticum from a host reserved for the purpose. Seventh-century references to viaticum are frequent, and the obligation of reserving the Eucharist for the purpose was inserted in the Statutes of Saint Boniface according to King, *Eucharistic Reservation in the Western Church*, 5.

30. We have used "underground" for in *cisterna*. Cox notes that the author may have been trying to emphasize the humbleness of Gertrude's grave compared to Wulftrude's marble tomb.

Of Miracles Performed After the Death of the Holy Abbess Gertrude

■

1. How can so many people, our own contemporaries, live the angelic life, unless their minds and consciences have been rooted in eternity? Though they live in the flesh here among us, must not their hearts dwell incessantly in divine contemplation while they barely subsist in the body? Thus, although Christ's servant Gertrude, whose life and behavior we have recorded from her earliest youth, lived in the flesh here among mortals and acted as regent over the men and women who lived as Christ's servants under her authority, she never forgot her perpetual interior life nor relaxed her standard of rectitude nor her serious manners nor her rigorous discipline even for a moment. Accordingly, it became clear that the omnipotent Lord granted more than a few things to be accomplished through her virtues after her death. For, as everyone familiar with her life and physical deprivations knows, they can now obtain help through prayer. For the Lord has deigned to show signs to those who humbly pray at her sepulchre with faith so that, to some extent we may remember hereafter and present them to the public.

2. There was a certain abbess in a monastery of Trier named Modesta who had been similarly consecrated to God in infancy. She was bound familiarly to holy Gertrude in divine friendship.[31] For a long time they had lived in separate homes and many miles and lengths of earth lay between them physically so that they could not see one another directly with their eyes. But they were always lovingly together in their hearts and minds, for they performed their military service equally and served the Lord equally, without guile, in sincerity of heart.[32] Much time passed and then something happened which I wish to recall to your minds by telling about it. One day, God's servant, Modesta, entered the church in her monastery to pray and prostrated herself before the altar of Blessed Mary Ever Virgin. When her prayers were finished, she arose. As she looked about her, she suddenly saw and perceived holy Gertrude standing on the right side of the altar in the same habit and form as she herself had been fashioned. She said to her: "Sister Modesta, receive this vision that you may know for certain and without any doubt that today at this same hour I have been freed from my fleshly habitation. I am Gertrude, whom you have loved much." And having said this, she

---

31. The "familiar" bond probably implies a blood relationship; Glodesind's sister gave her instruction in an unnamed convent at Trier. Oda, the wife of Arnulf of Metz and mother-in-law of Gertrude's sister Begga, also retired to a convent in that city.

32. See Benedict's Rule, c. 2.

was swept from her sight. Then she thought silently within herself about what such a vision might mean. And all that day she breathed no hint of the vision to anyone. But early on the following day, the Bishop of Metz, Clodulf, came to the monastery of the said servant of God, Modesta.[33] Among other conversation, the virgin questioned the bishop about holy Gertrude, particularly as to her habit and her appearance. Immediately, he described in detail her physical appearance and how beautiful she was. From the bishop's descriptions, the blessed Modesta understood that what she had seen was true and she said to him: "Now I confess to you what I concealed before: that yesterday about the sixth hour it was revealed to me that on that day and at that hour, she passed over." And after she disclosed all things in order to the bishop, Clodulf confirmed the day and hour and found that all things in order were as the Abbess had indicated.

3. Ten years after the saint's death, a fire broke out in the monastery of Nivelles which the saint had governed when she lived in the flesh. They say that the flames erupted so violently that none of the monks or virgins or men running together to the place had any hope of saving the monastery from fire. Thus the handmaids of God, who had already gathered, fled outside the monastery wall to a place nearby. Then one man, who had been entrusted with the responsibility of running the monastery, suddenly raised his eyes and saw holy Gertrude standing at the peak of the refectory in her old form and habit. With the veil that had covered her, she fanned the flames back from the house. The man was not terrified by the image but, full of joy, exhorted his companions to act resolutely. He ran quickly, ascending on high to see what was happening and, with wonder, they all saw the monastery rescued from fire in the same hour.[34]

4. Another time, through a vision to some of the sisters, they were warned that no other person should dare to rest in that little bed where Saint Gertrude was wont to lay her weary limbs after the labor of vigil and prayer. Then God's servant, Abbess Dominica, Saint Gertrude's niece who was brought up at her feet, was filled with joy that the Lord deigned to distinguish her with so many miracles of signs.[35] She convoked the whole congregation and they

---

33. Clodulf was Arnulf's second son and therefore Begga's brother-in-law. Cox notes that Clodulf commissioned the *Vita Sancti Arnulfi* (in Krusch, ed., *MGH*, *SRM* 1) and that a life of Clodulf himself was produced in the ninth century (*AS*, June 2, 127–32).

34. According to Cox, Arnulf of Metz was also a great firefighter, having saved the city of Metz from incineration.

35. The author appears to have confused the fourth abbess, Dominica, with Wulftrude, the second abbess. For a further interpretation, see Herbillon, "Dominica, Dominicana, pseudo-abbesse de Nivelles," 316. "Miracles of signs" appears also in the *Life of Aldegund*, c. 6, which was also written at

took up the little bed and carried it with great honor and praise of God and deposited it in the basilica of Saint Paul the Apostle where now the Lord has deigned to display many signs and wonders.

5. In that country, there was a certain girl who was burdened with a very heavy illness for many years and no doctor could cure her. Finally the sight left her eyes and she was blind. Then her folks took her up and brought her with them to the monastery of Nivelles where they hoped to find other doctors who might be able to cure her. There in the night Saint Gertrude appeared to her in a vision and said to her: "Girl, do not doubt but believe in the Lord Jesus Christ and go to the bed where Gertrude used to rest, which is placed in Saint Paul the Apostle's church. There you will receive a cure for all troubles which you now suffer in your body." Because of the gravity of her illness, the girl could not come there until the third day. Then, at Terce, the whole congregation gathered for divine service and when they had finished God's Work, the sick girl came forward. The sisters supported her and led her to the little bed where she had been commanded to go. And when, praying to God, she stretched out and bowed to the bed, her eyes were immediately opened and her whole body which before had been weakened was suddenly well and without injury. And she gave thanks to the Lord and was filled with joy and returned to her family exulting.

6. After this deed was performed, Saint Gertrude's niece, who had followed her as regent of the monastery of Nivelles migrated from this light. Then the entire conventual family unanimously chose as their abbess a girl from a noble family named Agnes, who had also been raised by blessed Gertrude. She is the one who later built a church in honor of Christ's virgin, Saint Gertrude. On the same day when the church was built, the bed was carried in with honor and all the sisters kept solemn vigil in the church on that night. When Matins was finished and the service of God complete, they extinguished the seven lamps which [now] always burn in that oratory. But in the morning when the sisters entered the same chapel for prayer, they saw all those lights, which they had earlier snuffed out, burning away. When this miracle was divulged, the fame of her virtues spread over the whole region so that everyone came from near and far to the blessed virgin's sepulchre seeking remedy for soul and body alike. And with God's aid, all who sought the help of divine love there, returned healthy and whole.

7. There was a certain man in the neighborhood whose wife had been blinded. He took her up and led her to the monastery of Nivelles where the

---

Nivelles or by someone close to that monastery. It may also have a relationship to the "signs of miracles" in Austreberta, c. 2.

holy virgin rested. When they entered the church, she stood beneath a lamp which suddenly overflowed, spilling its oil upon her cloak. All who were there saw a miracle! Taking a drop of that oil, they anointed her eyes and immediately the woman's eyes were opened which had been blind before. The next day, comforted by faith and hope and the virtues of the holy Gertrude, she returned to her home whole. However, it would take too long to set out everything in order that God did through her. God did so much that all who took refuge in her and prayed to her for health, returned home whence they came healed through God's aid. All who called her name in faith were freed from whatever trial oppressed them with an angel of the Lord for their helper.

8. On another occasion, thieves captured a certain boy and bound him, keeping him in chains because they wished to sell him into slavery outside the country. Suddenly, the boy remembered the name of Saint Gertrude and called upon her confidently to come to his rescue. Immediately, the chains fell in pieces from his bound hands and he began to run in order to escape. And the men who had captured him began to pursue him hoping to catch him. But they could not and the boy was freed from the hands of the thieves, his enemies.

9. A while after, a certain man was caught in great crimes. Thereupon his lord ordered that he be detained and confined in chains. The unhappy one was confined and reduced to terrified trembling for no one there expected him to live very long. But the captive was comforted by hope and prayed to the holy woman that she might help him in his misery. And at once the irons which bound him were broken. Bearing them with him to the monastery of Nivelles, he found all the doors and gates of the church open. He came to the holy bed and was freed by the holy virgin's virtue.

10. In the thirty-third year after the blessed Gertrude's death, by the Lord's inspiration, it came into her sister Begga's heart that she wished to found a monastery for herself.[36] Accordingly, she came to the said monastery of Nivelles and asked the Abbess Agnes with the whole congregation to give her help in this holy cause, whence she might have the best of everything she needed to establish this devotion. The entire congregation received the petition in the most loving spirit and, as she asked, they gave her relics and books of Holy Scriptures. Likewise, they gave her some of the sisters who were spiritual seniors in the holy habit who could teach the discipline of the regular life in her monastery and establish the norms of religion. And they gave her a piece of the bed from which Saint Gertrude, her sister, had migrated to Christ. Then the most Christian matron accepted all that per-

36. Andennes.

tained to the reverence of religion and in all honor and reverence bore them to her monastery filled with great joy and exultation.[37] And when they drew near the monastery to which they were headed, they raised crosses and sang canticles praising the Lord. They carried the relics and the holy bed which they bore with them and placed them near an altar dedicated to the virgin Saint Genovefa.[38] How can human words tell how many were daily cleansed of demons, cured of infirmities and freed of all tribulation? And in the following year all being perfected and well disposed, the matron migrated to the Lord.

11. After a few days, a certain religious woman came to that same monastery. Generated from a noble root, her name was Adula and in all things she was truly a handmaid of Christ, modest in dress, humble in religion, not false in charity but generous in alms to the old and poor, hospitable to the needy and to pilgrims. However, she had some doubts whether or not the Lord truly deigned to show so many signs through blessed Gertrude's merits. Whence it happened that an argument arose, as though in jest, between that matron and a handmaid of God here in the monastery. One day, the matron asked her, "On what day will the feast of Saint Gertrude be?" She responded, "In the fifth week of Lent on Friday."[39] And [Adula] said, "Far be it from me to wish to add anything out of the ordinary to our meal on that feast, beyond the usual servile portion." The girl said in answer, "If she can obtain anything from God, let her do it for you, so that on that day, willy nilly, you shall take the charity."[40] And when the day came, everyone who had gathered for the solemnity, man and woman, monk and virgin of Christ, were celebrating the day with honor and reverence. After the completion of solemn mass, they received food and drink with thanksgiving and rejoicing for all the things they were allowed to eat in that Lenten season.[41] Only the matron did not feast that day. Her little son whom she loved with much love was with her. Coming to her, the child asked if he might be allowed to play and she said to him, "Do what you like with yourself." And the little one laughed and ran this way and that. Suddenly, there was an accident. He fell into the well which was there.

37. Begga (d. 693), the widow of Arnulf of Metz's son, was Pepin of Herstal's mother. Popular tradition associates her with the foundation of the beguines, although the first of these groups do not appear in surviving texts for several centuries after her death.
38. See chapter 1 for similar use of a bed as relic.
39. Krusch calculates that this would be March 17, 691. The Friday before the beginning of Holy Week is traditionally a particularly solemn day of fasting and penitence.
40. The "charity" here is a technical expression defined by the CCSL, Lexicon as "an extraordinary repast given by monks to celebrate a feast day or anniversary of reception." Adula was refusing to eat anything beyond the usual lenten fare.
41. Borst, Mönche am Bodensee, 71, sees this banquet as a sign of deteriorated asceticism in the Adelskirchen of late Merovingian times.

And he lay there a long time until the sisters arose from table full of joy, happy and well fed. Then one of the sisters came in and said, "Do you know that the matron's son is dead?" They interrogated her about what had killed him. She answered: "He fell into the well where he was drowned." Then that nun who had before been contending with the matron over the virtues of Saint Gertrude cried out in a loud voice, saying: "Saint Gertrude, you have done this because the child's mother did not wish to believe in the miracles that God has worked through you!" And then she said, "I entreat your sanctity, holy Gertrude, virgin of Christ, and I adjure you through our Lord Jesus Christ, that as God gave you the power, you will resuscitate him." And she began to go hastily seeking the child. And his mother went and met her and asked what she was doing, saying, "What are you doing sister?" And she, answering for the third time, with an oath, said: "What I do, do you likewise. Believe in the truth, for in this hour Saint Gertrude will restore your son to you alive." Thus she bore the child and placed him by the blessed Gertrude's bed. Soon to the wondering eyes of all, the child who was dead arose. And from that day, the matron began to believe in the virtues of Saint Gertrude. Indeed, calling her whole household together in the same hour, she feasted [them] from the charity which she had previously refused. The next day she celebrated Mass in honor of Christ's virgin Gertrude and took refreshment with all the sisters. And the child, quite unhurt, served them and with his hands offered a drink to each in turn. And for this, the matron adorned the holy bed with gold and precious gems and most beautiful hangings. And, lest any find this incredible, I invoke God's witness that I saw all that I have written with my own eyes or heard it from reliable witnesses. And now, I have said enough of the virtues and miracles. For we can never explain everything in order that God deigns daily to do in her name. Therefore, now we pray the Lord that He will deign to help us through her prayers and to Him be all honor, virtue and power and glory, from everlasting to everlasting. Amen.

13

Aldegund, Abbess of Maubeuge (d. ca. 684)
Waldetrude, Abbess of Mons (d. ca. 688)

Aldegund and Waldetrude were sisters born in the reign of Dagobert I between 628 and 639, and therefore contemporaries with Sadalberga, Rictrude,
and Gertrude. Like those three women, they were ultimately settled in
monasteries in the northern frontiers of Christian Frankland under the influence of Saint Amand.[1] They are the best documented members of a family of
saints that includes their father and mother, Waldetrude's husband, Vincent
of Soignies, and her daughters Madelberta and Aldetrude. Aldetrude has also

Following our policy throughout of preferring the oldest available life, we have taken this translation of Aldegund's life from Smet's edition, *Acta Sanctorum Belgae*, 4:291–326. Levison stripped this life
of its mystical content for the MGH edition, 6:79–90. In addition he used the vita prepared in the
ninth century by Hucbald of Saint Amand, the author of Rictrude's life, among others. We have
made note of several variants found in Hucbald for the sake of readers interested in the changes
made by later hagiographers in primitive texts. This life appears to be a direct transcription of the
notes assembled by "a certain religious abbot named Subinus" and another anonymous brother
(*AS*, January 30, c. 5) to whom Aldegund had entrusted her own description of her visions. The text
is, therefore, particularly interesting in that it provides direct insight into this woman's interior life,
as noted by Wemple, "Female Spirituality." Chapters 20–24 appear to be an additional collection of
wonders collected from various witnesses including sisters of her community and her sister
Waldetrude. We have supplemented our translation with notes and some insertions from the oldest
life in *AS*, January 30, 649–62, which appears to be a rewrite, possibly on the occasion of her
translation to Maubeuge under the direction of her niece Aldetrude. It is particularly interesting
because the substantive differences (exclusive of the more elaborate interpretive passages) incorpo-
rate material from Waldetrude's visions and material about Aldegund's relationship with her
mother Bertilla, which may well have come from her older sister. Therefore, we are tempted to
advance the possibility that the second life may have been written by a nun under the direction of
Waldetrude herself or her daughter Aldetrude, abbess of Maubeuge.
This account of Waldetrude was taken from *AS*, April 9, 826–33. This redaction is late, dating from
the time of Waldetrude's official canonization in the thirteenth century. It represents a much older
cult reaching back to the seventh century and claims to be based on contemporary testimony.
Possibly the author's restraint in omitting legends of her travels with her husband in Ireland may
support his claim to reliability.
1. For more on these relationships, see Ewig, *Spätantikes und fränkisches Gallien*. 192ff.

merited inclusion in the *Acta Sanctorum*, but we have omitted her vita from the present collection because it generally repeats material incorporated into the lives of her mother and aunt. She succeeded Aldegund as abbess of Maubeuge from 684 to 696. Like her aunt, she was prone to visions of the saints encouraging her vocation.

The life of Aldegund links Maubeuge with Nivelles through visions, which suggests a possible family connection with Gertrude.[2] Neither the first nor the second edition of Aldegund's life are clear about where she actually lived or what the chronological relationships between her life and that of Waldetrude might have been. The last paragraph of the second edition indicates that she was never abbess of Maubeuge, despite the appellation given to her by all her historians.[3] Apparently she was consecrated soon after her first visions but remained at home (possibly while her mother still lived). Although the life mentions "sisters" and suggests that she lived for part of her life in a community, there is no mention of any monastic foundation. Possibly she simply gathered some women into her home and used the local church for devotions, as c. 12 of the second edition seems to suggest. She and Waldetrude clearly spent time together, but this may have been before the latter founded Mons (possibly only at the end of her life). Certainly the visions that Waldetrude had of Aldegund's impending "marriage," or death, seem to verify that they were living apart at that time. If we are to rely on the thirteenth-century version of Waldetrude's life included here, Aldegund must have been very much younger than her sister who had been married, borne children, and spent some years alone before she built the monastery to which she invited Aldegund. On the other hand, there is no indication of the date at which Aldegund took over the raising of Waldetrude's daughter Aldetrude. She may have taken the child into her mother's home at some time between Waldetrude's renunciation of the world and her own departure to her sister's side. Waldetrude's life is unusual for a female saint of this period because she is depicted as having spent some part of her career as a hermit before she was induced to found a community. This may be simply a reflection of a high medieval female spirituality that promoted the reclusive life for women. Of course, any number of women in the wildernesses of Frankland in those years may have lived as recluses. It is a comment on the ecclesiastical politics of the age that without institutional backing and well-connected relatives, their cults never sufficiently impressed their contem-

---

2. Aldegund's birth from "royal stock" is interpolated in the second redaction, possibly simply to lend dignity to the subject. Van der Essen, *Etude critique*, 223. If she were connected with the Carolingian family, however, they may already have replaced the Merovingian as "royal" when the life was written.

3. See note a in *AS*.

poraries to ensure that their light could not be hidden. The late date of the present life may also explain why Waldetrude, who was presumably as wealthy as her sister, was obliged to ask a male relative to build her convent.

A final peculiarity in the life of Waldetrude that might reflect the conjugal values of a later age is her apparent difficulty with sexual temptations. None of the Merovingian women, even those who had been successfully married like Rictrude and Sadalberga, are depicted by their contemporaries as being regretful for their carnal pleasures. This, however, seems to be a serious difficulty for Waldetrude. Her husband, Madelgar, is entered in the calendar of saints as Vincent of Soignies, his monastic name. Agnes Dunbar notes an Irish tradition that he came from that land as a soldier in Dagobert's service named Maguire, and later returned with his wife for Irish monks and books when they embarked on the monastic life.[4] This might conceivably refer to the period of Dagobert II's exile and attempted return in 676 which caused such difficulty for Saint Amatus.[5] If the family were involved with that disaster, it might account for their sudden flight to the cloister, and a sense that pervades Waldetrude's life that she was slow to adjust to the outcome.

Aldegund, Abbess of Maubeuge

∎

1. We assist at the feasts of holy virgins revolving in a cycle of anniversaries celebrated by Christ's conscientious prelates, while the cloudy courses of this world pass on and the waxing and waning of our years runs out. Thus while we give to the flesh what belongs to the flesh, we supply spiritual needs in equal measure to the Lord of spiritual things, which He, Who ordered us in His mighty voice to give Caesar the coin which belongs to him, commanded us not to neglect. Therefore, examples of the virtues of God's chosen should be related so that those who hear what good people have achieved may be joyful, enlightened, and set afire from this good memory, whence they may aspire to the joy of the eternal fatherland. Thus, to deserve help from their intercession, we celebrate these votive offices every year.

2. The Virgin Aldegund, loveable to Christ, is remembered to have been from an ancient line in the time of the great King of the Franks, Dagobert. She did not pull back from holy deeds in her childhood years but exulted, longing with great love to follow the footsteps of those who conquered the weak enemy. The Mediator of God and Man, Our Lord Jesus Christ, Who by His own will stooped to loose the knots of Tartaros and, triumphant as a

---

4. Dunbar, *A Dictionary of Saintly Women.*

5. Eddius Stephanus, *Life of Wilfrid,* c. 28 and 33, in *The Age of Bede;* also see herein chapter 12, Introduction, and chapter 16.

victor over the conquered enemy, by His power leads our captivity captive[6] and gives gifts to humanity, granted her His instrument of peace, that is love of charity. He Who created all things from nothing conferred strength on the fragile sex. In the human condition, she was known to be from noble stock. Therefore let us briefly note her lineage so as to leave later generations in no doubt. Her father was the venerable Waldebert and her mother Bertilla.[7] They were married in the flesh but, burning with divine radiance, they chose the spiritual life imitating Paul's example, who says, "They that have wives should be as though they had none."[8] Her two uncles were Gundeland and Landeric, remembered in the land as first in battle, whom we might, like Greek scholars, call Bellatores.[9] Their human state was wonderful but God's power is more wonderful. So one of such high birth was made poor for the love of Christ and from that poverty we are all made rich, as the witness says: "Blessed are the poor in spirit for theirs is the kingdom of Heaven."[10]

3. Instructed in the spiritual things she heard, struck with heavenly lightning, burning for Christ to enter into the heavenly company of those two travelling companions, fasts and prayers, the blessed virgin Aldegund began to think how she might give up the world for the sake of the Lord's name and celestial love. Her eagerness in all prosperity for alms and vigils with her pious mind intent, assiduous in reading, endured through more tribulations than we have revealed in our account.[11] Because when the time approached for marriage, the debt the soul owes to carnal desires, her mother, ignorant and wishing to discover her intent, said: "I want to be taught the counsel of human fragility, which God inspires. Dearest daughter, do you want to be married in the maternal way?" With her customary goodness, she deferred to her wise mother, saying: "I don't know the counsel of Almighty God and don't deny the words so much from my own free will as by God's inspiration. I want to serve under Christ's yoke and follow His precepts to humble the lurid pomp and vanity of this world so that I will be able to win Christ's prize of eternal bliss and, sheltered in His holy arms, climb to the heavenly Jerusalem with my feet unobstructed. Thus I shall deserve to be gathered within the gates of Paradise. This that you hear, oh dearest mother, I desire more

---

6. Ephesians 4:8.

7. Levison, MGH, SRM 6:86, n. 6, identifies Waldebert as the *domesticus* of Clothar II mentioned by Fredegar, CL 4:54, anno. 626–627.

8. 1 Corinthians 7:29.

9. Levison, MGH, SRM 6:86, n. 8, identifies Gundeland as the Neustrian mayor corrupted by Lombard bribes, ca. 616, LHF, 40. Ebling, *Prosopographie*, 228–29, is more discreet but does not dispute it; on 165 and 179 he identifies Landeric as Clothar's commander and the purported lover of Fredegund. Fredegar, CL 4:25–26.

10. Matthew 5:3.

11. These tribulations may be the opposition of her mother to her wish to consecrate her virginity to God, which is delineated in the second edition.

than all holocausts.[12] Instruct me in those things. Teach me that, my most faithful mother, because that is my will and my prayer."[13]

4. This was her desire, when the Lord shares the comfort of His piety with all who seek and plainly opens the good mysteries of His largesse to those who knock and does not desert those who are coming to Him but permits them to be gathered in the safest fortress. He doubled His help for His beloved virgin Aldegund and amplified His gifts to her from one bright lode of ore. For He kindled a fire of love in her sister Waldetrude and she began to pursue her own decision and sweat with good works. Seeing her thus constrained to God's will, her blessed husband Madelgar's heart filled with thanks to Almighty God Who had deigned to shower His spiritual gifts on His faithful and he said in a great voice: "Remember us, O Lord, with the pleasure that Thou bearest unto Thy people: Oh, visit us with Thy salvation."[14] And even before he completed this versicle, he turned toward the monastery called Hautmont that under the holy rule of monks he might begin to follow the spiritual life and persevere in good actions.[15] And as he went he sang the psalm: "Lead me in thy truth and teach me: for thou art the God of my salvation; on Thee do I wait all my days."[16] So afterwards according to His own will, the Lord sent a small fire of sparks to His near ones, one by one. Carnal ambitions vanished, doused by the dew from the heavenly fatherland, and they all flowered with aromatic shoots. Since her husband had become remote from carnal desires, strongly burning with the flames of faith, she took the consecrated Pallium from Bishop Audebert who advised her to be enclosed in the monastery which she had already begun to build.[17] And she obeyed, and at the same time implored God to help her tear her sister from

12. Mark 12:30.

13. The second edition, possibly expanded by Waldetrude, gives her a much more exhausting debate with her mother. "*Then the mother revealed her own desire: she showed her a large household, rich with infinite property, a wealth of farms and a full treasury. She urged her daughter to agree with her mother that she be joined with a husband and said that her father and all their friends were ready to add to these blandishments for they wanted to celebrate a wedding which would join her to a most noble, rich and beautiful youth. But God's virgin Aldegund had already considered it all in her heart. Filled with the breath of Divinity, the Spirit itself, she said: "Lady genetrix, sweetest mother, why do you burden my mind with all these honeyed words? Don't you remember what things I have disclosed to you? I have shown you what I desire. For I want a spouse whose estates comprise the heavens and earth and the oceans; whose wealth will not fail through all eternity, whose riches grow daily and in no way diminish. If you can, mother, get such a spouse for me—not a man of sin and caprice who will surely die." The mother heard this and could not move the mind of the virgin from her constancy. But still she tried often with feminine wiles to tempt her regarding the marital condition.*"

14. Psalms 106:4.

15. See the life of Waldetrude herein. The lives of Vincent/Madelgar are discussed by van der Essen, *Etude critique*, 241. Saint Autbert is discussed in ibid., 273.

16. Psalms 25:5.

17. Mabillon reads pallium to mean veil in this instance (2d ed., c. 4): "She gave herself to the monastery she built in a place called Castrilocus which, we understand, got its name because there was once a Roman camp there." Now it is Mons.

the jaws of this world so that she might render that interest to God which He expects from His sluggish servant, as He says in the teachings: "Bad servant, you knew that I was an austere man, taking up what I laid not down and reaping what I did not sow. Wherefore then gavest not thou my money into the bank that at my coming I might have required my own with interest?"[18] Hearing this, she feared that, if she left the blessed virgin [Aldegund] behind her, she might apostatize from good deeds. She sent letters to her mother Bertilla asking her to send [Aldegund] to her on a visit.[19] She was moved by piety to agree that she should go and so ordered it and it took place. And as she went, [Aldegund] said: "Hold up my steps, Lord, in thy path that my footsteps slip not."[20] And considering all this in her heart the blessed virgin indeed desired that her sister might, by accepting the privilege, become a mother of souls.[21]

5. Now while she still remained in her carnal condition busy at her parents' hearth, she heard the Most Blessed, through a vision, [say] that she was to have the highest measure of wealth. Marvelling, the girl's mind was able to believe in that unfamiliar showing of this vision though she did not know what the enigmatic vision wanted. Reflecting on Christ's secrets, she now found herself led to the gate of a great house supported by seven decorated columns and she looked in at bright ornaments [breathing] aromatic fragrance, imbued with the wonderfully sweet aroma of Christ. And as she began to see more clearly, as scales fell from her eyes, she was promised that she would receive the celestial gift from Him Who said "Come unto me, all ye that labor and are heavy laden, and I will give you rest."[22] Indeed with God helping, the two of them joined in the unity of the Holy Spirit and the chains

18. Luke 19:22–23.

19. There is some confusion here with pronouns. The virgin must be Aldegund because Waldetrude was married with children. However, the letter-writer must be Waldetrude because Aldegund is still living at home. The story is told more plainly in the second edition, c. 4.

20. Psalms 17:5.

21. This sentence is made clear by a convention that often appears in seventh-century texts. Waldetrude is called *sua germana*, whereas in later portions of the text Aldegund's spiritual sisters are consistently called *sorores*. She wishes her to become a *mater animarum*, whereas throughout the text Bertilla and even the Virgin Mary are designated by the term *genetrix* to distinguish physical from spiritual motherhood.

22. Matthew 11:28. This vision was omitted from the second edition, but the meaning of the following sentence, where *ambae* (both) is ambiguous, may relate back to that version, c. 4, which amplifies her partnership with Waldetrude: "Now Waldetrude had vowed that, once her sister Aldegund had taken the veil, she would give her care of the sisters living there. Unquestionably the Holy Spirit was at work that they should be of one mind in serving God and live in common habitation in this world. Steel is sharpened on steel, as it is written, and so one is sharpened by a friend's attention. They shone like two splendid lamps, offering the other sisters guidance to the eternal light of Our Lord Jesus Christ which they deserved to achieve with them."

of peace, moving as one. More and more, they followed the way to the Lord after revealed truth, refuting the lurid, vile and novel, hurrying on twin wings, joined wings extended, to the stars, like those of whom the Lord said: "Who are these that fly as a cloud and as doves to their windows?"[23] They shall deserve to take up the pairing of the apostles, who, as truthful reading attests, were sent preaching two by two; singing psalms and following the oracle saying: "Keep us Lord as the apple of Thine eye and hide us under the shadow of Thy wings."[24]

6. When Aldegund, a consecrated virgin daily devoted to Christ, stayed long at her prayers, the Lord began to show her, through nocturnal visions, gleaming miracles of signs of His majesty.[25] Seeing an angelic man standing nearby as though elevated from earth, his reflection veiled with exceeding splendor, the holy virgin never doubted [him] to be benevolent. Desiring to obtain information from him, she said: "Oh good Planter, expound what you may foresee of my fortune." Soon the interrogated one offered spiritual words, saying: "I see something like letters circling your head."[26] And when she requested a second admonition, he said: "I see a straight rod from your head reaching even to Heaven." To the third inquiry, he said: "I have heard a voice in Jerusalem that you will be a nun." Recall the Celestial of celestials Who said: "He that is of earth speaketh of earth; He that cometh from Heaven is above all."[27] Thus by her speaking and hearing of [Heaven], it is proved. And the more she fanned the sparks of faith, the more her love of Christ flamed up. After this support had withdrawn, raising her eyes to Heaven and praying, she said: "Oh tremendous Ruler of Eternal Salvation, Who deigned to visit your unworthy handmaid through an angel! Honor and power to you through infinite cycles of ages." To come to the end, she heard the angelic voice saying to her: "Oh flowering virgin, bound to the celestial Gardener, if you would know the gift promised you from your Heavenly Father, you must hold the semblances of this world as nothing." Speaking more plainly, it said: "You must have no other spouse but Christ the Lord." And it comforted her

---

23. Isaiah 10:8.
24. Psalms 17:8.
25. This is analogous to the "miracles of signs" found in the life of Gertrude of Nivelles. Along with chapters 19 and 29, it suggests a linkage to Nivelles. Indeed, van der Essen, *Etude critique*, 220, thought that the author might be a monk or nun at Nivelles.
26. This vision was also omitted from the second edition. Throughout, the vision seems to be informed by iconography. What the angel describes is a pictorial representation of a saint with her name inscribed in her halo and holding the palm that designates her sacrifice. A similar instance of transferring visual cues appears in the eighth-century life of Saint Leoba, who sees a purple ribbon coming from her mouth as she preaches.
27. John 3:31.

saying many things about the Kingdom of God, she held them deep in her heart with joy, saying: "Let it be done to your handmaid according to your word."[28]

7. And the following night after matins, in a vision, she remembered seeing that she had a precious dress which was beyond description, utterly unlike any garment ever seen on earth, and she was standing in His presence Who was clothed in the beautiful shape of a little boy Who said: "If you would know how this celestial *stola* looks which the Lord will give you, there is nothing like it![29] For it shines like the sun and the moon in my Father's kingdom." And while they spoke thus between themselves, someone else radiated in the bright light, with a hesitant breath: "Who do you think that is, Oh Salvifica, Who is speaking with you?" And she thought it to be a vision of an angel. But he said plainly: "This is Christ the Son of the Living God, who is speaking to you, the Hope of consolation and the Virtue in good works, the Superstantiality of bread Who has said of Himself: "I am the living bread which came down from Heaven."[30] Rejoicing and exulting in her heart, now having had a foretaste of the sweet food of Christ, with growing signs and portents of miracles, she further saw herself with a palm flowing with light in her hand, bright to all eyes, and likewise crowned with royal gold and gems not woven or made by human hands but only shaped in Heaven by God. And soon she longed to give up all human things to acquire these, considering the teaching of the Apostle saying: "Every man that strives for the mastery is temperate in all things. Now they do it to obtain a corruptible crown; but we an incorruptible."[31] And she desired to gain the prize of the eternal kingdom and possess eternal life.

8. Behold now as she pursued her good works, the Devil confronted her like a ravening wolf. The ancient enemy was like a roaring lion gnashing her teeth, accustomed to wander with unslaked jaws, leaving her young, through the forests and ravines seeking someone to devour. With importunate tongue, he said: "Why are you like an immoveable column, mocking me? The Almighty will give you the kingdom which I lost. Oh, how I hate your virginity and how I have plotted to tear it from you. But there is no way." And indeed Aldegund, Christ's stouthearted virgin, scolded him, saying: "Oh

28. The second edition does not follow the same order in these visions of Aldegund's courtship. C. 7 supplies an additional detail: "After her mother Bertilla had left this life, she appeared to her daughter, Aldegund, to inform her that an angel had said, "So now shall this blessed virgin become the habitation of Christ her spouse."

29. A *stola* is the traditional dress of a Roman matron. When she appeared so dressed in public, all pedestrians were supposed to defer to her married dignity by stepping out of her way.

30. John 6:51.

31. 1 Corinthians 9:25.

you poison-bearing pest of the furies! You malevolent mind! Our Lord Jesus Christ will trample you under His feet and likewise all your savagery against the humanity made in His image. Just you try to spread the death-bearing flames among the men and women who serve God! for their inmost veins burn with the spirit of chastity like a torch of Christ. Apostate! I order you in the name of Our Lord Jesus Christ, Who triumphs with the Father, overcoming you in Heaven, to go down into your infernal prison." Confounded, the hostile Devil vanished on the spot and the Lord's virgin remained with her faith unshaken. And immediately the angel of the Lord came to comfort the blessed virgin Aldegund, saying: "Peace be to you. Be comforted. Act manfully. The Lord is with you. Blessed art thou among virgins, for your name is written in the Book of Life and your true portion will be found among the number of the holy virgins. However, oh blessed virgin, you must preserve your virginity if you want to gain that crown which the Almighty showed to you in the night by a vision, the highest gift among all things visible and invisible, and if you want to escape all the wickedest snares of that tempter." And with these exhortations and admonitions from the Angel of the Lord, God's virgin Aldegund sang psalms without ceasing, saying with tears of joy: "I will freely sacrifice unto thee. I will praise thy name Oh Lord, for it is good." And again, she said: "Unto thee, O Lord, will I sing. I will behave myself wisely in a perfect way. Oh, when wilt thou come to me?" And again: "Show me a token for good; that they which hate me may see it and be ashamed because thou Lord, hast holpen me, and comforted me."[32]

9. Now the blessed virgin knew that she had been relieved of the burden of the millstone of sin and the yoke of carnal cares. She was burning with Christ, having felt His breath of eternal grace in many ineffable showings. She knew that she had been torn like a sheep from the jaws of the wolf by the hand of Christ the Good Shepherd and led to the fold of the eternal King by His watchful care. Constantly she prayed Almighty God for victory: "Let this immaculate and captivated spirit return there through the path of justice and come where she once came through Your largesse. Though You do wonders in little things, yet You perform more marvelously in greater things! For You water the arid bosom from the abundance of the fountains of Paradise and You gave witness by saying: 'If you thirst come unto me and you will never

---

32. The second edition, c. 8, prefaced the confrontation with the devil: "*Sometimes God's handmaid heard spiteful words directed against her: that her ways were perverse and slothful. But when her mind had long been tormented with such things, the angel came as usual, consoling her and promising her a heavenly seat. Indeed, eternal punishment and infernal pain threatened her envious and slothful detractors unless they came to their senses.*" It also adds the vision of Amand, given as c. 14 in this version, implying that, like Rictrude and others, Aldegund may have had Amand's help in achieving her goal. The confrontation with the devil in that version is reduced to a few lines and deprived of its energy.

thirst again, for the waters flow like rivers from my belly.'[33] For You have revealed your secrets to unworthy me, my God, to Whom belongs praise and power through the infinite cycle of the ages. Amen."

10. For while she stood praying with desire for the road to the eternal kingdom and begging in the path for a long time, by divine permission there came a maiden of wondrous beauty whose lips were pale. And she said in friendly fashion: "Chaste sister, the mother of the lord Jesus Christ sent me to discover what you want." And swiftly she said to her: "I need nothing more, oh admirable daughter of the roses, than to be able to do His will in all things Who, when a servant asked, 'Master, what shall I do to inherit eternal life?,' answered: 'Thou shalt love the Lord thy God with all thy heart and with all thy soul and with all thy strength and thy neighbor as thyself.'[34] This I desire above all to be taught, oh chaste root of many vines." And she vanished into the air, flame-haired with her yellow locks streaming to the stars. And even as she stood there marvelling, another one appeared in bright light coming down the road she was facing, with the eyes of a dove and the face of an Apostle. And he faced her and said: "Why are you surprised? I am Peter the Apostle, who has the power of binding and loosing, sent by Jesus Christ to you. You have been counted in the number of the saints, oh modest maid. Go forth, for the Lord desires you and your pain will endure as long as you linger in the world. Fear not. 'He that feareth is not made perfect in love; but perfect love casteth out fear, because fear hath torment.' "[35]

11. One day when she was in the secret chamber of her house, praying with the door to the outside closed, the Holy Spirit emitted rays upon her like the sun and the moon shining through the inserted windows. Startled by the overwhelming splendor, she fell to her knees and saw an angel of the lord standing in the air who said to her: "You have found grace with the Highest. Don't you see the great splendor of the sun and the moon shining upon you?" And answering, she said: "I see, my lord, but I don't know what it means." The Angel spoke for Him Who never wished goodness to be hidden but to be exposed like a candle; not under a bushel but on a candlestick, placed as a beacon to all in the house. Therefore, revealing the celestial mysteries from a mellifluous mouth, he said: "The lord Jesus Christ is meant by the rays of the sun, even He Who said to you: 'I am the true light.'[36] The moonlight must be understood as the reward of the just in eternity of whom

33. John 7:37–38.
34. Luke 10:25–27.
35. 1 John 4:18. The second edition, c. 10, adds that the apostle gave her "white bread" from his hand, which strengthened her with joy.
36. Cf. John 1:9.

the Gospel says: 'He shall gird himself and make them to sit down to meat and will come forth to serve them.'[37] And so did the Lord instruct His faithful when He said, 'Hear me, for I am mild and humble of heart and you will find rest for your souls. For my yoke is sweet and my burden light.' "[38] May I speak or should I be silent? The miracles of Christ taught me to speak more [powerfully] than authority bade me be silent so that the more brightly the light of faith is kindled, the more cloudy it becomes when the bushel is overturned. So does Our Lord deign to reveal the spiritual concerns of His salvation to our human gaze. Thus He might tame the stony heart by stony portents and through angelic visions restore the skills of nobles. But to go on like this is only to delay.

11.[39] *Now one day, when holy Waldetrude, that same sister whom we have already mentioned, gave herself to sleep, she was rapt in ecstasy and saw someone coming from Heaven. When she asked anxiously whether the Lord took note of her penitence, he nodded. And when she asked about her sister Aldegund, she heard: "Your sister has promised herself as a spouse to Christ." And she heard that King David was about to come for the dowry contract. A certain man of religion, who knew nothing of these things, came to bear witness saying: "It has been revealed to me through the Spirit that Christ will send messengers. And when I asked the cause of this legation I was answered that he would take the virgin Aldegund to wife, who has made her body a worthy habitation and prepared an immaculate marriage bed for Christ in her soul." Hearing this, the most holy virgin did not puff herself up with pride for so much honor. But with patient humility, she awaited the advent of her Lord and Savior.*

12. *She saw herself standing in a street, with a crowd of people all around to left and right. A fiery globe suddenly appeared to them, coming from heaven full of the greatest splendor. And when she asked the bystanders what it was, a man standing at her right said: "The Holy Ghost shall come upon thee and the virtue of the Highest shall overshadow thee."[40] And suddenly the vision vanished from her eyes. Four days later, about the middle of Sunday night, the blessed virgin arose to go to matutinal vigils. And one of the sisters coming out of the church just as she was going in, saw the street which had previously appeared in her vision shining with a great light. She marvelled, wondering whence so much light might have come when the whole earth was covered with darkness and she understood it to be from heaven. When day dawned, she*

---

37. Luke 12:37.

38. Matthew 11:29.

39. The first edition gives no concrete information regarding Aldegund's passage to the consecrated life, being exclusively concerned with her visions. The second edition is more detailed about her stay with her sister Waldetrude and, by rearranging the order of her visions, suggests that Saint Amand had somehow concerned himself with the course of her vocation. At this point we have interpolated material from the second edition that describes her sister's involvement in her betrothal to Christ.

40. Luke 1:35. Compare the alternate version of this story.

told the other sisters. They all wondered what had caused so much splendor but it remained unknown to all except blessed Aldegund to whom the vision had appeared before. And she glorified God Who did not despise those who hope in Him.

13. *And after the turning of the year, King David again appeared to [Waldetrude] revealing the glory of the saints and the peace of the faithful and their association in perpetual life.*[41]

12. Another night while she was performing her customary *cursus matutinarum*, one of her sisters was keeping her company. Black night enclosed them in impenetrable silence. She stood before the open doors of the house and, looking about, saw that the street was suddenly gleaming as something like globes of fire descended together. And knowing it to be a true angelic vision, she ran with a joyful soul within her.[42] On bended knee, as usual, she prayed in her accustomed manner, "Oh good Preceptor, Author of the Triple Light, Who restores our minds, look down upon the company here. Praise, honor and power befit You, Oh good Christ of glory. Christ, Savior of Man, do the good which we desire." With thundering voice, the Father of Heaven seated on high [said]: "I have betrothed you, I have given the dowry, I have adorned you with holy jewelry. Come, receive what I have made." And the woman who was with her ran quickly to tell the sisters saying: "Come see the wonderful thing that has come to our Lady. A burning fire was in the middle of the street which suddenly went away!" And rejoicing with a single voice they said: "We give You praise, Christ, Who placed us under the spiritual yoke of this mother. The highest praise is due to You."

13. For then it happened that through a divine vision she was shown her exit from human fragility. Two men, flowing with light, stood before her telling her about how the just received eternal reward, to each according to her deserts. And knowing that the light-flowing messengers came from the Lord to comfort her lest she be afraid of her passing, she gave warm thanks. And another day, she heard a warning angelic voice in a vision, saying: "The Lord has betrothed you in eternity that you may gain an incorruptible crown." And

---

41. Hucbald, in the ninth century, puffed up the tale of her final consecration with what appear to be stock legends of her flight from marriage into the wilderness. However, some credence might be given to his story of the hapless maiden crossing a violent river with the help of miracles by a third anonymous life cited by Smet, in his introduction, 293, which, in c. 7, refers to "a fisherman whose son, now betrothed, is known to us, who could testify to the deadly power of that river." In his *Vita Aldegundis*, 4:14, Hucbald added a tale that became a signature to the saint's iconography for later devotees: "*the Holy Spirit in the form of a dove appeared and slowly descending held the elevated veil in which she would be consecrated by its feet and mouth. Lest there be doubt concerning the miracle, those who were present saw the veil raised on high and placed on the head of the virgin. Then the dove sent from Heaven immediately disappeared before their eyes.*" The original life continues with an alternate version of the story above.

42. The two visions recounted previously (Aldegund's prophetic one and the later manifestation shown the sister coming out of church) seem to have been conflated here so that "she" is said to be standing at the door, running, and kneeling at the same time.

suddenly she saw herself dressed by Him in bridal clothing and she was filled with joy and asked: "What is your name?" And he answered, "My name is Glorious."[43] This should not surprise the understanding of the faithful, coming from Him Who said: "Heaven is my throne."[44] And, "The soul of the just is the seat of wisdom."

14. At that time, there was a certain bishop named Amand who was close to her in spiritual friendship. One night a dream was sent to her and the blessed virgin saw him crowned by the Lord and a great troop of souls with him to receive the beatitude of Christ. And the angels cried: "Behold the loveable gift! What his preaching mouth won, he brings to the Lord." And the blessed virgin rejoiced as she watched, exulting in her heart over her friend's salvation.[45]

15. On the way, the Devil met her and, acting out of his great envy for her, he said: "You have kept the faith of the first fathers and receive the secrets of Paradise in your bosom. Through obedience in this slimy place, you will soon get the mansion I lost through disobedience. For I was confounded and led astray by envy." To which the blessed virgin retorted: "Now I have told you, you fraud of savage malignity, you, who shall always dwell in misfortune, shall not shake me in my fortune. Our Lord Jesus Christ, triumphant by conquering you in Heaven, Who is not bounded but forever confirming our eternal happiness, rebuilt Chaos for you that you might remain in concealment forever accursed." He vanished, made frantic by hearing her words.

16. Some days later, she was fasting from carnal food and drink prostrate in her usual prayers, without which this sort of thing is not cast out. It was Good Friday. At dawn on Holy Saturday she saw an angel of the Lord speaking to her and saying: "I promise you from the Lord that you will soon receive His reward and, the affliction which will strike you in this world soon passing away, He will crown you as one of us." And hearing that, she fell joyfully on her face. But then he immediately receded. And while she remained in such suspense she thought of Him by Whom she would be saved, Who had comforted her amid many afflictions and strengthened her: "A mansion is prepared for you in Heaven filled with light."

17. And since God wished to prove her like gold purified in the furnace, the virgin consecrated to Christ began to sicken. Her body was afflicted with overpowering weakness. In the middle of the night, when she was seized with a sickness of thirst and heat, she responded by bearing that heat and

---

43. Judges 13. The second edition placed this story among the early intimations that Aldegund would become a nun. Here, however, it indicates that the betrothal was complete when she entered the religious life and that her wedding will be on the day of her death.

44. Acts 7:49.

45. Amand died in about 679, when Aldegund was about forty. C. 8 of the second edition states that Aldegund saw herself counted in the company of souls he had saved.

thirst until dawn when she would rise. And as day broke she saw the ancient enemy Satan, flame-haired, blowing his breath around the place where she lay. And he said to her: "I admit, I have been compelled by angelic threats and that is why I dare once more to make you suffer, when I have by now been put to rout so often, my face blushing. By my own envy, I admit the mother coerced me to do this who tramples me from her flowering seat." And then the wicked enemy vanished, excommunicate, and Christ's virgin was freed from suffering and gave herself to her usual prayers.

The second edition adds here: *And, after that temptation from the Devil, she had this divine consolation. In a vision, she saw someone standing before the horns of the altar in sacerdotal garb. When she understood it to be the God of Heaven, she prostrated herself in adoration and said: "My Lord God, concede to me a sinner that I may remain in your love to the end." And nodding the Lord promised it to her.[46] . . . And when the most prudent virgin had absorbed these visions into her mind thirsting for her eternal crown, someone came to her and said: "Lady, a most venerable sight appeared to me: clearly, the Lord Jesus with a band of angels came and spoke to you before the horns of the altar. And when you saw him you said: 'Behold the lamb of God! Behold Him Who takes away the sins of the world.'" And when the blessed virgin asked at what hour this vision had appeared to the man, she knew it was at the same time that it had been shown to her.[47]*

And that fourth day, a little boy near to death was brought to her whose relatives despaired of his life. She ordered the holy worshippers of Christ to place him by the horn of the altar in the spot where the Lord stood before her and by the virgin's prayer the innocent was immediately restored to health. And when the servants would have given her thanks for the child's health, she was quick to maintain that the power came from God. "Not from my merits," she said, "but the Lord restored him for I am useless in every way."

18. Oh ineffable mystery of Christ! What can reflect the gifts of the Holy Spirit, or what words can explain or deeds affirm them? For if a third of what I have heard of her from the mouths of faithful witnesses were unwound in order, the bright day would be ended and evening would enclose Olympus while the text of the reading was still being explicated to us. But we saw or heard so much about her from those same witnesses that I have attempted to write, ordered by Christ and obeying your command. Now lest the little pages in our rude manner generate boredom in our readers or listeners, let us return to the order of our titles. Aldegund, servant of God, told all in order about the visions that Christ, her bridegroom, revealed to her to a religious

---

46. From c. 10.

47. From c. 13. Waldetrude's vision of King David was inserted between the two accounts of this same vision.

man, Subino, abbot of Nivelles monastery.[48] And he put it into writing. And from our smallness, he ordered a little maid to read it in his presence. And we were all amazed because before that time we had not heard the like and what we heard we believed to be true.[49]

19. And when she was still a little girl in her parental home, she grew in love for the celestial life and care of alms for Christ's poor. And, some months, when she did not have as much as she required for generous alms to the poor, her mother had hidden monies which she often counted. By Christ's virtue, the holy virgin Aldegund knew that she ought to give them to Christ's poor. But she awaited some revelation that she might know Christ's will for certain. Then one day her mother sought them where they were hidden which she left intact on several occasions. And then God's chosen received her own offering which she distributed for love of Christ to the poor.[50] But when she was mother of the community and before she was perfect in good works and filled with examples by divine grace, she sent a servant to buy garments for the poor from that money.[51] And he went and did as he was told and what remained was returned to God's servant. The moment she placed the remainder of the purchase price on the scales she found the same weight and even as she and her sister stood wondering, the weight grew.[52] And immediately they recalled the place in Scripture where it says: "Whoever hath, to him shall be given."[53] That is, the fruit of what you give as alms for the needs of Christ's littlest brothers, you will gain many times over in eternal coin.

---

48. Because Nivelles was ruled by an abbess, clearly there is some mistake here. It is possible that he was the governor of the monks attached to the monastery to do its external business.

49. The use of the first person in this passage seems to indicate that the present manuscript was based on Subino's original text but expanded with the chapters below by someone, possibly one of the nuns who heard the original reading. Aldegund's community at that time was apparently at her original home, but it had some contact with Nivelles. The author could belong to either community.

50. The lack of clarity in this story may be the result of discretion because the sign required was Bertilla's death. The editor of the second edition, once again, has placed the mother in a harsher light: "*c. 15. It is the way with timid and fragile humans that they prefer to serve money and keep faith with Mammon rather than return what they received from the Creator for a hundred fold interest in perpetual life. Thus the virgin's mother Bertilla had accumulated no small amount of money. But she could not hide it from Christ's virgin. So by the grace of God, the daughter did well to distribute publicly what the mother did ill to hide in a sack. Though she knew where her unwilling mother's treasure was, she took none of it before her death. But when she finally succeeded to her parents, she dispersed her mother's treasure to Christ's poor.*"

51. Her own mother, as is common in these texts, was called *genetrix* to distinguish her from Aldegund, who became a spiritual *mater*.

52. Here, *germana* indicates that the sister is Waldetrude, not a *soror* from the community.

53. Matthew 13:12.

20. And it also happened that her fisherman one day caught an immense fish and pulled it alive from the river and brought it to the Lady Aldegund. And she ordered him to throw it still living into the fountain. The fish, floundering in the unfamiliar water, soon leaped to dry land. And birds flying together in the nearby trees longed to devour the fish with their rabid beaks. But a year-old lamb was nearby, grazing on the grass. Seeing the crows above the fish, it ran fearlessly and chased them with its hooves so that [the fish] would not be eaten. And the nuns, seeing this from afar, marvelled to see the lamb running so. Hurrying they found the fish alive and carried it to the spiritual mother. And the lamb followed them. Seeing all, the handmaid of Christ, Saint Aldegund, was full of joy and all the sisters were astonished at what had happened, never doubting that it was done for her merits.

21. One night, the God's servant Aldegund and her sister [Waldetrude] were conversing together in their home about love and the behavior of the holy flock who lived under their teaching and example when the candle which had been placed before them fell on the ground and went out. They waited awhile, as the attendant was going for another maiden to bring a light. Then, leaning over, the blessed mother took the candle from the ground and in her hand it shone again with the brightest light. And she glorified her Father in Heaven Who comforted her in so many tribulations.

22. A few days later, when she was instructing the senior [nuns] who generally administered the internal affairs of the monastery about the care of the flock and its stability,[54] she and Waldetrude [the *germanas*] came at the hour of sext to the church for prayer and knocked at the gate.[55] But the ministers of the church were not there. Who knows what purpose had caused them to go away? While [the women] stood waiting, suddenly by God's order, without human help, the gate was seen to open. Wondering at the miracle, they gave themselves to prayer and returned glorying to their dwelling.

23. The handmaid of God always kept in mind the Lord's command, remembering the Lordly response, saying: "If thou wilt be perfect, go and sell that thou hast and give to the poor and thou shalt have treasure in Heaven: and come and follow Me."[56] Considering this the virgin took all that she had received by hereditary right from her kindred, her own things, gold, silver, precious stones, wonderful garments, and with a sane mind and with sober advice, she distributed it for church ornaments and provisions for the poor,

---

54. These would be the appointed internal administrators, following the plan of Nivelles, see chapter 12.

55. Again, we have used the second edition, c. 18, which explains that the sisters were abroad on the business of the monastery, to clarify a confused sentence.

56. Matthew 19:21.

keeping only cheap clothing and enough for her own daily sustenance: because through diverse testimonies of Scripture it is better to give one solidus to the poor with your own hands than to promise a hundred after death.[57] And what she understood from reading she performed in life.

24. Then on a later night when the servants brought her drinking water from the well as was customary, it was swiftly changed to give off the odor of wine.[58] And there can be no doubt that this was meant as a sign that she had obeyed Our Lord Jesus Christ's command in all things. And again it happened that one of the holy virgin's servants filled a basin of water for washing her hands and suddenly, when she turned it over, she found it was empty. Trembling, she ran back swiftly to the well. And when she returned she found it full by the order of God so that there was reason for wonder at these things.

25. A certain priest of good reputation who had served the monastery from boyhood truthfully told us certain things. When he was in front of his house early in the night, he saw a globe of fire seemingly covered with peacock feathers, descending from the air. It rested on the house where the holy virgin lay sick. After the nocturnal and matutinal vigils, a sister from the monastery gave herself over to sleep and God showed her a mystic vision of Aldegund of holy memory standing before the altar in the priest's place. And she was breaking the Mass offerings into the chalice with her hands.[59] And she turned to the sister and said: "Go and tell the priest that he should chant the solemnities of the Mass over this chalice, because yesterday a serious sickness in my limbs prevented me from communion and today with the Lord's help I want to participate in the body and blood of Christ." And that day the priest proceeded to bless the bread and the chalice in the customary way when suddenly he saw it hanging in the air where it remained steadily for an hour. Afterward the girl and the priest together told God's servant about the vision

57. The second edition is more formal, referring to charters and public donation. The editors of *AS* note that a will exists claiming to be Aldegund's, although they have trouble reconciling the date, the twentieth year of Dagobert's reign, because he did not live that long. It could, however, be a reference to Dagobert II, whose return in 676 could have involved this family as it involved St. Amatus. It also cites the "Emperor Childeric," who could only be the son of Clovis II who died in 675. Moreover, it is "witnessed" by Saint Ouen, Abbess Gertrude, Abbess Aldetrude, and Abbess Madelberta as well as Gundeland, and it is difficult to make them contemporary.

58. The second edition is more explicit in relating this to the wedding at Cana, John 2:11.

59. Aldegund appears to be consecrating the wine by putting the consecrated bread into it. Jungmann, *The Mass of the Roman Rite*, 2:383, n. 66, refers to a Frankish extract from *Ordo Romanus I*, from the seventh century: "Sanctificatur enim vinum non consecratum per sanctificatum panem." Liturgists differ on the meaning of "consecrated" in this connection, but the usage was widespread, especially in giving communion to the sick.

and the suspended chalice. And silently within herself she determined that it meant that soon she would be able to lay her little body down.

26. One day when the sisters had built a fire for boiling water, one of them stepped on the coals. And the envious enemy who never ceases daily to fight the souls of holy people, suddenly, with a shove, cast her into the flames and coals where the copper vessel hung above full of boiling water. But calling on the name of Aldegund of good memory, she escaped unharmed from the threat of fire and the power of the enemy through the intercessory merits of the holy virgin by the Lord's order.[60]

27. And another maid, her niece Aldetrude, was trained in taking charge of monastic affairs from the cradle, nourished in the rule at the mistress' feet. The blessed mistress ordered her to melt fragments of wax into a single lump and chill it in the dust. While she was turning away from the place, the liquified wax, sputtering with fire and flames, fell down. Seeing that and doubtlessly upset by the accident, she ran and with her bare hands pulled the vessel and the wax from the fire. She put her arms and limbs and hands into the fire and pulled the spilled boiling wax to the pavement. And with the intercessory merits and prayers of the blessed virgin it happened that no sign of fire or hurt appeared on her flesh or skin. By the Lord, she looked whole amidst the fire's dangers.

28. A senseless man was fettered by sin and brought to the virgin's attention by his parents who despaired of his life. And they described to her how the infirmity had seized him. And she ordered him brought before her at vespers and placed the sign of the cross upon him. Returning home, he took food and drink and the next night he fell into healing sleep and remained in good health.

29. And the fifth day before her death, her sister (Waldetrude) had a great and glorious revelation that her sister holy Aldegund was taken to her ethereal seat by the apostles sent by Christ or flocks of angels.[61] In the monastery of Nivelles, a sign was given which I confess to be less wonderful but we know that it was witnessed by at least two people.[62] On Good Friday, before the Saturday of God's handmaid Aldegund's dormition, a certain sister who had been veiled three years earlier with pure simplicity and obedience lay on

60. The second edition, c. 21, adds that the sister was wearing one of Aldegund's old habits.
61. According to the second edition, c. 24: "Five days before the death of the blessed Aldegund, a vision appeared to her sister Waldetrude. She saw Blessed Mary, ever virgin, and the princes of the Apostles, Peter and Paul, come with a band of saints to lead her sister into the celestial kingdom to enjoy the fruit of their society eternally for the example of meritorious life she had lived in this world." We have also amended Smet's punctuation that implies that the ethereal seat was in Nivelles. The second edition places "In Nivelles" in a new sentence.
62. The tone here seems to indicate strongly that the author was someone at Nivelles.

her bed to sleep after her labors. In the middle of night the young woman saw the brightest light coming through the window so that the whole house from the pavement to the tree tops shone like the rays of the noonday sun. And while she was experiencing the wonderful miracle with her ears, she heard a psalm-singing choir of diverse voices great and small in the church of the blessed Apostle Peter, where Christ's holy virgin Gertrude rests in her body with other holy virgins. And in that moment, the light and the sound of the psalms swelled alike in her ears. The stupefied nuns conferring among themselves, knew that the blessed virgin Aldegund had passed over and that the wonders were done by the Lord in virtue of her merits. The third night of her leaving her body, we came from various places going out by reason of piety and visitations. The next day God's servant's sister (Waldetrude) told us how a certain sister, who was praying around midnight and standing before the door of her house watching, saw a great brightness descending upon the dwelling where God's chosen gave up her uncontaminated spirit and [music] spread in the heavens.[63] Oh wonderful piety of God! You present such things to human gaze that, lest any of the faithful doubt the grace Christ gives for the saints' sake, they receive from God so much brightness and wonderful clarity. Hither and yon, the sound of the psalms from the celestial flock was heard and many innumerable signs from the Lord were done at the exit of virgin men and women that governed in the land with His approval and were brought by His help to heaven. The virgin of Christ Aldegund imitated them when she lived on earth. She is now in their happy company in Heaven by order of the Lord Jesus Christ Whom this virgin served intact and inviolate. For He with the Father in unity with the Holy Spirit reigns, God, through the infinite cycle of the ages. Amen.[64]

The second edition adds a final two paragraphs.

26. *Praise and exult, Oh convent of Maubeuge, ruled with the support of such a mother. Strive to follow in her footsteps. Rejoice in the Lord, that you have the blessed virgin Aldegund, God's best beloved, to pray for your sins and reconcile your wickedness. For her merits, she rejoices in the celestial court with a chorus of angels; happily she revels in the company of the archangels for, when her body was still on earth, she strove to behave as though in Heaven. She was a witness to Jesus and the common hope, just like those who faced Nero's furious mobs and Diocletian's cruel persecutions and the deceptive persuasions of Julian, who corrupted many more with handsome rewards than others destroyed by torture. For the holy mother, venerable Aldegund, resisted every temptation. Overshadowed by the Holy Spirit, she vanquished the*

---

63. Again it is the *germana* who tells the story of the *soror's* vision. Perhaps this sister was at Waldetrude's community in Mons.

64. Her death date is highly uncertain but van der Essen assigns 684 as the most probable choice.

Devil's power, overcame the weakness of the female sex, manfully rising above worldly delights, visibly retaining nothing of the joys of the present world, lest in her crossing to the Lord she should dash her foot on a stone.

27. Then the best beloved virgin, a spouse of the Lord and habitation of the Holy Spirit, was buried on her domain where she had rendered up her soul to her creator in the villa called Curtissolra, where both her parents are said to have been buried.[65] Later the virgin's body was translated to the town of Maubeuge by King Sigebert and the blessed virgin Abbess Aldetrude.[66] There, as we have from an entry in the cartulary, she built a foundation where her memory is kept green with many miracles and great prodigies flourish.[67] And in this place, the maiden's flock fattens and is filled up with many servants of God. There are frequent cures of the sick, illuminations of the blind, hearing for the deaf, restorations of weak limbs and remission of sins for the petitioning faithful through the intercession of the most blessed and excellent virgin to whom we pray that she will deign to intercede for us with the Lord Jesus Christ, her spouse Who is equal in majesty with the Father and the Holy Spirit with immortal honor, incomparable power, eternal glory, ineffable praise, now and forever, world without end. Amen.

Waldetrude, Abbess of Mons

∎

Prologue

1. As ancient custom dictates, the venerable deeds of saints ought to be passed on in writing for the stimulation of the living. Such a volume of these has been left to us that we can scarcely count the number. Provoked by their example and compelled by the love of so many brothers and sisters in religion, I have presumed to attempt this work. May I exhort my prudent reader to spare the author's rusticity, and act as a benevolent corrector rather than a nagging pedant. For you should know that it has been my intention lucidly to present the truth contained in her deeds to her brothers and sisters rather than to keep the rules of grammar.

2. After His Ascension, the Redeemer of the world deigned to appoint chosen apostles as followers of the apostles to light the way to eternal life for all faithful Christians. They lived righteously bearing up bravely against adversity, disdaining the visible and temporal and longing for the invisible and eternal, preaching and watching, to reveal to all wanderers the lost joy of the

---

65. A place between Maubeuge and Lobbes where the remains of her parents were preserved.

66. The Bollandists point out that Sigebert II died in 656, many years before Aldegund. They believe the king in question would have to be Theuderic III (d. 690–91), son of Clovis II and Balthild, or one of his sons.

67. In 1984, the town of Maubeuge continued to celebrate Aldegund as its foundress with an exhibition of her relics and other memorabilia to mark her thirteen-hundredth anniversary.

eternal kingdom and, as I have said, like stars shining with the great grace of the Spirit, to light the way out of error's darkness for those who wished to return there. But because people of primitive times were carnal, believing only in the existence of what is visible, they did not long for the invisible, having no hint of its existence. The example and preaching of the saints was not sufficient to provoke faith in the invisible; therefore miracles were added so that a display of power might illumine faith in the word. Visible miracles gleamed to draw the listeners' hearts to faith in the invisible. External wonders were accomplished that the greater miracle within us might be experienced. Now, since, by God's work, the number of believers has multiplied in the world, these corporal miracles have generally ceased. It is not that those who live virtuous lives in the church do not perform physical signs, but that they are not necessary to us in this age. Whence the voice of the Apostle says: "Tongues are for a sign, not to them that believe but to them that believe not."[68] Therefore an external miracle is performed in vain if it does not work within us. For we should seek life, not the sign. And the value of true life is achieved in virtue not in a show of signs. Indeed, when they occur, they bear witness to a good life. And they inspire the hearts of neighbors to imitation. Whence doubtless we believe and hold firm in faith, for we wish to give over everything founded on earthly things and leave the broad and spacious avenues of this world which lead to perdition and follow our Redeemer's strait and narrow way which leads us to life, wherefore we would go forth and be not a little useful. So we draw examples from the lives of holy men and women who preceded us on this road, led by grace, and left their own footprints behind. Thus all that may have seemed impossible to them has been made easy to the hopeful who can see how others made the same crossing. Often, the saints' example excites the hearts of the sluggish and torpid to love of God and desire for eternal life better than preaching. For those who consider their works or sublime miracles, blush to consider their own foul weakness. Whence speaks the Lord: "that they may see your good works, and glorify your father which is in heaven."[69]

I. Saint Waldetrude's Family, Marriage, and Continence.

Therefore, helped by the grace of God, we shall write down a few of the many signs of the life and holy miracles of the most blessed Waldetrude, handmaid of Christ, whose deeds were done not very long ago, according to what certain truthful witnesses revealed who deserved to see and hear them to the glory of God and the edification of others.[70] She sprang from royal

68. 1 Corinthians 12:22.

69. Matthew 5:16.

70. Such references suggest that the thirteenth-century editor was copying more or less directly from the old text to which he refers at the end of this paragraph.

stock in the time of Dagobert, King of the Franks, of most noble and famous lineage.[71] Her father was Waldebert and her mother Bertilla and she was a sister of that most holy virgin named Aldegund who ruled the monastery of Maubeuge for many years leading a life full of virtue and keeping strict continence.[72] A little book of her life and works exists which those who wish to know how she stood in the grace of God and the angels and how she was dear to the people and how many and what kind of virtues the Lord showed in her, may easily discover. But let us return our pen to the subject.

3 [sic]. Blessed Waldetrude was still adolescent when she was sent from her parental home. Her parents, who loved her greatly, saw fit to give her to a husband in marriage according to God's ancient ordinance and the example of the patriarchs. For she was fair of face and beautiful of form, though more lovely still in faith, modesty and chastity. By secret disposition of the Lord, she who was betrothed by the ring of faith was yet predestined to share the company and inheritance of her sister the virgin Aldegund in the glory of the eternal kingdom. Nor could any union of flesh change that. For from the beginning of the world, almighty God drew her swiftly to her reward with gifts of piety. Her heart burning with love of Him, she easily refrained from all carnal desires and immoderate temporal appetites, to her altered mind, what pleased her once became vile to her then: and what first delighted her spirit became ever more burdensome. So she strove to set aside the cares of this world and fasten her sight on eternal longings only; generously and with all alacrity to give her substance to the poor, to orphans and widows; to redeem captives and assemble guests and pilgrims, thus seeking to uproot vice not only from her corporal deeds but even from the musings of her heart.

4. Meanwhile, not content with her own salvation, she labored daily with sweet and salutary words to inspire her yokemate, her noble husband Madelgar, to the love of God and arouse him to observe castimony.[73] And the fire of love which glowed sweetly in her sufficed to kindle his mind. And because carnal affection greatly tends to distract the mind's intentions and to obscure its understanding, she began to abhor the coupling of flesh. Not that she spurned God's gift conceded to man for the propagation of children, but because she knew the Apostle's teaching: "The unmarried woman and the virgin careth for the things of the Lord, that she may be holy both in body and

---

71. Thus she was born before Dagobert's death in 638.

72. Because this life was written centuries later, it cannot be used to confirm Aldegund's foundation of Maubeuge in contradiction to the second edition of Aldegund's life.

73. Castimony generally appears in conciliar legislation as a parallel to matrimony, when the behavior of religious women is being regulated. In this case, it is unclear whether the author means that she is urging her husband to become a monk or simply to observe continence within their marriage.

in spirit; those who are married think of the things of the world, that she may please her husband."[74] So, desiring to devote herself to God alone, she feared the burdens of carnal marriage as a stumbling block. She prayed daily with tears and sighs that she might be free, by God's favor, and that in her the Lord's will might be done. But almighty God, who had mercifully insinuated this disposition into His handmaid's heart, gave her help. For her husband, Madelgar, filled with divine inspiration and aflame with love, dissolved the bonds of marriage but kept his love for her. He proceeded to the monastery called Hautmont. There, taking the habit of a monk, he completed the course of his temporal life in holy deeds.[75]

5. Meanwhile Christ's religious handmaid, Waldetrude, continued to care for her household, still wearing a secular habit though in no way relaxing her strength of mind.[76] For she was given to acts of mercy and intent on good works, studied hospitality, serving with fasts and prayers day and night. So it was that almighty God, Who knows how to cultivate the palm to bring forth more fruit, deigned by a celestial vision to stimulate His handmaid to greater profits of sanctity by faithfully administering the gifts she had received. Thus one night, worn out from her labor, she gave herself to sleep to refresh her body. Soon she was deep in slumber and in a dream she seemed to enter the basilica in a town which the vulgar call Bossu. And, lo, the most holy man, Bishop Gangeric appeared to her shining with great light and showed her the greatest honor and reverence.[77] And in the vision, he gave her a chalice full of wine. When she had drunk it, he said to her with serene and happy face: "Do as you have been doing: the things you do please me greatly." Strengthened by this vision, she became drunk, as I might say, with the wine of divine grace. She began to scorn the world and blaze brightly with the love of heaven. After one sip, little by little, she thirsted more avidly for the sweetness of eternal life.

6. But when the ancient enemy is grieved by the progress of the good he seeks ways to bring the bad yet lower by evil craft. The servant of God humbly confided her vision to some of her gossips and they repeated it to the ears of vulgar commoners. The enemy of humankind, desiring to resist her holy plan at its inception, set the hearts of the reprobates on fire with envy of the vision. He inspired them to bear false witness, slander and opprobrium against her. I might say he armed those who opposed Christ's servant with

---

74. 1 Corinthians 7:34.

75. Madelgar was the name of the bishop of Laon in 692, who challenged the property rights of Saint Anstrude. We can find no connection to link the two men.

76. She had four children: Landeric, who succeeded his father as abbot of Soignies; Aldetrude and Madelberta, both nuns at Aldegund's convent at Maubeuge; and Dentelin, whose fate is unknown.

77. The feast of Saint Gangericus, bishop of Cambrai, is celebrated on August 11.

venomous tongues. Thence it is written: "the sons of men, whose teeth are spears and arrows and their tongues a sharp sword."[78] But almighty God came speedily to his servant's aid as she staggered under the diabolic blow. For her mind, naturally still unripe, was wearied and excessively troubled by this derision and insult. And she took to her bed, oppressed by the heavy sorrow. Soon, a heavenly angel in the form of a man shining with light appeared standing near her. He spoke familiarly, asking the cause of her sorrow. "Why," he asked, "Are you so weighed down with sorrow? Wherefore do you darken the happiness of your spirit with clouds of grief?" She answered that it was because she was so beset with her fellow citizens' derision, insult and falsehood instigated by the ancient enemy. The angel replied, saying: "Be comforted, and be strong against your detractors and slanderers. For it is written: 'Yet is he not crowned, except he strive lawfully.'[79] Therefore do not be concerned over the vain ashes of words whose flames are quickly quenched. For the prophets, apostles and martyrs who came before you suffered in the same way. Whence the Lord says in the Gospel: 'The disciple is not above his master.'[80] And a little later: 'If they have called the master of the house Beelzebub, how much more shall they call them of his household?'[81] Thus with little homilies and proofs from Scripture, he comforted her with overwhelming spiritual joy and soothed the useless sorrow which diabolical frauds had insinuated into her heart. Oh, what love the Lord shows who permits no slightest sorrow!"

II. Her solitary, then monastic life. Colloquy with Saint Aldegund.

7. Meanwhile, there was a certain priest named Gislenus living in a deserted place by the river Haina.[82] What his appearance in a monk's habit proclaimed, his behavior proved. He was reverenced by all who knew him for the worth of his holiness. Under divine orders, he was accustomed often to attend upon Christ's servant Waldetrude to instruct her, taking care to refresh her mind with the food of God's word. Thus, when the man of God understood that she had become cold to worldly desire and burned with heavenly desire for the habit of the holy life, he called her attention to a certain mountain now called Castrilocus.[83] With careful admonitions, he persuaded her to take the veil and have a cell built for herself there in which to serve almighty God. This cell would be located on that mountain, in a higher part of the wilderness about four miles from that of the man of God

---

78. Psalms 57:4.

79. 2 Timothy 2:5.

80. Matthew 10:24.

81. Matthew 10:25.

82. Saint Ghislain, October 9, gave his name to the town that now occupies the site.

83. Presently Mons, where an impressive collegial church still marks the site of her monastery and celebrates her cult under her modern name of St. Waudru.

Gislenus. Freely and gratefully, the blessed Waldetrude heeded his admonitions, and brooked no delay in completing the work to which almighty God had ordered her through his servant. She sent to a certain famous man named Hildulf, preeminent and noble and most powerful in worldly dignities at that time, who was related through his wife to God's servant.[84] Therefore, she asked him to buy the place which Divine Clemency had designated through His servant from its possessors for a given price and he did not refuse to prepare a place where she could serve God. Agreeing freely to her prayer, he undertook to provide what the servant of Christ asked and skillfully built a place for her on a mountain peak by tearing up trees and briars by the roots. Nor should we pass over in silence the miracle which almighty God granted to show concern for His handmaid in her first course of holy training. For when Christ's most religious recruit approached the home he had prepared, her eyes flinched away from its broad, high spaces, for all this magnificence greatly displeased them. Humbly she sought a little dwelling on earth out of human sight that she might gain a sublime place in heaven in the company of angels. Soon something wonderful and stupendous happened. For the servant of Christ having turned away, that night the whole fabric of the house was thrown down from its foundation by a whirlwind and divinely pitched far away. Then, on the same mountainside, Hildulf reconstructed a small dwelling and dedicated an oratory fitting for holy religion to Saint Peter the Apostle as she directed.

8. Meanwhile, Christ's most beloved servant, Waldetrude, longing with fervent spirit more and more for heaven, went to blessed Autbert on the advice of the man of God Gislenus whom we mentioned before.[85] She asked to be judged worthy of the holy veil and that was swiftly granted. Accepting the garments of a nun from him she immediately gave herself and all she had over to almighty God. She enclosed herself in the cell she had built for herself. Thus she gave an example to all of uncommon behavior. For she was grave of habit, sober of mind, gentle of manner and incomparably moderate in words. She perfected herself in charity to God and neighbor, provided for the poor and pilgrims and gave herself to fasting and prayer and vigils. With all her mind, she strove to mortify the flesh, to break her will and avoid the tumults of man and daily pour out her tears to the Lord on the altar of the heart.

9. Wherefore, the ancient enemy of human kind, who had attempted to frustrate her good works from the beginning, burned with flames of envy and piled up temptations on her with all his might. Because he mourned what he had lost in the public strife, he resorted to secret contests. So he began to try

84. Aya, who gave Waldetrude the monastery from her own inheritance.
85. Autbertus died about 670.

to erode her spirit's faith and hope in Jesus with temptation, importunately to infect her heart with various illicit thoughts. First, he insinuated memories of her noble family, responsibilities for her household, love of possessions, the superfluous glory of the world, various delectable foods and other blandishments of the life she had given up. Thus, he tested arduously the limits of her strength, her greatest efforts, even the fragility of her body for a long time.[86] With these and like temptations he aroused dark thoughts in her, seeking to coax her from her holy vow. But the strong hand of the almighty God easily defeated these pestiferous assaults of the Devil. For her respect for divine grace soon returned to her. Aware that she stood in battle with the hosts of Satan, she hastened to take up arms. She gave herself to lamenting, praying, to the Lord with tears and trembling that he would deign to comfort her in this battle, lest she succumb. Thus day and night, she prayed steadily to the Lord for remedy and thus it happened that she was up all night in prayer. And, behold, the old enemy in a man's shape pretended to assault her. Extending his hand, he placed it upon her breast but, when she promptly called Christ's name, the enemy soon sought flight. The intrepid one routed her persecutor strengthened with an angel's help, and chased him with vituperations and fit opprobrium. She said: "Well has it happened to you, miserable one! Well has it happened! You are one who has said in your heart: 'I will exalt my throne above the stars of God . . . I will be like the most High.'[87] Behold, for your pride, you were thrown down from the heavenly seat to the dead in Tartaros. So you deserve to be persecuted by a woman. And Christ, humbled, has redeemed with His blood the place you lost for your pride and restored it to human kind." Hearing this, the enemy blushed for shame and soon vanished in a puff of smoke and no longer presumed to weary the mind of Christ's handmaid with these temptations. For when he attempts to overcome anyone, by the power of almighty God he is compelled to serve her with an occasion for victory over him.

10. Temptation thus receding, Waldetrude began to bear fruit like cultivated land when the thorns have been uprooted. For the fame of her extraordinary way of life grew, spreading far and wide to women of noble families who began to gather dedicated to serve God in chastity, under this mistress. For freed from temptation, she became by right a mistress of virtue. Then her sister, the most holy virgin Aldegund, whom we mentioned above, used to come from her own monastery to visit her on certain days. They transfused one another with the sweet life-giving words and the soft bread of the

86. If she was born between 628 and 638 ("the time of Dagobert") and veiled before 670, these temptations must have extended into her forties.
87. Isaiah 14:13–14.

heavenly homeland. For as yet they were unable to rejoice perfectly, but they tasted it in hope. Once Aldegund noticed the smallness of the place, seeing that as yet but a few nuns belonged to her sister's service. Pulsating with human love, she urged compassionately that, because of her poverty, she should leave the place that they might hasten together to her monastery. But almighty God's servant, loving to weary herself in his service more than to gather the honors of transitory human life, would in no way consent, for she feared to lose the security of her poverty like a miser guards perishable wealth. Nor must we pass over the miracle which almighty God deigned to show His maidservants. When they met as usual one day for fruitful discussion of eternal life, a reason for the monastery's good arose for them to go a little way outside the walls. Having disposed of the business for which they went out, they returned to the monastery to find the gatekeeper absent. All the gates were closed and tightly barred. But soon something wonderful happened. For as the servants of Christ came to the basilica entrance, immediately the gates were divinely shaken and sprung open as if horrified to impede their prayers.[88]

11. After Christ's servant, venerable Waldetrude, left the allurements of the world, she did not refuse to submit humbly to the service of the King of Heaven. In turn she deserved to be borne sublimely to contemplation of the heavenly city. In spirit, she saw again a man descend from heaven and she trembled when, through the spirit, she recognized him as an angelic power. She strove to learn how she and her sister would be treated in the divine examination, humbly asking if they would be worthy of divine grace. The angel taught her to be comforted for the Lord always looked after her with serene piety as the prophet said: "To this man will I look, even to him, that is poor and of a contrite spirit, and trembleth at my word."[89] Whence the Psalmist says: "The eyes of the Lord are upon the righteous, and his ears are open unto their cry."[90] After that, it was divinely revealed to her that she and her sister, the blessed Aldegund, would inhabit one mansion and equal beatitude in the kingdom of God for the reward of their labors. So, each in her own way, they would arrive at that mansion. Instructed by this divine revelation, the handmaid of almighty God did not elevate her mind boasting in foolish pride but, keeping herself in the ark of humility, she afterwards devoted herself even more to the Creator in thanks for his grace as she saw him multiply his benefits to her. So she became swifter in good works and

---

88. See the life of Aldegund above. In this thirteenth-century version, cloistering seems to be assumed, and the monastery rather than the church is barred.

89. Isaiah 66:2.

90. Psalms 34:15.

surer of the promise. Meanwhile almighty God did not wish to hide his handmaid in solitude any longer but deigned to declare her merits with many signs that she might shine as a lamp on a lamp post for all in the house of God. We will narrate a few of these good virtues which we recall that many might be pondered from these few.

III. Miracles and death.

12. When she had meditated day and night on the law of God and ardently sought how to augment the profits of piety for herself, she determined to ransom some captives. Accordingly, she called one of the boys among her servants and gave him money to redeem the prisoners. And she placed it on the scales so that she could ascertain whether it was enough to do what she wanted. But, it is written: "To him that has, it shall be given and it will increase."[91] So she began to put the money into the scales and wonderfully it began to increase and outweigh itself.[92] And the boy saw this with wonder and awe. Forcefully, she instructed him to tell no one of the miracle while she yet lived in this body. For clearly she feared that if the things done by her virtue gained earthly fame, her inward self would weaken even while she appeared outwardly strong to people. She followed the example of the Master who taught His disciples about himself that we might be instructed in the way of humility, saying: "Tell the vision to no man until He be risen from the dead."[93]

13. Another time, when the said handmaid of Christ sat down to eat, one of the maids went as usual to the cellar to fill a vessel with drink to take to Christ's handmaid for her meal. But she walked carelessly on the way back and suddenly her foot stumbled, the fallen vessel emptied and the whole drink was poured on the ground. Rising fearfully, she thought to return to the cellar to refill the vessel. But when she looked again at the vessel she found it had become suddenly full in her hand as though it had never lost a drop.[94]

14. After this, a certain man one day became demented from the fatigue of an illness which had long afflicted him. And lo, he saw himself being pulled about by demons. But when he cried vociferously upon blessed Aldegund and her sister Saint Waldetrude to help him with their prayers and merits, he suddenly felt himself ripped from their hands and he emitted no more insane voices. Then he asked those who were nursing him to carry him into Waldetrude's presence. As he asked, he was brought before her in a chair and the handmaid of Christ seeing that he was suffering from extreme emaciation and

---

91. Matthew 13:12. The miracles that follow are closely patterned on those of her sister Aldegund, as though to illustrate the argument that they were destined to share a single mansion.

92. See the life of Aldegund above, c. 19.

93. Matthew 17:9.

94. See the life of Aldegund above, c. 24.

weakness, was moved by pity. She put her hands forth in prayer and placed them on his head. With the sign of the cross, all the languor which had held him fled. He was restored to pristine health so that he rose from the chair in which he was carried and walked and could eat normally again, though those who bore him there claimed that he had not been able to touch any food for thirty days. About four days later, a woman came to her with a little boy burdened with grave illness and prayed earnestly that she deign to touch her sick son with her hand. As she was merciful, the handmaid of Christ agreed, filled with compassion for a mother's sorrow. Humbly she put her hands on the half-dead boy and he was immediately healed. He took food and drink from her table and sucked as usual from his mother's breast though he had not eaten for four days. Then another little boy, but half-alive, was offered to her who had not yet been sprinkled with baptismal water. His mother implored with insistent prayers for him that, through her merits, he might deserve to come alive to the grace of baptism. Quickly, strengthened by divine help, the handmaid of Christ laid hands on him and pressed the sign of the cross on his head and the boy's body trembled wonderfully and his voice cried out and his eyes, which had been closed, opened and from that day he gained health and afterwards was ordained a priest and persevered in that life until old age.

15. Many other deeds of strength were done through her miraculously which we will have to leave out partly from lapse of memory and partly because of the need for brevity lest too much prolixity bore the reader when they have read the little that we have told of all that we witness daily done through her most sacred relics to abundant witness of her holy life. For how can we tell the many works of her life when even now, her body still testifies to so many virtues? For light comes to the blind, the lame walk, the sick are healed. Daily she is entreated that what she did when she was alive may be continued by her dead bones. For it is no wonder that her dead bones still live in wonder-working when she did such wonders in her life.

16. Saint Waldetrude died on 5 Ides April, taken up by angels and led into celestial dwelling places.[95] She lives with Christ, rejoices with patriarchs and prophets, exults with apostles, triumphs with martyrs, and associates with confessors on equal terms with virgins. So may we proceed with prayer and praise, asking that she may deign to remember us; that she gain forgiveness for our sins from Him who renders generous rewards for all labors. To Him be honor and glory, praise and power with the Father and Holy Spirit from everlasting to everlasting. Amen.

95. April 9.

14

Balthild, Queen of Neustria

(d. ca. 680)

Traffic across the English channel was busy and varied in the seventh century. Missionary monks, nuns in training, and pilgrim bishops took ship readily for the continent. Slavers also made the passage, taking Anglo-Saxon captives to sell in Frankland and even Italy.[1] Balthild was a victim of such a raid, but her future as queen of the Franks in Neustria and sainted foundress of Chelles was hardly typical. Still, she was not the first Merovingian queen to begin her career in servitude: the redoubtable Fredegund, mother of Clothar II; Bilichild, wife of Theudebert of Austrasia; and possibly Nanthild, mother of Clovis II, are so described. Nanthild may also have been an English woman.[2] All proved to be able partners in power. In fact, it is possible that their slave status, which kept them dependent on the good will of their husbands, made them the preferred confidantes of kings who had all too many reasons to fear their aristocratic associates.

Balthild began her career in the household of the Neustrian mayor of the palace, Erchinoald, who was related to King Dagobert's mother, Aldetrude. He was probably the brother of Saint Rictrude's husband, Adalbald, and uncle of her son Maurontus, who was actively involved in court service in his secular life.[3] How she rose from being Erchinoald's chambermaid to the

---

Vita Sanctae Balthildis, in Krusch, ed., MGH, SRM 2:477–508. We have translated Life A, which Krusch believes came from Chelles. It has generally been attributed to a nun of Chelles shortly after Balthild's death in 680; see Wemple, *Women in Frankish Society*, 182. The author claims, c. 3, to be writing during the reign of one of her sons. Life B, which the editor also included, is a later redaction expanded with the typical pieties and biblical citations admired by Carolingian authors but with no substantial material added. Krusch believes that it was written in conjunction with Balthild's translation under Abbess Hegilwich in 833; see MGH, SS 15:284.

1. Levison, *England and the Continent*, 8–11.
2. LHF, 42.
3. Geary, *Aristocracy in Provence*, 131–32, n. 22, supports the claim in the *Annales Marchianensis*, MGH, SS 16:611, that Erchinoald was Adalbald's brother. Because the claim comes from a dedication of the chapel in the castrum of Douai that Maurontus repaired and dedicated to Saint Amatus, Geary

conjugal bed of Clovis II, king of Neustria and Burgundy (639–657), is discreetly veiled. However, it seems highly likely that Erchinoald, soon or late, proved to be an active and able political mentor for the young woman who married a man who "had every kind of filthy habit. He was a seducer, and debaucher of women and a glutton and a drunk."[4] The discreet historian even hints that Clovis may have come to a violent end that he richly deserved. Clovis and his half-brother Sigebert, king of Austrasia, died within a year of one another. Balthild therefore took up the regency for her son Clothar III in the confused period of Grimoald's supremacy and attempted coup.[5]

Balthild must have continued to be on friendly terms with her former owner, for he held the office of mayor of the palace beyond Clovis's death in 657 until his own death in 658.[6] In that capacity, he supported Balthild's regency for Clothar III. Their joint reach extended even into Austrasia through Queen Himnechild, who brought her daughter to their court in the wake of Grimoald's coup and married her to Balthild's younger son, Childeric.[7] Balthild gave Himnechild her support in securing the fall of Gertrude of Nivelles' brother and made her regent for Austrasia during Childeric's minority.

As queen and regent, Balthild had a mixed reputation. This biography was probably written by a nun of Chelles, who was anxious to emphasize her saintly qualities. Her abbess, Bertilla, actively promoted Balthild's cult, dedicating several churches in her honor after her death.[8] This view was supported by the eighth-century historian who called her "beautiful, clever and strong of character."[9] Balthild was a patron and favorite of an ecclesiastical party that included Philibert, founder of Jumièges; Dagobert's former minister Ouen, who became bishop of Rouen; and Waldebert, abbot of Luxeuil. They all rallied behind Ebroin, whom she appointed mayor of the palace.[10] With his wife, Ebroin constructed a female monastery that followed

thinks it probably correct despite its thirteenth-century insertion into the chronicle. The name Aldetrude also has resonance, hinting at a possible relationship between the queen and saints Aldegund and Waldetrude (whose daughter was named Aldetrude).

4. LHF, 43–44.

5. Whether the coup occurred immediately upon Sigebert's death or in 661, Grimoald's policies in Austrasia confronted Balthild's in Neustria-Burgundy.

6. In later years, after the long period of Ebroin's domination, Erchinoald's descendants recovered the Neustrian mayoralty. See Geary, *Aristocracy in Provence*, 131.

7. See chapter 12, Introduction.

8. Folz, "Tradition hagiographique," claims that this was her own innovation.

9. LHF, 43.

10. Ebroin, with Brunhild, are the two active villains in the hagiography associated with the aristocracy. Graus, *Volk, Herrscher*, 373, attributes this to their efforts to strengthen royal power at the expanse of the nobility. Fischer, *Der Hausmeier Ebroin*, defends Ebroin as a victim of Carolingian propaganda. A full-scale treatment of Ebroin's policies can be found in Ewig, *Spätantikes und fränkisches Gallien*, 1:210ff.

the Benedictine-Columbanian Rule under Abbess Aetheria.[11] This suggests that he was Balthild's partner in a monastic policy that may have been designed to balance or even neutralize the efforts of the aristocratic opposition. Her biographer stresses her beneficent influence on public affairs and her use of the royal treasure to fund the establishment of monasteries. St. Denis, Corbie, Jouarre, and Chelles among other foundations profited from her patronage and became centers of royal influence. Balthild and Ebroin seem to have aspired to follow Dagobert's policy of making ecclesiastical appointments from their own court circles. This put them on a collision course with the aristocratic bishops who used monasteries and bishoprics as nuclei for local power concentrations.

Balthild's role in the ongoing drama seems to be lost beyond recall. She and Ebroin apparently followed a systematic policy of recentralizing the monarchy. Having placed Austrasia under her son Childeric, Ebroin expelled the Burgundian mayor of the palace. When his son sought vengeance, Ebroin defeated and killed him. Aunemund, the aristocratic bishop of Lyon, began to celebrate his deathday as a martyr's feast, a sort of cosmic retaliation also described in the life of Anstrude. Aunemund was a patron of Wilfrid of York whose English biographer Eddius Stephanus likened Balthild to a new Jezebel who caused the deaths of nine Frankish bishops.[12] Unaccountably, Eddius mistook the name of Bishop Aunemund for that of his brother Dalfinus, Count of Lyon, but this does not invalidate his charge. Aunemund was indeed killed, and Balthild appointed her supporter, Genesius, to his See. At the same time, she installed another friend, Leodegar, as bishop of Autun. The bishop of Paris, Sigobrand, was also a victim of this civil strife. Although Balthild's biographer is discretion itself, she assures us that he deserved to die. However, she claims that Balthild would have prevented the murder had not the nobles "allowed" her to become a nun at Chelles before the crime.

Thus Balthild's regency ended in mysterious circumstances. Her last known official act was a charter for the monastery of Corbie in 664.[13] At some date thereafter she resigned her power and retired into a monastery. Her biographer states that the nobles relaxed their opposition to her conversion because they wanted to be free to kill Sigobrand without fearing that she would punish them. Sigobrand was still alive in 667.[14] If she entered Chelles between 664 and 667, she was already out of the picture when Clothar III died in 670. At that

11. *DACL*, 2474.

12. Eddius Stephanus, *Life of Wilfred*, c. 6, in *The Age of Bede*, 111.

13. Nelson, "Queens as Jezebels," 64. Krusch gives the date as February 663, in Pertz, ed., *MGH, Diplomata* 1:32.

14. Krusch notes this from a charter.

time, a new power struggle developed that may have driven Maurontus into the religious life. However, in the absence of established dates, it remains possible that all these events link to that ongoing struggle in which old loyalties were realigned.

Did Ebroin kill the bishop of Paris and force Balthild into the convent when she objected?[15] Or was her entry connected to the ecclesiastical opposition that turned against Ebroin and supported Erchinoald's son Leudegisus? Ebroin was out of power between 673 and 675 and shared his exile at Waldebert's monastery of Luxeuil with Leodegar of Autun.[16] They apparently conspired together in 675 to murder Balthild's son, Childeric II, king of Austrasia. Soon after, however, while the Austrasians were attempting to restore Dagobert II, Ebroin came into conflict with Leodegar and Erchinoald's son, Leudegisus, whom he killed. Thereafter, until he died in 680, Ebroin successfully governed Neustria and Burgundy through Balthild's youngest son, Theuderic III.

It is fairly clear, even in this discreet biography, that her "success" in gaining permission to convert to religion is a hagiographer's euphemism. There was something so questionable about that conversion that the nuns of Chelles hesitated noticeably before admitting her into their congregation and the biographer was still sensitive enough to the problem to feel that she could not leave it out. The queen's retirement into monastic sanctity resembles the career patterns of the male saints of Dagobert's court, but it may also represent an ideal of sacral queenship first found in Clothild's life.[17] Certainly the author of her life saw her as one in a chain of saintly queens.[18]

However she came to be a nun, Balthild appears to have lived at Chelles for many years. She died in the same year as Ebroin, and it is all too likely that she occupied herself with more than the exercises in humility praised by her biographer, who does credit her with continued influence on behalf of the monastery. The struggles of her old friends, not to mention the fate of her three sons, could hardly have failed to move the retired queen, although she had ceased to be a major player in the political game. In any case, she survived two of her three sons. Soon after her death, Ebroin, who had dominated their reigns, was murdered. During the continuing reign of Theuderic III, the

15. Fisher, *Der Hausmeier Ebroin*, 90, holds this view and dates her retirement between 664 and 667.
16. See ibid., 76–104, for a detailed account of their relationship.
17. Wittern, "Frauen zwischen asketischem Ideal," argues that Balthild's systematic institutional approach to good works in contrast to the individual approach of Radegund supports the idea of the *Adelheiligkeit* of the seventh century advanced by Prinz. However, hers is a specifically royal approach that may fit an anti-aristocratic policy as well as a tradition of sacral queenship explored by McNamara in "Imitatio Helenae."
18. Folz, "Tradition hagiographique."

center of power in Frankland passed from Neustria to Austrasia and to the domination of Pippin of Herstal, nephew of Gertrude of Nivelles.[19]

Here Begins the Prologue to the Life of Lady Balthild the Queen

∎

1. Most beloved brothers, I have been commanded by the prelate Christ, to accomplish a simple and pious work.[20] My lack of skill and experience prevents me from setting forth an exquisite narrative in learned language. But the power of heartfelt love more strongly commands us not to be puffed up with vain glory and simply bring the truth to light.[21] For we know that the lord Jesus Christ asked for fruit from the fig tree, not leaves. And likewise we have determined that the fruit of truth shall not be hidden but shine forth upon a candlestick for the advancement and edification of many. Though less skilled in scholarship, we are all the more eager to cultivate a plain and open style so as to edify the many people who, like prudent bees seeking sweet nectar from the flowers, seek from simple words the burgeoning truth that edifies but does not flatter and puff up the one who hears it. Thus may the compendium of piety be thrown open to those who desire to imitate her. Therefore in what follows we have shown forth the truth as best we can, not for detractors but rather for the faithful.

Here Begins the Life of the Blessed Queen Balthild

∎

2. The blessed Lord, who "will have all men to be saved, and to come unto the knowledge of the truth," works "all in all" both "to will and to do."[22] By the same token, among the merits and virtues of the saints, praise should first be sung of Him Who made the humble great and raised the pauper from the dunghill and seated him among the princes of his people.[23] Such a one is the woman present to our minds, the venerable and great lady Balthild the queen. Divine Providence called her from across the seas. She, who came here as God's most precious and lofty pearl, was sold at a cheap price.

19. This traditional interpretation has recently been disputed by Fouracre, "Observations on the Outgrowth."

20. This text has often been attributed to a nun of Chelles, and it was customarily read to the community on the saint's feast. It is unclear, therefore, why the authors of both versions address it to "brothers," who were certainly subordinate to the abbess and the nuns in the community.

21. The author has changed in midsentence from the first person to the authorial "we."

22. 1 Timothy 2:4; 1 Corinthian 12:6; Philippians 2:33.

23. Psalms 113:7.

Erchinoald, a Frankish magnate and most illustrious man, acquired her and in his service the girl behaved most honorably.[24] And her pious and admirable manners pleased this prince and all his servants. For she was kindhearted and sober and prudent in all her ways, careful and plotting evil for none. Her speech was not frivolous nor her words presumptuous but in every way she behaved with utmost propriety. And since she was of the Saxon race, she was graceful in form with refined features, a most seemly woman with a smiling face and serious gait.[25] And she so showed herself just as she ought in all things, that she pleased her master and found favor in his eyes. So he determined that she should set out the drinking cup for him in his chamber and, honored above all others as his housekeeper, stand at his side always ready to serve him. She did not allow this dignity to make her proud but rather kept her humility. She was all obedience to her companions and amiable, ministering with fitting honor to her elders, ready to draw the shoes from their feet and wash and dry them. She brought them water to wash themselves and prepared their clothing expeditiously. And she performed all these services with good spirits and no grumbling.[26]

3. And from this noble conduct, the praise and love of her comrades for her increased greatly. She gained such happy fame that, when the said lord Erchinoald's wife died, he hoped to unite himself to Balthild, that faultless virgin, in a matronal bed. But when she heard of this, she fled and most swiftly took herself out of his sight. When she was called to the master's chamber she hid herself secretly in a corner and threw some vile rags over herself so that no one could guess that anyone might be concealed there. Thus for the love of humility, the prudent and astute virgin attempted to flee as best she could from vain honors. She hoped that she might avoid a human marriage bed and thus merit a spiritual and heavenly spouse. But doubtless, Divine Providence brought it about that the prince, unable to find the woman he sought, married another wife. Thereafter it happened, with God's approval, that Balthild, the maid who escaped marriage with a lord, came to be

24. In 641 or 642, Erchinoald succeeded Ega as mayor of the palace in Neustria; see Ebling, *Prosopographie*, 137–38. How Balthild was brought to Clovis's attention is not clear, but Erchinoald was a personal patron of the Irish monk Fursey and collaborated with Saint Eligius, whose influence at court was still strong in the promotion of the Irish mission. Balthild later hastened to Eligius's bedside and procured his relics for Chelles as soon as he died. The advancement of a pious captive from overseas with an attachment to the church and the monastic system may not be as accidental as the biographer suggests.

25. Chelles was a popular training center for Anglo-Saxon nuns. If the author was indeed a nun there, she could conceivably be Saxon herself.

26. In all probability, the author is making deliberate reference to the rules for nuns then in use and the standard virtues of nuns in their communities (chapter 15).

espoused to Clovis, son of the former king Dagobert. Thus by virtue of her humility she was raised to a higher rank. Divine dispensation determined to honor her in this station so that, having scorned the king's servant, she came to be coupled with the king himself and bring forth royal children. And these events are known to all for now her royal progeny rule the realm.

4. She upon whom God conferred the grace of prudence obeyed the King with vigilant care as her lord, acted as a mother to the princes, as a daughter to priests, and as a most pious nurse to children and adolescents. And she was amiable to all, loving priests as fathers, monks as brothers, a pious nurse to the poor. And she distributed generous alms to every one. She guarded the princes' honor by keeping their intimate counsels secret. She always exhorted the young to strive for religious achievement and humbly and assiduously suggested things to the king for the benefit of the church and the poor. For, desiring to serve Christ in the secular habit at that time, she frequented daily prayers commending herself with tears to Christ, the King of heaven. The pious king, impressed by her faith and devotion, delegated his faithful servant the abbot Genesius as her helper.[27] Through his hands, she ministered to priests and poor alike, feeding the needy and clothing the naked and taking care to order the burial of the dead, funneling large amounts of gold and silver through him to convents of men and virgins. Afterwards that servant of Christ, Genesius, by Christ's order, was ordained bishop of Lyon in Gaul.[28] But at that time, he was busy about the palace of the Franks. And as we have said, by King Clovis' order, Lady Balthild followed the servant of God's advice in providing alms through him to every poor person in many places.

5. What more? In accordance with God's will, her husband King Clovis migrated from the body and left his sons with their mother.[29] Immediately after him her son Clothar took up the kingdom of the Franks, maintaining peace in the realm, with the most excellent princes, Chrodebert, Bishop of Paris, Lord Ouen and Ebroin, Mayor of the Palace with the rest of the elders and many others.[30] Then to promote peace, by command of Lady Balthild with the advice of the other elders, the people of Austrasia accepted her son Childeric as their king and the Burgundians were united with the Franks.[31]

---

27. The author flatters Clovis II or, perhaps if she were a nun of the next generation, she is simply ignorant of his bad reputation as a liar, a glutton, and a womanizer. For Genesius, see chapter 15.
28. The author slides discreetly past the murder of Aunemund.
29. About 657. Balthild had three sons; Clothar III succeeded his father in Neustria and was followed in turn by Childeric and Theuderic.
30. For Chrodebert, the bishop of Paris who appears in charters of 654 and 660, see Ebling, *Prosopographie*, 112–13. Ouen (d. 685–86) figures in the life of Bertilla. For Ebroin, see Ebling, *Prosopographie*, 131–33, and Fischer, *Der Hausmeier Ebroin*.
31. Nelson, "Queens as Jezebels," 50, points out the echo of Ezechial 36, which gives resonance to the author's vision of Balthild as a peacemaker. For a discussion of the place names, see Ewig, "Die

And we believe, under God's ordinance, that these three realms then held peace and concord among themselves because of Lady Balthild's great faith.

6. Then following the exhortations of good priests, by God's will working through her, Lady Balthild prohibited the impious evil of the simoniac heresy, a depraved custom which stained the church of God, whereby episcopal orders were obtained for a price. She proclaimed that no payment could be exacted for receipt of a sacred rank. Moreover, she, or God acting through her, ordained that yet another evil custom should cease, namely, that many people determined to kill their children rather than nurture them, for they feared to incur the public exactions which were heaped upon them by custom, which caused great damage to their affairs.[32] In her mercy, that lady forbade anyone to do these things. And for all these deeds, a great reward must surely have awaited her.

7. Who can count how many and how great her services were to religious communities? She showered great estates and whole forests upon them for the construction of their cells and monasteries. And at Chelles, in the region of Paris, she built a great community of virgins as her own special house of God.[33] There she established the maiden Bertilla, God's serving girl, as the first to hold the place of their mother. And there in turn the venerable lady Balthild had determined she would finally go to live under the rule of religion and to rest in peace and in truth she fulfilled her desire with willing devotion.[34] Whatever wonders God works through His saints and His chosen ones should not be passed over, for they contribute to His praise. For, as Scripture says, "God does wonders in his saints."[35] For His Holy Spirit, the Paraclete, dwells within and cooperates with the benevolent heart as it is written: "All things work together for good to them that love God."[36] And thus it was spoken truly of this great woman. As we said, neither our tongue nor any others, however learned as I believe, can give voice to all the good she did. How much consolation and help did she lavish on the houses of God and on the poor for the love of Christ and how many advantages and comforts did she confer on them? And what of the monastery called Corbie

---

fränkische Teilungen," 153. Fischer, *Der Hausmeier Ebroin*, 73, indicates that Childeric had already been associated in the regency of his aunt Himnechild for a year in the absence of the vanished Dagobert II before he married her daughter Bilichild, who was murdered with him in 675.

32. This sentence is highly obscure; we have had recourse to Life B for *exactiones* in place of *actiones*. For the ongoing problem of infanticide, see Coleman, "Infanticide in the Early Middle Ages."

33. For the wider ecclesiastical context, see Ewig, *Spätantikes und fränkisches Gallien*, 180.

34. This rather heavy-handed emphasis on her intention is probably designed to suppress the notion that her eventual entry into Chelles was forced.

35. Psalms 37:38.

36. Romans 8:25. As usual, we have cited the King James version, but the passage as cited here actually reads: "For God is co-worker with everyone who wills what is good."

in the parish of Amiens that she built at her own expense?[37] There the venerable man, Lord Theofredus, now a bishop but then the abbot, ruled a great flock of brothers whom Lady Balthild had requested from the most saintly Lord Waldebert, then abbot of the monastery of Luxeuil, who wondrously had them sent to that same convent which all agree in praising to this very day.[38]

8. What more? At Jumièges, the religious man lord Philibert, was given a great wood from the fisc where his community has settled and other gifts and pastures were also conceded from the fisc for the building of this same monastery.[39] And how many great farms and talents of gold and silver did she give to Lord Lagobert at Curbio?[40] She took off a girdle from her regalia, which had encircled her own holy loins and gave it to the brothers to devote to alms. And she dispensed all this with a benign and joyous soul, for as the scripture says: "The Lord loveth a cheerful giver."[41] And likewise to Fontanelle and Logium, she conceded many things.[42] As to Luxeuil and the monasteries in Burgundy, who can tell how many whole farms and innumerable gifts of money she gave? And what did she do for Jouarre, whence she gathered the lady Bertilla abbess of Chelles and other sacred virgins? How many gifts of wealth and land? And similarly she often directed gifts to holy Fara's monastery.[43] And she granted many great estates to the basilicas of the saints and monasteries of the city of Paris, and enriched them with many gifts. What more? As we have said, we cannot recount these things one by one, not even half of them and to give an account of all the blessings she conferred is utterly beyond our powers.

37. Krusch, MGH, SRM 2:477, refers to appropriate charters in Pertz, ed., MGH, Diplomata 1:35–47. He notes that Corbie was originally among the estates of Gundeland, the Neustrian mayor of the palace related to Aldegund and Waldetrude.

38. Waldebert had succeeded Eustasius at Luxeuil and was a ready source of instruction in the Columbanian monastic discipline. He was the mentor of Burgundofara and Sadalberga and author of a popular rule for women that was used widely in these Frankish foundations. Krusch tries to establish Theodefred's episcopacy but cannot tie him to any city. See MGH, SRM 2:491, n. 1.

39. *Vita Filiberti* 6, ASOSB, saeculum 2, 319. For more on Saint Philibert, see chapter 17, which relates the process of Jumièges' fission from a double monastery into separate institutions for women (at Pavilly) and men.

40. Today Saint-Laumer-de-Moutier; this redistribution of royal wealth, principally accumulated as loot, seems to have been a queenly office (chapters 2 and 4).

41. 2 Corinthians 9:7.

42. Krusch, MGH, SRM 2:492, nn. 1, 2, establishes these as Saint Wandrille and Logium, a convent for girls in Normandy. Ibid., n. 3, notes that Mother Melona and the recluse Willa are named in *Gesta abb. Fontanelle*, 4.

43. Faremoutiers, where Anglo-Saxon nuns were in evidence from the life of Burgundofara, a connection extended to Chelles in the time of Bertilla and that may have strengthened Balthild's association with the Irish monks of Luxeuil, headed by Waldebert.

9. We should not pass over, however, what she did in her zealous love of God for the older basilicas of the saints, Lord Denis and Lord Germanus and Lord Médard and Saint Peter or the Lord Anianus, and Saint Martin, or wherever something came to her notice. She would send orders and letters warning bishops and abbots that the monks dwelling in those places ought to live according to their holy rule and order. And that they might agree more freely, she ordered their privileges confirmed and granted immunities that it might please them all the more to beseech Christ the highest King to show mercy to the king and give peace. And let it be remembered, since it increases the magnitude of her own reward, that she prohibited the sale of captive Christian folk to outsiders and gave orders through all the lands that no one was to sell captive Christians within the borders of the Frankish realm.[44] What is more, she ordered that many captives should be ransomed, paying the price herself. And she installed some of the captives she released and other people in monasteries, particularly as many men and women of her own people as possible and cared for them. For as many of them as she could persuade thereto, she commended to holy communities and bade that they might pray for her. And even to Rome, to the basilicas of Peter and Paul, and the Roman poor, she directed many and large gifts.[45]

10. And as we have said before, it was her own holy intention to convert to this monastery of religious women which she had built at Chelles. But the Franks delayed much for love of her and would not have permitted this to happen except that there was a commotion made by the wretched Bishop Sigobrand whose pride among the Franks, earned him his mortal ruin.[46] Indeed, they formed a plan to kill him against her will. Fearing that the lady would act heavily against them, and wish to avenge him, they suddenly relented and permitted her to enter the monastery. There can be no doubt that the princes' motives were far from pure.[47] But the lady, considering the

44. Thus effectively blocking the slave trade, of which she had been herself a victim, on both ends.

45. Nelson, "Queens as Jezebels," 69, outlines a more general ecclesiastical policy from these devotions. She argues that it constituted a taxation of bishops in favor of monasteries. Graus, Volk, Herrscher, 413, notes that compared to Clothild and Radegund, Balthild's sanctity rests directly on her use of royal authority.

46. Krusch identifies Sigobrand as Chrodebert's successor at Paris, Gallia Christiana 7, 26, citing a charter of 667. Nelson points out that he was one of a succession of royal appointees to bishoprics since Dagobert's time who probably attracted hostility as instruments of royal power and possibly his own efforts to restore wealth to his diocese after Landeric's forced donations to Saint Denis.

47. Fischer, Der Hausmeier Ebroin, 98, interprets this passage to mean that Ebroin who owed his position to the queen forced her into the cloister, between 664 and 667 on the basis of coins and charters. From 673 to 675 Ebroin himself was in exile at Luxeuil. On his overthrow and death in 680, Waratto of the Erchinoald family succeeded him, and Anstrude, the widow of his son Bercharius, married a son of Pippin II, tying the two great mayoral families together.

will of God rather than their counsel, thought it a dispensation from God so that, whatever the circumstances, she might have the chance to fulfill her holy plan under Christ's rule. And conducted by several elders, she came to her aforesaid monastery of Chelles and there she was received into the holy congregation by the holy maidens, as was fitting, honorably and with sufficient love. But at first she had no small complaint against those whom she had so sweetly nurtured. For they suspected her of false motives or else simply attempted to return evil for good. Hastily conferring with the priests about this, she mercifully indulged them in the delay and begged that they would forgive the commotion in her heart. And afterwards by the largesse of God, peace was fully restored between them.

11. And indeed, she loved her sisters with the most pious affection as her own daughters and she obeyed their most holy abbess as a mother. She showed herself as a servant and lowliest bondwoman to them from holy devotion, even while she still ruled over the public palace, and had often visited the community. One example of her great humility was the way she would valiantly take care of the dirtiest cleaning jobs for the sisters in the kitchen, personally cleaning up the dung from the latrine.[48] And she did all this gladly and in perfect joy of spirit, doing such humble service for Christ's sake. For who would believe that one so sublime in power would take care of things so vile? Only if she were driven by the fullest love of Christ could it be expected. And she prayed constantly, persistently, devoutly, tearfully. She frequently attended divine reading and gave constant comfort to the sick through holy exhortation and frequent visits. Through the achievement of charity, she grieved with the sorrowful, rejoiced with the joyful and, that all might be comforted, she often made suggestions for their improvement humbly to the lady abbess. And that lady amiably gave heed to her petitions for truly in them as in the apostles, there was but one heart and one soul, and they loved each other tenderly in Christ.

12. Then the lady Balthild became physically ill of body and suffered wearily from pain in the bowels caused by a serious infection, and but for the doctors' efforts she would have died. But she always had more confidence in celestial medicine for her health. So, with a holy and pious conscience, she never ceased to thank God for chastising. She gave her astute advice at all times and—example of great humility—she provided a pattern of piety in her service to her sisters. She often consulted with the mother of the monastery as to how they might always call on the king and queen and their honored

48. The author is looking beyond the expectation of all the rules that every sister would take her turn at cooking. Her inspiration is the *Life of Radegund*, which Krusch thought she used as a model throughout (478).

nobles with gifts,[49] as was customary, that the house of God might continue to enjoy the good fame with which it began. Thus it would not lose but always remain in loving affection with all its friends and grow stronger in the name of God, as it is written: "It is fitting to have good report of them which are without."[50] Particularly, she urged them always to care for the poor and for guests with the utmost zeal, out of love and mercy and the mother of the monastery heard her salutary admonitions willingly for love of Christ and did all with gladness of heart. Nor did she ever cease to carry out all this and to increase the rewards of her community.

13. And as her glorious death approached, a clear vision was shown to her.[51] Before holy Mary's altar, a ladder stood upright whose height reached the heavens. Angels of God were going up and down and there the Lady Balthild made her ascent. Through this revelation, she was clearly given to understand that her sublime merit, patience and humility, would take her to the heights of the eternal King who would swiftly reward her with an exalted crown. The lady knew, from this clear vision, that it would not be long before she would migrate from her body and come where she had already laid up her best treasures. And she ordered that this be concealed from her sisters so that until her passing the vision was not revealed lest it cause painful grief to the sisters or the mother of the monastery.[52] But she on her part devoted herself with ever greater piety and good spirits to holy prayer, commending herself ever more zealously, humbly, and in contrition of heart to the celestial king, the Lord Jesus Christ. As much as she could, she concealed the weight of her pain and consoled Lady Bertilla and the rest of the sisters saying that her illness was not serious, that she was convalescent, dissimulating what was to come so that afterwards they took comfort in believing that the blow fell suddenly and she went unexpectedly from life.

14. And when the lady felt her end to be truly near, she raised her holy mind to Heaven. And having made certain that she would be awarded the great prize that the blessed receive, she vehemently forbade her attendants to

---

49. Eulogies. See discussion in the life of Genovefa, n. 18.

50. 1 Timothy 3:7. The grammar in this passage is impenetrable, but it seems clear enough that the dying queen had lost none of her political acumen. Nelson, "Queens as Jezebels," 72, credits her with laying the foundations for a structural change in the Merovingian church that would tie it to the prestige of the crown, ultimately leading to the sacral kingship of Carolingian times.

51. Life A says simply *ei*, but Life B modified this to *ei conveniens*, which might suggest that someone else saw the vision, which would accord with subsequent events.

52. It is not clear to whom Balthild gave these orders. The B version that is basically an expansion of Life A says she was speaking to the sisters who were conscious of the vision. But A does not mention anyone else involved in the vision, which suggests that perhaps she simply confided her experience to someone she trusted to reveal it after her death.

say how sick she was to the other sisters or to the abbess who was ill herself lest she be distracted by a multitude of even heavier sorrows. At the time there was an infant, her goddaughter whom she wished to take with her. And she was suddenly snatched from her body and preceded her to the tomb.[53] Then full of faith, she crossed herself. Raising pious eyes and holy hands to heaven, the saint's soul was released from the chains of her flesh in peace. And immediately her chamber glittered brightly with the light of divine splendor. And no doubt with that light, a chorus of angels and her faithful old friend Bishop Genesius came to receive that most holy soul as her great merits deserved.

15. For a little while, the sisters attending her, stifled their sorrowful groans. They said nothing of her death and, as she had ordered, remained silent and told only those priests who commended her most blessed soul to the Lord.[54] But when the abbess and all the congregation learned what had happened they asked tearfully how this universally desired jewel could have been snatched away so suddenly without warning, without knowing the hour of her departure.[55] And stupefied, they all prostrated themselves on the ground in grief and with profuse tears and fearful groans, gave thanks to the pious Lord and praised Him together. Then they commended her holy soul to Christ, the pious King, that He might escort her to holy Mary in the chorus and company of the saints. Then they buried her with great honor and much reverence as was proper. And Lady Bertilla the Abbess, with solicitous striving for piety, earnestly commended her to the holy priests in several churches that her holy name be carefully commemorated in the sacred oblations.[56] And they still celebrate her merits in many places.

16. To her followers, she left a holy example of humility and patience, mildness and overflowing zest for loving; nay more, infinite mercy, astute and prudent vigilance, pure confessions. She showed that everything should be done as a result of consultation and that nothing should be done without consent but that all actions should be temperate and rational. She left this rule of piety as a model to her companions and now for her holy virtues and many

---

53. Krusch notes, citing the history of her translation in 833 (MGH, SS 15:285), that a seven-year-old named Radegund was buried in the same tomb with Balthild. The naming of this god-daughter seems to suggest that Balthild was quite conscious of the earlier queen as an exemplar for her own life, and that similarities should not be entirely laid at the door of the author.

54. The later Life B adds "that He had already received it." Presumably, this refers to the vision of the ladder in c. 13.

55. See chapter 9 for the regularity of a saint's prophecy of death. The two monasteries were close together, and Balthild had been a patroness of both of them. Bertilla was expecting what seems to have become a traditional guarantee of sanctity.

56. At the oblation prayer during Mass, the names of the dead are commemorated.

other merits she has received the prize of the crown that the Lord set aside for her long ago. So she is happy among the angels in the Lord's sight and as His spouse rejoices forever among the white-garbed flock of virgins enjoying the immense and everlasting joy she had always desired. And in order to make known her sublime merits to the faithful, God in his goodness has effected many miracles at her holy tomb. For whoever came there seized by fever, or vexed with demons, or worn with toothache, if they had faith, was immediately cured through divine virtue and her holy intercession from whatever plague or illness. Safe and sound, they went out in the Lord's name as was manifested not long ago in the case of a certain boy.

17. A certain venerable man, Bishop Leudegund came from Provence, a faithful friend to the monastery of Chelles. His son was possessed by a demon so violent that his companions could only control him if his hands and feet were bound, for with great cruelty he tore apart all he could reach. But when they brought him into the place of her holy sepulchre and laid him half-alive on the pavement, the ferocious demon grew stiff and terrified with fear of God and fell silent. Divine power made him flee from the boy forthwith. And the boy rose up confidently, crossed himself and, giving thanks to God, returned to his own unharmed and in his right mind.

18. Now let us recall that there have been other noble queens in the realm of the Franks who worshipped God: Clothild, King Clovis' queen of old, niece of King Gundobad. Her husband was a mighty pagan but she drew him, with many other Frankish leaders to Christianity and the Catholic faith by holy exhortations. She led them to construct a church in honor of Saint Peter at Paris, and she built the original community of virgins for Saint George at Chelles and in honor of the saints and to store up her future reward she founded many others which she endowed with much wealth. And likewise we are told of Queen Ultragotha of the most Christian king Childebert, that she was a comforter of the poor and helper of the monks who served God. And also, there was the most faithful handmaid Radegund, King Clothar's queen of elder time, whom the grace of the Holy Spirit enkindled so that she relinquished her husband during his life and consecrated herself to the Lord Christ under the holy veil. And we may read in her acts of all the good she did for Christ her spouse.

19. But it is only right that we meditate instead on her who is our subject here, lady Balthild whose many good deeds have been done in our time and whose acts are best known to us. We have commemorated a few of these many acts and cannot think her merits inferior to those who came before her for we know she surpassed them in zealous striving for what is holy. For after performing many good deeds to the point of evangelical perfection, she at last surrendered herself freely to holy obedience and happily ended her life

as a religious, a true *monacha*. Her sacred obit and holy feast are celebrated on the third calends of February.[57] She lies entombed in Chelles, her monastery, while truly she reigns gloriously with Christ in Heaven in perpetual joy never, we trust, to forget her faithful friends. And as well as we could, if not as much as we ought, in fervent charity we have striven to follow your orders. Forgive our lack of skill and for our sins of negligence we pray for charity's sake that you ask the good Lord to exonerate us. May the peace of the Lord be with you to Whom be glory from everlasting to everlasting. Amen.

57. January 30, 680.

15
Bertilla, Abbess of Chelles
(d. ca. 700)

The life of Bertilla illustrates the working of familial networks among the saints of this age and their admirers. She was trained at the abbey of Jouarre in Brie on the Marne near Faremoutiers.[1] The founding of Jouarre was noted by Jonas of Bobbio who wrote about 642.[2] The founders were Ado, son of Autharius and Aiga, who, with his brother, Saint Ouen, was consecrated by Columbanus.[3] The life of Ouen, from the early eighth century, notes that the monastery derived its name from *Jovis ara*, the altar of Jove, having been built on the site of an ancient pagan temple haunted by brigands and lost women.[4] It was endowed with privileges by Burgundofara's brother Faro, Bishop of Meaux, and housed monks as well as nuns according to the Irish custom and the Rule of Columbanus. The first abbess, who would have trained Bertilla, was Theudechild, niece of Moda, second wife of Autharius. Moda's other niece, Agilberta, was second abbess, and her sister, Balda, third abbess. Agilberta's brother was bishop of Paris and is believed to be related to Sadalberga.

Genesius, bishop of Lyon, recommended Bertilla to the English Queen

---

Vita Bertilae abbatissae Calensis, in Levison, ed., MGH, SRM 4:534–46. This life of Bertilla seems to have been derived in the eighth century from several sources. Levison thought it was primarily from the Life of Balthild with additions from other sources. Mabillon, ASOSB, saeculum 3, 1:25, thought it was put together at Chelles about six or seven years after her death. The present manuscript is Carolingian, and ornamentation and grammatical correction by a later scribe are probable. Bertilla's dates are uncertain. The author of this text states she lived at Chelles for forty-six years after its foundation, but the founding date is unknown and her death has been set anywhere between 692 and 708. It was certainly established by 660 when Saint Eligius died and Balthild bestowed his relics on the convent.

1. Formerly Evoriacus, founded by Burgundofara.

2. Jonas of Bobbio, *Vita S. Columbani*, 1:50.

3. Jouarre was probably founded somewhere between 635 and 642. For its use as a prestigious center for family tombs, see Geary, *Before France and Germany*, 179.

4. This and the following summary of Jouarre's history are drawn from Guérout, "Les Origines"; see also Ewig, *Spätantikes und fränkisches Gallien*, 183–91.

Balthild as first abbess of Chelles, and she came with a cadre of recruits from Jouarre.[5] Chelles was soon a vital link between Frankland and the British Isles. The connection began with the marriage of Charibert's daughter Bertha, who invited Roman missionaries into her kingdom of Kent at the end of the sixth century. The relationship was reinforced by the growing influence of Luxeuii and the Irish monks, such as those at Nivelles and Fosse. About the middle of the seventh century, Bede noted that Hereswith, sister of Saint Hilda of Whitby, was a nun at Chelles.[6] This was no accident, but a policy Balthild actively promoted after she had become queen of Neustria.

As a training ground for missionaries of monasticism and a center for the conversion of the countryside through dispensation of communion and confession, Chelles was concerned with the exemplary qualities of hagiography. The life of Bertilla is not distinguished for its miracles or even for the heroic qualities of its heroine. The author presents the abbess, as she presented herself in life, as a mirror of monastic living, a practitioner of the rule in all her ways. Thus the life is replete with references to the rules of Benedict, Caesarius, Donatus, and Waldebert. Because it was read to the community at meals and on feast days, it would have translated the abstract demands of these rules into the common life of their own convent.[7]

Saint Bertilla, Abbess of Chelles

■

1. The brighter the religious life of holy virgins shines in merit, the more it is celebrated by word of mouth and praised in the tongues of all people.[8] For as long as it presents an example of good behavior to others, it should move every voice to praise. Blessed Bertilla, a virgin native to the province of Soissons, sprang from parents of the highest nobility. As worthy seed gives birth to yet worthier children, she amplified the honors she received from her birth by the merits of her blessed life when Christ chose to be glorified in her and to make her glitter so that many would imitate her. From the beginning of her earliest youth, she showed so much fervor in the faith that she willingly relinquished her parents for love of Christ, though as long as she

---

5. For Balthild's English background, see chapter 14.

6. Bede, HE, 4:23.

7. McNamara has explored these questions further in "Living Sermons" and "The Ordeal of Community."

8. *Vita virginum*, the use of the singular *life*, may be intended self-consciously to echo Gregory of Tours's *Vita patruum*, the sense that all saints share a single life, which is brilliantly elucidated in the first chapter of Heffernan, *Sacred Biography*.

was a child she always yielded swiftly to their desires. As soon as she reached her adolescence, the age of understanding, she desired Christ the Lord and planned, with a heart full of love, to enter His service. When questioned by the most faithful man Dado, called Ouen, as to whether she wished to serve Christ, she answered with thankful spirit that she had been devoted to Him from infancy when she had sworn to gain Christ, the Son of God, for her spouse.[9] But she had not dared to announce this publicly for she knew that her parents were strongly opposed and would rather impede her with their prohibitions than give her their consent. But while she was still of tender age, she astutely followed divine counsel and secretly begged help most assiduously from God that her piety might produce profits and He might ordain that she be led into a suitable consortium of holy women or one of their communities. Considering her devotion, Divine Piety Which never fails those who place their hope in It, soon sent divine grace to her aid. At last, she gained her parents' consent and her devoted brothers and sisters encouraged her to persist in holy devotion and consecrate herself as an intact virgin to God. By the Lord's inspiration, they freely gave her encouragement and soon brought her, according to her vow, to a nearby monastery of women called Jouarre.[10] She arrived there and was commended to the Lady Abbess Theudechild, who received her with honor among the holy women.[11]

2. Thus the noble maiden Bertilla gave many thanks to Christ, whose piety guided her from the tempest of the world to the snug harbor of the community. And from that day, in that same place, she set herself to be pleasing to God with so much humility of soul that, except for the honorable way she behaved, she took no pride in the nobility of her stock. For sprung from free people at birth, she voluntarily consented to become a slave. In the holy community, she behaved herself so admirably and praiseworthily under the norms of the holy rule, that she soon achieved senior status in holy obedience. She hastened devoutly with fervent mind to prayers and to the divine office. She behaved properly with all gravity, gentleness and temperance, winning the admiration of the holy congregation. She kept the fear of God always before her eyes, walking with a heart perfected by the purity of confession. Humble and obedient, she was always pleasant to her seniors and served her elders in every way, as the mother ordered her. She strove to do everything most faithfully with a willing spirit, trusting in the consolation

9. Soissons was in the diocese of Rouen where Ouen was bishop from 641 to 684.

10. Jonas of Bobbio, *Vita S. Columbani,* 1:26.

11. As far as possible without a contemporary vita, the life of Theuthilda has been reconstructed for the *AS,* October 10, 114–20. She spent most of her life in the convent from its foundation, and her tomb still remains there in the crypt. She died in about 660, the last possible date for the founding of Chelles.

of divine grace and did all that was enjoined upon her without a murmur.[12] Thus she profited, making daily advances in her exercises. She rose steadily above herself, not simply to surpass the others in merits but to triumph in taming her own body. Who now can recollect or tell all that there was to tell of what Christ's servant Bertilla did in that time? She was foremost in the stringency of her fasting and readier in love of vigils, more laudable in assiduity of prayer, more lavish in charity, more careful in reading Holy Scripture and more remarkable in works of mercy. Despite her youth, she was an elder in her habits of obedience and so mature in the treading down of vice that, in her juvenile inexperience, she was an example of understanding to her seniors, a solace to her companions and a model of the saints' ways to her juniors.[13] While she lived, she wished to be wholly in Christ and with Christ. Not voluptuous in her gaze nor wanton of ear, not turning her mind to pleasure, but always restraining herself with the anchor of gravity, she so worked within the monastery walls that, in many useful matters, she resembled the spiritual mother. Considering her most faithful ministry, the abbess enjoined more and heavier duties upon her than others below her. Thus, while she was trained in many holy and religious ways she behaved with pious solicitude to other sisters under the mother's direction. The care of the sick, of children and even guests was frequently entrusted to her.[14] All of this, she performed most blessedly with a spirit of grace and equanimity, as though under divine guidance. She was chosen by the Lord for all the offices of the monastery and held the chief office second only to the mother abbess. She discharged all with flawless obedience for the love of God. She always maintained sobriety and peace with an untroubled mind so that no provocation ever moved her spirit to scandal. And more, if she discerned any commotion or heard any sisters murmuring, for zeal of piety she strove to soothe and pacify them, to curb malicious whispers so that she might administer charity and piety by divine grace to their hearts.[15]

3. So that the great merit in Christ's servant, Bertilla, might be shown to others, a great miracle was done through her. For once, when one of her sisters, whose spirit was troubled, spoke wrathful words to her, she called

---

12. The Rule of Columbanus requires regular confession of all faults (c. 10). It puts primary emphasis on obedience (c. 1) and provides penalties for murmuring and protesting. Thus, the author is presenting Bertilla as an exemplum for other nuns.

13. Donatus of Besançon, *Regula ad virgines*, c. 66, provides that "age" ranking in the monastery must follow order of conversion rather than order of birth. Having entered at an early age, Bertilla would probably have become a "senior" while still young.

14. Benedict, c. 31, and Donatus, c. 61, prescribe these qualities as suitable to the celleress, whose appointment is at the discretion of the abbess.

15. Donatus, c. 28–29, gives specific application to Columbanus, c. 18, "on discretion."

down divine judgment upon her. Although, as was seemly, the fault was mutually forgiven, Lady Bertilla continued to be fearful about the divine judgment she had summoned. Then the sister who had angered her died unexpectedly, choked by asthma. Hearing the signal, the rest of the sisters gathered for the funeral, to perform the customary prayers for the soul that had been taken from them so that the Lord might decree a warm welcome for her into His perpetual peace.[16] Not having been told, God's servant Bertilla asked what caused the resounding chorus of psalms. One sister answered her: "Did you not know that the tones are ringing out because that sister's soul has left her body?" Hearing that, she trembled greatly because of the words they had had between them. She ran speedily, hurrying with great faith, to the place where the little body of the defunct sister lay lifeless. Entering, she immediately laid her right hand on the breast of the deceased adjuring her receding soul through Jesus Christ, the Son of God, not to leave but, before she spoke with Him, to forgive her anger against her. God permitting, at her commanding voice, the spirit which had left the body returned to the corpse and to the stupefaction of all, the revived cadaver drew breath. Looking at the servant of God, she said: "What have you done, sister? Why did you retrieve me from the way of light?" To which God's servant Bertilla said humbly: "I beg you sister to give me words of forgiveness, for once I cursed you with a troubled spirit." To which she said: "May God forgive you. I harbor no resentment in my heart against you now. Nay, rather, I hold you in fullest love. I pray that you will entreat God for me and permit me to go in peace nor cause me delay. For I am ready for the bright road and now I cannot start without your permission." And to that she said: "Go then in the peace of Christ and pray for me, sweet and lovable sister." How great was the faith in God that permitted her to recall a soul when she wished and return it when she pleased! From that miraculous deed, let us recognize how much constancy of faith God's servant had that enabled her, strengthened inwardly by the gift of celestial piety, to recall a soul indubitably gone from the body, to reanimate a cadaver. She spoke with her as she wished. And when the talk was ended, she permitted the soul to leave. Thus in the blessed Bertilla was the scripture fulfilled: "All things are possible to him that believeth."[17] For nothing is impossible to one who confides in God with all her heart, as this miracle makes clear.

4. Now this was in the time after the decease of Lord Clovis the King.[18] Queen Balthild, his most noble wife, with her little son Clothar, governed the

16. Caesarius of Arles, *Regula*, c. 10.
17. Mark 9:22.
18. Clovis II (639–57); for events of this period, see chapter 14.

Kingdom of the Franks without reproach.[19] All the bishops and nobles and even the commoners of the kingdom were compelled by her merits to love her with wonderful affection. For she was religious and much devoted to God and took care of paupers and churches. With great strength of soul, she governed the palace manfully. She took counsel with pontiffs and primates of the people and proposed to build a monastery of maidens at a royal villa called Chelles. For she announced that she had made up her mind that when her son, the said Lord Clothar, reached his majority and could rule for himself, she would enter that monastery under religious orders, leaving royal cares behind. And because she loved everyone with wondrous affection and everyone loved her, her counsel pleased the company and they all gave their assent to it. And, prudent and wise as she was, she ordered the monastery to be built with all haste. Foreseeing the future needs of God's handmaids, she provided the necessary substance. Then, with the convent diligently prepared, she resolved in her mind to seek a woman of worthy merits and honesty and maidenly behavior to whom she could entrust a flock of holy virgins gathered there under the rule of holy religion. Rumors of the blessed holy maid Bertilla were on many tongues and, through many tales told by the faithful, came at last to the ears of the royal lady Balthild, the most glorious and Christian Queen. She rejoiced at the news of her sanctity and took counsel on the spot and decreed that [Bertilla] should be constituted mother over the holy women whom she had gathered for the love of Christ and reverence of holy Mary in the above-named convent. This, by God's dispensation, she afterwards brought to pass. With great devotion and humility she entreated the lady abbess Theudechild to designate some servants of God from her monastery to govern her community. After long urging, she could not deny the queen's supplication and freely granted the glorious lady's petition. She ordered the Lady Bertilla with several holy maidens to proceed to the convent at Chelles, to the spiritual mother Lady Balthild with the greatest care and fitting honor. As is proper, through the great priest Genesius, the whole congregation was commended to her as spiritual mother and he presently relayed to the Lady Queen his confidence in her religion and modest manners.[20] Accordingly, the glorious queen, Balthild, received her as a heavenly gift, with great honor and, by mandate of Lady Theudechild, imposed the burden of ruling the whole convent upon her and ordered her to be its abbess.

19. Clothar III (657–73).

20. See chapter 14, c. 4, and *AS*, November 1, 352–56. He became bishop of Lyon in 658 or 659 when Chelles was probably founded. "Great priest" is interpreted by the Bollandists to refer to his position as chief chaplain of the palace, or to be a contemporary usage for Bishop.

5. Now truly I cannot express with what prudence and utter blamelessness the venerable servant of God Bertilla prepared herself to take up the cares of governance. She was not puffed up by the honor she had assumed or the abundant wealth or the surrounding crowd of servants of both sexes. She continued to remain in herself what she had been before: humble, pious, benignant, modest, virginal and, what supercedes everything, charitable. Assiduously, with complete faith, she prayed God, Who had consoled her in all things since her infancy, to help her and give her both strength and astute counsel to govern her holy community so that it would please Him Who had deigned to call her to this dignity. With the help of divine piety, she was able, through priestly counsel, to govern the community manfully with the highest sanctity and religion and guide it wonderfully under the holy rule so that she was pleasing to God and to the holy queen in all things. For she loved each of her sons and daughters like a mother and all returned that love. So she was loved when she was angry and feared when she laughed. She fortified her daughters and others under her governance against the devil's insidiousness and used spiritual arts as precautions to lead them to good deeds. She showed herself as a shining example in every good work and provided abundantly for their physical needs.[21] Her sober and beneficent demeanor attracted many women and even men whose hearts were faithful.[22] As the holy woman's fame spread, even more men and women hastened to her, not only from neighboring provinces but even from across the seas, leaving parents and fatherland with love's strongest desire. And with pious affection, God's servant Bertilla received them all as a mother to her darling little ones and cared for them lovingly, instructing them with holy lessons to live justly and piously that they might be pleasing to Christ the King.

6. Now, through her continence and fullest love, blessed Bertilla was an example and model of piety to all. She carefully taught religious customs to her subjects not only through holy speech but even more through her own sanctity, so that they might love one another in charitable affection and behave purely, soberly and chastely in all things and be ever ready for offices and prayers and to take care of guests and the poor with fond concern and to love their neighbors. Through holy communion, she drew the monastic household and its near neighbors to do the penance given for their sins in confession.[23] Thus she gained the improvement of many and gained much

21. Caesarius, *Recapitulatio regulae ad virgines*, 10.
22. Ibid., c. 6.
23. Mabillon's edition, *ASOSB*, saeculum 3, 1, 60, no. 80, omits "per sanctam communionem." Levison notes a discussion of this pastoral work by Malnory, *Quid Luxorienses monachi*, 75. Confessional practices were particularly associated with Irish discipline. Donatus, c. 23, recommends it at

profit for their souls and rewards for herself. Christ's servant Bertilla had the highest devotion and diligence for the adornment of churches and altars for Christ. She ordered her priests daily to offer their sacred hosts to God for the salvation of the souls of the faithful and the right state of God's Holy Church. She was always assiduous in vigils and prayers and abstinence from food and above all it was wonderful how little she drank. And in constancy of faith, she kept her unswerving mind always on the Lord Jesus Christ. And when she carried out these and other most honest customs, her holy example was edifying to the Christianity of her brothers and sisters; meanwhile paupers and pilgrims were comforted by her munificent largesse. Through her, the Lord collected such great fruits for the salvation of souls that even from over the seas, the faithful kings of the Saxons, through trusted messengers, asked her to send some of her disciples for the learning and holy instruction they heard were wonderful in her, that they might build convents of men and nuns in their land.[24] She did not deny these religious requests which would speed the salvation of souls. In a thankful spirit, taking counsel with her elders and heeding her brothers' exhortations, with great diligence and the protection of the saints,[25] she sent many volumes of books to them. That the harvest of souls in that nation might increase through her and be multiplied by God's grace, she sent chosen women and devout men.[26] And we trust that this has been fulfilled to the praise of God and Lady Bertilla.

7. Meanwhile the glorious servant of God, Queen Balthild, who had been bound to government service and the care of the affairs of the principality, felt love of Christ and devotion to religion possess her mind, even as she labored under the heavy burden. With the consent of his optimates, she abandoned care of the royal palace to her adult son Lord Clothar and enlisted as a soldier of the Lord Christ in the monastery which she had built. There, as we wrote above, she submitted herself in obedience to the abbess Lady Bertilla.[27] Received by her and by the whole flock of holy maidens, with great veneration, as was right and proper, she determined to remain in holy religion even

---

every hour of every day, "nothing to be hidden from the spiritual mother." At the Council of Chalons-sur-Saone (October 24, 647), Irish representations secured the adoption of the auricular confession in the Frankish church. The confessional role of the abbess suggests that the practice did not at that time have a settled sacramental function.

24. Balthild was English and interested in the fate of her countrywomen, see chapter 14. The training of young women at Chelles to rule new English houses is confirmed by Bede, *HE*, 3:8, in his account of Hereswith, mother of the East Anglian king. Bede also notes (4:23) that Hilda, foundress of Whitby, was diverted from her original plan to follow the same route.

25. *Patrocinio* is read as *relics* in *AS*, November 5, 93, n. 4.

26. *Personas* and *homines*: the difference in gender could be no more than a grammatical accident.

27. This biographer slides gracefully over the difficulties associated with Balthild's retreat into Chelles.

to her dying day. By common counsel and dual example of sanctity, [the two women] adorned the conventual buildings and offices. They shone like two of the brightest lights placed on a candlestick for the clear edification of many. By apostolic custom, through the grace of the Holy Spirit, they were one heart and one soul, and their minds were always ready to act for the good.[28] It was wonderful what delight and charity there was between them all their days. They mutually exhorted one another, that their rewards might increase in abundance. And after Lady Balthild the Queen had completed her devotions in all ways and migrated in peace to Christ, her body was placed with honors in the grave.[29] Then the servant of Christ, Lady Bertilla, a few of whose many deeds we here commemorate, continued to occupy her office according to God, working in this convent while forty six years ran their cycle. More and more, she grew in good works and progressed from strength to strength even to the day of her perfect death.

8. Blessed Bertilla would gladly have bowed her neck to gratify her great desire for martyrdom, had there been a skilled executioner ready for the task. But we believe that even though that passion was not fulfilled, yet she completed her martyrdom through mortification of her own body and blood.[30] For when she had reached an advanced age, she drove her weary and senescent members to spiritual service. She did not follow the common custom and modify her life in old age or seek for better diet. As she had begun, she went on ever more strongly never taking enough of anything but barely sustaining her aged body, lest she might weaken from within. She indulged in a modicum of food and drink to force her weakening limbs into their nightly vigils. You yourselves have seen the many admirable deeds she performed which you will remember in full. So it is fitting that we proclaim them, though with our poor little words we could never tell you how much she loved you. And when Divine Piety had determined to reward her for so many merits, her body was stricken with a slight illness and she lay feverish on her cot. So confined to her bed of sickness, she strove to give thanks to God in psalms, hymns, and spiritual canticles admonishing those standing by to sing to God. Without being too much troubled by bodily illness, she happily scaled the heights of beatitude, with eyes raised up and holy hands stretched to heaven. The soul so dear to God was torn from the world and released in Heaven, living with Christ while the angels applauded. Then there was sorrow in the whole convent among Christ's servants. What a multitude of mourning brethren arrived immediately, their lamenting voices choked up

28. An echo of Caesarius, *Regula*, 18.

29. This was in 680.

30. The *AS* supplies references to similar attitudes in the *Vita S. Albini*, 18:50, and Sulpicius Severus, *Epistolae*, 3:14.

with welling tears! It is impossible for us to tell and only those who were there in person will believe what happened. Plangent sounds reverberated, as though thunder struck the place. Nothing could be heard among the bitter sighs except everyone clamoring: "Pious nurse, noble mother! Why do you desert us and why do you leave us behind whom you have nurtured so long a time with sweet and maternal affection? Why make us derelict today, orphaned and pitiable? In your death, all of us have died too." For three days, these and similar complaints went on without intermission. On the fourth day, with fitting honors, they conducted her blessed little body, anointed with balsam, to the grave. There by the Lord's grace, for the salvation of human kind, she proved worthy to perform many miracles. Daily the prayers of the faithful are heard demanding her intercession and a variety of illnesses and infirmities are cured.

9. Therefore, for the edification of the faithful, we have been pleased to write here a few of the many deeds in the life of the servant of God, Bertilla of blessed memory. Then anyone who likes may carefully consider and imitate, as in a clear mirror, those examples of virtue, particularly humility which is the mother of virtues and the fullest loving charity, the sharpest abstinence and the prudence of astute counsel and fortitude of faith and piety of generous mercy and, the reward of integrity, holy modesty of virginity with most devout insistence on prayer and wondrous peace and fervor of holy zeal which far surpasses every beauty. Almighty God chose whatever might be pleasing from these most brilliant gems to adorn the spirit of his servant Bertilla. As He well might, He desired to conserve her, with Christ presiding, to be a participant in the rewards of the just. For this evangelical virgin of Christ could claim a hundred-fold reward and life eternal. We have no doubt that she has achieved eternal life associated in eternal glory for her holy and splendid labors. She ran first in the race with the help of Christ and happily finished it and received the reward of the crown of eternal life in the flock of the just where she remains from everlasting to everlasting. Amen.

16

Anstrude, Abbess of Laon

(ca. 645, d. before 709)

Anstrude was the daughter of Saint Sadalberga and succeeded her mother as abbess of her convent in Laon. She entered the community around 657 to avoid marriage with a suitor named Landramnus. The beginning of her life as a religious therefore coincided with Grimoald's attempt to secure the kingship of Austrasia for his son by sending the Merovingian heir, Dagobert II, into Ireland. In 661 Grimoald was defeated by Ebroin, Balthild's mayor of the palace.[1] As we have seen, her son Childeric and Himnechild's daughter Bilichild then took the throne of Austrasia.

Sadalberga died about 670, and Anstrude succeeded her as abbess just as the death of Balthild's son, Clothar III, precipitated a new power struggle between Neustria and Austrasia. Ebroin's attempt to place Balthild's third son, Theuderic, on the Neustrian throne was frustrated by the Austrasians, and Ebroin was exiled to Luxeuil. Childeric and his wife moved to Neustria, leaving Austrasia to her mother's government. They installed the Austrasian Wulfold, who may be the relative of Anstrude mentioned in her biography, as

---

Vita Anstrudis abbatissae Laudunensis, in Levison, ed., MGH, SRM 6:64–78. Krusch, in his edition of the Life of Sadalberga, denies that Anstrude was the saint's daughter and condemns her vita as worthless. Levison, however, readily concedes that Anstrude was believed to be Sadalberga's daughter and does not challenge the basic outlines of her story. He argues that the text he edited was based upon an older one written by someone in the convent, as indicated by references to "this city" in c. 4, 9, 15 and direct references to the sisters in c. 3 and 10. He thinks that it had been expanded and "improved" by a ninth-century hagiographer, based on a style found in the introduction that Levison connects to Carolingian chanting and to the final miracle which, he argues, was far removed in time from the rest. He suspects that the historical content could have been drawn from other chronicles to defend the monastery's privileges against Carolingian bishops. However, where we have been able to compare ninth-century hagiographical texts with their Merovingian sources, we have found that the later writers do not tamper with factual data so much as empurple the prose and embellish it with edifying texts from scripture. We have no particular reason to suppose that Merovingian bishops were less likely to threaten monastic privileges than Carolingian ones.

1. For an overview of Ebroin's career, see Fischer, Der Hausmeier Ebroin.

mayor of the palace in Neustria. He barely escaped with his life when Childeric and Bilichild were killed in an ambush, probably arranged by Ebroin and his fellow exile Leodegar of Autun.[2]

Anstrude's story unfolds in the context of the subsequent violence. Although it may seem excessively lurid to us, there is nothing in it that would outrage the credulity of her seventh-century contemporaries. Childeric's death opened the way for Theuderic to succeed to all the Merovingian kingdoms. It also gave the exiled Ebroin his opportunity to escape from Luxeuil, renounce his tonsure, and regain his lost power. The sinuous course of Ebroin's plots and counterplots made it almost impossible for any noble to avoid a charge of treason at one turn or another. Anstrude had brothers and sisters active in the outside world, and the story suggests that at least one of them was involved in some political turmoil. She was related to the influential Wulfold and through him to Gertrude of Nivelles and the family of Pippin.

Ebroin first attempted to support one of Clothar III's children as king of Austrasia and subsequently abandoned him when Theuderic offered him a favorable alliance. Meanwhile, Himnechild discovered that her long-lost son, Dagobert II, whom Grimoald had exiled in Ireland, was still alive. She secured the help of Wilfred, archbishop of York, in bringing him home to Austrasia.[3] Wilfred's English biographer blamed the "Jezebel," Balthild, for the deaths of various bishops in the subsequent struggle. In this tangled conflict of loyalties, Ansegisus, the son of Gertrude's sister Begga, was murdered by an adoptive son (or godson) who was a partisan of Ebroin. He, in turn, was murdered by Pippin, who, with his adoptive brother Martin, had succeeded Wulfold as mayor of the palace in Austrasia under Dagobert II in 676.[4] That year, Ebroin turned on his old political partner, Balthild's friend Leodegar of Autun, besieged him in his cathedral city, and killed him.[5] In 677, the war foretold in the life of Sadalberga broke out in the area of Langres.[6] The Neustrian forces headed by Ebroin defeated Pippin and Martin, who fled into refuge in Laon.[7]

---

2. LHF, 45.

3. Eddius Stephanus, *Life of Saint Wilfrid*, 25, 33. Ebroin tried Wilfred for assisting the defeated Dagobert. He claimed that the young king "laid waste our cities, spurned the advice of our elders, acted like Solomon's Rehoboam in imposing tribute on his people, and despised the church of God and her rulers." Wilfred was in Frankland because of yet another political involvement in his native Northumbria. Queen Etheldreda made the preservation of her virginity a condition of her marriage with King Egbert. After some time, the king tried to break the promise, and Wilfred helped the queen flee to her aunt's convent at Coldingham, where she took the veil. Bede, HE, 4:19.

4. LHF, 46.

5. DACL, Saint Leger.

6. See chapter 10.

7. Huguenin, *Histoire de royaume*, 460–64, believes that Anstrude was not only instrumental in sheltering the Carolingians but also urged the citizens to defy Ebroin.

There is more than enough skullduggery in this history to involve a noble clergyman from Laon in a tale of foresworn safe conducts and murder. Ebroin or one of his agents may well have been the instrument of the murder of Anstrude's brother Baldwin, or some other enemy may have seized the opportunity offered by the turbulence of the time. Anstrude's relative, the mayor of the palace, Martin, was enticed from the safety of Laon by bishops acting as agents of Ebroin. His safe conduct was ignored, and he was murdered. Anstrude's confrontation with Ebroin would then have occurred somewhere between his defeat of Martin and Pippin in 677 and his own murder in 681. The dramatic scene of their reconciliation in the chapel may reflect the reconciliation of Pippin and Theuderic around 679. Pippin once more became Austrasian mayor of the palace. He settled the widow and daughters of the dead Dagobert II on various estates and eventually they entered religion, founding a pair of female establishments near Trier, an area popular with Pippin's family since the days of Glodesind. According to later legends, Pippin's own daughter, Hadeloga, fled from an intended marriage to live in the forest in that neighborhood until her father relented and gave her an endowed monastery at Kitzingen.[8]

Here Begins the Life of the Holy and Blessed Anstrude, Virgin of Our Lord Jesus Christ

■

1. Baso was a noble man in this world, who lived in the time of King Dagobert. He sprang from a stock which was noble by nature and through grace his behavior became nobler still. On the advice of some Frankish nobles, he took to wife Sadalberga, the religious daughter of the high-born and religious man Gunduin.[9] After a barren period, she bore her spouse an elite troop of children including a daughter named Anstrude.[10] She was carefully nurtured by her parents and brought to the Christian religion with much diligence, learning her letters in the days of her tender childhood. The newborn virgin went from strength to strength, beyond the capacities of her girlish age. As soon as she ceased being rocked in her cradle, she learned to sing the praises of the Virgin's Son. Through divine clemency, she exercised her capacious memory for reading and listening, training herself in the mastery of learning. She possessed carnal distinctions by birth, but she became

8. For Hadeloga, see AS, February 2.

9. Sadalberga's biographer ascribed their marriage to the king's order rather than the advice of the nobles.

10. Electam turmam (crack troops) is a military term popular with the ninth-century hagiographers of Remiremont. Folz, "Remiremont," 20, n. 49.

more distinguished still for her holy mind. Precious was the sight of her face, but more precious still her heart and it became clear to the world that she was filled with eloquence and, more important, wisdom. Beloved of God and man, she grappled the anchor of her will to virtue. Above all, she was so full of grace that the ways of her maturity could be discerned in her first years.

2. When she was in her twelfth year, a certain noble lad of noble parentage, Landramnus, asked for her hand. He brought much gold with him and gems and clothing which he gave into the hands of her parents that he might gain the virgin Anstrude for his wife.[11] But it was to prove vain, and vain to promise more, for she had given herself as a spouse to God. The virgin refused, rejecting perishable wealth and transitory nuptials. Her mind dwelt not on a marriage bed but on the gospel. Fortified by the walls of her virginity, she spurned a husband with a dower of worldly wealth. And happily, Landramnus was seduced into the fields of chastity where he thought he might espouse the virgin now espoused to Christ. For the earthly suitor's eye had not seen the ring of faith sent to the virgin by her heavenly spouse. What more? Finally she had to speak about him in his presence to some girls destined for her service: "Did you really say that this person was to be my husband? Mark my words, I will never be joined to a carnal spouse under the law of marriage." So saying, burning with ardor for her heavenly spouse, she abandoned the temporal attachments of this world with all her heart and soul to join the chorus of the clergy singing psalms in the church.

3. And when this daughter of the nobility was thus enlisted for God, the clerical order rejoiced. Carrying lighted candles and carrying crosses in their hands, the priests at her offering gave praise to God for all the virtues that they knew to be in the virgin Anstrude. Thus with great devotion she followed the singing clerks even to the monastery wherein Sadalberga, the holy mother of a holy maid, piously commanded a troop of nuns. For that holy virgin, guided by God, was not overwhelmed by the sapphires of vice nor deceived by precious colored gems on which worldly women set their ambitions. Avarice, which seduces faith and honesty and good arts in greedy minds, never ruled her. Behold how the prudent virgin, a careful sailor avoiding the shipwreck of the world by flight among earthly tempests, the habitation of her breast wisely preserved by God, is now cherished. For there is no greater wealth than to be poor in Christ. The possession of wealth is not praiseworthy in the church but rather we despise it for Christ's sake. For the virgin who

11. Her earliest education was attributed to her *progenitores*, whereas the plan for her marriage is ascribed to *parentum*. According to the life of Sadalberga, c. 2, both her parents had entered the monastic life at some point after the birth of their children. This text suggests that Anstrude was not living with her mother. "Parents" may therefore refer to some other kinfolk.

spurned worldly pomp had filled her vessel with oil. So, dearest sisters, the lamp of the glorious Anstrude was never extinguished because, as you have heard, she was remote from worldly pomp. So it will be sweeter for you to pursue the glory that follows victory with this virgin than suffer the ignominy that follows fleshly ruin without her.

4. Meanwhile, the venerable abbess Sadalberga, feeling her body's dissolution to be near, committed her pastoral care to her daughter Anstrude, who had been consecrated to God after her flight from marriage. She bade her have a care for Christ's sheepfold. So she was consecrated abbess under royal license and episcopal benediction, by advice of the provincial bishop and the consent of the nobles who ruled the province, and the agreement and election and acclamation of the sisters then gathered in the place.[12] She was around twenty years old when she took Christ's flock under her care.[13] She considered God in all things for neither by day or night was she far out of communion with divine mandates. Oh virgin so replete with the grace of God! She wished to be more beautiful in faith than in face, more powerful in chastity than elegant of body. She was attentive to fasts and devoted to prayer, sedulous in vigils, assiduous in sobriety, ecclesiastical in manner, generous in alms-giving, most joyful in giving away her goods, most gentle to her flock and mild in speech. She proved to be humble and pious to her subjects and hospitable to guests. Her doors were open to the needy and to pilgrims. She took care of those who were confined to prison or held in chains. She was untiring in her mercy for widows and orphans, wards and paupers, expending offerings of food to the hungry, drink to the thirsty, consolation to the bereaved, cheer to the sorrowful, visiting the sick, calming the angry, restoring disputants to peace, and finally burying the dead. And her good works spread her fame among the kings of Francia and the great ones of the land and her name was great with honor for love of God. But she took no credit for goodness to herself; she attributed it all to God for she so clung to Him that all her demeanor, in word, look and walk, seemed to be a lesson in virtue.

5. But in this world, there is never an absence of depraved perfidy to test the patience of the good. It is ever the part of evil to attack the pious party, whence Cain struck his brother in the throat with a hoe. While the blessed virgin Anstrude strove to spend all the days of her life praising God, the enemy of human kind secretly made arrows of sorrow for her. For her

---

12. Laon is on the border between the kingdoms then ruled by Balthild's elder son, Clothar III (Neustria) and her second son, Childeric II (Austrasia). The community numbered about three hundred women according to the Life of Sadalberga.

13. Anstrude would have entered the convent around 657, when she was twelve. Sadalberga died about 670, so presumably the new abbess was then about twenty-five.

brother Baldwin was most dear to her. People who posed as friends and followers of the virgin and her brother, instigated by the Devil, conceived and carried out evil against him. Rare indeed is good faith among men of whom it is written: "Hypocrites at heart heap up wrath."[14] For when a servant of Satan, sick with envy, called Baldwin to an assembly at a villa in the province of Laon, his sister's most tenderly beloved answered, in the simplicity of his heart. He took but two riders with him and, for pleading the case, he went at once as the third to his cruelest enemies, the wickedest of all the men who ever lived on earth. Deceived by a peace made under false colors, he was stabbed with their swords. Thus do the impious appear at the murder of the just, seeming to be their friends. But we would not injure their name and lineage by setting them down here.[15]

6. When news of her brother's death came to the sister's ears, she blessed the name of the Lord through bitter tears, like guileless Job when he had lost his numerous children. "With the heart man believeth unto righteousness and with the mouth confession is made unto salvation."[16] Knowing how fragile is the state of the human condition, she said: "Though I may be desolate today and bereft of my brother, still I gave many thanks to You, God, and render praise and honor to Your Majesty. Most pious Christ, I beseech that I will not feel the wrath of Your judgment and that You will not turn away the face of Your mercy from my tearful eyes. But grant me strength to bear up patiently and to regret the untimely bitterness in my disordered heart which suddenly swept over me for the loss of my murdered brother. I praise and glorify and bless the name of Your glory which is holy, that You have taken away the brother that You gave to me." And again, she said, "Alas for me, innocent brother, that I sent you off at the advice of those cruelest men! Oh, would that case had never been brought to court, that I persuaded you to attend! Oh, brutal murder! You were the staff of my weakness!" And, because fraternal love knows no bounds, she broke out again weeping: "Now may those who have brothers in the flesh be mindful of mercy and have compassion on my sorrowful tears. Let them not condemn my weeping but be moved to pity by my cries while I mourn my brother bitterly. He alone

14. Job 36:13.

15. Levison, the editor of the Latin edition suspects (65) that the [Carolingian] author omitted the names out of ignorance, but it may have been simple discretion if the murderers were attached to the Carolingian family. Krusch, *Vita Sadalbergae*, 45, who questions Baldwin's existence, conceded that his name appears in the psalter of Emma, tenth-century queen of England, which suggests some connection between the young man and the party of Dagobert II, who returned from his English exile at this time. This would also connect with our speculation that his father had some connection to this incident.

16. Romans 10:10.

remained to me and this day I have lost him. Oh, God, be merciful to me. Be my keeper and my comforter."

7. After these tears and complaints, though her brother's suffering still troubled her heart, she presented a reasonably calm and manly face. For her sorrow was tempered by the sweetness of the Holy Spirit who rested in her. The congregation of nuns, seeing and hearing of the abbess's sad misfortune, beat their breasts, not without tears, for the sister's mourning and the murdered brother's martyrdom. Groaning prostrate on the pavement, each one showed how she sorrowed with the sorrowing and wept with the weeping. Thus it is written: "Whether one member suffers, all the members suffer with it."[17]

8. The abbess was greatly moved by her sisters' sighs, as they lay prostrate with pity on the ground, writhing about on the pavement in uncontrollable grief. With other people's hands holding her up, she came to them. For she could not walk steadily, fatigued as she was with weeping and wailing. Standing before the altar, barely imposing silence with her raised hands, her voice restraining her tears, she said: "Listen to me, most beloved sisters and daughters. Don't cry out so, with such misery and harsh clamoring. Only keep in memory how sweetly and steadily my brother, who was so unjustly murdered today, loved all of you. For you all know what a wealth of true love he had for you and how he sought to enrich you and procure your well-being. I pray you, despite my own pain at the loss of my brother, that you will remember his soul in your prayers so his cruelly slaughtered soul may possess the joy of Paradise."

9. Thereafter she went out with her sisters and took comfort, for the quality of her strength was more of the manly than the feminine kind. No sooner had the holy virgin ended her weeping when, standing on the peak of Laon's rock, she suddenly saw the bier in which her brother's body was enclosed. It is written: "Love will never be idle; if it exists it does great things."[18] Directing her glance to the murdered one, she said: "Now, now you come back to me dearest brother. Yesterday you were alive, today slaughtered. Yesterday, I sent you out unhurt; today I receive you back for burial. Brother, brother, best loved of my soul! Why was your life torn away by such unworthy men when you were so young? Yet though your killers bring you to me, I reckon to be more joyful than sorrowful at your murder. For it is surely better that you have lost your life while still innocent. You have only forfeited dishonor and flight and exile and indigence and the dangers of this world and all else that can sweep over mortals. Called to that court, you made but a third with two

17. 1 Corinthians 12:26.
18. Gregory the Great, *Homilies in Evangelium* 30, 2, PL 76:1221.

others. Now you return with your many friends grieving for you. Because you were simple and innocent of fraud and you believed in the deceitful friendship of your enemies, you have left me, your sister, alone." And who is there with breast so steely that would not be moved to compassion for the virgin at her brother's murder? But no one can tell in detail how much lamentation and sorrow there was in the city of Laon for many days, not only among those for whom the man had been teacher and pastor, but even among the towns-people. But the most blessed virgin, who understood that everything in this world is transitory, armed herself with the shield of patience. For in the midst of prosperity, she had learned to be humble and steady in adversity and therefore, like choice myrrh, she gave a sweet fragrance to Christ.

10. Nor is it wonderful, dearest sisters, that such a man should be killed by limbs of Satan, as you have heard, for you must understand that this martyr was a limb of Him Who was crucified by the zeal of the Pharisees for the salvation of the world. For from ancient times, the envious have always persecuted the virtuous.[19] Maybe these things happen so that God, the font of piety, may mercifully receive those whom the world has beaten down. For those who displease the world always please God. The afflictions of the elect are but temporary in this world and they bring rewards in celestial glory while peace of mind never lasts in this world. Therefore, it was not without reason that the Apostle Paul forbade mourning for the dead, relegating sorrow to those who have no hope of resurrection. He who has left his body is not dead but sleeping and in Holy Scripture it is called a dream. For the substance of human corporeality is not consumed but it will be reconstituted through the glory of resurrection in eternity perpetually through Him Who destroyed death by His death. So we conclude that he who was killed for Christ will die happily as a conqueror. For that man is safe ruling with Christ: "He was taken away lest that wickedness should alter his understanding."[20]

11. Meanwhile, the killers of such a man, who were hateful to God, did not cease trying to injure God's handmaid Anstrude, using all their evil fraud and clever depravity against her. For making light of the just man's blood which they had shed, filled with malicious rage, they went to Ebroin, Mayor of the Palace, who was at that time wealthy and most powerful in all King Theuderic's counsels.[21] Accusing the innocent virgin, by pouring false testimony into that prince's ears, they moved his power to anger and persuaded him to

19. To reinforce the topos, Levison cites Jerome, *Epistola* 108, 18, itself drawn from Horace, *Carmina*, 2:10, 11.

20. Wisdom 4:11. Levison, *Vita Anstrudis*, breaks off his text here, claiming that "the paragraph goes on in the same vein."

21. In 674, the succession of Theuderic to Austrasia as well as Neustria was challenged by the returning son of Childeric and Himnechild, Dagobert II.

act against her by depriving the consecrated abbess of her power to rule souls and driving her from her monastery. So it is written: "Evil communications corrupt good manners."[22] The heart of the earthly prince was kindled with wrath against the gentle virgin.

12. Now it happened by chance rather than design that King Theuderic entered the city in arms and Ebroin came with his army.[23] Calling the accused virgin to mind and desiring to serve Theuderic rather than God, Ebroin went to the convent of maidens. Not as one desiring good will but rather as a rapacious wolf seeking to scatter Christ's sheep, he ordered the nuns' spiritual mother into exile. In fact, no sooner did the raging man look into the Abbess's maidenly face than he began to abuse her most harshly. But God's renowned handmaid, with mild and humble heart, returned a few soft words patiently showing herself unafraid of the proud tyrant's threats and rash insults.

13. With Ebroin speaking evil and threatening worse, a certain well-intentioned man named Agilbert approached some of the sisters of mature age and good life.[24] He said to them: "Handmaids of God, act manfully and seek comfort in the Lord. Cry out all together, unanimously in one voice, upon the majesty of the Lord, urging Him that none may separate you today from your spiritual mother." Then the cohort of nuns, with repeated prayers, exhorted God Almighty that He might tear His Abbess from the hands of the enemy and the power of the adversary. And when Ebroin's satellites and companions heard the chanting nuns, they were seized with excessive fear. Raising their gaze to the towers of the church, they saw a globe of fire rising even unto Heaven. Trembling uncontrollably, they quickly revealed this sign to Ebroin and hearing of it he was excessively terrified. Hastily he transformed his ferocity into the smoothest manner. Throwing himself humbly at the feet of the spiritual mother, he asked her forgiveness with a devout spirit. He vowed that he would heap up honors for the rest of his life in veneration of God's handmaid and promised to devote himself in faith and friendship to the service of their convent. Thus he, who had been an enemy of God's beloved virgin, returned to the palace as a friend of religion.

14. Several days later, a certain man named Cariveus, instigated by the Devil, shamelessly began to contend against God's handmaid Anstrude.[25] Full of

22. I Corinthians 12:16.

23. Pippin of Herstal and his brother Martin took refuge in Laon about 680. Martin went to Ebroin on a safe conduct borne by Agilbert and Reolus, bishop of Reims. He and his companions were killed treacherously. LHF, 46; Fredegar's continuator, 8.

24. Levison, *Vita Anstrudis*, 72, n. 1, notes that this man is mentioned in 677 in a charter of Theuderic III as his referendary. See MGH, *Diplomata,* 55.

25. Ebling, *Prosopographie,* 102.

evil, he chased her into the church of Saint Mary Ever Virgin and even drew his sword from its sheath to kill her. Standing valiantly against the horn of the altar, arms outstretched, the Lord's virgin prayed confidently to God. Then the impious persecutor saw how she despised his threats with firm faith and did not dare come nearer to her. Fearing divine judgment, he reversed himself and humbly begged her indulgence, prostrate upon the ground. And seeing him thus beg favor and forgiveness, the Lord's handmaid was immediately moved by mercy and kindly pardoned him for all her injury. For she was mindful of the Lord's saying: "Forgive and ye shall be forgiven."[26] Still, Cariveus came to the end of his life in a few days and was buried in that same place where he had attacked the handmaid of God. The most blessed one permitted it for, according to Apostolic teaching, she did not return evil for evil but prepared his burial place with great care.

15. Two years later, a certain young man named Ebroard entered the citadel of Laon with his accomplices in the night and angrily set the greater part of the town on fire because he desired to spill the blood of his neighbor Giselard.[27] Knowing that Ebroard had come for that purpose and seeing the city in flames, Giselard doubted that he could survive for the space of another hour. He fled as fast as he could and thus escaped his enemy. For a long time, Ebroard sought the fugitives without finding their hiding place. Wrathfully, he hurried to the lady Anstrude and began to revile her harshly saying she was his enemy and had befriended those who despised his lordship. Ferociously, he ordered her: "Bring me all the keys to this monastery." Quickly, to calm his madness, Christ's virgin ordered them to be brought. But the Highest Judge gave a nod and at the dawn of the very day after he had taken her keys, right before the monastery gates, the intruder met the cruel death he deserved. Witnessing this, God's handmaid took back the monastery keys and kindly brought his miserable little corpse to burial, thus obeying the precepts of the Lord, who said: "Be ye merciful, as your Father is also merciful."[28] And again, "Do good to them that hate you."[29]

16. In princely Pippin's time, Madelgar, who was pontiff of Laon, wished to usurp blessed Anstrude's convent from her.[30] In no way bending to the Prelate's will, the handmaid of God prudently denied him so that a great altercation rose between them. Not having the strength to bear such conten-

---

26. Luke 6:37.

27. Levison, *Vita Anstrudis*, 72, n. 3; Giselard signed a charter from Laon in 666/7.

28. Luke 6:36.

29. Matthew 5:44.

30. His name is the same as Waldetrude's husband, but we can find no relationship. Here he is called pontiff; the word *antistes*, which we have usually translated in that way, does not appear in these later lives.

tion, God's virgin wisely sent word to Pippin of the bishop's cupidity through her relative Wulfold.[31] Pippin received the holy virgin's delegation with honors and directed his son Grimoald to go respectfully to Laon with instructions to see that Bishop Madelgar caused God's beloved virgin no anxiety.[32] Is it any wonder that God snatched her quickly from this tribulation when she had relinquished her own will and the cares of the flesh in this world and had no desire but to see the living God?

17. Except on solemn feast days—that is, the Lord's nativity, Easter day and Sundays—she took neither food nor drink until she had chanted the offices of the psalter with hymns and spiritual canticles to the Lord. Nor was she wont to be refreshed except at the hours of nones or vespers. In the nocturnal hours, she exercised herself with so many vigils and psalms that it would take too long to tell of it. Indeed she chose the last place for herself, behind the church door, where she placed a little chair to sit and rest a little when she had completed the offices for each of the hours. For sometime before, she had given up the last cover of her bed. At daybreak she would quickly stand up and make the rounds of the churches asking help from the saints as her assistants. Then with every pious care she would visit the cells of the infirm. She made every effort to subject herself to all the Lord's precepts so that in no moment of any hour might she be found without some divine work.

18. Now we must not leave out the first marvel the lord deigned to perform through her. When a certain woman in the household lost the light of her eyes, the chosen virgin appeared to her in a vision.[33] She said: "How are you doing, sister?" And she answered "Well, lady. But I pray you will be merciful to me, sinner that I am." And she said to her, "I may return here next Sunday to gratify you." And immediately she receded. When Sunday came, at the hour of sext, the aforementioned Sister Chramnegundis asked to be led by the hand to the blessed Anstrude. She met her on the threshold and said to her: "I beseech you, lady, to lay your hands upon my eyes." Considering herself unworthy, Anstrude began stoutly to refuse but the blind woman clamored more and more saying: "I swear I will not go from here until you

---

31. Madelgar was bishop of Laon in 692, when he signed a charter cited by Levison, *Vita Anstrudis*, 73, n. 1. Wulfold was a count in the territory of Verdun who built the monastery of Saint Michael. Ibid., n. 2. We cannot be certain whether he is the same person, or related to the person, who was mayor of the palace under Childeric. Ebling, *Prosopographie*, 243–46, discusses him in some detail, but his genealogical chart does not include Anstrude.

32. Grimoald II was mayor of the palace from 697 to 743. Levison, *Vita Anstrudis*, 73, n. 4, notes that Mabillon added to her second vita: "thereafter the bishops of Laon had no power over the nuns except to give the abbess his blessing after her election."

33. Considering that Anstrude was still alive and reluctant to attempt the cure, the "electissima virgo" of the vision may be Mary.

touch me and restore my sight." And, hearing this, God's virgin began to weep saying naught but raising her eyes to Heaven. She placed her right hand on the sister's eyes and immediately all their original light was restored.

19. Another time, a certain handmaid of God named Adalsinda could not even raise her head, it had been aching so long. God's virgin Anstrude came to her for a visit and placed her hand with the sign of the cross on her head and at once all the pain vanished.

20. And, on another day, Lady Anstrude, through the Lord, raised a certain handmaid of God named Scholastica from the sleep of death, though she had been counted dead because no breath came from her mouth or nostrils. This and much else the Lord deigned to do through the hands of his maiden while she lived.

21. As the day of her soul's departure drew near, she called her troop of sisters and indicated that the day of her death was swiftly approaching. She forgave each of them and asked that they forgive her. Then two days before she migrated to the Lord, Whom her soul loved, an immense brilliance shone around that house in which Christ's virgin lay exhausted. And from it, a brightness like a shining star lay on her breast and entered into her mouth. In that same hour when her sainted soul left her body, like a snow white dove, it issued from her mouth, which all bystanders saw, and flew to heaven.[34]

22. And when her body, composed according to custom, was brought to burial, the people at the gates wept bitterly. And behold, two birds, gleaming with ineffable splendor, flew from the secret places on high and sat on the roof of the house until the holy body was carried away with all tenderness. And when the holy body had been carried on its bier to the basilica of Saint John, a certain sister who had a wound under the armpit came up to the bier. With all reverence, she placed the saint's hand on her wound and it was immediately cured as though nothing had ever been amiss.

23. And the day after the holy body was laid in the tomb, a certain woman filled with a demon who came quickly to the tomb was cured.

24. After that, a certain paralytic woman who was consecrated to God lay there. Falling into sleep, she saw Christ's servant Anstrude standing before her bed, throwing a cloak she had been wont to wear over her. Immediately she rose up from her sleep, all her limbs restored. And she walked unhurt before the gaze of all the sisters.

25. A prisoner in bonds who was being led to execution saw all his hope fading. "Woe is me," he said, "woe is me, poor thing. Lady Anstrude, in other days when you were alive you might have set me free. Now I go to my death and you are already dead. You can no longer help me." Immediately on these

---

34. Levison, *Vita Anstrudis*, 75, n. 1, dates her death on October 17, prior to 709. He refers to similar miracles in Gregory the Great; see *Dialogue*, 4:10, and the *Vita Solemnis*, 11.

words, the rope was torn from his hands and the prisoner, with no one following him, fled through the opened doors, escaped and ran swiftly to the virgin's sepulchre.

26. At the same time, a certain sister who had lost the sight of her eyes lay on the holy virgin's sepulchre and prayed. At some point, she fell asleep and woke with her lost light regained.[35]

27. Then a girl named Helena, both blind and mute, was led by her sisters' hands to that same holy sepulchre. With her help, in a single night, she received the light of her eyes and the speech of her tongue so that it seemed she had never had a care.

28. Now let us recall to mind that sister Oda, Duke Gautsuin's daughter, was gravely harassed by demons from infancy. With such an infirmity she had received a nun's habit and for fifteen years as a *monacha* suffered from that affliction in the monastery at Laon. One Saturday, as dawn was breaking, it seemed as though Anstrude's voice came to her asking her to arm herself strongly with the sign of the cross and get up from her bed with all haste and hurry to the virgin's sepulchre where she should bite the stone three times.[36] Hearing this admonition twice, she did not dare to rise for she was terribly afraid. But the third time the voice scolded her saying: "Why do you doubt, girl? Rise up quickly! Do not be afraid or fall into dread but go to my sepulchre and I will go with you. Bite that stone three times and you will be healed." Rising quickly, she went to the sepulchre and, lo, the church doors which were usually firmly closed and locked with keys at that hour stood wide open. Going in, she prostrated herself and bit the stone three times as she had been bidden. Then she was immediately cast into the sweetest sleep and she heard the voice of Saint Anstrude as she had first spoken to her saying: "Rise up, daughter, for now you are healed of this infirmity which has afflicted you since infancy." And, made whole, she walked with great joy among the other virgins.

29. And another of the sisters suffered severely from a flow of blood. In her sleep, she saw a certain *monacha* admonishing her that she should take no other medicine but dust scraped from the holy virgin's sepulchre and drunk in warm wine. Waking, she carried out the order and in that moment the flow of blood was cured.[37]

---

35. In this life, all the miracles at the tomb are performed for the benefit of women, very likely women who were sisters in the monastery. In some cases, the women appear to be in the monastery because of chronic disabilities, which suggests that the institution may have been used as a nursing home, even excluding the possibilities of miracles.

36. The text actually says "in Trinity."

37. Van Dam, *Leadership and Community*, 275, notes the frequent use of dust as an agent of healing and suggests that it reinforces the faith of the receiver in the miraculous qualities of the body within the tomb, itself in the process of turning to dust.

30. Then that maiden whom Anstrude raised up, as we told above, was tormented by being seized with a demon.[38] Catching her, they placed the possessed one on the holy virgin's tomb. There she sank into sleep and was cleansed of the demon and went out with all her limbs free.

31. Another maiden, whom hydropsy had deprived of the use of all her limbs, came on that same day when, according to custom, Anstrude's deposition is venerated with great honors In the sight of all, she prostrated herself on the sepulchre of the holy virgin and fell asleep. Roused, that maiden whom two women could barely carry there, recovered all her limbs and walked home by herself unhurt.

32. Then a certain sick woman, Sigrada, lay paralyzed for eight years so that she could not raise her hand to her mouth. And in sleep, she saw the holy Anstrude in shining garments, holding in her hand a vessel of most glittering crystal full of oil and she began to anoint her in the form of a cross, on the arms, hands and her whole body. Roused from this vision, she had herself carried to the basilica of Saint John the Baptist and placed by the chair where Saint Anstrude was wont to sit praying. Immediately, she recovered all her health as at first, feeling no pain.

33. And one Saturday, while she prayed, a nun fell into sleep and saw Saint Anstrude near her chair in Blessed John the Baptist's basilica. She said to her, "Sister, go to God's handmaid, Abbess Adalsinda, and tell her to have a couch built quickly on this spot where you see me standing. Let those sisters who wish come here to have their prayers answered."[39] At these words, the sister rose and followed her orders and told the mother of the family what she had seen and heard. She understood the couch to mean an altar and obediently had one constructed in that place where the faithful who prayed in the name of Jesus might obtain what they asked.

34. Another sister had suffered for four years from a flow of blood and was cured of her infirmity by coming to this holy place to pray.

35. Another sister was gravely wounded and doctors could do little to heal the affliction. Then she was carried to that chair of Saint Anstrude and, through its power, she was healed and had no swelling left on her body from the wound.

36. A maid named Petronilla, nourished in this holy convent from infancy, was so violently sick and wasted that she could scarcely breathe without a moan and her other limbs were so weak that she couldn't even open her eyes. Truly, her nurse was already mourning her death and carried her on her

38. See c. 20.

39. See c. 19 for Adalsinda's cure. Levison speculates that she may have been the wife of Anstrude's kinsman Wulfold, who is noted in the charters.

shoulders to the place where Anstrude was buried and laid her out there most devoutly. Which done, helped by blessed Anstrude's merits, the maid's eyes opened and she began to speak and was healed with the use of all her limbs restored.

37. And it happened recently that a certain woman of noble stock with her daughter and two maids were all gravely troubled by demons.[40] Bereft of all their faculties, they gave themselves in full devotion to the Lord that they might take on the habits of holy nuns in this convent. But when, as is the custom, they had been sequestered at the far top of the monastery, they were so cruelly vexed by savage demons that the sisters hardly dared to go near them except to put food down at some distance and flee. But through the approval and holy merits of Anstrude, after the celebration of the Lord's nativity, about midnight, the said matron with her daughter and the maids, were struck with excessive trembling. They ran from the place where they were, proceeding to the basilica of Holy Mary Ever Virgin where the saints of God (Anstrude and Sadalberga) were seen to lie.[41] They came and lay there for two days before the holy sepulchre. And on the third day, at cock's crow, the light from the lamp which hung over the grave of the saints was extinguished, and after an hour was lit again, and extinguished and lit again for a third time. Then the whole church burst into a splendor of brilliant light. Seeing this, the aforesaid woman and her companions were seized with the greatest terror. They had gone to sleep and heard the sounds of their own limbs stricken with uncontrollable trembling. And they cried out in loud voices fearing that their lives were at an end. And when the bright light of day shone they stood on their feet. Whence, with God's help, through the intercession of Saint Anstrude, the matron, her daughter and both maids were freed from the vexation of demons and appeared purified. And none of them ever were disturbed by demons again even to the day of their deaths.

38. And God, Who always does wonders in His saints, especially His holy and blessed handmaid, the virgin Anstrude, showed many other miracles which do not now spring to mind. Daily benefits were given at her sepulchre by her prayers to all the petitioning faithful, through our Lord and Savior Jesus Christ Who lives and reigns with the eternal Father, Son and Holy Spirit from everlasting to everlasting. Amen.

40. Levison, Introduction, Vita Anstrudis, believes that this miracle was added by the Carolingian editor, as indicated by the word "recently."

41. Levison, Vita Anstrudis, 77, n. 2, quotes Mabillon's note that a twelfth-century copyist added that Anstrude's body was moved from the church of St. Mary's and translated with the bones of her mother Sadalberga to the church of St. John the Baptist.

17

Austreberta, Abbess of Pavilly

(650–703)

In 687, with his victory at Tertry, Pippin II united the thrones of Neustria, Burgundy, and Austrasia under Balthild's last living son, Theuderic III. Once Ebroin's puppet, he became the first of the "do-nothing" kings whom Pippin's descendants would ultimately replace. Thus, our final story leads us into the new proto-Carolingian age, abandoning the tangled dynastic schemes and monastic politics of the Merovingian age. We began the seventh century with a glimpse of the Christian aristocracy converted or "discovered" by Columbanus and his disciples in the pagan countryside just north of Paris. Throughout the century, the evangelizing mission spread from the center at Luxeuil to the Gascon south, the Frisian north, the German and Saxon borders, and to that coast which in later years would be called Normandy.

Yet another group of saints once associated with the court of Dagobert undertook the evangelization of the relatively peaceful, remote lands of western Neustria. Saint Omer, who gave the veil to Austreberta, was abbot of Saint Ouen's foundation at Rebais and then bishop of Thérouanne, where she was born. He had been trained at Luxeuil and brought three saintly missionaries from there to convert his new diocese: Momelinus, Bertin, and Ebertramnus. It was about 656 when he placed Austreberta in the convent at Port-le-Grand in Ponthieu.[1] He continued to rule his see until his death in 667.

De S. Austreberta virgine in Belgio et Normannia, AS, February 10, 417. The editor believed that this vita was written soon after the saint's death by a contemporary who was familiar with the internal life of the convent, either one of the nuns or a monk or chaplain attached to their service directly or as part of the life of their brother institution, Jumièges. This seems to be confirmed by several references within the text to persons or events as though known to the sisters who are to read the book. There are, however, several conventions that appear to relate the text to later authors. The writer mentions a supervisor or patron with the power to rewrite or rearrange the text, similar to the situation found in Hucbald's work. The counting of kings from Clovis also found a reflection in the Carolingian author, as did the story of the heavenly veil, which appears more elaborately in the life of Glodesind and in Hucbald's version of the life of Aldegund.

1. Luxeuil and its trainees also formed a focal point for relations between Neustria in the northwest and Provence in the south. In the early eighth century, the archbishop of Vienne was named

Sometime after 670, Saint Philibert, who had been involved in the political tangles of Ebroin's grab for power, was exiled to the diocese of Rouen under the supervision of Ebroin's friend, Saint Ouen.[2] He occupied his time by establishing the monastery of Jumièges, patronized by Balthild who was then a nun at Chelles. At first, it was a double monastery but, as it grew, it split into separate establishments for women and men. The former was absorbed by the community at Pavilly established by Austreberta, and the two monasteries formed a long-standing partnership. Austreberta was thus part of a systematic plantation of female communities in the area that included Saint Godeberta, brought by Saint Eligius to found a nunnery at Noyon, and Saint Angadrisma, whom Saint Ouen contributed to the Thérouanne group. The latter is said to have prayed herself into leprosy to evade her threatened marriage.[3]

In brief, a thriving and prosperous network of monasteries had been established in western Neustria by the time Philibert died in 685 at his island retreat of Noirmoutiers. The Christian aristocracy, through its patronage of monasteries and its cooperation with noble bishops, laid down an infrastructure upon which the spirituality of later centuries could safely rest.[4] This and the preceding lives of the great abbesses of the age have demonstrated the vital role played by women in that process. The eighth-century saint Boniface, who brought cadres of nuns headed by Saint Leoba to Germany to provide a support network for his mission, was merely replicating a situation that already existed in seventh-century Gaul.

Saint Philibert was the last of the great Dagobertian missionary saints. His patronage of Austreberta resembles the work of Amand and Waldebert, but once she was established in her monastery, her life turned inward, concerned with her pastoral tasks and not with the turmoil of the world outside. Even after her death, Austreberta's spirit concentrated on the discipline of her community, only slowly turning outward to the surrounding countryside, which still respects and maintains her cult. In the ninth century, many of these foundations were destined to be obliterated by Viking raiders and nearly forgotten. Pavilly and its surrounding territory was so devastated that the convent became nothing but a shadowy memory. A later author, resurrecting Austreberta's cult, wrote:

In that place, there lived a most faithful man and two women of probity, one a nun. Though they lived in separate little huts, one night a single

---

Austrobertus, a native of Normandy; see Geary, *Aristocracy in Provence*, 139. He held estates near those of Waratto, the successor of Ebroin, and may have been allied to him in the struggles of the earlier period.

2. Ewig, *Spätantikes und fränkisches Gallien*, 217.

3. No contemporary lives exist for them although they enjoyed active local cults.

4. This is the felicitous concept of Werner, "Le rôle de l'aristocratie," in *Structures politiques*, 1.

voice spoke to all of them together: "Why are you sunk in deepest slumber? Don't you know that the feast day of your venerable patroness Austreberta has arrived? Get up and hasten to the church." Having been unaware of this, they rose quickly and ran to the church. Within they heard voices already present celebrating together in the night the feast of the virgin in heaven. And soon, sharing the exultation, the pious ones joined in emulation. But when they arrived at the temple door, there was absolutely no sound to be heard. Still a fragrance lingered of inestimable sweetness. There things clearly show that the same solemnity of the blessed virgin which the angels observed should be honored on earth.[5]

Austreberta, Virgin and Abbess of Pavilly

∎

Prologue

1. Venerable mother Julia, disciple of Christ: for a long time now you have begged me with all your might, in importunate prayers, to try with my pen to compose the most blessed virgin Austreberta's life so that the publicity might bring that bright gem to a wider audience. Often have you urged this upon me, admonishing me and accusing me of torpor and idleness, recalling the stupidity of the servant in the Gospel who earned a harsh sentence of condemnation from the Divine One because he hid his lord's money in the earth rather than enlarging it by putting it out to interest. Conscious of my ignorance, for because of my lazy nature I have as yet barely learned the rudiments of letters, I have hitherto refused to undertake this task. I have hesitated to lift a weight unequal to my strength. I have greatly feared lest my untutored eloquence seem to cast a cloud before the most splendid light of our time. For who has words sharp enough and rhetoric so facile as to be worthy of her? Who can sufficiently herald her innumerable virtues? For like the holy prophet Jeremiah, she was known to God before she was formed in the womb, as angelic oracles attested; sanctified by heaven before emerging in birth, she strove in every way to lead the angelic life and afterwards she merited the indescribable glory of the angels. Whence I am not wrong to fear attacking such a mass of material. I do believe that Homer himself, should he emerge from the underworld, or the wondrously eloquent Tully, must succumb and be overcome by so much virtue. For I fear lest I suffer what I have heard happened to another author. Someone asked him to write the life and habits of the most reverend Philibert, former abbot of the monastery of

5. *AS*, February 10, 427.

Jumièges, and with diligent pen he strove to do so. And when it came to the patron's hand to be read, he despised and mocked it and finally changed it into quite a different sort of text. Whence I have deferred serving Your Devoutness, lest perhaps those who applaud their own philosophic skills and mangle the knowledge of simple folk may blame me for hasty presumption because I appear to explicate the blessed virgin's famous deeds with unskillful words.[6]

2. However, since God holds worldly wisdom for foolishness, we will stop making excuses. For the profit of many and as her perpetual memorial, we shall undertake with true and faithful pen to produce a truthful narrative from what we have learned from her followers.[7] Therefore, animated by the merits of this glorious patron who rejoices in her happy marriage with the Celestial Emperor, obeying your orders with pious devotion, I shall now put my mind to writing of her holy birth, customs, and death and how through her the Lord made signs of miracles. The preservation of the virgin's precious works will be my reward, even though I do what was asked of me with a barbarous pen which lacks all urbane wit and relate the divine wondrousness all too briefly with a stuttering tongue. Surely one who contemplates the wisdom of God the Father from end to end, reaching and disposing of these things in weight and number, must give a faithful account. Therefore, let us praise the Redeemer as we approach the beginning of her life and ways, so signs of virtue may be glorified in Him Who is wonderful and glorious in His saints.

I. Birth of Saint Austreberta and her monastic life in the convent of Portus.[8]

3. After the Universal Lord, Who is at once the Author and Redeemer of human salvation, bent the savage necks of the Gauls to His power, four kings followed Clovis, who first received the rule of Christian religion through Remigius' mediation, until Dagobert, most glorious prince, famous in nobility, prepotent in power, strong in arms, devoted entirely to the King of Kings, Christ, took the reins of the Frankish kingdom by God's will.[9] In his time, holy mother church flowered again as a palm tree in Gaul, adorned with the diverse virtues of holy priests and monks and virgins dedicated to God. So, as the apostle Paul so truly said, "Where sin abounded, grace did

---

6. The author appears to be someone quite confident of the abbess's good will to risk the mildly satirical tone of this introduction.

7. This seems to indicate that the author was working within the lifetime of Austreberta's contemporaries and had ready access to them. The story in c. 10 suggests that she or he also spoke to the nuns at Portus, Austreberta's first monastery.

8. Port-le-Grand in Ponthieu.

9. This chronology only works if the author is counting generations rather than individual monarchs or entirely cutting out Sigibert and his descendants. This would make the four after Clovis, Clothar I, Chilperic, Clothar II, and Dagobert.

much more abound."[10] Among them, a star more glittering than the rest, the Lord's man, Philibert, famous pastor of monks, noble founder of convents, established a monastery in the dale of Jumièges, from the aforesaid Dagobert's largesse. He built it up from the first stone and adorned it with a noble congregation of monks in the service of God. At the same time, as his reputation for goodness grew, he built another convent, through the largesse of the famous Amalbert on his farm called Pavilly about ten miles from the aforesaid Jumièges where he gathered a small congregation of God's handmaids.[11]

4. At this time, in the aforesaid King Dagobert's palace, there was a man of honest life and venerable customs, famed for wisdom and prudent counsel, born from the race of the first kings. His name was Badefridus and he held the office of Count Palatine. He took a wife named Framechilda who was descended from the King of the Alamans. She was elegant of face but far more elegant in her sanctity. For she lived in such a manner on earth that today her glory is proclaimed through miracles to the people.[12] As we have said, the couple were high in the perishable honors of this world but higher in holy probity of mind, firm faith, great charity, renowned justice, long-suffering hope, almsgiving and solicitous hospitality for the poor. Adorned with such flowers of virtue, they deserved to be called temples of the Holy Spirit as was manifested afterwards by abundant signs. As the new mother of the Lord's precursor, Elizabeth, was filled with the Holy Spirit and, as the Gospel tells, deserved the divine favor of feeling rather than seeing her child before his birth, so the God-pleasing mother Framechilda through the same illuminating Spirit foresaw long before that she would bear a child of her own sex who would be a mother in the Lord's house and a pillar to the Christian people.[13]

5. And as the time drew near when a clear light should break over the shadowy mists of this world from the darkness of her womb, the mother earned the honor of an angelic vision which announced the name of the virgin about to be born and told her that she would deserve to come before God. Therefore, that glory among maidens, who was to be called Austreberta according to the revelation, sprang from those parents in the land of Thérouanne. For she was chosen by God before she was conceived in her mother's belly. She

---

10. Romans 5:20.

11. The author seems to have jumped forward with a standard account of Philibert's achievements. Ebling, *Prosopographie*, 46–48, lists three Amalberts from the sources of this period but connects none of them with Austreberta.

12. *Vita beatae Framechildis viduae, Analecta Bollandiana* 72 (1954): 155–61, does not differ appreciably from her daughter's life except that it gives no hint that she opposed Austreberta's vocation while, paradoxically, retaining the account of the girl's flight and its accompanying miracles.

13. Austreberta is going to become a *mater*, whereas Framechilda is called *genetrix*.

was known to the assembly of angels before she was born into the world. Before her limbs appeared, her deeds were foretold to the people. Diligently her careful parents nurtured her and gave her strict masters for her instruction. And, as she passed the years of her childhood simply at home, the fervor of sanctity grew so great in her that none could doubt that the Lord had chosen her for His handmaid before her nativity. Firmly, she began to put the world aside, manfully with all her strength to despise all delightful pleasures and to desire heaven from the bottom of her heart. Before she was even ten years old, the Holy Spirit so filled her that her mind panted to be in a monastery or church. For while she was still in the rude years of childhood, the devout girl planned what she later fulfilled.

6. One day, as children do, she was contemplating the shape of her face in the water. Suddenly, a veil appeared to have been placed on her head. That sign meant so much to her that from that day she burned with desire. When her parents wished to give her to a mortal husband, she was so aware that she wanted to cling only to an immortal one that in tearful prayers she begged the Lord incessantly to fulfill in fact what He had deigned to show her as a shadow. Nor from that time did she ever suffer anything to stifle her determination to fulfill with works what she had seen with her eyes and conceived with her mind, with the aid of divine grace. She was aflame with that evangelical fire which our Savior Jesus Christ kindled upon the earth, when He came to separate son from father and daughter from mother. Secretly, she bore it in her breast, enduring the unquenchable heat. Neither by day nor night could she cease from prayer and divine colloquy, waiting for the right and proper time to come when she might receive her desired consecration in a nun's habit. And then, by chance, she read, or heard someone read, the reproachful saying of the Apostle James: "If any be a hearer of the word and not a doer, he is like a man beholding his natural face in a glass: for he beholdeth himself and goeth his way and straightaway forgetteth what manner of man he was."[14] So, from this blessed handmaid of God's example, let them who know not learn how this sentence of Holy Scripture is to be imitated, that they may not be like that oblivious man but become doers, not just hearers, of the word. So may it please them to be like that handmaid of God who considered her natural face in a mirror and did not forget what she had seen. Therefore those who would imitate her must not be forgetful listeners but should be doers of deeds. And they who persevere in this work will be blessed.

7. As time went on, her parents, who too little favored her happy acts, accepted a pledge of earthly love and fixed a day for her appointed marriage.

14. James 1:23.

Thrown into anguish, she racked her brain for something she could do. Finally in sorrow she took furtively to the road, bringing her brother with her though he was but a child. As they went along together, he asked her where they were heading and she answered, to a nearby villa. They came to the river Cange, where there was a bridge. They found the river running swiftly, swollen with flood water whose waves hid the bridge, denying passage to all travellers. Then at last she confessed to her brother where she was going in such eager haste. At that time there was a holy man named Omer, great with merit before God, who was bishop of the town of Thérouanne in which diocese the noble maid was born. She was running to him to be consecrated with the holy veil. She had many companions with her on the road and they, seeing the difficulty in crossing, trembled with fear and did not dare go forward. With common sense, they began to leave the place and return to their original road. For they could not even get across by boat. But God's holy handmaid, devoted to Christ and illumined with the grace of the Holy Spirit, first said a prayer and then, making the sign of salvation, walked onto the bridge submerged by the flood, calling upon the others to follow her. And, lo, the nature of certain elements was fundamentally changed: for the water became solid as wood beneath her feet and then the wood liquid as water. God's handmaid with all her companions crossed unharmed on a road so dry that no drop from the flood touched them. Then, having crossed the stream, swiftly hurrying, they came to the man of God and flying to his feet the maid obtained her desire. For she was consecrated to Christ and, taking the veil, her soul clove to Him ever after and the right hand of Christ received her. So it was in vain that they had sought to couple her with an earthly man who was to be joined in heaven with Christ.

8. The man of God, knowing her parents would be disturbed by these things, sought to visit them with consolation. Bringing God's handmaid with him, he cleansed their spirits with pacific words and treated them mildly and gently, reminding them of their original affection. The father embraced his daughter and the brothers their sister and each of them kissed her as they glorified God together. Indeed, it was an act of divine dispensation that those who first despised her in mockery were afterwards the most reverent in their devotion. And as soon as she had settled in her parents' home, she began to implore her mother and brothers that they would no longer oppose her vow but would rather help her to enter a monastery, to be associated with holy virgins, where, clearly, she was to live under another power. They consented kindly and not only gave her free leave to depart but even accompanied her hastening to the monastery.

9. Now that monastery had been built by the river Somme and was called Portus. There the spiritual mother Burgofled presided who rejoiced when

they had explained everything to her, and took her as a daughter and placed her among the other sisters. And the blessed handmaid of God entered into Christ's sheepfold, joined the holy flock and became a sheep. She sowed the seed of the primary virtue, humility, in her heart serving not only her spiritual mother but each of her sisters as a handmaid, subjecting herself to all of them, rendering service to each as becomes a servant. Proclaiming herself inferior, judging herself more vile, she considered herself below all others. She pronounced herself an unhappy sinner who had wasted her time serving the world rather than God. Rather, she called them blessed who strove to please Christ the King, with tireless intention serving under the discipline of the rule. They, who had been trained to overcome the impulses of the flesh in battle with God's help, had become equal to the combat against spiritual iniquities. God Almighty always enriches the humble with grace. So the more she appeared vile and despicable in her own eyes, the more she became glorious to God and honored among men. For by unanimous choice and the mother's consent, she was made prioress despite her unwillingness.[15] And because of that she began to humble herself even more as she progressed from strength to strength, confronting rudeness with patience, displaying long-suffering to the pusillanimous and demonstrating gravity to the reckless that the ignorant might seek to be taught. She preached vigilance to the sleepy, not by words but by deeds, being first to appear when the signal sounded.

10. The following example will demonstrate the power of her obedience. It was the custom of the monastery for the sisters to take turns in baking the bread. One day the task fell to our handmaid and she worked with an adolescent whom she was training. As long as she lived in the flesh, that girl was wont to tell of this miracle. When the oven had been fired up and the bread quickly readied for baking, the fire was pulled out and the girl was supposed to clean out any remaining live coals or glowing ashes. But a little bundle of twigs on top of the wood fell and totally burst into flames. When God's handmaid noticed, she clapped her hands together groaning loudly and cried: "Woe to us! What shall we do? The bread will be ruined for such a thing cannot be fixed!" Running quickly, she barred the door of the house. Then, armed with the sign of the cross, she went straight into the smoky fire of the oven and, seizing the sleeves she wore on her arms, she cleaned the whole thing out. When she had carefully completed the whole job, she came out. The fire had not presumed to touch a hair of her head nor a fiber of her

---

15. Donatus, "Rule of Donatus," c. 8, describes the prioress chosen by the abbess with the advice of the elders as one with more "holiness, wisdom, humility and fear of God" than the rest. She acted as the abbess's second in command.

garment. Then she told the girl to open the door of the house and admonished her with many words to tell no one what she had seen. But to avoid the vice of presumption, she recounted the miraculous thing that had happened to a servant of God. And that most ingenious man understood that God's grace had been granted because of her simplicity which is how the Lord distinguishes such virtue. Wishing to simulate, he answered her as though in reproach: "Daughter, I don't want you to tell or even repeat this, lest Satan attack you strongly." But since, as it is written, a city on a hill cannot be hidden, the sisters told it afterwards, referring to the man of God. For it was not God's will that this handmaid should spend the rest of her life in that monastery. But by her example she was the salvation of many in the fourteen years she stayed there.

II. The government of the convent at Pavilly committed to holy Austreberta.

11. At that time, there lived a man of venerable life named Philibert whom we mentioned above. Since his works and teachings in faith and religion were respected and considered outstanding by everyone, a powerful man named Amalbert asked him to undertake the regulation of a monastery he had founded on his farm at Pavilly where his little daughter Aurea and others consecrated to God in Christ had vowed to serve. Though the man of God taught these handmaids of God through frequent readings and instructed them with holy preaching, it was still necessary for them to absorb such rudiments in the regular discipline of the rule as were inherent to their own sex.[16] Thus the said servant of God sent messengers to Christ's handmaid, Austreberta, for he had heard of her fame. Two of his monks went to her to ask her to come to the place. The handmaid of God had long been burning with desire to be trained in this holy man's discipline, like a firm and steady pillar, remembering Saint Paul's sentence: "Be not soon shaken . . . neither by word nor by letter."[17] Not knowing whether this was pleasing to God, at first she refused to go. The messengers returned and God's man was compelled to attend personally on His handmaid. Then indeed did a holy contention arise. For all God's servants, weeping and wailing, lifted up their voices crying: "Why, holy father, would you cheat us this day? Why would you take the light from our eyes and leave us in darkness?" Responding to them, he said: "Don't, daughters, don't talk like that. For in no way will you be left in

---

16. It is likely that Philibert was training them in the Benedictine Rule, which was gaining headway at the time. The story of the nuns trying to murder Austreberta as well as the miracle in c. 16 parallel the life of Saint Benedict as told by Gregory the Great.

17. 2 Thessalonians 2:2.

darkness, you who are the light of the world. But don't keep others from sharing in your light. Rather you should extend charity to those who are waiting." And thus he preached and more in the same vein to God's handmaids and the altercation was silenced and peace restored. The Holy Spirit, through the mouth of the man of God conquered them and they acquiesced. Then each one kissed her with God's blessing and, taking two sisters with her, she went with the man of God to take up the charge of ruling that place.

12. Now, God help us, we must discuss how cunningly the Devil worked to prevent her holy teaching from gaining strength. Holding strongly to her proposed rigor, she deviated neither left nor right. What her tongue preached to others, they saw her do first. But, like unbroken horses never pulling in harness, they resisted in every way the performance of what God's handmaid did in the cause of salvation. They were so infected with the ancient enemy's venom that they conspired, with great hatred, to kill her. And when, God preventing, they failed, they complained to Amalbert when that man, great in the world but not with God, visited them. With prefabricated lies, they made the most serious accusations against her. And as he was cruel of mind and terrible of aspect he believed the lies and had God's handmaid brought before him. He began to insult her in the harshest terms. Filled with rage, he tore out the sword which he had girded on and attacked her. She thought her time for martyrdom had come. Proving that the heart in her breast was in no way feminine but virile, she drew the finely woven veil she wore on her head smoothly about her throat, extended her hands and bowed her head to expose her neck to the blow. And, as they tell it, he stood astounded and immobile admiring such fortitude in a woman as he had never seen in a man. Quaking, he restored the sword to its place. From this affair it can be seen that if she had lived when the blood of martyrs was cleansing the land of filthy idolatry, she would not have been dragged as a resisting victim to the executioner's waiting services but, on the contrary, would have presented herself for torment to be the first victim to gain the palm of blood. Previously, she had not feared the Babylonian punishment when she unhesitatingly entered a burning fire for the sake of a few loaves of bread to save her monastery from harm. She would have stepped into a furnace seven times hotter for the sake of the kingdom of heaven.[18] By these signs, the Lord Christ proved that His handmaid did not fear martyrdom, for it was not she who faltered but He Who failed to make her a martyr.

13. The years ran by as blessed Austreberta ruled that convent called by the ancient name of Pavilly. At first, it was small and modest but little by little it

18. Daniel 3:19.

became great thereafter. There were fewer than twenty-five handmaids of God with her but they clove to her in mind and body so that not one of them would part from her until the day of their calling. There, God's servant built a wonderful monastery dedicated to Mary, God's mother. She also constructed basilicas to Saint Peter, Saint Martin and other saints, housing them as saints should be, with all prepared swiftly and properly. Seeing which, recognizing the goodness of God in her, no tongue will ever be able to give voice to how the holy and most blessed Austreberta was snatched like a bird from the jaws of the venomous serpent or how swiftly a place was prepared for her to dwell or how she took up the care of many souls or how many and what sort were those of whom she took charge. How charity adorned her and her goodness prospered! The purity of her mind and simplicity of her heart shone forth and her long-suffering blazed up before everyone from a frugality which we have not the power to evoke. For she was often reading, keeping vigil and praying through the night; she was prompt to fast and wear cheap clothing, most constant in tribulation and faithful in temptation.

14. And all Quadragesima, except for the Lord's Day, she ate but three times a week. She punished her body and enslaved it by self-denial and followed the Lord bearing her own cross. She loved everyone and they all loved her. Modest in all things, she appeared joyful and happy. When quarrels sprang up, as they usually do, she could calm every mind with just a few words. She undertook to eat more sparingly than people usually do and never failed in sobriety. She was chaste, circumspect, mild and quiet in all her ways. Her manners were accommodating and her conversation most gracious. So none who joined her for any reason ever left her without a pang of the heart. All who lived in the neighborhood, seeing her example and teaching, not only came to offer sons and daughters to God but many hurried to the monastery themselves, relinquishing their own marriages, casting off husbands and wives. And the spouses, in the cause of sanctity, spurned those who spurned them.

15. Indeed the blessed virgin never lost the humility she had first assumed. It was her custom to watch over the Lord's flock like a good shepherd. By day and night, she circled about to investigate anything that might happen. In that crepuscular light when dawn drenches the earth, after Matins had been discharged and the sisters, weary from their labors, rested their bodies in bed, she would wander slowly through the dormitory wanting to assure herself that all were at peace, inspecting each one on her couch. Once, not knowing that it was God's handmaid, the waking prioress reproved her, saying: "Why do you behave like this sister? Wherefore do you disturb the sleepers? Go to the cross." And she hurried there joyfully and stood immobile, singing

psalms until the hour of meeting when all rose together at the signal.[19] And, in fact, when the prioress saw what she had done, she fell at her feet, praying for forgiveness.

III. Miracles and Death of Saint Austreberta.

16. Once the gravest suffering overcame a sister whose face got so swollen that her eye was almost hidden. But when God's servant visited her, as usual, she touched her painful and swollen jaw and immediately she was restored to health. Again, at the beginning of Quadragesima, about midnight, a voice came to a sleeping sister saying: "Rise, sister, run quickly and tell the abbess to get up and rouse the sisters to God's service." But, sunk deeply in sleep, she failed to rise. A second time, the voice came and said the same thing but again she did not rise but continued sleeping. A third time, the voice reproached her indignantly: "Why do you sleep, sister, letting your cares slip away in slumber? Are you so far gone that I must repeat my orders a third time? Arise," it said, "tell the abbess that she must get up and give the signal and rouse the sisters to God's work." Fearful and trembling, she ran quickly and found her keeping vigil in the church and told her what happened. As soon as the signal was given, in the space of a moment, they all gathered in the church with only two little infants missing. Everyone marvelled that they could assemble so quickly for none could remember it happening before. No sooner had they embarked upon a psalm than the center of the dormitory collapsed with a great concussion. They were all struck dumb with terror at the noise which was like a great thunderbolt and started to go out to see what had happened. But God's handmaid stopped them, saying: "No one is to dare to leave the church. Go back inside and do God's work, pray and sing psalms and complete our office." Armed with the sign of the cross, with a burning lamp before her, she went out of the church. In fact, when she realized what had happened she began to worry about the babies. But behold, she found one of them under a table and the other in the ruined window. Indeed, the walls on both sides of the window had fallen to the ground and only the window which sheltered the infant stood firm. Now, how they got into those places or who saved them remains unknown to us even to this day, though it is not hidden from God. Meanwhile, one sister who was related to one of the infants, disobeyed holy mother Austreberta's orders and left the church whereupon she found herself in immediate danger. For, as she ran back and forth, trying to uncover a corpse somewhere, the ruined wall fell on her and struck her and smashed her whole body. Not only her head, but every bone

---

19. The editors suggest that she was performing a penance common among Belgian monks of standing with outstretched arms as though crucified.

in her body was broken. Hearing the sound of the second collapse and the sister's cry, everyone ran to the spot. Gathering the disobedient one in a rug, they carried her to the infirmary. There Austreberta visited her at dawn and, anointing her shattered limbs with blessed oil, restored her to pristine health.[20] Moreover, with God's help, by the feast of the Lord's Resurrection, the beloved abbess restored the house that had collapsed at the beginning of Quadragesima. In fact, careful mortaring made it better than before.

17. Now, having touched a little upon the life and virtues of the holy virgin, let us recount briefly, lest boredom disgust our readers or they think us frivolous, how her present life ran its course. Having fought the good fight, run the race and kept the faith, her holy soul was freed from the flesh. Therefore, Almighty God, pious remunerator of His faithful, determined to call the blessed virgin Austreberta from this world of calamity and darkness to eternal and boundless beatitude. Seized with a mild fever, God's beloved began to sicken. She gathered the sisters in one place and told them to expect the day of her death. The day being Sunday, seven days hence she would migrate to the Lord as, she said, an angel had revealed to her in a vision. Therefore, proffering many testimonies of divine scripture from the treasury in her heart, she instructed them about those who belong to the Kingdom of God, about contempt for the world, the glory of the righteous and the punishment of reprobates. Indeed, she urged them to have every care to maintain the bonds of charity and patience, saying to them that Christ could not live in a heart that burned with flames of envy. Rather they should burn to do their neighbors good. With a kiss for each, at peace with all, the venerable mother was laid, as was her noble custom, on a horsehair spread. There she lived on for a few days, never ceasing to multiply interest on the talents the Lord had entrusted to her.

18. When that Sunday came, since fame of her goodness and virtue had spread through the length and breadth of Gaul, a crowd of priests and clerks, abbots and monks and a multitude of people of both sexes flowed to the place of her passing. Meanwhile the hour of the blessed woman's reward was imminent. Summoning all to her, the most holy and venerable mother made her last farewell to each according to her order of dignity.[21] She exhorted that none should desert the road of holy religion on which they had begun. Finally, having received the sacrament of the Lord's body, armed with the standard of the cross, she bade farewell to the sheep entrusted to her by

---

20. A similar miracle occurs in Gregory the Great, *Life of Benedict*, in *Dialogues*, book 2, 17.

21. This would be the prescribed order in processions and in chapter; it reflected each nun's seniority in entering religion.

Christ. She said: "Well, then, sisters and daughters most beloved to me in Christ, today I am going the way of all flesh. If you love me with true love, keep all my admonitions in mind and never seek to desert the road of religion once you have started forth. I commit your care to the highest Christ: He will be your pastor and guardian forever." At this, the assembled nuns broke out in a single lament, hair unbound and breasts bared.[22] "Why us, Lady, why do you desert us, holy mother? To whom do you commit your vigilance and pastoral care? You would go today to the homeland of endless glory. To whom will you leave us, desolate in this vale of tears? Take us with you by your prayers. For we would rather die with you than live blindly in a world from which you are absent."

19. Moved by these tears, the pious mother poured out a prayer: "Immortal God, ruler of men and angels, we pray You to be eternally the guardian of these your bondwomen. Until now, You have kept them in my custody. But now watch over them even as You kept watch over Israel, never sleeping. Behold, I come to You Whom I have loved! I hasten to You Whom I have desired. To You I come thirsting Whom I have ever loved with most ardent love. In You I trust; I will not be put to shame. In You I hope; I will not be confounded. Take my spirit to Your eternal peace lest the spears of the enemy prevail against me. But, this I pray, eternal King, that You will deign to reward with peace and health from Heaven any who keep my memory on earth." So saying, she fell silent for the hour of her reward had come. Meanwhile, those who stood around her were singing psalms and saying the names of the saints in order. Then in as strong a voice as she could, she interrupted them, saying: "Quiet, brothers mine, quiet.[23] Don't you see what a joyous procession comes here? As you invoke their names, a vast multitude of saints are coming forward." And so seeing what her mind had so long thirsted to see, her holy soul was freed from the flesh. And thus the glorious virgin crossed over on the fourth ides of February on the Lord's day, at daybreak—the same hour when Christ rose victorious from Hell.[24] Oh, truly holy and venerable virgin

22. The editor of *AS* discreetly noted that this was probably an expression of the author's poetic style, not a genuine ritual gesture.

23. It is unclear who these "brothers" were. Presumably they were among the people seen arriving at the beginning of c. 18, but that does not explain why they are singled out here. They could have been monks of Jumièges, which was paired with Pavilly, or a small contingent assigned to the nuns' service. Possibly the singers were all monks, which could happen in the Irish system. That is unlikely, however, as the text indicates that the sisters customarily did the offices themselves. The reference might be a subtle variation of the common conceit that virgins were manly—or perhaps the author's pen simply slipped.

24. February 10.

at whose passing a multitude of angels attended! What a procession of martyrs garbed in purple! An assembly of virgins, white as lilies, joined with our virgin, rejoicing and exulting from everlasting to everlasting.

20. She was buried in the basilica of blessed Peter, prince of apostles, where she rested over the course of several years. Our words cannot tell how many wondrous prodigies the Lord deigned to perform in that place to show the merits of the most excellent virgin to the faithful after she had passed to glory. For demons fled from the bodies they possessed. The blind were illuminated; malformed hands repaired; the lame restored to walking; the strongest fevers expelled and many types of diseases cured. So may the famous virgin be with us who celebrate her memory; may she pray for her servants that their sins be pardoned and after this life ends, may she lead us by her holy prayers into the society of the saints. Amen.

Miracles of Saint Austreberta[25]

∎

I. Blessings Saint Austreberta bestowed after death on her people at Pavilly.

1. After her glorious death, some sisters became so undisciplined that they dared to lie down at noon or any other hour of the day on the bed where she died. Visiting them in frequent visions, the holy virgin protested and said that if they did not obey her she threatened swift punishment for their correction. One woman, more impudent than the rest, persisted in her presumption and even began to use it for her own bed. Soon she lay in extremis gripped by fever. For one or two days, she remained sick in bed. The others cared for her but she grew steadily worse. Finally she turned to her nurse and said: "I know that I am about to die but still I pray that you will gain me a little relief by moving me to another place. For I fear that if my soul departs from here I will be damned for the obnoxious sin I committed against her. For I have presumed to use the marriage bed of God's holy woman for myself." Consenting to her request, they took her to the infirmary. There she recovered within the hour and was restored to health. Fearing lest in future others might repeat her crime, she accepted the punishment for her fault for her own profit and that of others. Since she had refused to heed the reproof as the others did, she brought punishment on her own body. Through this, she learned that the saints' relics can never be disdained in the least but must be greatly venerated and never delegated to human uses.

2. At this time, another sister had a terrible sore on her jaw, so putrescent

---

25. The editors of the text in AS believe that the following text should be attributed to the anonymous author of the preceding vita.

that her throat swelled inwardly and she could swallow neither food nor drink. She could not even sleep for the agony. If anyone put a little liquid in her mouth, she rejected it and it spilled out with her phlegm. Finally, none could go near her because of the stench. But when she was carried to the holy tomb, she fell asleep there and in a dream someone in a virgin's habit appeared to her with an apple which she said Saint Austreberta sent. Taking it, she ate and awoke with her mouth full of immense sweetness like a honeycomb. And she rose from the place and went to her bed and while she was resting there she felt a hand touch her head with great tenderness. Opening her eyes, she saw a splendid face shining with great light. Then in the twinkling of an eye, the one she had seen was gone. But at once she asked for food, ate and was healed.

3. When the day of the anniversary of her deposition came, the sisters arose in the night to praise God in her memory. One of them, her body overcome by sleep, neglected to rise and slept while the rest were singing their psalms. She saw blessed Austreberta, preceded by three girls carrying lamps, walking around the whole dormitory.[26] When they stopped before her bed, the saint looked at her and spoke in a voice full of reproach: "Why are you sunk in slumberous torpor? Why do you, dissolved in sluggish slumber, shirk all your duty while others are wakeful and praising God?" Then she reached out and struck her in the face. Turning to the maidens who were with her, she said: "Grab her and throw her out of doors." And, awakened by the blow, she rose from her bed and began to run right away. And lo, behind her back there was a sound of running steps and she entered the church in great trembling. And confessing what she had suffered, she vowed to do better in future. Throughout the whole of the next year, she continued to suffer the box on her ear which she had received from her. But when the feast came round again, she said a prayer and Almighty God released her and she was restored to health.

4. Another time, while they commemorated her by celebrating solemn mass, a certain maid wishing to save her soul, asked to join the holy congregation. But in times past she had often been a postulant in that same cause and all had denied her the right to enter. Despairing that the grace she sought could come to her from man, she confided rather in God's mercy and the saint's prayers. In that hour when the Lord God of hosts is thrice called Holy by all, she ran to the holy sepulchre.[27] Grabbing the pall of God's blessed bondwoman in her hands, she said she would never go back from there unless forced against her will for she feared that her soul would perish if she were thrown out and then her blood would be required from those who

---

26. A vision that calls to mind the saint's habits in life, c. 15.
27. Probably referring to the "Sanctus" of the Mass.

impeded her devotion. The mother of those handmaids of God who was ruling the monastery at that time waxed indignant at what she had done and ordered that she be removed from the place and expelled in disgrace saying: "You were born a servant in this monastery and you ought to do servile work as you would have to do outside. Do you dare to imagine that you can make yourself a lady by stealing the corpse of another nun?"[28] But the following night, when the abbess gave herself up to sleep, a grave fever attacked her continuously so that she was disturbed all night long. And as the fever worsened at dawn, she commanded the priest to come and all the sisters with him. She indicated that she thought she was near death and that she suffered on account of that girl. She asked them all to receive her into the congregation. But they, who had unanimously striven against the girl's reception, still questioned whether she was the cause of the illness. They took counsel saying: "First, let's go to the body of God's holy handmaid and there we will pray for you, vowing that if the Lord has mercy on you and cures you, we will help you do yourself what you now ask from us." They did so and immediately the fever left her. Rising from her bed she ordered the girl to return and received her as a daughter and made her a sister to the others. Then she remembered well what she did ill to forget before: that the Lord is no respecter of persons, that in Christ there is neither bond nor free, but all are one and we are all enlisted under a single lord. Thus is the Lord pleased with those who fear Him and put their hopes in His mercy.[29]

5. Another sister was crippled by illness with one part of her body drawn downward from the kidneys so that she lost the power to walk and was thus tortured for five years. One night, she had reached the last gasp and could scarcely draw a breath. In a dream, a voice told another sister to rise and carry the invalid to the body of Christ's handmaid. Thrice roused, she came to the invalid and told her what had happened. Thinking her end must be near, she agreed and the nun laboriously bore her across her shoulder to the place and laid her down there. At once she slept while the other, lingering nearby, awaited the outcome of the affair. She heard a sudden sound like the wings of a dove flying and resting above the holy sepulchre. And when it subsided a

28. It appears that a low-born woman had attempted to provide herself with a more comfortable life than she was born to by joining the monastic community. This is strictly forbidden in the "Rule of Donatus," c. 9, where it is coupled with the demand that those who were well-off in the world give up their advantages.

29. It is tempting to see in this miracle some attempt to stem the inexorable move toward an aristocratic monopoly in contemporary convents. There is at least some evidence that in the earliest period some class mixture appeared that gradually gave way before or during the eighth century, see McNamara, "The Ordeal of Community."

little, the invalid arose feeling no illness and stood on her feet giving thanks for the return of her health. She then went out uninjured.

6. At the same time, one of the maids whose fingernail had been fixed into the palm was unable to use her hand. When she came, out of faith, to pray at the tomb she was cured as soon as she invoked the name of God's handmaid, Austreberta.

7. And another nun, overcome by bodily illness, lost the use of her tongue and remained mute for four days unable to emit any sound or word.[30] On the fifth day that she continued speechless, she saw God's blessed handmaid in a dream who said: "When you get up at dawn, go to pray and the Lord will be your helper." And so at dawn, she went out mute and returned speaking; she went out silent and returned preaching: "Blessed be God who does such and so many works through his servant Austreberta."

II. Translation of Austreberta's body and subsequent miracles.

8. Meanwhile the holy body was translated from the place where it first lay: but not without miracles. For almighty God often revealed to one of His servants that she should be raised up from there since water was touching the surface of her stone. And it was found to be as the angel announced.

9. Moreover, after this when her holy feast came, a certain woman whose hands were paralyzed arrived who had come there with faith to be healed. The sisters conducted a vigil through the night with psalms and spiritual canticles and around midnight the use of her hands was returned to her and at dawn she left healed and giving thanks to God.

10. Another sister of the servants of God lost the light of her eyes and the chains of blindness bound her for twelve years. When she was praying before the venerated one's sepulchre, she received sight and the shadows of darkness were thrown off.

11. A certain adolescent with one lame foot kept watch in prayer through the night of the same feast for the venerated one. At day, when dawn shone forth, she received the ability to walk and went back home by a straight road.

12. And here is another marvel. A woman who had lost the use of one hand, came from far away, hurrying to arrive on the night when the commemoration of her solemn feast was celebrated. But the lateness of the hour prevented her from coming in for the outside doors were all fastened. Therefore, she spent the night in vigil at that place; when dawn came, she went in through the opened gates and offered a ring from her crippled hand

---

30. The text reads *ex monachis*. Even though *monacha* is a rather rare usage in these compositions, we have decided arbitrarily to make this person feminine in the absence of any clear indication of gender.

for a gift. Indicating that she had been favorably heard even from outside, she testified that her hand had been restored during the night.

13. The mother of a rich and noble family, who had formerly enjoyed the friendship of God's holy woman, was struck by the pestiferous and incurable disease which doctors call cancer. For nine years it tore at her chest until her breast was nearly consumed. On the day when the holy deposition of the blessed virgin is celebrated, she came and prostrated herself with devotion and faith before the venerated one's sepulchre. With many tears flowing because of her suffering she prayed intently for a long time. Then on another day, after she had returned home, the wound putrefying in her flesh was pulled out by the roots, a flood of bloody matter streamed out and within a few days she was restored to health.

14. A certain little boy was troubled by a demon and when his father brought him to the body of God's blessed handmaid and laid him there, the demon fled immediately and his health was restored.

15. A certain adolescent girl had a demon and could not rest day or night, crying out and tearing herself apart until her parents could not bear the disturbance. Her mother brought her to the holy tomb where the demon was expelled and the mother brought her home cured.

16. Meanwhile let us omit several things lest reading so much disgust our audience. We think it gratifying to have noted so many excellencies, but let a little suffice for much that almighty God did through His handmaid. For it is proper now that we should be silent; every book must have an end. Not that her deeds have ceased but human eloquence has wearied and, as they say, "Now is the time to loosen the necks of our steaming horses."[31] Their necks were not bent to the yoke or broken to the horses' reins just so that they might be freed, steaming after work, but [this horse has been] most scrupulously searching in its secret heart, not without labor, for what is worthy and fitting to say to others. Now, after many exertions, steaming in a great lather, it seeks the time of release.[32] So I admonish you who read this that you will pass over discussion of syllables and style and parts of speech and clauses of the sentences and periods. Rather choose to consider the sense of the matter and imitate it in your spirit. Do not be put off by the dirty dress of our style and you will find the beautiful body within.

17. May the most holy virgin protect us with her prayers and defend us from evil and guard and keep us. This may He deign to concede Who lives

---

31. Virgil, *Georgics*, 2.

32. This little joke, referring back to the introduction, seems to prove that the miracles were written by the same author as the life.

with the Father and Holy Spirit, God, Who reigns from everlasting to everlasting. Amen.

III. Saint Austreberta's power against demons; defense of chastity. Remuneration for services and other cures.[33]

18. In the province of Rouen, one of the priestly order by the hidden counsel of God was troubled by unclean spirits and tirelessly tortured day and night. His relatives led him to many saints' places and finally to the church of blessed Austreberta at Pavilly and left him there. And the next night, Christ's virgin appeared to him, wonderfully adorned, and ordered him to rest a while. At her voice, the ancient enemy fled, deserting God's creature. At dawn, the people gathering found that he was healed and giving thanks.

19. And another miserable person was seized by a legion of demons and tortured within by malign spirits as well as agitated without by dire furors of motion. And when he was so insane that he broke the chains and cords that bound him, his parents seized him and confined him in a wooden stall and brought to the virgin's oratory where they left him alone. And, wonderful to say, people later coming to the church to pray, saw him whom they had left enclosed in wood prostrate before the altar in the shape of a cross blessing and praising God with all his bonds placed on the altar. Greatly astonished, they asked the cause of this prodigy. Tearfully, he said, "Blessed Austreberta came to me a little while ago and cured me of my trouble and freed me from my chains and ordered me to put them on her altar as a gift."

20. In the province of Rouen, in a villa called Clavilla by the inhabitants, a poor woman lived with her husband. When he was absent one day and shades of night were falling, she was sitting, as usual, before the fire. Suddenly the ancient enemy appeared before her in the guise of an Ethiopian of sootiest blackness. He threw himself at her trying to snatch the little son hanging at her breast. Turning pale and trembling, she invoked Saint Austreberta who sprang first into her mind. At the sound of her voice, it was as though a thunder clap struck the wicked and shameless predator. As she called the name three times, he swore horribly at the woman and fled away unwillingly, to appear no more. And he who fled with terror at the invocation of the holy virgin, had not dared to lay a finger on the little one. But by divine command rather than his own will, he had stricken the mother with blindness. Not only was she deprived of light but lost the very pupils of her eyes themselves. She was bereft of sight for a year, becoming more of a burden than a solace to her husband's poverty. One night in sleep she was admon-

---

33. This is an addendum which, as the editors noted, does not appear in every extant manuscript.

ished to hurry to Saint Austreberta's church which was near by and wash her eyes in the fountain signing herself with her name. At dawn she told her husband what she had heard and urged that they carry out the order quickly. But he held the words cheaply in his rude mind, attributing them to fantastic illusions. "You're a fool," he said. "I don't think it's possible to restore sight to you when no trace at all remains of your eyes." But he was overborne by her prayers and importunities and finally agreed to lead her to the holy virgin's oratory. There she prayed devoutly prostrate on the ground. Then, according to custom, she offered a candle. Dipping her hand in the liquid from the fountain under the holy altar, with faith, she thrice washed her eyes. Wonderful to tell! Suddenly, like two shining stars falling from heaven, her eyes were restored to their proper place just as to the one born blind at the pool of Siloam.[34] And she saw the monastery clearly, a comfortable place where Saint Austreberta had lived for a little while among the celibate and meditated, contemplating Heaven. And she gave thanks to almighty God.[35]

21. And another woman of the city of Rouen was so tortured in feet and legs that she could barely walk and suffered night and day. Therefore she was put on a donkey and brought by her relatives to the blessed virgin who restored her to perfect health. But then she spoke to a certain little woman of her perfect health and recent cure who said "I know a herb of such power that as long as it was bound to my feet such an infirmity could in no way attack me." And soon she talked her round. She who had received healing from Heaven placed the lethal juices on her healthy limbs. Immediately, by divine command, the former pain invaded her feet worse than before. And then the miserable one repented and mounted her animal once more and returned to the pious merciful one. But she did not deserve to receive the medicinal work quickly as before. Eight days of penance before the altar were exacted before she was again restored to health.[36]

22. A lewd fellow desired forcibly to seize the shameful parts of a certain honest woman dwelling near the Seine. She fought off the violation and fled precipitously from her house. Quickly calling for help from Christ's holy virgins, Austreberta in particular, she came to the rapid currents of the river. Pursued by her enemy who was behind her whichever way she turned, she

---

34. John 9:11.

35. This spring still marks the site of the long-vanished monastery in the village of Sainte-Austreberte near Pavilly. A modern chapel has been built over the spring, and pilgrims are still encouraged to make use of its waters.

36. Van Dam, *Leadership and Community*, 261ff., notes that miracles of this sort are common among the Gallic saints to impress worshippers with the superior healing powers found in church as against those commanded by local wise women or even miraculous cures associated with old pagan shrines.

could neither flee forward nor turn back. Choosing death before shameful rape she gave herself to the river with a leap. But a wonder, worthy of note, appeared in the liquid element. By divine favor, the wave smoothed and became like a boat to carry the modest woman leaving her on dry land uninjured on the opposite bank of the river.

23. A virgin from her first nature, undeservedly reduced to poverty, was accustomed to give service to the virgin Austreberta. As long as she breathed with the air of health, she was accustomed to sweep the pavement of the church with a broom every Saturday and clean it diligently. In spring, summer or autumn she sprinkled diverse flowers and aromatic herbs on the ground and on the holy tomb of the blessed virgin. Finally this present life ran toward an end and the time of her calling was known. The blessed virgin, by no means unmindful of her servant, appeared in a vision where she lay in bed. Fine and admirable of form, sweet as a mother, she said, "Sister, don't be afraid or troubled. This coming Saturday you will cross over from labor to rest in eternal life." And when, as usual, some of the faithful visited her, she told them that her end was coming and revealed the prophecy from above. At the day and hour when Christ's servant customarily cleaned the floor of the sacred oratory, when she was wont to circle the virgin body's resting place with flowers, after partaking of viaticum and commending her spirit to Christ, she migrated from this dirty dwelling to the holy Lord's tabernacle where unquestionably she had earned the patronage of blessed Austreberta for whom she had done such faithful services. For her bare poverty on earth, she was compensated copiously with immortal wealth.

24. Meanwhile, our Lord declared the merits of His servant Austreberta far and wide. Wherever basilicas or oratories were named in her honor, He did not shirk from showing the strength of her influence. In the province of Le Mans the faithful built a little church rather austere of design but neatly decorated with signs. Three women living together in that neighborhood endured different infirmities: for one of them was blind, another contracted in the feet and a third languishing with a long illness. They made vows to blessed Austreberta to whom they sent candles in her little house. And immediately they got help according to God's clement custom. They went devoutly to Pavilly to give thanks at her tomb and discharged their vow with praise of Almighty God.

25. And a certain demoniac and a mute, as in the Gospel, was led to the blessed virgin Austreberta at Pavilly and within a few days the demon was expelled and the office of the tongue restored by the blessed virgin's merits.

Bibliography

Wherever possible, we have favored English translations in this bibliography.

Aigrain, René. *L'hagiographie: ses sources, ses méthodes, son histoire.* Paris: 1953.
——. *Sainte Radegonde.* Reprint. Parthenay: Les Trois Moutiers, 1987.
——. "Le voyage de Ste. Radegonde à Arles." *Bulletin d'Histoire et philologie de comité des travaux historiques* (1926–27): 119–27.
Allen, Michael, and Daniel G. Calder. *Sources and Analogues of Old English Poetry: The Major Latin Texts in translation.* Totowa, N.J.: Rowman and Littlefield, 1976.
Aubrun, Jean. *Radegonde: Reine, Moniale et Sainte.* Poitiers: Abbaye de Sainte-Croix, 1986.
Bachrach, Bernard S. "Procopius and the Chronology of Clovis' Reign." *Viator* 1 (1970): 21–32.
Barroux, R. *Dagobert, Roi des Francs.* Paris: Payot, 1938.
Bateson, Mary Catherine. "Origin and Early History of Double Monasteries." *Royal Historical Society Transactions* 13 (1899): 137–98.
Beck, Henry G. J. *The Pastoral Care of Souls in Southeast France during the Sixth Century.* Rome, 1950.
Bede. *History of the English Church and People.* Translated by Leo Sherley-Price. Baltimore: Penguin Books, 1968.
Benoit, F. "Topographie monastique d'Arles au VIe siècle." *Etudes mérovingiennes: Acts des journées de Poitiers, 1–3 mai 1952,* 13–17. Paris: Picard, 1953.
Bernoulli, C. A. *Der Heiliger der Merovinger.* Tübingen: Mohr, 1900.
Besse, J. M. "Les moines de l'ancienne France." *Archives de la France monastique* 2 (1906).
Borst, Arno. *Mönche am Bodensee (610–1525).* Sigmaringen: Thorbecke, 1978.
Bravé, John Rahm. *Uncle John's Original Bread Book.* New York: Galahad Books, 1965.
Brown, Peter R. L. *The Cult of the Saints: Its Rise and Function in Latin Christianity.* Chicago: University of Chicago Press, 1981.
——. *Relics and Social Status in the Age of Gregory of Tours.* Reading: University of Reading Press, 1977.
——. *Society and the Holy.* London: Faber and Faber, 1982.
Bullough, Vern L., and Cameron Campbell. "Female Longevity and Diet in the Middle Ages." *Speculum* 55, no. 2 (1980): 315–25.
The Burgundian Code: Book of Constitutions; or The Law of Gundobad. Translated by Katherine Fischer Drew. Philadelphia: University of Pennsylvania Press, 1972.
Catholic Encyclopedia. Vol. 12. New York: Encyclopedia Press, 1913.
Cassian, John. *Institutions cénobitiques.* Sources Chrétiennes 109. Paris: Editions du Cerf, 1971.
Chadwick, Nora K. *Poetry and Letters in Merovingian Gaul.* London: Bowes and Bowes, 1955.
Chamard, François. *Histoire écclésiastique du Poitou.* Poitiers, 1874.

Chapman, John. *Saint Benedict and the Sixth Century.* London: Sheed and Ward, 1929.

Chaussey, Yves, ed. *L'Abbaye Royale Notre Dame de Jouarre.* Paris: Bibliothèque d'Histoire et d'Archéologie Chrétienne, 1961.

Cherewatuk, Karen, "Female Personae in Radegund's Letters to Hamalafred and Artachis." In *Dear Sister: The Correspondence of Medieval Women,* ed. Ulrike Wiethaus and Karen Cherewatuk. In press.

Clarke, H. B., and M. Brennan, eds. *Columbanus and Merovingian Monasticism.* B.A.R. International Series 1113. Oxford, 1981.

Coleman, Emily. "Infanticide in the Early Middle Ages." In *Women in Medieval Society,* ed. Susan M. Stuard, 47–70. Philadelphia: University of Pennsylvania Press, 1976.

Columbanus. *Regula S. Columbani.* In *PL,* ed. J. P. Migne, vol. 80.

Concilia Galliae. In *CCSL,* vol. 148, ed. C. Munier; vol. 148A, ed. C. de Clercq. Turnholt: Brepols, 1963.

Constable, Giles. "The *Liber Memorialis* of Remiremont." In *Religious Life and Thought.* London: Variorum Reprints, 1979.

Coudanne, Louise. "Baudonivie, moniale de Sainte Croix et sa biographe de Sainte Radegonde." *Etudes Mérovingiennes: Acts des journées de Poitiers,* 1–3 mai 1952. Paris: Picard, 1953.

Couturier, M. J. *Sainte Balthilde.* Paris, 1909.

Delaruelle, Etienne. "Sainte Radegonde et la Chrétienité de son temps." *Etudes Mérovingiennes: Acts des journées de Poitiers,* 1–3 mai 1952, 65–74. Paris: Picard, 1953.

Delehaye, Hippolyte. *The Legends of the Saints.* Translated by Donald Attwater. New York: Fordham University Press, 1962.

———. *Les origines du culte des martyres.* Brussels, 1933.

De Long, Nicholas. *Histoire écclésiastique et civile du Diocèse de Laon.* Chalons, 1783.

Donatus of Besançon. "The Rule of Donatus of Besançon: A Working Translation." Translated by Jo Ann McNamara and John E. Halborg. *Vox Benedictina* 2, no. 2 (1985): 85–107.

Dronke, Peter. *Women Writers of the Middle Ages.* New York: Cambridge University Press, 1984.

Dubois, Jacques, and Laure Beaumont-Maillet. *Sainte Geneviève de Paris.* Paris: Beauchesne, 1982.

Duby, Georges. *The Early Growth of the European Economy: Warrior and Peasants, 7th–12th centuries.* Ithaca: Cornell University Press, 1974.

Duchesne, Louis. *L'Eglise au sixième siècle.* Paris: E. de Boccard, 1925.

Duckett, Eleanor S. *The Wandering Saints of the Early Middle Ages.* New York: W. W. Norton, 1959.

Dumas, Auguste. "Sainte Clothilde." *Dictionnaire d'histoire et de géographie écclésiastique,* 1965.

Dunbar, Agnes. *A Dictionary of Saintly Women.* London: G. Bell and Sons, 1904–5.

Dürig, Walter. *Geburtstag und Namenstag.* Munich, 1954.

Dupraz, Louis. *Contribution à l'histoire de Regnum Francorum pendant le troisième quart du VIIe siècle (656–680).* Fribourg, 1948.

Ebling, Horst. *Prosopographie der Amstrager des Merovingerreiches.* Beiheft der Francia 2. Munich, 1972.

Eckenstein, Lina. *Women under Monasticism, 500–1500.* Cambridge: Cambridge University Press, 1896.

Eddius Stephanus. *The Life of Saint Wilfrid,* translated by J. F. Webb. In *The Age of Bede,* ed. D. H. Farmer, 105–83. New York: Penguin, 1983.

Evans, Robert F. *Pelagius: Inquiries and Reappraisals.* New York: Seabury Press, 1968.

Ewig, Eugen. *Spätantikes und fränkisches Gallien.* 2 vols. Beihefte der Francia 3, no. 1/2. Munich: Artemis Verlag, 1976–1979.

Fischer, Johannes. *Der Hausmeier Ebroin.* Bonn, 1959.

Folz, Robert. "Remiremont dans le mouvement colombanien." In *Remiremont: L'Abbaye et la Ville,* ed. Michel Parisse, 15–28. Nancy: Service des Publications de l'Université de Nancy II, 1980.

———. "Tradition hagiographique et culte de sainte Balthilde, reine des Francs." *Académie des Inscriptions et Belles-Lettres Comtes Rendus des séances pour 1975* 3 (1976): 369–84.

"Fontinus." *Encyclopedic Dictionary of Religion.* Washington, D.C.: Corpus Publications, 1979.

Fortunatus, Venantius. *Carmina*. In *MGH, AA* 4/2:55–64.

Fouracre, Paul J. "Observations on the outgrowth of Pippinid influence in the *Regnum Francorum* after the Battle of Tertry (687–715)." *Medieval Prosopography*, 5, no. 2 (1984): 1–32.

Fredegar. *Chronicorum Liber quartus cum continuationibus*. Translated by J. M. Wallace-Hadrill. London: Nelson, 1960.

Gaiffier, Baudouin de. "La lecture des Actes des martyres dans la prière liturgique." *Analecta Bollandiana* 72 (1954): 145–51.

———. "Un prologue hagiographique hostile au décret de Gélase." *Analecta Bollandiana* 82 (1964): 341–53.

———. "Sainte Angadrisma. (VIIe siècle): A propos de son culte." In *Pietas: Festschrift für Bernhard Kotting*, ed. E. Dassmann and K. Frank. *Jahrbuch für Antike und Christentum* 8 (1980): 280–84.

Gallia Christiana. 16 vols. Paris, 1715–1865.

Gauthier, N. *L'évangelisation des Pays de la Moselle. 2–8 siècles*. Paris: Boccard, 1981.

Geary, Patrick J. *Aristocracy in Provence: The Rhône Basin at the Dawn of the Carolingian Age*. Philadelphia: University of Pennsylvania Press, 1985.

———. *Before France and Germany: The Creation and Transformation of the Merovingian World*. New York: Oxford University Press, 1988.

———. *Furta Sacra: Thefts of Relics in the Central Middle Ages*. Princeton: Princeton University Press, 1978.

Geberding, Richard A. *The Rise of the Carolingians and the Liber Historiae Francorum*. New York: Oxford University Press, 1987.

Gerontius. *Life of Melania the Younger*. Translated by Elizabeth Clark. Lewiston: Edwin Mellen Press, 1988.

Goffart, Walter. *Barbarians and Romans AD 418–584: The Techniques of Accommodation*. Princeton: Princeton University Press, 1980.

Graus, Frantisek. "Die Gewalt bei den Anfängen des Feudalismus und die 'Gefangenenbefreiung' der merowingischen Hagiographie." *Jahrbuch für Wirtschaftsgeschichte* 1 (1961): 61–156.

———. *Volk, Herrscher und Heiliger im Reich der Merowinger*. Prague, 1965.

Gregory the Great. *Dialogues*. Translated by G. F. Hill. London, 1911.

———. *Registrum epistularum*. Edited by Dag Norberg. Turnholt: Brepols, 1982.

Gregory of Nyssa. "Life of Saint Macrina." In *Ascetical Works*, translated by V. W. Callahan. Washington, D.C.: Catholic University Press, 1966.

Gregory of Tours. *Glory of the Martyrs and Glory of the Confessors*. Translated by Raymond van Dam. Liverpool: Liverpool University Press, 1988.

———. *History of the Franks*. Translated by Lewis Thorpe. New York: Penguin Books, 1974.

———. *Liber de miraculi S. Martini, libri quatuor*. In *PL*, ed. J. P. Migne, 71:913–1008.

———. *Life of the Fathers*. Translated by Edward James. Liverpool: Liverpool University Press, 1986.

———. *De virtutibus S. Martini*. In *MGH, SRM*, ed. Bruno Krusch, 1:584–601.

Grisard, Maurice. "Histoire et légende: Les saints mérovingiens de Consolre: Aldegonde, Ealkert, Bertile." *Publications de la Société d'histoire de France* 6 (1968): 67–92.

Guérout, Jean. "Les origines et le premier siècle de l'abbaye de Notre-Dame de Jouarre." *L'abbaye royale de Notre-Dame de Jouarre* 1:1–67. Paris, 1961.

———. "Le testament de sainte Fare: Matériaux pour l'étude et l'édition critique de ce document." *Revue d'histoire écclésiastique* 60, nos. 3–4 (1965): 761–821.

Guillaume, Jean-Marie. "Les abbayes de femmes en pays franc des origines à la fin du VIIe siècle." In *Remiremont: L'Abbaye et la Ville*, ed. Michel Parisse, 29–46. Nancy: Service des Publications de l'Université de Nancy II, 1980.

Hagiographie: Cultures et sociétés, IVe–XIIe siècles. Actes du Colloque organisé à Nanterre et à Paris 2–6 mai 1979. Paris: Etudes augustiniennes, 1981.

Hay, Denys. *Europe: The Emergence of an Idea.* Edinburgh, 1957.

Head, Thomas, "Bodies, Fire, and Salvation." Paper delivered at the Twenty-fifth International Congress on Medieval Studies, Kalamazoo, Mich., 1990.

Hefele, O. J., and H. Leclercq. *Histoire des conciles.* Paris, 1910.

Heffernan, Thomas J. *Sacred Biography: Saints and Their Biographers in the Middle Ages.* New York: Oxford University Press, 1988.

Heinrich, Mary. *Canonesses and Education in the Early Middle Ages.* Washington, D.C.: Catholic University Press, 1924.

Heinzelmann, Martin. *Bischofherrschaft in Gallien: Zur Kontinuität römischer Führungschichten vom 4. bis zum 7. Jahrhundert. Soziale, prosopographische und bildungsgeschichtliche Aspekte. Beihefte der Francia 5.* Munich, 1976.

———. "Les changements de la dénomination latine à la fin de l'antiquité." In *Famille et Parenté dans l'Occident Médiéval,* ed. Georges Duby and Jacques LeGoff, 19–42. Paris: Boccard, 1978.

———. "Une source de base de la littérature hagiographique latine: La recueil de miracles." In *Hagiographie: Cultures et sociétés, IVe–XIIe siècles,* 235–59. Paris: Etudes Augustiniennes, 1981.

Heinzelmann, Martin, and Jean-Claude Poulin. *Les vies anciennes de Sainte Geneviève de Paris.* Bibliothèque de l'école des hautes études, scientifiques, historique, et philologique 329. Paris, 1986.

Herbillon, Jules. "Dominica, Dominicana, pseudo-abbesse de Nivelles." *Bulletin de la Société Royale le vieux-Liège* 10, no. 220 (1983): 316.

Herlihy, David. "Land, Family and Women in Continental Europe, 701–1200." In *Women in Medieval Society,* ed. Susan M. Stuard, 13–46. Philadelphia: University of Pennsylvania Press, 1976.

Hermas. *The Pastor.* In *The AnteNicene Fathers,* ed. Alexander Roberts and James Donaldson, vol. 2. Grand Rapids, Mich.: Eerdmans, 1975.

Higounet, Charles. "Saints mérovingiennes d'Aquitaine dans la toponymie." *Etudes mérovingiennes: Acts des journées de Poitiers,* 1–3 mai 1952, 155–67. Paris: Picard, 1953.

Hillgarth, Joyce N. *The Conversion of Western Europe, 350–750.* Englewood Cliffs, N.J.: Prentice-Hall, 1969.

Hilpisch, Ferdinand (dom Stephanus). *Die Döppelklöster: Entstehung und Organisation.* Dissertation, Münster-in-Westphalia, 1928.

Hincmar of Reims. *Vita Remigius.* In MGH, SRM 3:814–17.

Hlawitschka, Eduard. "Studien zur Abtissinnenreihe von Remiremont." *Veroffentlichungen des Instituts für Landeskunde des Saarlandes* 9. Saarbrucken, 1963.

Hoare, F. R., ed. and trans. *The Western Fathers.* New York: Harper, 1965.

Hoebanx, Jean Jacques. *L'abbaye de Nivelles des origines au XIVe siècle. Mémoires de l'académie royale de Belgique* 46. Brussels, 1952.

Hucbald of Saint-Amand. *Vita S. Aldegundis virginis.* In AS, January 30.

Huguenin, Alexandre. *Histoire du royaume mérovingienne d'Austrasie.* Paris, 1862.

Huyghe, H. *La clôture des moniales des origines à la fin du XIIIe siècle: Etude historique et juridique.* Roubaix, 1944.

Isidore of Seville. *History of the Goths, Vandals, and Suevi.* Translated by Guido Donini and Gordon B. Ford, Jr. Leiden: E. J. Brill, 1970.

James, Edward. *The Origins of France: From Clovis to the Capetians.* New York: St. Martins, 1982.

Jerome. *Letters.* Translated by F. A. Wright. Loeb Classical Library 262. Cambridge, Mass.: Harvard University Press, 1963.

Jonas of Bobbio. *Vita S. Columbani abbatis discipulorumque eius, Liber II.* In MGH, SRM, ed. Bruno Krusch, 4:822–27.

Jungmann, Joseph A. *The Mass of the Roman Rite.* New York: Benziger Brothers, 1953.

King, Archdale A. *Eucharistic Reservation in the Western Church.* New York: Sheed and Ward, 1965.

Knowles, David. "Great Historical Enterprises: The Bolandists." *Transactions of the Royal Historical Society,* ser. 5, no. 8 (1958): 147–66.

Kohler, C. *Etude critique sur le texte de la vie latine de Ste. Geneviève.* Paris, 1881.

Kroll, Jerome, and Bernard Bachrach. "Medieval Visions and Contemporary Hallucinations." *Psychological Medicine* 12 (1982): 709–21.

Krusch, Bruno. "Die fälschung der Vita Genovefa." *Neues Archiv der Gesellschaft für ältere deutsche Geschichtskunde* 18, no. 1 (1892): 9–50.

Kurth, Godefroy. "Etude critique sur la vie de sainte Geneviève." *Revue d'histoire écclésiastique* 14 (1913): 9–16.

———. *Etudes franques.* 2 vols. Paris: Champion, 1919.

———. *Sainte Clothilde.* 2d ed. Paris, 1897.

Labande-Mailfert, Yvonne. "Les débuts de Sainte-Croix." In *Histoire de l'abbaye Sainte-Croix de Poitiers: Quatorze siècles de vie monastique,* ed. Edmond-René Labande. Poitiers: Société des Antiquaires de l'Ouest, 1986.

Lambot, C. "Le prototype des monastères cloîtres de femmes: L'abbaye de S. Jean d'Arles." *Revue littéraire et monastique* 23 (1938): 171.

Laugardière, M. de. *L'église de Bourges avant Charlemagne.* Paris, 1951.

Leclercq, H. "Sainte Geneviève." *DACL,* 6, 1, 960–990.

Lesne, Emile. *La propriété écclésiastique en France aux époques romains et mérovingienne.* Paris, 1910.

Levillain, L. "Le testament de Sainte Fare." *Revue d'histoire écclésiastique* 60 (1965): 761–821.

Levison, Wilhelm. *England and the Continent in the Eighth Century.* Oxford: Oxford University Press, 1973.

Liber Historiae Francorum, ed. and trans. Bernard S. Bachrach. Lawrence, Kans.: Coronado Press, 1973.

McCarthy, Mary Caritas, trans. *The Rule for Nuns of Saint Caesarius of Arles.* Washington, D.C.: Catholic University Press, 1960.

McNamara, Jo Ann. "Cornelia's Daughters." *Women's Studies* 11, nos. 1 and 2 (1984): 9–27.

———. "Imitatio Helenae: Sainthood as an Attribute of Queenship in the Early Middle Ages." In *Saints and Sainthood,* ed. Sandro Sticca. Binghamton, N.Y.: MRTS, in press.

———. "A Legacy of Miracles: Hagiography and Nunneries in Merovingian Gaul." In *Women of the Medieval World: Essays in Honor of John Mundy,* ed. Julius Kirschner and Suzanne Wemple, 36–52. New York: Basil Blackwell, 1985.

———. "Living Sermons." In *Medieval Religious Women,* vol. 2: *Peace Weavers,* ed. John A. Nichols and Lilian T. Shank, 19–38. Kalamazoo, Mich.: Cistercian Publications, 1987.

———. "The Need to Give: Economic Restriction and Penitential Piety Among Late Medieval Nuns." In *Images of Sainthood in Medieval and Renaissance Europe,* ed. Renate Blumenfeld-Kozinski and Timea Szell, 199–221. Ithaca: Cornell University Press, 1991.

———. "The Ordeal of Community: Hagiography and Discipline in Merovingian Convents." *Vox Benedictina* 3 and 4 (1986): 293–326.

———, and Suzanne F. Wemple. "Marriage and Divorce in the Frankish Kingdom." In *Women in Medieval Society,* ed. Susan M. Stuard, 95–124. Philadelphia: University of Pennsylvania Press, 1976.

———, and Suzanne F. Wemple. "The Power of Women Through the Family in Medieval Europe: 500–1100." In *Women and Power in the Middle Ages,* ed. Maryanne Kowaleski and Mary Erler. Athens: University of Georgia Press, 1988.

Malnory, A. *Quid Luxorienses monachi ad regulam monasteriorum atque ad communem ecclesiae profectum contulerint?* Paris, 1894.

Margin, Paul Edmond. *Etudes critiques sur la Suisse à l'époque mérovingienne 534–715.* Geneva, 1910.

Marignan, A. *Etudes sur la civilization française.* Vol. 2: *Le culte des saints sous les mérovingiens.* Paris, 1899.

Meisel, A. C., and M. L. del Mastro. *The Rule of Saint Benedict.* New York, 1975.

Melin, A. *Une Cité Carolingienne: Histoire de la ville et du Ban d'Andenne.* Liège: Vaillant-Carmanne, 1928.

Metz, René. "La consecration des vièrges en Gaule des origines à l'apparition des livres liturgiques." *Revue de droit canonique* 6 (1956): 321–39.

Meyer, Bruno. "Das Testament der Burgundofara." *Mitteilungen der Oesterreichisches Institut für Geschichtsforschung* 14 (1939): 1–12.

Moreau, E. de. *Saint Amand: Apôtre de la Belgique et du nord de la France.* Louvain, 1927.

Murray, Alexander C. *Germanic Kinship Structure: Studies in Law and Society in Antiquity and the Early Middle Ages.* Pontifical Institute of Mediaeval Studies and Texts, 65. Toronto, 1983.

Nelson, Janet L. "Queens as Jezebels: The Careers of Brunhild and Balthild in Merovingian History." In *Medieval Women,* ed. Derek Baker, 31–78. Oxford: Basil Blackwell, 1978.

Nisard, Charles. "Des poésies de Radegonde attribuées jusqu'ici à Fortunatus." In *Fortunatus, Opera Poetica,* ed. Nisard. Paris, 1887.

Nolte, Cordula. "Klosterleben von Frauen in der frühen Merowingerzeit: Überlegungen zur Regula ad virgines des Caesarius von Arles." In *Frauen in der Geschichte VII,* ed. Werner Affeldt and Annette Kuhn, 257–71. Düsseldorf: Schwann, 1986.

Parisse, Michel, ed. *Remiremont: L'Abbaye et la Ville.* Nancy: Service des Publications de l'Université de Nancy II, 1980.

Peeters, P. *L'Oeuvre des Bollandistes. Mémoires de l'Académie royal de Belgique, Classe des Lettres,* 14:5. Brussels, 1961.

Peters, Edward, ed. *Monks, Bishops and Pagans.* Philadelphia: University of Pennsylvania Press, 1975.

Prinz, Friedrich. *Frühes Mönchtum im Frankreich.* Munich, 1965.

———. *Grundlagen und Anfänge: Deutschland bis 1056.* In *Neue Deutsche Geschichte,* vol. 1, ed. Peter Moraw, Volker Press, and Wolfgang Schieber, 63–64. Munich: C. H. Beck Verlag, 1985.

———. "Heiligenkult und Adelsherrschaft im Spiegel merowingischen Hagiographie." *Historische Zeitschrift* 204 (1967): 532.

Richards, Jeffrey. *Consul of God: The Life and Times of Gregory the Great.* London: Routledge and Kegan Paul, 1980.

Riché, Pierre. "Columbanus, His Followers, and the Merovingian Church." In *Columbanus and Merovingian Monasticism,* ed. H. B. Clarke and M. Brennan, 59–72. B.A.R. International Series 1113. Oxford, 1981.

———. "Interêts historiques de la vie de Ste. Geneviève." *Montagne Ste-Geneviève et ses Abords. Société historique et archéologie du Ve arrondissement* 210 (1978): 52–55.

———. "La Vita S. Rusticulae: Note d'hagiographie mérovingienne." *Analecta Bollandiana* 72 (1954): 369–77.

Sainte Fare et Faremoutiers. Faremoutiers, 1956.

Salin, Edouard. *La civilisation mérovingienne.* Paris: A. and J. Picard, 1949–59.

Salmon, Pierre. *The Breviary through the Centuries.* Collegeville: Liturgical Press, 1962.

Scheibelreiter, Geary. "Königstochter im Klöster. Radegund (ob. 587) und des Nonnenaufstand von Poitiers (589)." *Mitteilungen des Institut für österreichisches Geschichtsforschung* 87, no. 1 (1979): 1–37.

Schulenberg, Jane T. "Sexism and the Celestial Gynecaeum from 500 to 1200." *Journal of Medieval History* 4, no. 2 (1978): 117–33.

———. "Strict Active Enclosure and Its Effects on the Female Monastic Experience, 500–1100." In *Medieval Religious Women,* vol. 1: *Distant Echoes,* ed. John A. Nichols and Lilian T. Shank, 51–86. Kalamazoo, Mich.: Cistercian Publications, 1984.

———. "Women as Proselytizers in Germanic Society." Paper delivered at the Tenth International Congress on Medieval Studies, Kalamazoo, Mich., 1975.

Straw, Carole. *Perfection in Imperfection: Body, Soul, and Spiritual Progress in Gregory the Great.* Berkeley: University of California Press, 1988.

Sullivan, Richard E. "The Papacy and Missionary Activity in the Early Middle Ages." *Mediaeval Studies* 17 (1955): 46–106.

Taft, Robert A. *The Liturgy of the Hours in East and West.* Collegeville: The Liturgical Press, 1986.

Talley, Thomas Y. *The Origins of the Church Year.* New York: Pueblo Publishing, 1986.

Tessier, Georges. *Le Baptême de Clovis.* Paris: Gallimard, 1964.

Theis, Laurent. "Saints sans famille? Quelques remarques sur la famille dans le monde franc à travers les sources hagiographiques." *Revue Historique* 255 (1976): 3–20.

Thiébaux, Marcelle. *The Writings of Medieval Women.* New York: Garland Publishing, 1987.

Thurston, Herbert. *Lent and Holy Week.* New York: Longmans, 1904.

Van Dam, Raymond. *Leadership and Community in Late Ancient Gaul.* Berkeley: University of California Press, 1985.

Van der Essen, L. *Etude critique et littéraire sur les vitae des saints mérovingiens de l'ancienne Belgique.* Louvain, 1907.

Van Uytfanghe, Marc. "La controverse biblique et patristique autour du miracle, et ses répercussions sur l'hagiographie dans l'Antiquité tardive et le haut Moyen Age latin." *Hagiographie, Cultures et Sociétés, IVe–XIIe siècles,* 205–33. Paris: Etudes Augustiniennes, 1981.

Verdon, Jean. "Recherches sur les monastères féminins dans la France du sud aux IX–XI siècles." *Annales du Midi* 88 (1976): 122.

"Vita beatae Framechildis viduae." *Analecta Bollandiana* 72 (1954): 155–61.

"Vita Caesarii Arelatensis." In *MGH, SRM* 3:32.

"Vita S. Germani Autisiodorensis episcopi." In *Etude critique sur la vie de S. Germain d'Auxerre,* ed. Narbey. Paris, 1884.

"Vita Patrum iurensium." *Sources Chrétiennes* 142, ed. F. Martinez. Paris: Editions du Cerf, 1968.

Vogel, Cyrille. *Medieval Liturgy: An Introduction to the Sources.* Translated by William Storey and Niels Rasmussen. Washington, D.C.: Pastoral Press, 1986.

Waldebert of Luxeuil. *Regula cuiusdam patris ad virgines.* In *PL,* ed. J. P. Migne, 88:1053–70.

Wallace-Hadrill, J. M. *The Frankish Church.* New York: Oxford University Press, 1984.

———. *The Long-haired Kings and Other Studies in Frankish History.* New York: Barnes and Noble, 1962.

Warren, F. E., ed. *The Antiphonary of Bangor.* London: Harrison and Sons, 1893–95.

Weber, Katharina. *Kulturgeschichtliche Probleme der Merowingerzeit im Spiegel frühen Heiligenleben. Studien und Mitteilungen zur Geschichte des Benediktinerordens und seine Zweige* 18. Munich, 1930.

Weinberger, Stephen. "Peasant Households in Provence." *Speculum* 48 (1973): 247–57.

Wemple, Suzanne F. "Female Spirituality and Mysticism in Frankish Monasticism: Radegund, Balthild, and Aldegund." In *Medieval Religious Women,* vol. 2: *Peace Weavers,* ed. John A. Nichols and Lilian T. Shank, 39–54. Kalamazoo, Mich.: Cistercian Publications, 1987.

———. *Women in Frankish Society: Marriage and the Cloister, 500–900.* Philadelphia: University of Pennsylvania Press, 1981.

Werner, Karl Ferdinand. *Structures politiques du monde franc. VIe–XIIe siècles.* London: Variorum Reprints, 1979.

Whatley, E. Gordon. "The Earliest Literary Quotations from the *Inventio S. Crucis:* A Note on Baudonivia's *Vita S. Radegundis.*" In press.

Wittern, Susanne. "Frauen zwischen asketischem Ideal und weltlichem Leben. Zur Darstellung des christlichen Handelns der merowingischen Königinnen Radegunde und Balthilde in den hagiographischen Lebensbeschreibungen des 6. und 7. Jahrhunderts." In *Frauen in der Geschichte VII,* ed. Werner Affeldt and Annette Kuhn, 272–94. Düsseldorf: Schwann, 1986.

Wood, Ian N. "Gregory of Tours and Clovis." *Revue belge de philologie et d'histoire* 63 (1985): 249–72.

———. "Kings, Kingdoms, and Consent." In *Early Medieval Kingship,* ed. Peter H. Sawyer and Ian Wood, 6–29. Leeds: University of Leeds Press, 1977.

———. "A Prelude to Columbanus: The Monastic Achievement in the Burgundian Territories." In *Columbanus and Merovingian Monasticism,* ed. H. B. Clarke and M. Brennan, 3–32. B.A.R. International Series 1113. Oxford, 1981.

Index

About the Editors Jo Ann McNamara is Professor of History at
Hunter College, City University of New York. Her publications
include *Gilles Aycelin: A Servant of Two Masters, A New Song: Celibate
Women in the First Three Christian Centuries, Daily Life in the World of
Charlemagne,* by Pierre Riché (English translation), and *Women and
the Structure of Society: Selected Research from the Fifth Berkshire Conference
on the History of Women* (coeditor with Barbara J. Harris). John E.
Halborg serves as a priest at St. Thomas More Church in New
York. E. Gordon Whatley is Associate Professor of English at
Queens College and the Graduate Center, City University of
New York. He is the author of *The Saint of London: The Life and
Miracles of St. Erkenwald.*

Library of Congress Cataloging-in-Publication Data
Sainted women of the Dark Ages / edited and translated by
Jo Ann McNamara and John E. Halborg with Gordon Whatley.
Includes bibliographical references and index.
ISBN 0-8223-1200-X (alk. paper). — ISBN 0-8223-1216-6 (pbk. : alk.
paper)
1. Christian women saints—France—Biography—Early works to
1800.   2. Women, Catholic—France—Biography—Early works
to 1800.   3. France—Church history—To 987—Sources.
4. Christian hagiography.   I. McNamara, Jo Ann, 1931–   .
II. Halborg, John E.   III. Whatley, E. Gordon, 1944–   .
BX4656.S28   1992
282′.092′244—dc20
[B] 91-24544 CIP